H A

D0679039

PHILADELPHIA

KARRIE GAVIN

Contents

Discover Philadelphia

Philadelphia's been getting a lot of press about becoming America's "next great city." And though I'm pleased to see my city getting the recognition it deserves, I need to set the record straight. As any proud local will tell you – and we are all proud – Philly has *always* been a great city, and it keeps getting better all the time.

As you're exploring the streets of Philadelphia (some paved and some still cobblestone) in the footsteps of Benjamin Franklin, history is always present. Though Center City has blossomed into a world-class downtown, new skyscrapers, restaurants, theaters, and galleries still mingle with the well-preserved homes and churches of the founding fathers.

While visiting the Liberty Bell and jogging up the famed Art Museum steps à la Rocky, be sure to indulge in the activities that locals enjoy. Relax in Rittenhouse Square. Grab lunch in Reading Terminal Market. Stroll along the Schuylkill River Trail. See a play on the Avenue of the Arts. In the colorful neighborhoods beyond Center City, you'll discover family-run greasy spoons where you'll be called "Hon," charming BYOBs, and dive bars where Quizzo and karaoke rival the 76ers, Eagles, Phillies, and Flyers as serious competitive sports.

Philadelphians have an innate and unshakeable hometown pride, and we couldn't be happier that millions of visitors are flocking to see for themselves what we've known all along. But let's be clear: Philadelphia will never become "the next" Boston, San Francisco, or New York. There is no city in the world quite like Philly – and that's just the way we like it.

Planning Your Trip

▶ WHERE TO GO

A horse and buggy ride is a popular way to tour Old City.

Old City

Most first-time visits to Philadelphia begin here. Independence National Historical Park is home to the most popular historic attractions including Independence Hall, the Liberty Bell, and the National Constitution Center. Old City has a wealth of dining and hotels, and the liveliest nightlife in the city.

Society Hill

A tranquil neighbor to Old City, Society Hill boasts many of the finest and oldest homes and cathedrals in the city. Bordered by leafy Washington Square Park to the west and Penn's Landing, the waterfront strip, to the east, it is a lovely place to soak up American history.

Center City East

Broad Street, known as Avenue of the Arts just south of City Hall, divides the downtown business district into East and West. Center City East is home to Reading Terminal Market, Chinatown, and the Washington Square West neighborhood, the center of gay culture in the city.

Center City West

The west side of Broad Street is home to the most upscale restaurants, bars, and shops in the city. The action centers around tree-lined Rittenhouse Square and the chic Rittenhouse Row shopping district.

Benjamin Franklin Parkway/ Fairmount

The broad, diagonal Parkway is lined with flowers, sculptures, and flags from around the world. Here, the Philadelphia Museum of Art, the Franklin Institute Science Museum, and the Academy of Natural Sciences form the cultural center of the city. Just north, in the residential Fairmount neighborhood, lies the spooky Eastern State Penitentiary.

The Eagle sculpture by Alexander Calder, in front of the Philadelphia Museum of Art

South Street/South Philadelphia

South Street, with its eclectic mix of tattoo parlors, independent record stores, dive bars, and upscale restaurants, forms the northern border of South Philly. The Italian Market embodies the area's diverse mix of Italian and Asian influences. Further south, Passyunk Avenue has hip new restaurants and chic boutiques alongside centuries-old family-run pizza joints and tchotchke shops.

A spring day brings joggers, rowers, and bladers to the Schuylkill River Trail.

West Philadelphia/ University City

The University of Pennsylvania and Drexel University live just blocks apart in University City, the part of West Philly nearest to Center City. There are excellent museums, affordable ethnic restaurants, and plenty of shopping in the surrounding streets.

Northern Liberties

For many years considered the up-and-coming neighborhood, No-Libs has officially come up. Chic boutiques and the Edgar Allen Poe House draw a sprinkling of visitors by day, but the area—with its great restaurants and nightlife—truly comes alive at night.

Fairmount Park

The largest urban park system in the nation boasts miles of hiking, biking, and jogging trails. The Schuylkill River Trail is a paved loop that spreads out on both sides of the river. In addition to endless recreational opportunities, the park is home to historic sights, gardens, and the Philadelphia Zoo.

Northwest Philadelphia

Separated from the rest of the city by a short drive, Northwest Philadelphia is worth the trip. Highlights include: Main Street in Manayunk, a high-end strip of boutiques and restaurants; the historic homes of Germantown; shopping on Germantown Avenue and gawking at the mansions in Chestnut Hill; and best of all, hiking in the peaceful Wissahickon.

▶ WHEN TO GO

To enjoy the best weather, avoid the largest crowds, and be assured that all seasonal attractions are open, visit in May–June or September–October. If you don't mind longer lines for popular attractions and rising hotel rates, the city comes alive in summer with festivals, fireworks, and parades—especially during the week of Independence Day. And if you don't mind bundling up, winter offers the lowest hotel rates, fewest crowds, and if you're lucky, perhaps a beautiful snowfall.

Explore Philadelphia

► THE TWO-DAY BEST OF PHILADELPHIA

While a week's vacation would allow you to take in all the major sights in Philadelphia, you can experience many of the highlights and get a feel for the city in just two days. Stay in or near City Center or Old City. From here it's easy to get around on foot, bike, or public transportation or take advantage of the hop-on hop-off tour buses that make key stops around the city.

You can easily spend an entire afternoon or even a day at the best sights, including the Constitution Center, Franklin Institute, and especially the Philadelphia Museum of Art. Keep moving if you want to hit multiple sights in a short time. And while this itinerary covers mostly sights and dining, you'll be in areas that also happen to be shopping havens. Feel free to skip some of the sights and hit the stores instead.

Day 1

Spend the day in Independence National Historical Park, where Philly's most famous historic sights are conveniently located within a few square blocks. Have breakfast at Metro Café and then head to Independence Visitor Center—your first stop. Get information and maps, watch the short introductory film, and reserve your free timed ticket for Independence Hall. Spend the rest of the morning at the National Constitution Center or take a Mural Tour in an open-air trolley.

Eat lunch at the Bourse Food Court, then visit the Liberty Bell and Independence Hall. If time allows, you can choose from nearby attractions such as Carpenters' Hall, Franklin Court, and the Betsy Ross House.

Old City is *the* place to be for an evening out. Try Amada for exquisite tapas or Philadelphia

Reaching For Your Star, by Donald Gensler, one of nearly 2,800 murals in the city

BEYOND CHEESESTEAKS

Everyone knows about the cheesesteak – as iconic to Philly as the Liberty Bell – but while you're in town, don't forget to try our other culinary classics.

HOAGIES

Often translated as Philly's version of the hero or sub, many locals would argue that hoagies are in a league of their own in the sandwich family. The main reason for this is the bread: Most hoagies are made on chewy Amoroso's rolls or gourmet bread. Try **Sarcone's** (734 S. 9th St.) for thin-sliced meats like prosciutto, topped with roasted red peppers and chunks of sharp provolone cheese, served on homemade crusty bread. Other favorites are **Shank's and Evelyn's** (932 S. 10th St.), **Koch's Deli** (4309 Locust St.), and **Dalessandro's** (600 Wendover St.).

SOFT PRETZELS

Their history dates to the early German settlers, but soft pretzels remain a strong local tradition. Indulge in a perfectly browned, chewy soft pretzel, topped with rock salt and smothered with yellow mustard. If it looks too hard or soggy, avoid it. Try **Center City Pretzel Co.** (816 Washington Ave.), best for a midnight snack when they're fresh out of the oven, or

Philly Pretzel Factory (1532 Sansom St.), a mostly local chain with multiple locations in the city.

WATER ICE

Pronounced "wooder ice," water ice is an essential part of summer in the city. Vastly superior to the supermarket variety of Italian ice or snow cones with syrup drizzled over an ice, a proper water ice is a perfectly smooth, creamy consistency – often blended with real bits of fruit. Try **John's** (701 Christian St.), a small South Philly joint, or **Rita's** (239 South St. and more), a Philly-born chain that's spreading real water ice throughout the country.

the historic Bourse building

Fish & Co. for excellent seafood. Or immerse yourself in history on the Independence After Hours Tour where actors reenact events from the American Revolution during a meal at City Tavern. The tour ends with a Lights of Liberty laser lights show in Independence Park. If you're ready to return to the present, hit the many bars in Old City.

Day 2

Today tour the rest of Center City and the Parkway. Try an egg-and-cheese sandwich from a food truck or more refined breakfast offerings at LeBus. Take a stroll through Rittenhouse Square and the ritzy

Franklin Institute Science Museum

surrounding shopping district. Stop at City Hall and ride the elevator to the base of the William Penn statue (weekdays only) for a spectacular view of the city. If you have time, tour the majestic Masonic Temple across the street.

Have lunch at Reading Terminal Market and burn it off with a walk on the picturesque Parkway, where you can take your pick of museums. The Philadelphia Museum of Art—complete with Rocky statue and the famous steps—is top-notch, or if you prefer science to art, visit the Franklin Institute Science Museum. If time allows, check out the Fairmount Water Works and Boathouse Row.

Head back into Center City for endless dining and nightlife options. Oh—and if you somehow haven't yet, have a cheesesteak already! Tony Jr.'s is a nearby favorite.

TOP 10 FOR KIDS

- Join in a real archaeological dig at the **Academy of Natural Sciences** (p. 113).
- Take the RiverLink ferry across the Delaware to the **Adventure Aquarium** in Camden, New Jersey (p. 53).
- Tour the **Betsy Ross House,** with an audio tour and scavenger hunt designed just for kids (p. 23).
- Explore historic Philadelphia in an amphibious **Duck Tour** (p. 17).
- Walk through the giant human heart model and visit the IMAX theater at the **Franklin Institute Science Museum** (p. 113).
- Ride the carousel and play mini-golf at the historic-themed course in **Franklin Square** (p. 25).
- Take part in interactive exhibits at the **National Constitution Center** (p. 20).
- Visit the hands-on petting zoo and Treehouse and ride in the Zooballoon at the **Philadelphia Zoo** (p. 46).
- Discover one of the world's best interactive kids' museums, the **Please Touch Museum** (p. 114).
- Play in Fairmount Park's sprawling indoor and outdoor **Smith Memorial Playground and Playhouse** (p. 127).

SIGHTS

Millions of people come each year to soak in the rich history of our nation's birthplace—and for good reason. A 2007 *Travel + Leisure* survey ranked Philadelphia second only to Washington, D.C., among U.S. cities, for its wealth of historical sights and monuments. The majority of pivotal events leading to the formation of the United States happened on local ground, including Revolutionary War battles and the formation of the Declaration of Independence and the Constitution. Philadelphia also served as the nation's capital for its first ten years, and a wealth of interesting, interactive monuments and museums keeps that history alive.

Independence National Historical Park encompasses several square blocks in the heart of Old City, rightfully dubbed "America's most historic square mile." Many of Philadelphia's most famous sights—including the Liberty Bell and Independence Hall—are conveniently located within this compact and attractive area. As you walk the streets—complete with tour guides dressed in colonial garb—it is easy to imagine the founding fathers, Benjamin Franklin among them, inhabiting these same streets. Philadelphia's favorite son, Franklin, is connected to practically every pivotal decision, event, and invention in the city's early history.

In the past decade, this bustling area has been given a boost with the addition of the interactive multimedia Constitution Center, a new and improved museum to house the Liberty Bell, and a major renovation of Franklin Square. The area will continue to

PHOTO BY K. CIAPPA FOR GPTMC

HIGHLIGHTS

LOOK FOR ◖ TO FIND RECOMMENDED SIGHTS.

◖ **Most Momentous Building:** Both the Declaration of Independence and the Constitution were debated and drafted in **Independence Hall,** where you can almost picture the visionary leaders coming together to create history (page 18).

◖ **Most Iconic Philadelphia Landmark:** The **Liberty Bell** is the image most commonly associated with the City of Brotherly Love and the United States' independence from England. At the Liberty Bell Center you'll learn more about its history and the many other freedom movements that claim the bell as their symbol (page 20).

◖ **Most Modern Old City Attraction:** Offering a refreshing and fascinating contrast to the many historic buildings, the world-class **National Constitution Center** delights with its high-tech interactive exhibits highlighting the history and meaning of the U.S. Constitution (page 20).

◖ **Most Beautiful Office Building:** Philadelphia's **City Hall** is the largest municipal building in the nation and arguably the most breathtaking. This impressive work of architecture is crowned by a 37-foot-tall William Penn – the largest statue atop any building in the world (page 31).

◖ **Most Secretive Sight:** A tour of the **Masonic Temple** reveals a lot about the magnificent building, and even a little about the oldest, most mysterious fraternal order in the world – the masons. The building is considered one of the three most impressive Masonic temples in the world (page 34).

◖ **Most Historic Market:** Where else but the **Reading Terminal Market** can you eat delicious international fare and shop for unique goods in a former railroad station more than 100 years old? Go hungry: The smells are simply irresistible (page 35).

◖ **Spookiest Sight:** The **Eastern State Penitentiary,** the first of its kind, mixes past and present with artist installations placed

© KARRIE GAVIN

Eastern State Penitentiary

throughout the grounds in addition to all those creepy cells (page 36).

◖ **Best Art Museum – Inside and Out:** Before entering the world-renowned **Philadelphia Museum of Art,** be sure to take in the stunning Greek-revival building – and stand at the top of the "Rocky steps" to survey the city (page 39).

◖ **Coolest Cemetery:** If wandering around a cemetery isn't your idea of a good time, then clearly you've never visited **Laurel Hill Cemetery.** The centuries-old architecture and beautiful view of the Schuylkill River from the raised, sprawling grounds make it a worthwhile stop. On a tour, you'll learn about the fascinating lives – and deaths – of many of Philadelphia's earliest residents (page 45).

◖ **Best Place to See Animals and Get High:** The **Philadelphia Zoo** is home to more than 2,000 animal species. While it is the nation's oldest zoo, it is regularly updated with all-new, cutting-edge attractions, including the Zooballoon, a hot air balloon that rises high above the city offering breathtaking views of the skyline, the Schuylkill River, and Fairmount Park (page 46).

improve in the coming years, with additions such as the President's House monument, on the ground where both George Washington and John Adams once lived. The Civil War and Underground Railroad Museum and the Museum of Jewish American History are also moving to new locations in the heart of Independence Park. Even the least patriotic among us find it hard not to feel a surge of national pride after spending time in this part of town.

While Old City is certainly the most popular area for tourists, you're never far from history with markers of the city's long life apparent from South Philadelphia to Germantown. As you explore, look for the National Historic Landmark symbol on homes, churches, cemeteries, hotels, and even buildings that now house modern shops and restaurants.

More recent historical and architectural gems include City Hall and the Grand Masonic Temple. Built in the mid-19th century, they now share the skyline with ultra-modern skyscrapers. Extending out from Center City, the broad Benjamin Franklin Parkway, often called the Museum District or the Cultural District, is a sight in its own right. Inspired by Paris's Champs-Élysées, it connects City Hall with the world-renowned Philadelphia Museum of Art and other famous museums of art and science. The already massive Art Museum expanded in 2007 with the addition of the Perelman Building across the street, so even repeat visitors never run out of something new to see. The one-of-a-kind Eastern State Penitentiary in nearby Fairmount rounds out the diverse sights in the area.

Just beyond, Fairmount Park extends on both sides of the Schuylkill River into the northwest section of the city. The park offers plenty of cultural and recreational opportunities, including the Philadelphia Zoo and a wealth of historic homes, gardens, and sculptures. Still more historic homes—some that were stops on the Underground Railroad or sites of Revolutionary battles—are open for tours in Germantown.

Meanwhile, local institutions like Reading Terminal Market have remained popular for more than a century, helping to connect Philadelphia's history with the present. In a place that has done an extraordinary job of preserving its past while keeping up with the times, there is no shortage of interesting sights.

Old City   Map 1

INDEPENDENCE NATIONAL HISTORICAL PARK

Operated by National Park Services, Independence National Historical Park is devoted to telling the history of American independence and democracy. Plenty of interesting sights and historic buildings are located within close proximity, and they are all free with the exception of the Constitution Center.

Your visit to the area should start at the **Independence Visitor Center,** and if you're here March–December this is where you'll need to pick up a free timed-entrance ticket to Independence Hall. Be sure to arrive before noon in the busy summer months or call or go online to reserve your Independence Hall tickets (800/967-2283, www.reservations.nps .gov). At the Visitor Center you can also reserve a ticket for a free tour of the Todd House and the Bishop White House.

This compact area is easily traversed on foot, but if you prefer, the Historic Philadelphia Trolley Loop runs 10 A.M.–6:30 P.M. in late May–September. It makes 10 stops throughout Old City, including Franklin Square, the Liberty Bell Center, and Penn's Landing, and offers continuous service every 15 minutes. An all-day pass is $2.

BISHOP WHITE HOUSE

309 Walnut St., 215/965-2305, www.nps.gov/inde

HOURS: Open by tour only, times vary with season, call ahead

COST: Free; tickets available at Independence Visitor Center (6th and Market Sts.)

Reverend William White (1748–1836) was the first Episcopal Bishop of Pennsylvania and founder of the American Episcopal Church. For nearly 50 years he lived in this home conveniently located between the two churches where he served as rector—Christ Church and St. Peter's Church. Many prominent 18th-century figures, among them George Washington and Benjamin Franklin, visited the home. Restored to look as it did in 1787, the elegant federal-style mansion offers a glimpse into the

life of an upper-class 18th-century Philadelphia family. It contains White's library, many of his personal items, and an early version of a flush toilet, or privy—one of the very first in a Philadelphia home. Tours are limited to 10 people and offered on a first-come, first-served basis combined with a tour of the Todd House (see listing later in this section).

CARPENTERS' HALL

320 Chestnut St., 215/925-0167, www.carpentershall.org

HOURS: Tues.-Sun. 10 A.M.-4 P.M.

COST: Free

Georgian-style Carpenters' Hall has a rich history despite its inconspicuous presence. Designed by Robert Smith, it was built in 1770

FUN AND FREE: PHILLY ON A BUDGET

With plenty of free sights and activities, you don't have to be rich to have fun in Philly. You can do all of the following for free – yes, you heard right, free.

SIGHTS

Nearly all the sights of **Independence National Historical Park** are free, including the **Liberty Bell**, **Independence Hall**, **Franklin Court**, **Carpenters' Hall**, **Bishop White House**, **Library Hall**, **Philosophical Hall**, **U.S. Mint**, and **Edgar Allen Poe House.**

Most churches and cathedrals are free to explore, including **Christ Church**, **Arch Street Friends Meeting House**, **Old Pine Street Presbyterian**, and **Mother Bethel A.M.E.**

TOURS

Free self-guided walking tours are offered at the **Independence Visitor Center.** While you're there, check out the free mini-museum and the film *Independence*.

Two of Philadelphia's most spectacular buildings – the **Kimmel Center** and **City Hall**, built more than a century apart – offer free tours.

MUSEUMS

On Sunday, pay whatever you wish at the **Philadelphia Museum of Art.**

At select times on Sunday, visit the following museums for free: **Independence Seaport Museum** (10 A.M.-noon), **Institute of Contemporary Art** (11 A.M.-1 P.M.), and **University Museum of Archaeology and Anthropology** (all day Sept.-May).

GALLERIES

Most art galleries are free, including the **Morris Gallery** in the Pennsylvania Academy of Fine Arts, presenting rotating exhibitions of regional artists. The best time to visit the galleries of Old City is in the evening on the **First Friday** of the month, when the galleries are free and open.

---

to serve as headquarters for the Carpenters' Company of Philadelphia. The company, founded in 1724, is today the nation's oldest trade guild. Carpenters' Hall is most famous as the site of the meeting of the First Continental Congress in 1774, when 12 men including George Washington, John Adams, Samuel Adams, and Patrick Henry met to discuss their discontent with their ruler, King George. They were particularly disgruntled with the taxes imposed on the colonies without the consent of colonists, which became popularly known as "taxation without representation." The meeting resulted in one of the earliest formal acts of rebellion against British rule—a trade embargo—and was the precursor to the Second Continental Congress, which met at the State House two years later to declare war.

Over its long history Carpenters' Hall has also been home to Franklin's Library Company, the American Philosophical Society, the First and Second Banks of the United States, and a hospital for American forces during the Revolutionary War. Inside, you'll find a scale model of the building, the original Windsor chairs used by members of the Continental Congress, and a banner carried during the 1788 parade celebrating the ratification of the Constitution.

CHRIST CHURCH

2nd St. btwn. Market and Arch Sts., 215/922-1695, www.christchurchphila.org

HOURS: Mon.-Sat. 9 A.M.-5 P.M., Sun. 12:30-5 P.M., closed Mon. and Tues. in Jan. and Feb., guided tours start on the hour

COST: Free, but suggested donation $3 adult, $2 student

In its heyday, among Christ Church's members were many of Philadelphia's elite—including a total of 15 of the signers of the Declaration of Independence. Basically, everyone who was anyone was a member. The first parish of the Anglican Church in Pennsylvania and the birthplace of the American Episcopal Church, it is also referred to as "The Nation's Church."

SAVE MONEY WITH CITYPASS OR PHILADELPHIA PASS

CityPass is a good option if you're planning to visit all or most of the attractions included: the Franklin Institute, Adventure Aquarium, Philadelphia Zoo, and either the Academy of Natural Sciences or the Independence Seaport Museum. It includes one day, or 24 hours from the time of validation, of hop-on, hop-off service on the Philadelphia Trolley Works, which conveniently connects all the attraction stops, among many others. The pass saves about 50 percent off the total cost of paying for each attraction individually. The passes, good for nine days, are available at the Independence Visitor Center, online (www.citypass.com/city/philadelphia.html), or at any participating attraction. The cost for adults is $49 (total value $94.65), and $34 for kids 3-12.

Another option is the **Philadelphia Pass**, which includes admission to 20 popular attractions and discounts on many others. It includes more sights and there is no limit on the amount you can do in one day. This may be a better choice if you're short on time and planning to do a quick whirlwind tour, but you'll have to move quickly to make it worth it since it is valid for less time than CityPass (one to five consecutive days). The price increases with the number of days it is valid: $47-110 adult, $35-95 child. The pass includes access to the Big Bus Company double-decker tour buses on each day of validity and can be purchased online (www.philadelphiapass.com) or by phone (888/567-7277).

At its founding in 1695, the modest brick-and-wood structure resembled the typical Quaker meeting houses that dominated early Philadelphia. It was a far cry from what you'll see today—one of the finest and most elaborate examples of colonial Georgian architecture in the world.

Rebuilt in 1727–1744, the church was designed by Dr. John Kearsley and modeled on the work of famed British architect Christopher Wren. The tower was added in 1754 with funds raised from a lottery organized by Benjamin Franklin, making the church the tallest structure in the colonies for 75 years to follow.

Inside, you'll see William Penn's baptismal font (donated in 1697 by All Hallows Church in London), a chandelier installed in 1740, and a pulpit built by Thomas Folwell in 1769. William White, church rector for 57 years, first Bishop of Pennsylvania, and Chaplain of the Continental Congress, is buried here. When the parish grew too large, St. Peters Church was established as an offshoot for Society Hill members. The church remains active to this day.

CHRIST CHURCH BURIAL GROUND

Arch St. btwn. 4th and 5th Sts.,
www.christchurchphila.org
HOURS: Mon.-Sat. 10 A.M.-4 P.M., Sun. noon-4 P.M. Mar.-Nov.; Sun.-Fri. noon-4 P.M., Sat. 10 A.M.-4 P.M. Dec., weather permitting; closed Jan. and Feb.
COST: $2 adult, $1 student, $10 for groups up to 25

In 1790, Ben Franklin's funeral was attended by more than 20,000 people. Here he rests, alongside his wife and young son and more than 5,000 other early Philadelphians. In 1719, the overcrowded grounds of Christ Church a few blocks away could no longer fit more bodies, so this plot was purchased on the "outskirts of town" to accommodate its members.

The historic site was closed to the public for 25 years, but it reopened in 2003 after an intensive renovation. More than 1,400 markers remain, but many are so old and worn down that the names are no longer visible.

During a tour you'll learn about the prominent figures and ordinary folks who were buried here. While 80 percent of the burials took place before 1840, the most recent was in 1994. Some think it's good luck to throw a penny on Ben's gravestone.

DECLARATION HOUSE (GRAFF HOUSE)

701 Market St., 215/965-2305, www.nps.gov/inde

HOURS: Daily 9 A.M.-5 P.M. summer, 10 A.M.-1 P.M. rest of the year

COST: Free

When bricklayer Jacob Graff Jr. decided to rent out rooms in the modest home he built in 1775, he never could have anticipated what would happen under his roof. Thomas Jefferson—a Virginia delegate to the Continental Congress and future president of the United States—was his boarder, and it was in these rooms that he drafted the Declaration of Independence. The small exhibit on the 1st floor contains rough drafts of the Declaration and a small theater for viewing the short film *The Extraordinary Creation.* The film reveals important details— like the fact that Jefferson's original version called for the abolishment of slavery, but it was eliminated because the committee, including Benjamin Franklin and John Adams, didn't feel people were ready for it. Upstairs, you can see Jefferson's bedroom and parlor, which include reproduction furnishings of his desk and his swivel chair.

FRANKLIN COURT

314-322 Market St., 215/965-2305, www.nps.gov/inde

HOURS: Daily 9 A.M.-5 P.M., hours may be reduced in winter, call ahead

COST: Free

At times it seems the entire city is one giant tribute to Benjamin Franklin, and nowhere is it more overt than at Franklin Court. Philadelphia's favorite son, who spent much of his life in the city, was a printer, diplomat, inventor, publisher, author, statesman, and postmaster. He founded the Library Company, Pennsylvania Hospital, Philosophical Society, the University of Pennsylvania, and more, so it's fitting that an entire court occupying a large portion of a city block is dedicated to him.

Franklin Court is on the site of Franklin's home for the final five years of his life after he returned from nearly 20 years of working as a commissary in France and England. Designed by world-famous architect Robert Venturi for the bicentennial, a "ghost structure" made of

steel outlines the area occupied by his original home, destroyed in 1812. Remains of the original foundation, underground kitchen, and privy pit (toilet) can be seen through viewing pits in the ground. Flagstones around the house have been carved with real correspondence that took place between Ben and his wife, Deborah, mostly about renovations to their home while he was away.

At the opposite end of Franklin Court, a row of homes built by Franklin in the late 1780s has been transformed into other Ben-themed structures, including the **Franklin Court Museum Shop** and the **B. Free Franklin Post Office and Museum,** highlighting postal history. Note that the post office is the only one in the country that does not display an American flag—since it had not yet been invented. The court also contains an archaeological display called "Fragments of Franklin Court" and a **Printing Office and Bindery.**

A highlight of Franklin Court is the **Underground Museum,** with its interesting displays, interactive exhibits, and a 22-minute film entitled *The Real Ben Franklin.* A phone bank plays audio testimonies about Franklin based on the words of other famous people in history. As with most major public figures, Ben was highly praised and highly criticized, but one thing is certain—he left quite a mark on Philadelphia and the world.

FREE QUAKER MEETING HOUSE

500 Arch St., 215/965-2305, www.nps.gov/inde

HOURS: Wed.-Sun. 1-5 P.M.

COST: Free

The Revolutionary War raised a major dilemma for many Quakers—whether to uphold their religious values or fight those darn Brits. Since one of the most important tenets of the religion is pacifism, those who decided to join the fight for independence were excommunicated and unwelcome at their meeting houses. So in 1783, they founded one of their own. The simple brick Georgian meeting house was designed by Samuel Wetherill, and its 200-plus members, who included Betsy Ross and Constitution-signer Thomas Mifflin, became

SIGHTSEEING TOURS

Taking a guided tour can be a fun and informative way to see and learn about Philadelphia. There are a variety of options – especially in Independence National Historical Park – ranging from your basic history tour to a bar tour led by guides in colonial garb. Old City is best explored on foot, with lots of sights within close proximity of one another. To cover farther-reaching areas of the city, or when hot summer temperatures make it unpleasant to do much walking at all, there are also bus, trolley, carriage, and boat tours to choose from.

ON FOOT

Constitutional Walking Tours (Independence Visitor Center, 6th and Market Sts., 215/525-1776, www.theconstitutional.com, $17.50 adult, $12.50 children 3–12, $55 for family of 2 adults and 2 children) let you see Independence National Historical Park through a variety of methods. Free self-guided map tours cover more than 30 historic sites; various audio tours that work with mp3 players and cell phones are available for purchase; or you can take a 75-minute guided tour that points out 15 popular sites. Note that the guided tour does not include entry to the sites.

Duck boats tour the Delaware River.

© KARRIE GAVIN

Once Upon a Nation is responsible for the knowledgeable colonial-dressed storytellers stationed at various benches throughout Independence Park, and they also offer a variety of entertaining tours led by well-trained costumed characters. Tours depart from the Independence Living History Center (115 S. 3rd St., 215/629-4026, www.onceuponanation .org, hours and cost vary). On the one-hour **Turmoil and Treason Tour,** you'll see actors debate going to war with England during a walk to Independence Hall. On the four-hour *Independence After Hours Tour,* you'll have a three-course dinner at the historic City Tavern and watch Revolutionary-era reenactments between courses; visit Independence Hall where you'll watch more reenactments between Thomas Jefferson, John Adams, and Benjamin

Franklin; and see the Lights of Liberty Show. On the **Tipplers Tour** (my favorite), you'll enjoy a drink at four different bars – Society Hill Hotel, The Plough & The Stars, Old Original Bookbinders, and City Tavern – during a two-hour bar tour while learning about the role of the local watering hole in colonial Philadelphia.

The **Friends of Independence National Historical Park** (143 S. 3rd St., 215/861-4971, www.friendsofindependence.org) offers **Twilight Tours** (early July–Labor Day, daily 6 P.M., free), hour-long walking tours of the area. Designed by the volunteer guides, each tour is a little different. The organization also offers **Open House Tours** (800/537-7676, prices and schedule vary), when private homeowners from around the region open their doors and let you explore the unique architecture, histories, and stories of their homes.

During a 90-minute **Candlelight Ghost Tour** (215/413-1997, www.ghosttour.com/Philadelphia.htm, 7:30 and 9:30 P.M. Apr.-Nov., $15 adult, $8 children 4–12, reservations required), you'll hear tales of countless ghosts believed to roam the city. Stops include Independence Hall and St. Peter's Cemetery, and ghosts include Benjamin Franklin. Tours depart from 5th and Chestnut Streets and tickets can be purchased at Independence Visitor Center, the gift shop (401 Chestnut St.), or online.

During the **Lights of Liberty Show** (6th and Chestnut Sts., 877/462-1776, $19.50 adult, $16.50 student and senior, $13 child 12 and under, Mar.-Oct., multiple shows each evening), you'll experience the American Revolution through state-of-the-art technology. The story is told through laser-light images up to 50 feet high projected onto the buildings of Independence Park, including some where the events actually took place. An accompanying audio tour includes a musical score by the Philadelphia Orchestra and the voices of Walter Cronkite, Ossie Davis, and Charlton Heston. It is available in English, German, Italian, Japanese, and Spanish, as well as a version geared toward children ages 6–12.

ON WHEELS
Philadelphia Trolley Works (5th and Market Sts., 215/923-8516, www.phillytour.com) operates narrated tours on open-air Victorian trolleys, double-decker London-style buses (Big Bus Company), and horse-drawn carriages ('76 Carriage Company). The buses and trolleys allow you to hop off at any of 20 stops, including Independence National Historical Park, Chinatown, City Hall, Eastern State Penitentiary, Philadelphia Museum of Art, Philadelphia Zoo, Franklin Institute Science Museum, Penn's Landing, and more. An all-day day pass costs $27 for adults, $25 for seniors, and $10 for children 4–12, with a $2 savings per ticket booked online. Carriage rides through Old City and Society Hill last 15 minutes to one hour

and cost $30–80 depending on length of tour for up to four people, with an additional $10 for each additional rider. Avoid taking a carriage ride on the hottest summer days – the horse is even hotter than you are.

If you can get past the outrageously cheesy factor and the annoying sounds of the Wacky Quacker, a whistle that makes quacking sounds that is given to each guest, the amphibious **Duck Tours** (6th and Market Sts., 877/887-8225, www.phillyducks.com, $25 adult, $24 senior, $15 child, free child under 2) offer a unique way to see the city on land and from water. The superhero-like open-air machines transform from land vehicles on wheels into boats when they drop into the Delaware River at Penn's Landing. The "Captain" tells stories of the city's history as you move through the streets and the water, and if you join in and make some quacking sounds of your own, it's much less annoying than listening to others do it.

ON WATER
With a bar and food at your disposal, a ride on **Riverboat Queen Fleet** (200 N. Columbus Blvd., Penn's Landing, 215/923-2628, www.riverboatqueenfleet.com, summer only) is a relaxing way to take in the scenery. Trips vary in length of time and price; one-hour tours without food and drink included start at $15 per person. The fleet also offers U-Pedal paddle boats for rental and Super Ducks, a variation of the duck boat available for private charter. A larger cruise ship, the **Spirit of Philadelphia** (Pier 3, Columbus Blvd., Penn's Landing, 866/455-3866, www.spiritcitycruises.com) is more than just a sightseeing tour. With a restaurant, full bar, and dance floor onboard, it offers lunch ($29–39), dinner ($50-75), and late-night ($21-26) cruises, as well as special events like theater and holiday cruises. There is no better way to take in the skyline than sailing along the Delaware River.

SIGHTS

known as the "fighting Quakers." After the war, most returned to their former meeting houses and by 1834, services were no longer held here. It has since been a school, an apprentice library, a plumbing warehouse, and headquarters for the Junior League of Philadelphia. There isn't much to see inside today, but take a quick peek at the two original benches and original window, and the five-pointed-star tissue pattern that Betsy Ross is thought to have used to make the first American flag. Descendants of the original group still hold annual meetings here, and it is now home to the offices of Once Upon a Nation, a nonprofit organization that operates many programs in historic Philadelphia.

◖ INDEPENDENCE HALL

Chestnut St. btwn. 5th and 6th Sts., 215/965-2305 or 877/444-6777, www.nps.gov/inde

HOURS: Daily 9 A.M.–5 P.M.; tours start every 15-30 minutes, last tour at 4:30 P.M.

COST: Free, but reserve a ticket at Independence

Visitor Center the day of your visit Mar.-Dec., or reserve in advance for a fee of $1.50 per ticket online or by phone

Independence Hall is the centerpiece of Independence National Historical Park. It sits on leafy Independence Square and is the southern boundary of Independence Mall, home to the Liberty Bell and Constitution Center. Sensing a pattern? If you slept through your grade school history class, this is where the United States' independence from England became official. Within these walls, the Declaration of Independence and the Constitution were debated, drafted, and signed, and our nation was formed.

Originally the State House, the classic Georgian structure was designed by Andrew Hamilton and Edmund Wooley and built 1732–1756. Of the many restorations it has seen, the most notable were those by Greek revival architect John Havilland in 1830 and by the National Park Service in 1950; the latter greatly restored the building to its late 18th-

© KARRIE GAVIN

The Declaration of Independence and the Constitution were drafted inside Independence Hall, formerly the State House.

century appearance. The furniture is mostly reproduction, since much of the original furniture was burnt during the winter of 1777–1778 when Philadelphia was briefly occupied by the British Army.

Independence Hall was the meeting place for the Second Continental Congress from 1775 to 1783, except during the brief British occupation. The most important decisions were made in the 1st-floor **Assembly Room,** home to George Washington's famous "Rising Sun" chair. This is where he was appointed commander in chief of the Continental Army (1775), the Declaration of Independence was adopted (July 4, 1776), the design of the American flag was agreed upon (1777), the Articles of Confederation were adopted (1781), and the U.S. Constitution was drafted (1787). Original copies of the Articles of Confederation, Declaration of Independence, and the Constitution are on display in the **Great Essentials Exhibit** in the West Wing of Independence Hall. You can also see the Syng silver inkstand that was used to sign the Declaration of Independence and the Constitution.

Independence Hall is one of a trio of matching Georgian buildings that housed the three branches of early government, and it makes sense to visit all of them together. Facing Independence Hall on Chestnut Street, the building on the corner of Chestnut and 5th Streets is **Old City Hall.** Built in 1790 by master carpenter David Evans, it was home to the United States Supreme Court 1791–1800. Once the capital moved to D.C., it became Philadelphia's City Hall until 1870.

On the corner of Chestnut and 6th Streets is **Congress Hall,** where the two branches of Congress met (1790–1800). The House of Representatives was on the 1st floor and the Senate on the 2nd floor. Built in 1787, Congress Hall was the site of the inaugurations of Adams and of Washington for his second term. It is also where the Bill of Rights was ratified. On the 2nd floor, notice the 19th-century fresco of an eagle holding an olive branch signifying peace, and a plaster medallion on the ceiling with an oval sunburst with 13 stars, designed to honor the 13 original states. The carpet features 13 state shields and cornucopias wishing for abundance in the new land. It's a reproduction of the original carpet made in the 1790s by William Sprague. Founder of the first woven carpet mill in Philadelphia, Sprague is credited with bringing the carpet industry to the United States.

INDEPENDENCE LIVING HISTORY CENTER

115 S. 3rd St., 215/629-4026
HOURS: Mon.-Fri. 9 A.M.–5 P.M.
COST: Free

The Living History Center contains an active archaeology lab devoted almost entirely to discovering and examining artifacts excavated on the site of the National Constitution Center. Large windows allow visitors to watch scientists work on thousands of artifacts that continue to reveal fascinating details about Philadelphia's early history. It is operated by Independence National Historical Park and Once Upon a Nation, a nonprofit that operates tours and programming in historic Philadelphia, many of which take place or depart from here. One of these programs is *1776: The Movie-Musical,* which plays every Friday in summer at 7 P.M. ($12 adult, $8 children 8–12, $10 senior, student, and military). The three-hour interactive event, with sing-alongs and props, is educational and enjoyable for the whole family, but is particularly a big hit with children under 12. Tickets can be purchased at the gift shop in the lobby.

INDEPENDENCE VISITOR CENTER

6th and Market Sts., 215/965-7676 or 800/537-7676, www.independencevisitorcenter.com
HOURS: Daily 8:30 A.M.–7 P.M. Memorial Day-Labor Day, 8:30 A.M.–6 P.M. Mar.-Memorial Day and Sept. following Labor Day, 8:30 A.M.–5 P.M. rest of year
COST: Free

This is your first stop on any visit to historic Philadelphia. In addition to maps and information galore, there is a free mini-museum and a 28-minute film, *Independence,* to introduce you to the history of Philadelphia. An automated kiosk provides information and allows you to book tickets to area attractions. The

SIGHTS

center has a gift shop, a café, and WiFi. This is also where you reserve your free timed tickets to Independence Hall and sign up for tours of the Todd and Bishop White Houses.

◖ LIBERTY BELL

Market St. btwn. 5th and 6th Sts., 215/965-2305
HOURS: Daily 9 A.M.-5 P.M., last admission 4:45 P.M.
COST: Free

This iconic symbol is associated not only with Philadelphia, but with democracy and the United States' independence from England, and with freedom in worldwide struggles, such as freedom from slavery and the women's rights movement. In fact, it didn't become widely known as the "Liberty Bell" until the abolitionists coined the phrase. So yes, you—along with more than a million other visitors each year—have to see it once in your life. Just don't set your hopes too high—it is just a bell after all—and not a very well-made one at that. But the real attraction is not the 2,090-pound piece of metal; it is what the bell has come to symbolize.

There is some debate over the details of its history, but it goes something like this: Originally built for the tower of the State House (now Independence Hall), it was cast in London and arrived in Philadelphia in 1752 to commemorate the 50-year anniversary of William Penn's Charter of Privileges. It suffered the first of several cracks during its first ring in a test run. It was recast two years later by two Philadelphians, John Stow and John Pass, who took the opportunity to carve their own names on it. The bell is said to have rung for several important events, including the first public reading of the Declaration of Independence in 1776. No one knows exactly when it rang for the last time, but it may have been for George Washington's birthday in 1846, at which point the cracks were so bad that the bell was rendered useless.

Housed in Independence Hall for more than 200 years, it was moved to Liberty Bell Pavilion in 1976 for the bicentennial. In 2003 it was moved again to its current home in the **Liberty Bell Center,** a modern glass-enclosed

PHOTO BY R. KENNEDY FOR GPTMC

The symbol of liberty is one of Philadelphia's most popular attractions.

mini-museum and multimedia gallery containing documents, images, and a short History Channel film exploring the facts and myths surrounding the bell, available in nine languages.

The bell's strategic position offers an uninterrupted view of Independence Hall, making it one of the most photographed spots in the city. On the bell, Pennsylvania is spelled "Pensylvania," which was one of several acceptable spellings at the time. It is engraved with the message "Proclaim Liberty throughout all the Land unto all the Inhabitants thereof." The message may present a conundrum considering slavery was still prevalent at the time, but it makes sense that so many groups later adopted it as a symbol for freedom.

◖ NATIONAL CONSTITUTION CENTER

25 Arch St., 215/409-6700, www.constitutioncenter.org
HOURS: Mon.-Fri. 9:30 A.M.-5 P.M., Sat. 9:30 A.M.-6 P.M., Sun. noon-5 P.M.
COST: $12 adult, $11 senior, $8 child, free for children ages 4 and under and active military personnel

This modern museum stands out among the

area's countless 17th- and 18th-century attractions. It is the only national museum entirely dedicated to telling the story of the U.S. Constitution, the seminal document that was drafted just a block away in Independence Hall. The museum opened on July 4, 2003, and immediately became one of the area's most popular attractions, bringing in more than a million visitors a year. Inscribed on the outside of the two-story structure are the first three words of the Constitution, "We the People."

A visit begins with *Freedom Rising,* a live-actor show complete with film, music, and lights that runs twice an hour. The show is pretty Hollywood, complete with dramatic voiceovers and music, but it's actually quite captivating and—dare I say—inspirational. The round theater is surrounded by a 360-degree exhibit space, where you can learn more than you were ever taught about the Constitution and the events, people, and ideas that formed it and remain part of our government today. Photographs, artifacts, and an original copy of the Constitution are on display. You can participate in interactive and multimedia exhibits, like trying on the judicial robes, taking a photograph of yourself projected realistically on a screen while taking the presidential oath of office, and voting for your favorite president. In Signers' Hall, life-size bronze figures of the Constitution's signers and dissenters are on display, and you choose for yourself whether to sign or dissent. It would take days to read everything on display, so you'll have to pick and choose, and allow a few hours to wander.

NEW HALL MILITARY MUSEUM
320 Chestnut St., 215/965-2305, www.nps.gov/inde
HOURS: Mon.-Sat. 9 A.M.-5 P.M.
COST: Free
Although this brick building is modest in appearance, it introduces visitors to one of the most significant developments of the colonial era: the early beginnings of the U.S. military. The museum is dedicated to the founding soldiers who sacrificed their lives for freedom and has exhibits on the past and present army,

navy, and marines. Educational seminars are given during the summer. The building is a reconstruction of the original built by the Carpenters' Company in 1791, which once housed the office of the first secretary of war, Henry Knox.

PHILADELPHIA MERCHANT'S EXCHANGE
143 S. 3rd St.
HOURS: Mon.-Fri. 8:30 A.M.-4:30 P.M.
COST: Free
This was essentially the first stock exchange building in the country, offering merchants a fabulous place to barter or sell their wares, which was previously done on the streets and in coffee shops and taverns. It is now headquarters for the National Park Service, and while the building is an architectural gem, there isn't much to see inside except for a small exhibition on the building's history. William Strickland, also responsible for the steeple atop Independence Hall and the Second Bank of the United States, designed the Greek-influenced structure built 1832–1834. The tower is based on the Choragic Monument of Lysicrates in Athens, and the resplendent Exchange Room (now closed to the public) was graced with a domed ceiling, mosaic floor, and marble columns. At the Exchange's dedication speech in 1832, solicitor John Kane aptly predicted: "The building which we have founded shall stand among the relics of antiquities, another memorial to posterity of the skill of its architect— and proof of the liberal spirit, and cultivated taste, which, in our days, distinguish the mercantile community."

PHILOSOPHICAL HALL AND LIBRARY HALL
105 S. 5th St., 215/440-3400, www.amphilsoc.org
HOURS: Library Hall Thurs.-Sun. 10 A.M.-4 P.M., Philosophical Hall Mon.-Fri. 9 A.M.-4:45 P.M.
COST: Free
Philosophical Hall is the only privately owned building on Independence Square, as property of the American Philosophical Society. Founded in 1743 by Benjamin Franklin to

"promote useful knowledge," it is the oldest learned society in the country. The word "philosophy" once had a much broader context, and the society was intended to encourage thinking about all sorts of topics, including science, nature, machinery, industry, and government. Its esteemed list of past and present members includes Benjamin Franklin, Charles Darwin, Madame Curie, Albert Einstein, Toni Morrison, Nelson Mandela, more than a dozen U.S. presidents, and 200 Nobel Prize winners.

The federal-style building was constructed 1786–1789 by Samuel Vaughan and remodeled in 1949 by Sydney Martin. It contains one of the nation's first museums, founded in 1784 by Charles Wilson Peale, artist, naturalist, and Society member. The museum closed in the early 19th century and did not reopen until 2001. Today, it features rotating exhibits of art, science, and early U.S. history.

Library Hall across the street is also owned by the American Philosophical Society and houses many of its most important collections, including original journals of Lewis and Clark, a copy of the Declaration of Independence in Jefferson's handwriting, and first editions of Sir Isaac Newton's *Principia* and Charles Darwin's *Origin of Species*. The original Library Hall was built in 1790 by architect William Thornton. It was home to the Library Company of Philadelphia, the first public library in the country, founded by Benjamin Franklin, and served as Library of Congress when Philadelphia was the capital. When the Library Company outgrew the space, it relocated to a larger location at 1314 Locust Street, where it operates today.

PRESIDENT'S HOUSE
5th and Market Sts., 215/965-2305,
www.phila.gov/presidentshouse
Next to the Liberty Bell stands the site of the President's House. When Philadelphia was the capital from 1790 to 1800, the presidents during that period, George Washington and John Adams, both lived and worked in this house, which functioned as the nation's first White House. At least nine slaves also lived in the house under Washington, during the time when the founding fathers were declaring independence, freedom, and that "all men are created equal." Plans are underway to build a monument on the site, and there has been much thought given as to how to highlight both the presidents' and the slaves' history, and acknowledge the conflicting values at work during the time of the Revolution, when so many founding fathers still owned slaves.

SECOND BANK OF THE UNITED STATES
420 Chestnut St., 215/965-2305, www.nps.gov/inde
HOURS: Wed.-Sun. 11 A.M.–4 P.M.
COST: $2
Designed by William Strickland and built 1819–1824, this is considered one of the finest examples of Greek revival architecture in the United States. Modeled on the Parthenon, the building served as a model for countless other U.S. financial institutions. The bank was chartered in 1816 during a time of massive currency fluctuations to provide credit for government and businesses— think of the Fed today. In 1832, President Andrew Jackson vetoed a bill to recharter the Bank because he feared it was creating an unconstitutional monopoly. While it has evolved greatly over the years, the banking system of today operates under many of the same structures and ideas.

Today, the building is owned by the National Park Service and houses the portrait gallery "People of Independence." Eighty-five of the portraits were painted by Charles Wilson Peale (1741–1827), the most famous portraitist of the 18th century. The 185 paintings of colonial and federal leaders, scientists, explorers, and officers include George Washington, Alexander Hamilton, Thomas Mifflin, Thomas Jefferson, Robert Morris, and the Marquis de Lafayette. If you've ever wondered what the Founding Fathers looked like, this is a good place to find out.

TODD HOUSE

4th and Walnut Sts., 215/965-2305, www.nps.gov/inde

HOURS: By tour only, times vary

COST: Free; tickets available at Independence Visitor Center (corner of 6th and Market Sts.) on first-come, first-served basis combined with a tour of the Bishop White House, limited to 10 people

In 1791–1793, future first lady Dolley Payne lived in this Georgian home with her husband, lawyer John Todd. Todd died during the 1793 yellow fever epidemic, leaving young Dolley to care for their son. She quickly attracted the attentions of many men, including a lawyer from Virginia, James Madison. They were married and he became president of the United States and she one of the favorite first ladies in history. The parlor of the house is believed to be where Madison—17 years her senior—first wooed young Dolley. On the tour you can see a reproduction of John Todd's law office and leather fire buckets hanging from the ceiling. Most of all, it exemplifies a middle-class American home in the late 18th century.

MORE OLD CITY SIGHTS

ARCH STREET FRIENDS MEETING HOUSE

320 Arch St., 215/627-2667, www.archstreetfriends.org

HOURS: Mon.-Sat. 10 A.M.-4 P.M., with meetings for worship Wed. 7 P.M. and Sun. 10:30 A.M.

COST: $2 donation suggested

The oldest and largest Quaker meeting house in the world fittingly occupies a piece of land donated by Quaker founder William Penn. In 1793, Penn donated the site to the Religious Society of Friends to be used as a Quaker burial ground. The large wall surrounding it was installed to keep cats and dogs out of the graves.

The building was constructed in 1804 by architect Owen Biddle at a slight elevation above the ground level to accommodate layers of graves beneath. The modest, symmetrical brick structure reflects the early Quaker values of simplicity.

There are three distinct sections inside. The East Wing is probably the most interesting to visitors, with its dioramas depicting the major events in the life of William Penn, and the "Drinker Dollhouse," a reproduction of the 18th-century home of a Philadelphia Quaker, Elizabeth Drinker. The West Wing was used for women-only meetings, some of which were attended by famous abolitionist Lucretia Mott. Today, men and women attend worship together in the Center section. Meetings are open to the public and last 45 minutes to an hour. Don't expect a sermon; meetings are not led by anyone and they are generally silent, unless the spirit moves someone to speak.

BETSY ROSS HOUSE

239 Arch St., 215/686-1252, www.betsyrosshouse.org

HOURS: Daily 10 A.M.-5 P.M. Apr.-Sept., Tues.-Sun. 10 A.M.-5 P.M. Oct.-Mar.

COST: $3 adult, $2 child (12 and under) and student, $4 audio tour includes admission

Did she or didn't she? The debate over whether or not Betsy Ross actually sewed the first American flag rages on, but the fact that she led a fascinating life is indisputable. Married and widowed three times, Betsy was shunned because her first husband was not a Quaker. She was eventually welcomed back into the Society of Friends when she married her third husband, a Quaker named John Claypoole.

Built in 1740, her "bandbox"-style home has one room on each floor and a winding staircase from the basement to the top. Betsy made a living as an upholsterer while she lived here from 1773 to 1785. And she wasn't the only one; a wide variety of shopkeepers and artisans lived and worked in the home over a 150-year-period, including a shoemaker, an apothecary, and a cigarmaker. Period furniture, including some of Betsy's belongings, can be seen in the seven tiny rooms. As you explore, you'll be struck by the narrow hallways and low doorways. A 25-minute audio tour gives a history of the house and of Betsy's life. An alternative tour is offered for kids—complete with a scavenger hunt. The site draws crowds in the summer, and you'll be moved through more quickly. If you're able to visit in fall or winter, you'll have the option of a longer, more in-depth tour.

CURTIS CENTER AND DREAM GARDEN MOSAIC

601-45 Walnut St., 215/238-6450

HOURS: Mon.-Fri. 8 A.M.-6 P.M., Sat. 8 A.M.-1 P.M.

COST: Free

Tiffany Studios and artist Maxfield Parrish combined artistic visions to brighten the Curtis Center lobby with the dazzling Dream Garden Mosaic. The 15-by-49-foot intricately designed mosaic combines light, glass, and color in a mesmerizing landscape. Louis Comfort Tiffany was hired to work with Philadelphian Parrish to execute a design based on Parrish's painting *The Dream Garden.* The mosaic was completed in 1916 and has been on display ever since—despite casino-owner Steve Wynn's attempt to take it to Vegas. Wynn purchased the masterpiece in 1988, but public outcry inspired Pew Charitable Trust to pay $3.5 million to keep it in place.

The building was commissioned by Curtis Publishing, one of the largest and most influential publishers of the early 20th century. Curtis was responsible for the still-popular *Ladies Home Journal,* founded in 1883, and the *Saturday Evening Post,* which was founded in 1728 but purchased by Curtis in 1897. Curtis Publishing operated out of this building, built in the 1890s, for many years. Since it is primarily an office building, the only reason to go is for a glimpse of the Dream Garden.

ELFRETH'S ALLEY

btwn. Front and N. 2nd Sts. and Race and Arch Sts., Museum Shop in House 124, 215/574-0560, www.elfrethsalley.org

HOURS: Mon.-Sat. 10 A.M.-5 P.M., Sun. noon-5 P.M. Mar.-Oct.; Thurs.-Sat. 10 A.M.-5 P.M., Sun. noon-5 P.M. Nov.-Feb.

COST: Tours $5 adult, $1 child (ages 6-18), free 5 and under, tours offered on the hour and half hour

Yes, it's cliché, but walking through this narrow cobblestone street is a bit like stepping back in time. Occupied since 1702, Elfreth's Alley is the oldest continuously occupied residential street in the United States. Federal and Georgian homes—complete with horse posts and shoe scrapes—have been immaculately preserved, and the entire street is listed on the Philadelphia Register of Historic Properties. Small by today's standards, one of the homes is said to have housed up to 27 people from eight different families at a time. There's very little car traffic and no modern appliances visible in the windows looking out on the 16-foot-wide street, making the bustle of Old City feel far away, even though it's just around the corner.

The street is named after blacksmith Jeremiah Elfreth, one of the 18th-century artisans and tradespeople who lived here, and who was responsible for building many of the homes. In 1755, he built the house that stands today as a museum and the only home regularly open to the public. If possible, visit on Fete Day, typically the first or second Saturday in June, when many homes on the street open their doors to the public, with music, a parade, and historical reenactments on the street. Or come for the holiday open house, usually the second Saturday in December; check the website for exact dates.

FIRST BANK OF THE UNITED STATES

116 S. 3rd. St., 215/965-7676

The building is closed to the public, but the outside of the oldest national bank in the country is worth checking out on your walk through Old City. The building was constructed 1795–1797 and designed by Samuel Blodgett and James Windrim in the classical revival style, influenced by the ancient Greeks. An eagle, then the relatively new national symbol, sits atop the portico. The bank institution was founded in 1791 during Alexander Hamilton's term as treasury secretary in an attempt to deal with the massive debt the government accrued during the Revolutionary War and to create standard currency for all states. The first charter was drafted by Congress in 1791 and signed by George Washington, and the bank was housed in Carpenters' Hall until 1795. The charter lasted 30 years, but was abandoned by Congress in 1811. The building was restored for the bicentennial in 1976, and is slated to become the new home of the Civil War and Underground Railroad museum in 2010.

FRANKLIN SQUARE

6th and Race Sts., 215/629-4026,
www.onceuponanation.org

HOURS: Sun.-Thurs. 10 A.M.-6 P.M., Fri.-Sat.
10 A.M.-7 P.M., extended hours in summer until 10 P.M.

COST: Park: free; Carousel: $3 adult, $2 child; Mini-golf: $8 adult, $6 child

One of William Penn's five original squares, Franklin Square was until recently a desolate, neglected piece of prime real estate in the heart of Old City. But in 2006, a $6 million renovation project transformed it into an attractive landscaped park, with an 18-hole mini-golf course, playground, and an old-fashioned carousel. Four brick paths lead to an original restored 1838 marble fountain in the center. On spring and summer days and nights, this is a lovely place to stroll, picnic, or enjoy the family-friendly facilities. Originally named Northeast Square by Penn, it was renamed in honor of Benjamin Franklin in 1825.

U.S. MINT

151 N. Independence Mall East (enter on 5th and Arch Sts.), 215/408-0110, www.usmint.gov

HOURS: Mon.-Fri. 9 A.M.-3 P.M., closed on federal holidays

COST: Free; government-issued ID required

From half-eagles of yore to George Washingtons of today, there isn't a penny, schilling, or bird you can't find in the U.S. Mint. Behind the concrete columns, enormous printing and coin presses make every variety of coin and bill in U.S. currency. Elite craftsmen—the national engravers—etch microscopic details into each mold and print, and money is processed, printed, and shipped five days a week. And in less than 24 hours the mint will have made one million dollars, so they can easily afford the free admission for guests.

The U.S. Mint is more than a workshop; it showcases the history of our nation's currency and coin-making process. On display are the presses and tools that crafted the first gold eagle coins (each coin was nearly handmade), and information on the development of the National Treasury and early mint facilities. This facility opened in 1969, Philadelphia's fourth mint.

carousel in Franklin Square

WELCOME PARK

2nd St. and Sansom Alley

This monument to William Penn doesn't begin to rival that of Ben Franklin's Franklin Court, but it's worth a quick stop on your way to get a drink at City Tavern, the watering hole of colonial leaders across the street, or to see a movie at the Ritz East next door. In 1982 the Friends of Independence National Historical Park created Welcome Park for the 300th anniversary of Penn's founding of Pennsylvania. Named after his ship, *The Welcome,* the open-air monument was built on the spot where he lived from 1699 to 1701. A dollhouse-sized replica of the home, the Slate Roof House, is part of the display. Penn's original plan for Philadelphia is etched in marble on the ground and a miniature version of the statue of Penn above City Hall occupies the center. Along two walls, a timeline of his life and early Philadelphia history is displayed.

Society Hill

Map 1

ATHENAEUM

219 S. 6th St., 215/925-2688, www.philaathenaeum.org

HOURS: Mon.-Fri. 9 A.M.-5 P.M.

COST: Free; valid photo ID required

The Athenaeum is a must-see for architecture and design enthusiasts, or anyone looking for a glimpse into the finest in 19th-century living. Established as a research library in 1814, its first member was renowned architect William Strickland in 1820. Strickland's 1839 proposal for a building to house the library on Washington Square was the first drawing acquired by the Athenaeum. It now contains more than a million books, architectural drawings, photographs, and manuscripts representing the work of more than 1,000 American architects, and is considered the premier landmark devoted to American architecture 1800–1945. The 1st-floor gallery is open to the public, but you'll need to make an appointment in advance to tour other areas. Designed by architect John Notman in 1845, the building is one of Philadelphia's first brownstones. The relatively simple exterior belies the ornate reading rooms and 24-foot ceilings inside.

HEADHOUSE SQUARE

2nd St. btwn. Pine and Lombard Sts.

One of the nation's earliest social scenes, Headhouse Square has brought the Society Hill community together since the 18th century. Most of the founders had homes within walking distance of this colonial square and since 1745, traders, artisans, and craftsman have sold and traded goods here on weekends. The Shambles, a covered brick courtyard stretching along 2nd Street between Pine and Lombard Streets, was built in 1803 for the community's "market master," the bazaar's official goods inspector.

The tradition continues today as locals and tourists stroll on the charming cobblestone street during seasonal craft shows, art exhibitions, and weekend farmers markets. Now home to stylish restaurants, cafés, bars, and shops, Headhouse Square maintains much of the energy it must have had 250 years ago.

MOTHER BETHEL A.M.E. CHURCH

419 S. 6th St., 215/925-0616, www.motherbethel.org

HOURS: Tues.-Sat. 10 A.M.-3 P.M., Sun. noon-1 P.M., call ahead

COST: Free

Former slave and preacher Reverend Richard Allen was forced to sit in the balcony of the mixed-race church he attended, St. George's Methodist. So in 1797, along with Absalom Jones and others, he founded Mother Bethel A.M.E., a place where African Americans could worship without restriction. The first African Methodist church in America occupies the oldest piece of land continuously owned by African Americans. The original building was a converted blacksmith shop, but the current building—the church's fourth

PHOTO BY G. WIDMAN FOR GPTMC

Mother Bethel A.M.E. occupies the oldest piece of land continuously owned by African Americans.

incarnation—is a stunning example of 19th-century Romanesque revival architecture built in the 1890s. Light streams through the expansive stained-glass windows and creates a warm glow on the elaborate woodwork.

The basement holds Allen's tomb and a small but fascinating museum highlighting the history of the church and of African American history in general. Allen, born in 1760, was a slave in Germantown who bought his own freedom in 1782. He became a prominent politician and abolitionist activist and the church was an important station on the Underground Railroad. It was also used as a school where slaves were taught to read. The museum's artifacts include the original pulpit constructed by Allen, his Bible, ballot boxes used to elect church officers, and a wooden pew from the original blacksmith's shop. The church also played a significant role in the birth of the first black periodical and insurance company, and Frederick Douglass and Sojourner Truth were among the famous leaders who spoke here.

OLD PINE STREET PRESBYTERIAN CHURCH

412 Pine St., 215/925-8051, www.oldpine.org
HOURS: Mon.-Sat. 10:30 A.M.-5 P.M., Sun. 9 A.M.-noon, call ahead
COST: Free

Old Pine became known as the "Church of the Patriots" because so many of its parishioners, including John Adams, were strong supporters of the Revolution. It was the third Presbyterian Church in Philadelphia, but is the oldest one standing today. The pale-yellow church blends into its tranquil surroundings despite its impressive size and imposing iron fence. Established in 1768, it stands on its original foundation and has its original brick walls, but was expanded twice during the 19th century. The church was almost destroyed after the British occupied it and used it as a hospital during the Revolutionary War, burning many of the pews for warmth during the cold winter. The stately Corinthian columns were added in 1830; behind the giant doors a bi-level sanctuary is lined with dark-red carpeting. The shaded graveyard holds more than 3,000 early Philadelphians, including at least 50 Revolutionary War soldiers; the site inspires many ghost stories. No formal tours are offered, but Old Pine welcomes visitors to come in and look around.

OLD ST. JOSEPH'S CHURCH

321 Willings Alley, off 4th St. btwn. Walnut and Spruce Sts., 215/923-1733, www.oldstjoseph.org

HOURS: Mon.-Fri. 11 A.M.-3 P.M., Sat. 11 A.M.-6:30 P.M., Sun. 8:30 A.M.-3 P.M.

COST: Free

A tiny chapel served as the city's first Catholic parish in 1733 for just 11 Philadelphia families. Despite the general unpopularity of Catholics in Philadelphia at the time, William Penn's 1701 Charter of Privileges called for religious tolerance, so the land was granted to the small group. This became the only place under British rule where Catholic Mass was legal. Ben Franklin advised church leaders to install an iron gate, which turned out to be a good call, considering Quakers once had to prevent a Protestant mob from interrupting services. The church was, however, damaged during anti-Catholic riots in the 1830s. The current building is the third on this site, dating from 1839, and the parish remains active. Notice the stained-glass windows above the altar, glass mosaics on the north and south walls, and the ceiling painting, *The Exaltation of Saint Joseph into Heaven,* by Italian artist Philippo Paggini, whose work also appears in the Capitol in Washington, D.C.

OLD ST. MARY'S CHURCH

252 S. 4th St., 215/923-7930, www.oldstmarys.com

HOURS: Mon.-Fri. 9 A.M.-5 P.M.

COST: Free

Old St. Joseph's was the first and Old St. Mary's was the second Catholic parish in Philadelphia. The two churches were run as one unit until 1830. Built in 1763 by master carpenter Charles Johnson, the church was enlarged in 1810 and has seen several renovations since. Notice the marble pieta crafted by French sculptor Boucher, the crucifix carved by William Rush, and the two stories of stained-glass windows. The church also contains a 1791 baptismal font, brass chandeliers from Independence Hall, and Bishop Conwell's chair.

The cemetery has been in use since 1759, when graves were transported here from crowded Old St. Joseph's and Washington Square. It is higher than street level because a top layer of graves was added after the 1793 yellow fever epidemic required much more space for bodies. Notable people buried here include Commodore John Barry (known as father to the U.S. Navy), General Moylan (aid to George Washington), Thomas Fitzsimmons (a member of the Continental Congress who helped draft the Constitution), and Michael Bouvier, great-great-grandfather of Jacqueline Kennedy Onassis.

PENN'S LANDING

Visitors Center: 301 S. Columbus Blvd. near Spruce St., 215/928-8801, www.pennslandingcorp.com

Penn always dreamed of building an attractive waterfront area lined with trees, but it didn't actually happen until about 300 years after he set foot in this area. Vacant and dilapidated until the late 1960s when the city and developers saw its potential, Penn's Landing is now home to a recreational park, several historic attractions, modern dining and entertainment options, and expensive condominiums. It includes roughly 10 blocks along the Delaware River from Vine Street to South Street, and four footbridges connect it to Old City and Society Hill over I-95.

While you're there, check out the **Benjamin Franklin Bridge,** the largest suspension bridge in the world when it was completed in 1926. Designed by Paul Philippe Cret, who also did the Benjamin Franklin Parkway, it was built to connect Center City with Camden, New Jersey. A lighting system added for the bicentennial celebration makes the view especially beautiful at night.

Near Market Street, you can tour the *Gazela* (215/923-9030) when it's in port. The

177-foot vessel, built in 1883, was originally a Portuguese fishing boat. It was used as late as the 1960s for cod fishing in Canada and still sometimes sails.

Nearby, the **Great Plaza** at Chestnut Street is home to a tiered amphitheater that hosts numerous festivals including a New Orleans–inspired festival on Memorial Day and a week-end-long blues festival in July. In summertime, concerts and events are often held here, including the fireworks display for the Sunoco Welcome America Independence Day celebration. Inscribed stones in the ground highlight Philadelphia as a "City of Firsts."

A few blocks south, check out the **World Sculpture Garden,** containing an obelisk celebrating the 500th anniversary of Columbus's arrival; *Sphere,* a 16-ton 8-foot-circumference monolithic stone from Costa Rica; a totem pole from Canada; a cow sculpture from India; and a bronze statue of William Penn at age 38, among others.

PENNSYLVANIA HOSPITAL

800 Spruce St., 215/829-3370,
www.pennhealth.com/pahosp
HOURS: Tues.-Sat. 10 A.M.-5 P.M., Sun. noon-5 P.M.
COST: Free, $2 to purchase visitors guide from gift shop
Although Benjamin Franklin was best known as an inventor and scientist, he also dabbled in medicine. Realizing the importance of a medical care facility, he consulted esteemed doctor Thomas Bond, and together they founded the nation's first hospital in 1751. The hospital sparked a boom of medical advancements and made Philadelphia the hub of medicine and surgery in the Western hemisphere.

Now part of the University of Pennsylvania health-care system, the hospital remains an integral place of medical research and teaching and one of the city's best hospitals in many fields. Since it is a functioning hospital, only a few areas are open to the public. Tours can be scheduled by appointment Tuesday to Sunday, or a $2 booklet that details the hospital's history can be purchased in the gift shop for a self-tour. Don't miss Benjamin West's epic painting *Christ Healing the Sick in the Temple,* the 13,000-volume library containing a preserved seven-pound tumor, or the oldest existing surgical amphitheater in the United States—which was constructed on the top floor in 1804 to take advantage of natural light.

PHILADELPHIA CONTRIBUTIONSHIP

212 S. 4th St., 215/627-1752, www.contributionship.com
HOURS: Mon.-Fri. 9 A.M.-4 P.M.
COST: Free
In 1736, Ben Franklin founded Philadelphia's first fire brigade, the Union Fire Company, and in 1752, he helped establish the first property insurance company in the country. The Philadelphia Contributionship for the Insurance of Houses from Loss by Fire laid the groundwork for modern insurance companies. Fire and fireproofing buildings were longtime interests of Ben Franklin, who once told a friend that in case of fire: "You may be forced to leap out of windows and hazard your neck to avoid being overroasted." John Stow, who recast the Liberty Bell after it cracked, was responsible for casting the Contributionship's official symbol, the hand-in-hand fire mark, which can be seen on buildings around town.

Constructed in 1836, the building remains the headquarters of the Contributionship and contains a small ground-floor museum that is open to the public. Among the memorabilia are fire marks, firemen's hats, miniature engines, lanterns, and a silver "speaking trumpet" used to convey orders at fire sites. You'll learn interesting tidbits about the history of firefighting—like how rival fire companies fought one another at the scenes of fires because whoever put out the fire received payment. Some members formed the city's most violent gangs. The museum maintains home surveys for many old Philadelphia residences, including those of Ben Franklin and John Penn (William Penn's son). These insurance surveys and records have been useful to present-day Society Hill residents in re-creating the original features of their homes. The elegant 2nd-floor rooms are open by appointment only.

PHYSICK HOUSE

321 S. 4th St., 215/925-7866, www.philalandmarks.org
HOURS: Thurs.-Sat. noon-5 P.M., Sun. 1-5 P.M., last tour 4 P.M.
COST: $5 adult, $4 student and senior, free under 6

Named after the "father of American surgery," Dr. Philip Syng Physick, the four-story federal-style home was built in 1768 by wine importer Henry Hill. It served as the home and office of Dr. Physick from 1815 to 1837. It was here that he designed numerous revolutionary operative instruments, invented the stomach pump, pioneered the use of autopsy for research, and advanced cataract surgery. He also offered medical advice to presidents and created America's first carbonated beverage. He even began an anti-smoking campaign way before his time.

The home was rehabilitated by the Annenberg family during the late 1960s, and it has been largely restored to its original character. French and colonial art and neoclassical furniture decorate the 1st floor, while the 2nd floor is entirely dedicated to Physick's work, showcasing his surgical inventions. The home contains one of the largest gardens in 19th-century Philadelphia, with a cobblestone path surrounded by lush plant life and grotto statuary.

POWEL HOUSE

244 S. 3rd St., 215/627-0364, www.philalandmarks.org
HOURS: Thurs.-Sat. noon-5 P.M., Sun. 1-5 P.M., tours on the hour, last one at 4 P.M.
COST: $5 adult, $4 student and senior, $3 pp for group of 10 or more, $12 families, free child 6 and under

Built in 1765, this stately Georgian mansion was the home of Samuel and Elizabeth Powel, a prominent 18th-century couple. It is the finest surviving example of an upper-class colonial townhouse. Samuel Powel was a third-generation Philadelphian who spent years traveling in Europe, like many wealthy young men of his time. He married Elizabeth Willing upon his return and became mayor of Philadelphia during the critical time of the Revolution. The Powels were friendly with all the VIPs of the period, including Benjamin Franklin, John

Adams, the Marquis de Lafayette, and George and Martha Washington. Political discussions and grand parties often took place in the Powel home in the evenings. Martha and George Washington celebrated a wedding anniversary here, and a thank-you note written by George after a lovely night is on display.

The British briefly took over the home during their occupation of Philadelphia during the war, during which time the Powels were allowed to stay in their servants' quarters. By the early 20th century, the home was in terrible disrepair and was almost converted to a parking lot. Miss Frances Wister, founder of the Philadelphia Society for the Preservation of Landmarks, raised money to buy it in 1931, and over the next decade it was restored to its appearance during the Powels' time. Among the trademarks of upper-class colonial America seen here are a decorative arts collection (including a china set given as a gift by Martha Washington), portraits of the Powels, and a formal walled garden.

ST. PETER'S EPISCOPAL CHURCH

313 Pine St., 215/925-5968, www.stpetersphila.org
HOURS: Tues.-Sat. 9 A.M.-noon
COST: Free

This Georgian-style building was designed by Scottish-born architect Robert Smith and opened in 1761. Built as an alternative to the overcrowded Christ Church, a far walk in the mud on rainy days for some residents, it was run jointly with Christ Church until 1832. In a stark contrast with the Quaker ideals that shun hierarchy, the church pews were for sale at St. Peter's, so the richest members could literally buy the best seats in the house.

The towering spire was designed by William Strickland in 1842. It was built to house a gift of eight bells given to the church by the Whitechapel Foundry in London, where the Liberty Bell was made. Among the famous members buried in the graveyard are portraitist Charles Willson Peale; chiefs of the seven Iroquois tribes who died during the smallpox epidemic in 1793; James Polk's vice president, George Mifflin Dallas; Benjamin Chew, owner of Cliveden, the site of the 1777 Battle of Germantown; and Nicholas Biddle, president of the Second Bank of the United States. No tours are offered, but you can look around the church and yard. Knock if the door is locked.

THADDEUS KOSCIUSZKO NATIONAL MEMORIAL

301 Pine St., 215/597-9618, www.nps.gov/thko
HOURS: Wed.-Sun. noon-4 P.M.
COST: Free

Thomas Jefferson said that Polish-born Thaddeus Kosciuszko was "as pure a son of liberty as I have ever known." A former Polish count, Kosciuszko developed innovative military engineering that contributed to several important victories in Revolutionary War battles. After the war, he returned to Poland, but

came back several years later to collect ¡ tary payment and consult with Dr. Ben, Rush about injuries he suffered while ur. cessfully defending his homeland against cza ist Russia. During his stay he was treated as a hero and visited by local leaders, including Vice President Jefferson.

The small Georgian-style boarding home where he stayed, built 1775–1776 by Joseph Few, has been converted into a memorial and museum maintained by Independence National Historical Park. The 1st-floor exhibits display his military innovations and the 2nd floor, his bedroom. In addition to entertaining the leaders of the day, he is rumored to have entertained many a young lady here as well. A short video reveals additional details about his life, and tours are available on request.

Center City East   Map 2

ARCH STREET UNITED METHODIST CHURCH

Broad and Arch Sts., 215/568-6250,
www.archstreetumc.org
HOURS: Tours Wed. 10 A.M.-3 P.M.
COST: Free

North of the Masonic Temple on Broad Street stands another architectural gem, the Arch Street United Methodist Church. The Gothic revival structure features a white-marble exterior, arched doorways, domed ceilings, dark wood, red-cushioned pews, and impressive stained-glass windows. It also houses a multistop Stanbridge organ made in 1870. The church was founded in 1862 and built on a former coal yard 1864–1870. The active congregation hosts many community and social events, including regular workshops about Native American heritage.

CHINESE FRIENDSHIP GATE

10th and Arch Sts.
There's no question that you're in Chinatown when you see the colorful Chinese Friendship Gate that forms an arch 40 feet above 10th

Street near Arch Street. Built in 1984, it was a collaboration between leading architect Sabrina Soong, other Chinese engineers and artisans, and members of the local community. In celebrating the traditional Qing Dynasty style, this grand gateway to Chinatown was partially constructed with tiles from Philadelphia's sister city, Tianjin. It was the first gate constructed by Chinese artisans outside of China.

◖ CITY HALL

Broad and Market Sts., 215/686-2840,
www.phila.gov/property/virtualcityhall
HOURS: Mon.-Fri. 9:30 A.M.-4:30 P.M.; building tours offered once daily Mon.-Fri. 12:30 P.M.; Tower Tours offered throughout the day, reservations recommended
COST: Free

City Hall stands proudly on the site of Center Square, one of William Penn's five original squares in his 1682 plans for the city. The city was originally concentrated in Old City along the Delaware River, where its earliest residents settled, so it made sense that local government offices were located nearby in

the Chinese Friendship Gate

PHOTO BY R. KENNEDY FOR GPTMC

Independence Hall, formerly the State House. But Penn predicted the city would eventually expand westward towards the Schuylkill River, and he envisioned this space at its geometric center as the perfect locale for government. Even though Penn left the city for good in 1701, his well-laid plan came to fruition two centuries later, when construction of the current City Hall was completed for city offices in 1901.

Renowned architects John McArthur Jr. and Thomas U. Walter designed the masterpiece that stands today at the city center—one of the world's finest examples of French Second Empire architecture. Construction began in 1871 and took 30 years and at least 1,000 people to complete. The design was influenced by the Palais des Tuileries and the New Louvre in Paris, evidenced in the turreted courtyard stair towers, slate mansard roof with dormer windows, and the paired columns that create the cozy illusion that the building is just three stories high instead of eight. A solid-granite ground floor is 22 feet thick in some areas, strong enough to support the brick structure faced with marble. The 548-foot center tower stands as the tallest masonry structure in the world supported without a steel frame.

Famed sculptor Alexander Milne Calder designed the more than 250 sculptures on the building's exterior. The symbolically rich sculptures include representations of seasons, continents, allegorical figures, and of course, the crowning jewel—the 37-foot-tall, 27-ton **William Penn statue** at the top. There was an unofficial but long-respected agreement that no building would be built taller than Penn's head, but the city's growth eventually demanded that it grow up (both literally and figuratively). In 1987, Liberty One was built, the first of a series of skyscrapers that now tower high above Billy Penn.

While City Hall looks small in today's skyline, it remains one of the most impressive and unique buildings. It is also the largest municipal building in the country, covering more than 14.5 acres of space on its eight floors. Just as Independence

Hall once housed the three branches of national government when Philadelphia was the nation's capital in the early 19th century, City Hall today houses segments of all three branches of city government as home of the mayor, city council, and civil trial courtrooms.

While the vast majority of the 700 rooms are standard offices, several of the spaces are truly spectacular. City Council Chambers, the Mayor's Reception Room, Conversation Hall, the Caucus Room, and the Supreme Court Room are lavish, impressive meeting rooms. Security measures require that you visit as part of a tour. The 12:30 P.M. weekday tour covers all the impressive rooms of the building that are not in use, including a Tower Tour to the base of the Penn statue. The full tour takes about 1.5 hours, but if you're short on time, you can just stop in for a Tower Tour throughout the day. A small elevator (capacity of four) takes visitors to an observation deck at the base of the Penn statue for a panoramic view of the city. The view from the top makes the site's prime location at the very center of Penn's

original Philadelphia apparent. Stop into the Visitors Center and Gift Shop in Room 121 of the East Portal for more information and for tours. Summer months can be busy, so plan to stop early in the morning to reserve a tour spot for later in the day.

LIBRARY COMPANY OF PHILADELPHIA

1314 Locust St., 215/546-3181, www.librarycompany.org

HOURS: Mon.-Fri. 9 A.M.-4:45 P.M., print room by appt. only

COST: Free

The country's first lending library was founded by Benjamin Franklin in 1731 when he was just 25 years old. In its original Old City location, today called Library Hall, it served as the Library of Congress when Philadelphia was the capital. The only intact colonial-era library and the oldest circulating library in the nation, it was also the largest library in the nation until 1850. It remains an excellent resource on 17th-to-19th-century American society and culture. In addition to its extensive circulating

© KARRIE GAVIN

City Hall is one of the finest examples of French Second Empire architecture in the world.

SCULPTURE AND SYMBOLISM NEAR CITY HALL

There are 250 sculptures adorning City Hall, but while you're in the area, be sure to see the many other sculptures nearby.

CLOTHESPIN

Just across the street from the west side of City Hall stands Claes Oldenburg's 45-foot steel *Clothespin*. Sleek and modern, it offers a stark contrast to City Hall. Oldenburg has linked the design to Constantin Brancusi's *The Kiss* in the Philadelphia Museum of Art, and many agree that the shape is reminiscent of lovers holding one another. The *Clothespin* can also be seen as a symbol of holding, or clipping, the old with the new in Philadelphia.

LOVE

At 15th Street and John F. Kennedy Boulevard stands John F. Kennedy Plaza, better known to locals as Love Park because of the sculpture by Robert Indiana at its center. It is said that the crooked "O" in the bright-red letters spelling "love" is there to remind us that nothing – including love – is perfect. Positioned at an angle so the Benjamin Franklin Parkway spreads out behind it with the Art Museum in the distance, it was installed for the bicentennial in 1976 and quickly became an iconic image for the City of Brotherly Love.

© KARRIE GAVIN

LOVE statue at Christmas time

GOVERNMENT OF THE PEOPLE

Across John F. Kennedy Boulevard, you can't miss Jacques Lipchitz's large *Government of the People*, one of several art installations in the plaza of the Municipal Services Building. The abstract bronze sculpture has a narrow base that widens at the top and includes hands and limbs gripping each other. It was built in the 1970s during the era of polarizing mayor Frank Rizzo. Nearby stands a large replica of Rizzo himself, who fittingly has his back to Lipchitz's statue. The story is that Rizzo hated the statue and cut off city funding for it. He was quoted as saying "It looks like some plasterer dropped a load of plaster." Ah, the history of Philadelphia municipal politics.

---

collections, the library holds more than half a million rare books, 75,000 graphics, 160,000 manuscripts, and an array of artwork, prints, and photographs of early Philadelphia. Since its opening, the independent research library has been supported by shareholders. Revolving free exhibits draw from the collections.

◖ MASONIC TEMPLE

1 N. Broad St., 215/988-1900, www.pagrandlodge.org
HOURS: Mon.-Fri. tours at 11 A.M., 2 P.M., and 3 P.M., Sat. tours at 10 and 11 A.M. Sept.-June, call ahead
COST: Library and museum entrance fee: $3; tour (including library and museum): $8 adult, $6 student, $5

child, senior, and freemason, $20 families of four or more

The Masonic Temple is a magnificent work of art and architecture both inside and out—as it should be, considering the giant fraternity house is built for and by masons. While the masons of today represent practically every profession, the earliest members were highly skilled stoneworkers. Completed in 1873, the temple designed by James Windrim took five years to complete. The interior was decorated under the supervision of artist George Herzog over a 20-year period.

Seven spectacular meeting rooms stand as a tribute to the seven "ideal" forms of architecture. Oriental Hall replicates parts of the

Alhambra; Gothic Hall is a tribute to the European Knights Templar made famous in Dan Brown's *The Da Vinci Code*; and Egyptian Hall is adorned with hieroglyphics so accurate that archaeology students from University of Pennsylvania sometimes visit to study them. Other styles include Renaissance, Ionic, Corinthian, and Norman, and each room is more fascinating and breathtaking than the one before. Look for one intentional mistake in the design of each room, placed there to acknowledge that only God is perfect and all man's work is flawed. Paintings of former Masonic Grand Masters, including Ben Franklin and George Washington, line the grand staircase and hallways. Hand-painted wooden sculptures by William Rush, the "father of American sculpture," are also on display. The library and museum contain artifacts galore from early masons, including George Washington's Masonic apron.

The Grand Lodge of England (GLE) was founded in 1717 and spread to the U.S. colonies by the 1730s, making Freemasonry the oldest continuous fraternal organization in the world. It is shrouded in mystery and many practices are known only to members. The Masonic Temple remains the meeting place for 28 different groups. Knowledgeable and friendly tour guides are willing to share information about many aspects of the history of the masons, but don't bother asking them to reveal their secrets, or explain why women are still not admitted to the group—believe me, I tried.

◀ READING TERMINAL MARKET

12th and Arch Sts., 215/922-2317,
www.readingterminalmarket.org
HOURS: Mon.-Sat. 8 A.M.-6 P.M., Sun. 9 A.M.-4 P.M.

Picture the Reading Terminal Market more than a century ago amid a mass of trains bringing goods and people in and out of the city, and you'll know how far it has come in its long history. Today, it is flanked on one side by the Gallery, a massive urban mall, and on the other by a state-of-the-art convention center. It has survived the Great Depression, World War II, and the decline of the railroads, and it is as

much a marvel today as it was at the turn of the 20th century.

It opened its doors in 1892 in response to a backlash against outdoor markets that were beginning to be viewed as a health hazard. The new market was laid out in a tidy grid system similar to the streets of downtown Philadelphia. Twelve aisles and four larger avenues were aligned in the spacious cavern beneath the elevated train shed of the Reading Railroad. Proximity to the railroad made it the perfect place for shipping and receiving goods and provided easy access for Pennsylvania Dutch merchants to peddle their wares.

In the 1970s, the Reading Railroad filed for bankruptcy and attempted to dismantle the market to make it easier to sell the terminal. Fortunately, they changed their minds and began efforts to revitalize it in the 1980s. What remains is one of Philadelphia's most proud and well-utilized sites.

Today the railroad runs underneath the market instead of above it, and Amish merchants still have a significant presence, bringing some of the best baked goods, meats, and produce. They have been joined by vendors selling everything from cheesesteaks to Vietnamese cuisine to fresh-baked cookies, making it an excellent place for lunch and one of the best spots in Philadelphia to buy affordable and delicious produce, meats, seafood, and a dizzying array of prepared foods. Philadelphia chefs from many local restaurants visit the market early each morning for the very freshest ingredients, and a wide assortment of lasting goods like wearable art, artisan candles, gourmet cookware, and crafts from around the globe are also available.

ST. STEPHEN'S EPISCOPAL CHURCH

19 S. 10th St., 215/922-3807, www.ststephensphl.org
HOURS: Tues.-Thurs. 11 A.M.-4:30 P.M. or by appt.
COST: Free

This is the only church designed by William Strickland, Philadelphia's leading colonial architect, that remains standing in Philadelphia today. Completed in 1823, it was modeled after

St. Stephen's Church in Vienna and was enlarged in 1878 by architect Frank Furness, responsible for the ornate stencils on the walls. The church's design marked the end of the neoclassical style and was one of the earliest examples of what became known as Gothic revival architecture. The site also happens to be where Benjamin Franklin flew the first kite.

Benjamin Franklin Parkway/Fairmount Map 4

CATHEDRAL OF SAINTS PETER AND PAUL

1723 Race St., 215/561-1313,
www.sspeterpaulcathedral.catholicweb.com
HOURS: Daily 8 A.M.-5 P.M., call for mass times
COST: Free

The Cathedral-Basilica of Saints Peter and Paul on the east side of Logan Circle is Philadelphia's largest brownstone and probably its most architecturally impressive Italian Renaissance structure. Home to the Archdiocese of Philadelphia and built 1846–1864, it was modeled after the Lombard Church of St. Charles (San Carla al Corso) in Rome. Four massive Corinthian columns, a vaulted copper dome, and eight side chapels only hint at the church's grandeur. Constantino Brumidi, also credited with painting the dome of the Capitol in Washington, led the design team. The ornate cathedral accommodates 2,000 people. The Crypt of the Bishops in the lower level holds the bodies of six Philadelphia bishops and archbishops.

EAKINS OVAL

Benjamin Franklin Pkwy. in front of the Philadelphia Museum of Art

Eakins Oval was named for Thomas Eakins (1844–1916), the famous Philadelphia realist painter best known for *The Gross Clinic* and *The Agnew Clinic.* The centerpiece of the oval is **Washington Monument,** designed by German sculptor Rudolf Siemering in 1897. The fantastic, symbolic statue was a gift from the Cincinnati Society of Pennsylvania, descendants of men who fought in the Revolutionary War. A bronze and granite replica of George Washington in uniform on a horse sits high atop a granite pedestal looking towards City Hall; his face was made from an impression taken during his life. Four pairs of Native American figures and animals each guard a pool of water representing the four great waterways of America—the Mississippi, the Potomac, the Delaware, and the Hudson. Thirteen steps that lead to the pedestal represent the original 13 states. Each side of the pedestal represents aspects of the American journey—the victory in the war, warning against the dangers of slavery, westward movement, and the march of the army.

The monument was dedicated in 1897 at the Green Street entrance to Fairmount Park and moved to this spot in 1928 when construction on the Parkway was completed. The southeastern side of the oval is used as a parking lot. You can sit on the statue, with the art museum or the Parkway and City Hall in the background, for a great photo op.

◖ EASTERN STATE PENITENTIARY

N. 22nd St. and Fairmount Ave., 215/236-3300,
www.easternstate.org
HOURS: 10 A.M.-5 P.M., last entry 4 P.M. Apr.-Nov.;
10 A.M.-8 P.M., last entry 7 P.M. June-Aug.
COST: $9 adult, $7 senior and student, $4 child 7-12, under 7 not admitted

A walk through Eastern State Penitentiary offers a glimpse into a world rarely seen by ordinary citizens. It forces one to imagine the lives of those behind bars and to examine the controversial history and ideals of the criminal justice system—past and present.

When it opened in 1829, the penitentiary's novel design and philosophy were considered radical experiments. Benjamin Franklin and Benjamin Rush, who were members of the first prison reform group

© KARRIE GAVIN

hallway in Eastern State Penitentiary

their cells, with an hour each day outdoors in a small private courtyard. When it was necessary to move through the public spaces, hoods were placed over their heads so they couldn't even see one another.

While the intentions of the founders were presumably good, the failings of the isolation system quickly became clear and the prison faced accusations of inhumane treatment. The first investigation into the possibility of questionable practices took place in 1832; in 1842 Charles Dickens visited and said: "The system is rigid, strict and hopeless solitary confinement, and I believe it, in its effects, to be cruel and wrong." It wasn't until 1913 that the confinement system was abandoned.

Among the famous prisoners who did time here was Al Capone, who was apparently given royal treatment during his eight-month stay. A peek into his restored cell reveals a cushy apartment with antiques, rugs, oil paintings, and the sounds of a waltz that frequently played on his radio.

In 1970, the prison closed, and there was talk of tearing it down and using the space for commercial property. Fortunately, a task force set out to preserve what is now considered a National Historic Landmark. In 1994, Eastern State opened for daily tours. Visitors are required to sign a waiver stating that they are aware of the poor condition of the building before entering, but the areas deemed unsafe are closed to the public.

Different tours take place throughout the day in which guides tell stories of prisoners, escapes, and more, but the well-made self-guided audio tour, "Voices of Eastern State," is the best way to get the full picture. Actor Steve Buscemi's voice, along with those of real prisoners and guards, guides you to more than 20 fascinating sites throughout the prison that reveal its rich history.

If you happen to be in town and have a high tolerance for fear, the already-spooky site is transformed into the annual Terror Behind the Walls, a haunted house, every night in October.

in history—the Philadelphia Society for Alleviating the Miseries of Public Prisons—supported the prison. Famed architect John Havilland won the design competition and one of his competitors, William Strickland, oversaw construction.

An alternative to the overcrowded prisons of the time, the Quaker-inspired goal of Eastern State was to reform criminals through strict isolation. It was founded on the belief that when left to their own devices without the influence of the outside world, prisoners would become "penitent," or remorseful. Both the concept and architecture soon became a model for prison design worldwide. Approximately 300 prisons on four continents were modeled on the innovative floor plan, in which a central guard post is flanked with multiple sections extending from the center. The castle-like structure occupies 11 acres in what was then considered the outskirts of town, today's Fairmount neighborhood. It was the most expensive structure ever built at the time. Prisoners ate, worked, and lived in

© KARRIE GAVIN

The water works once supplied water to the entire city.

FAIRMOUNT WATER WORKS INTERPRETIVE CENTER

640 Waterworks Dr., 215/685-0723,
www.fairmountwaterworks.org

HOURS: Tues.-Sat. 10 A.M.-5 P.M., Sun. 1-5 P.M.

COST: Free

Stroll above the scenic Fairmount Dam and learn about Philadelphia's 200-year relationship with the Schuylkill River at the Fairmount Water Works Interpretive Center. You will be in good company; out-of-town admirers have included Mark Twain and Charles Dickens, who praised the water works for its technical ingenuity and natural and architectural beauty. The nation's first municipal water-delivery system is just behind the Philadelphia Museum of Art within the original water works complex, now a National Historic Landmark. Classical architecture and unique, thoughtful landscaping make the site popular for wedding pictures and picnics.

Completed in 1822, the water works used steam engines and later waterwheels to pump water uphill from the Schuylkill River into a reservoir on the hill where the art museum now

stands. Exhibits in the interpretive center explain the importance of waterways to urban centers and illustrate the storied history of this once cutting-edge facility. Self-guided tours are available anytime, and regular guided tours are available on weekends. During the week, reservations must be made in advance for a guided tour. The water works site is now also home to the upscale, appropriately named Water Works Restaurant.

FREE LIBRARY OF PHILADELPHIA

1901 Vine St., 215/686-5322, www.library.phila.gov

HOURS: Mon.-Wed. 9 A.M.-9 P.M., Thurs.-Sat.
9 A.M.-5 P.M., Sun. 1-5 P.M., tour of rare books collection
Mon.-Fri. 11 A.M.

The central branch of the Free Library of Philadelphia opened in 1927. While parts are in need of updating, signs of the Beaux Arts building's original grandeur can be seen in the high vaulted ceilings in the main foyer, crown moldings in many of the reading rooms, and the Rare Books Collection on the 3rd floor. Twenty different signs throughout the building describe each space and its history.

During a tour of the Rare Books Collection, you'll see a cuneiform from 2800 B.C.; *Book of the Dead* scrolls; Charles Dickens' mummified pet raven, Grip, believed to have inspired Edgar Allen Poe's famous poem *The Raven*; and original manuscripts and first editions of both Dickens and Poe. The collection also contains the **William McIntyre Elkins Library,** transported from the collector's home in Briar Hill just outside Philadelphia panel by panel and beautifully re-created. It contains an extensive Dickens collection and Dickens' own desk and lamp.

A massive renovation and restoration project is in the works that will add a modern, state-of-the-art addition to the library, connected by bridges to the original building. The library regularly hosts free films, lectures, and children's programs, and rotating exhibits in the 1st-floor Fleisher Gallery. A roof deck affords a great view of the city, but is only open for special events—or if you can sweet-talk a staff member into taking you up for a peek.

◖ PHILADELPHIA MUSEUM OF ART

2600 Benjamin Franklin Parkway, 215/763-8100, www.philamuseum.org

HOURS: Tues.-Sun. 10 A.M.-5 P.M., Fri. until 8:45 P.M.

COST: $12 adult, $9 senior, $8 student, $8 child (13-18), free 12 and under, pay what you wish on Sun., not including special exhibits

Whether you've come to see the world-renowned art collection, to take photographs outside at one of the most picturesque spots in the city, or to run up the steps in the footsteps of Philly's Rocky Balboa (hopefully you'll do all of the above), just be sure to come. One of Philadelphia's most impressive monuments and the third-largest museum in the United States, the Philadelphia Museum of Art is a sight to behold. Rising high at the end of the Parkway and serving as the gateway to Fairmount Park, it is known to locals simply as "the Art Museum."

Founded during the nation's first centennial in 1876, it was originally a museum of decorative arts housed in Fairmount Park's Memorial

© KARRIE GAVIN

a Native American figure, designed by Rudolf Siemering in 1897, at the base of the Washington Monument sculpture, with Philadelphia Museum of Art in the background

ROCKY'S FOUND A HOME

Ben Franklin is certainly Philadelphia's most famous historical son, but almost equally revered is Rocky Balboa, our most famous fictional son. More than just a character in a movie, Rocky came to represent Philly's scrappy, fighting, underdog spirit. In the classic 1976 movie, Sylvester Stallone, aka Rocky, trained in and around landmark Philadelphia sights, from the Italian Market to the famous scene where he runs up the steps of the Philadelphia Museum of Art. The steps are even known to many visitors as the "Rocky Steps."

Since its construction in 1982, debate has ensued over where the bronze 8-foot, 6-inch, 1,500-pound statue of Rocky belongs. For many years, it was at the top of the Art Mu-seum steps, but some thought it was uncouth to have a movie character so prominently displayed in front of a world-class museum of art, so Rocky was relegated to a spot outside of the Spectrum sports arena. A compromise was finally reached in 2006 when he was re-turned to the Art Museum, although now he is on a street-level pedestal next to the East Entrance steps rather than at the top of the steps. It seems that Rocky has finally found a permanent home – we hope!

Run up the steps for a classic photo op; even us locals have done it at least once in our lives. Just don't make the mistake that some visitors do, and forget to actually go into the museum. While Rocky is great and all, the museum be-yond the steps is the real draw.

Hall. It moved to its current location in 1928. Its chief designer, Julian Abele, was the first African American graduate of the University of Pennsylvania's architecture school. Inspired by temples he saw while traveling in Greece, he designed the museum to look like three linked Greek temples. Made of Minnesota dolomite, the massive Greek revival building is adorned with rich color in the detailed friezes. Be sure to walk around outside and take in all the elaborate details, and don't miss the brightly painted sculptures lining the top. Rocky, or at least the bronze 8-foot, 6-inch, 1,500-pound statue of him, is located on a street-level ped-estal next to the East Entrance steps.

You can't possibly see everything inside in a day, so look at a map and plan accord-ingly, or simply meander through the many rooms and galleries and take in what you can of more than 200 galleries showcasing more than 225,000 works of art. Don't miss some of the 80-plus carefully decorated period rooms that will transport you through time all over the world. The museum also hosts some of the most famous traveling exhibits in the art world, often serving as one of, if not the only, U.S. stop, so be sure to check the website to find out what is current. If possible, visit on a Friday night for **Art After 5,** complete with live performances, food, and wine in the Great Hall, or come on a Sunday, when you can pay whatever you like.

With the 2007 addition of the **Ruth and Raymond G. Perelman Building** across the street, there's now even more to see. The pre-served art deco building is the first major ex-pansion in 80 years and the first phase of a major plan to modernize the museum. Modern gallery spaces, state-of-the-art visitor ameni-ties, study centers, and educational resources are just some of the features offered in the im-pressive new space.

South Street/South Philadelphia   Map 5

GLORIA DEI (OLD SWEDES' EPISCOPAL CHURCH)

Columbus Blvd. and Christian St., 215/389-1513, www.old-swedes.org

HOURS: Tours Wed.-Sat. 10 A.M.-4 P.M., call for times of services

COST: $2

Swedes settled along the banks of the Schuylkill and Delaware Rivers as early as 1638—long before William Penn arrived. The earliest church still standing in Pennsylvania was built for a group of early settlers 1698–1700. A massive Swedish-style marble baptismal font was crafted in Philadelphia and added to the church in 1731. Miniature wooden replicas of ships that carried Swedish settlers here in the early 17th century hang from the ceilings inside. Operated by Independence National Historical Park, a one-room museum displays a historical map and other artifacts from that time. Sea captains and Revolutionary War soldiers are among those buried in the cemetery outside. Swedish and Norwegian congregations use the church regularly, but the doors are open to the public.

ISAIAH ZAGAR'S MAGIC GARDEN

1020-22 South St., 215/715-4938, www.isaiahzagar.org

HOURS: Tues.-Sun. 11 A.M.-5 P.M.

COST: $3 suggested donation

In the 1960s, a group of young artists moved into a run-down section of South Street and helped transform the neighborhood into something beautiful. At the forefront were Isaiah Zagar and his wife, Julia, who returned from the Peace Corps in 1969 and opened the Eyes Gallery at 4th and South Streets to sell the textiles, woodcarvings, and ceramics they collected in South America. They decorated their store with anything and everything they found in the neighborhood, especially the many pieces they discovered in an abandoned glass warehouse. Isaiah began creating mosaics with a variety of materials—glass in particular—and hasn't stopped since.

Isaiah's trademark mosaics can be seen all over the city on homes, businesses, and in murals, but the pinnacle is his beautiful, trippy home and studio—the Magic Garden. Every square inch has been covered with colorful tiles, bottles, mirrors, and other everyday materials to create an abstract collage. A walk down nearby South Street or Bainbridge Street between 3rd and 11th Streets will reveal more of Zagar's unmistakable public works of art.

West Philadelphia/University City   Map 6

30TH STREET STATION

2951 Market St., 215/386-6426, www.30thstreetstation.com

HOURS: Daily 24 hours a day

Locals may forget to stop and appreciate the beauty of Philadelphia's 30th Street Station while they run for their trains, but it happens to be one of America's finest transportation hubs and one of the few remaining grand railroad stations in the country. The Pennsylvania Railroad needed a location between New York and Washington on what is now known as the

Northeast Corridor, so the neoclassical structure was built in 1929–1934 by Graham, Anderson, Probst & White. It is now listed on the National Register of Historic Places. The 90-foot-high ceiling creates a majestic atmosphere, and it's easy to imagine an early-20th-century bustle not all that different from today. Inside, you can see the sculpture by Walker Hancock created in 1950 to honor Pennsylvania Railroad employees killed during World War II; it includes an archangel Michael lifting the body of a dead soldier out of the flames of war.

CITY OF MURALS

With more than 2,800 murals spread throughout the city, Philadelphia boasts more impressive works of public art than any other city in the entire world. The colorful, larger-than-life designs brighten schools, community centers, businesses, and homes from the Avenue of the Arts to many outlying neighborhoods that most tourists and even many residents rarely visit. In many areas, especially in parts of North and West Philadelphia where urban blight is at its worst, the murals bring beauty to neighborhoods that need it most. Not only do the murals give the community something to be proud of, but the tours provide visitors with an excellent, and safe, way to visit.

The **Mural Arts Program** is an offshoot of the Anti-Graffiti Network. Mural artist and community activist Jane Golden was hired to lead the initiative of redirecting the energy of local graffiti writers into mural-making. The city was covered with graffiti throughout the 1980s, and the program has done much to alleviate the problem. Its enormous success has helped to empower young artists and contribute to youth development and neighborhood revitalization in many parts of the city. Professional artists are hired to work closely with residents to design and create the murals, so they represent the people, cultures, and issues of the diverse neighborhoods they inhabit. Each has a different theme and is created with a variety of materials, including paint, tile, and glass.

The two-hour guided **Mural Arts Tour** in a covered open-air trolley is one of the best ways to get off the beaten path and get a taste of the real Philadelphia. On a tour, you'll learn about the city's murals, and in the process, the diverse neighborhoods they inhabit. A different section of the city is featured each week: the first Saturday and Wednesday of each month, Center City; the second, North Philadelphia; the third, South Philadelphia; and the fourth, West Philadelphia. The fifth Saturday or Wednesday, if there is one, the tour is of Broad Street and the Avenue of the Arts. Tours depart from Independence Visitor Center at 6th and Market Streets on Saturday April–November and Wednesday May–November at 11 A.M. Tours cost $25 for adults, $23 for seniors, $15 for children 3-10, and are free for children under two. Reservations are recommended (215/685-0754, www.muralarts.org), since the tour closes when the trolley is full. You should arrive at least 30 minutes early in case there are lines at the Visitor Center.

The station was featured in the 1983 film *Trading Places* and M. Night Shyamalan's *Unbreakable* (2000), but its most famous screen moments are from the now-classic scene in *Witness* (1985), in which a young Amish boy traveling through Philadelphia with his mom witnesses a murder in the bathroom of the station. Fortunately, it was just a movie and the station is a relatively safe place.

UNIVERSITY OF PENNSYLVANIA
btwn. 34th and 38th Sts. and Walnut and Spruce Sts., 215/898-5000, www.upenn.edu

The Ivy League University of Pennsylvania, or "Penn" as it is locally called, is the oldest and most esteemed of the many universities in Philadelphia. The first official university in the country was founded in part by Ben Franklin in 1740. Franklin designed an educational program that included practical applications in commerce and public service along with classics and theology. This laid the groundwork for the multidisciplinary and liberal arts curriculums practiced at many modern colleges and universities today, so you can blame Ben for all those annoying general education requirements. The campus didn't move to its current site until the 1870s, after more than a century in Center City.

Today, the attractive campus is in the heart of University City, the most developed section of West Philadelphia just across the bridge from Center City. Be sure to stroll along **Locust Walk,** the typical ivy-covered walkway lined with trees and stately architecture. If school is in session, you'll be surrounded by Penn students promoting fraternity parties, groups, and events and enjoying college life. No matter when you come, you'll notice the many monuments to Ben Franklin along and around the walk. Sit next to his bronze sculpture on a bench near 36th and Walnut Streets for a popular photo op. A large statue of him sits on a pedestal on Locust Walk near 34th and Walnut Streets.

Across from the statue, you'll see a modern statue of a large broken button, courtesy of Claes Oldenberg, also responsible for the *Clothespin* sculpture near City Hall. Rumor has it that the ultimate feat for a Penn student is to have sex on the button—although it's hard to imagine this is possible considering the near-constant bustle of Locust Walk.

Beyond the button is the **Van Pelt Library,** an excellent place to study, read, or use the free Internet, or to visit the rare books room on the 6th floor. The library is open to the public with a photo ID. There are many notable buildings worth exploring on campus, but be sure to stop in at the rotating exhibit in the Arthur Ross Gallery in the stunning **Fisher Fine Arts Library** (across College Green from the Van Pelt Library). And all true sports fans will want to see the historic basketball arena, the **Palestra** (220 S. 32nd St.).

WOODLANDS CEMETERY AND MANSION

4000 Woodland Ave., 215/386-2181,
www.uchs.net/Woodlands/woodlandshome.html
HOURS: Cemetery always open, mansion hours vary
COST: Free

Famous Philadelphia lawyer Andrew Hamilton purchased the land at Woodlands, approximately 300 acres, in 1735. The mansion was built in 1787, long after his death; the carriage house and stable were built in 1792 under the ownership of his grandson William. The federal-style mansion was a 16-room manor and one of Philadelphia's finest estates for many years. William was an active botanist and the lands and greenhouses contained more than 10,000 different plant species, some grown from seeds harvested during Lewis and Clark's expeditions. More than 720 historic trees and plants have survived today.

After William's death in 1813, much of the property was sold and in 1840 the Woodlands Cemetery Company purchased the remaining grounds. Winding brick paths from the original landscape are now lined with headstones honoring notable Philadelphians including Thomas Eakins, Rembrandt Peale, the Drexel and Biddle families, surgical pioneer Dr. Samuel Gross, and railroad magnates Asa Whitney and John Edgar Thompson.

Woodlands, along with Laurel Hill Cemetery, served as an innovative improvement to the overcrowded city-church cemeteries that dominated early Philadelphia. Both were unique in their elaborate landscaping and architecture and in their isolated locations. According to an early advertisement for the cemetery, "the decaying bodies of the dead may securely moulder into kindred dust, with an abundant vegetation and free winds to absorb and dissipate all noxious effluvia."

Today, the Woodlands Cemetery Company, a nonprofit organization, works with the Friends of Woodlands and the University City Historical Society to preserve and maintain the mansion and cemetery grounds. If you visit when the office is open, grab a map showing where people are buried. You can also tour the mansion, which is undergoing a much-needed renovation but still serves as an impressive example of federal architecture.

Northern Liberties
Map 7

EDGAR ALLEN POE
NATIONAL HISTORIC SITE

530 N. 7th St., 215/597-8780,
www.nps.gov/edal

HOURS: Wed.-Sun. 9 A.M.-5 P.M.

COST: Free

One of America's most famous and unique writers, Edgar Allen Poe (1809–1849), lived in this three-story brick home with his wife, Virginia, and his mother-in-law, Maria Clemm. He was a Philadelphia resident for only a year before moving to New York City in 1843, but this was one of the most productive years in his life. It was here that he wrote *The Black Cat,* which describes a basement similar to the one in the home, and three of his most ac-claimed masterpieces: *The Tell-Tale Heart, The Fall of the House of Usher,* and *The Gold Bug.* This is the only one of the three homes Poe lived in that stands today. Visitors can tour the rooms, cellar, and exhibits and watch a short film about Poe, his family, and contemporaries. The site is operated by Independence National Historical Park.

THE NATIONAL SHRINE OF
ST. JOHN NEUMANN

St. Peter's Catholic Church, 1019 N. 5th St., 215/627-3080, www.stjohnneumann.org

HOURS: By appt.

COST: Free

Catholics come from far and wide to pray to the remarkably well-preserved body of St. John Neumann (1811–1860). Born in Bohemia, Neumann became an American Catholic Church bishop in Philadelphia in 1952. He died eight years later at age 48 and was enshrined in a crypt in the basement of Saint Peter's Church, as he'd requested. Devoted followers have come to pray to him ever since. Many people believed their prayers were answered by the journey, and with the miracles they experienced, his popu-larity soared. In 1977, he was canonized and declared "America's first saint" by Pope Paul VI. His life is depicted on stained-glass win-dows next to the glass case that holds his body. The baroque church is an active parish and not a major tourist stop, so call ahead to make sure it is a good time for a visit.

Fairmount Park
Map 8

BOATHOUSE ROW

Kelly Drive along the Schuylkill River behind the Art Museum

The historic homes of many of Philadelphia's rowing clubs also provide one of its most fa-mous sights—Boathouse Row, which is espe-cially pretty at night, when the lights outlining the homes reflect onto the Schuylkill River. Designed in 1979 by architectural lighting designer Raymond Grenald, the lights helped revitalize Boathouse Row and brought them renewed status. The boathouses are home to several active rowing clubs overseen by the Schuylkill Navy of Philadelphia, the oldest amateur athletic governing body in the coun-try, established in 1858. The organization has produced several Olympic-champion rowers, and today the organization hosts four annual regattas. But rowing isn't the only recreation that takes place here. Philadelphia's most pop-ular paved trail, the Schuylkill River Trail, is most crowded in this stretch with walkers, runners, bikers, and others out to enjoy the scenery.

HISTORIC RITTENHOUSETOWN

206 Lincoln Dr., 215/438-5711, www.rittenhousetown.org

HOURS: Weekends noon-4 P.M., last tour 3 P.M. June-Sept., and by appt.

COST: $5 adult, $3 senior and child

Cliveden, Upsula, Johnson House, and

© KARRIE GAVIN

Boathouse Row

Stenton offer a glimpse into Germantown as the summer retreat for wealthy Philadelphians. The Ebenezer Maxwell Mansion shows Germantown as the Victorian suburb. But only RittenhouseTown shows you the Germantown of its earliest settlers—the Germans. The group of small German-style buildings in a beautiful wooded enclave on the edge of the Wissahickon Creek transports you to a time before the Revolution—when Germantown was home to German immigrants drawn to Pennsylvania to enjoy religious freedom.

William Rittenhouse (originally Wilhelm Rittenhausen) was the leader and first minister of a small Mennonite community. He built North America's first paper mill on this site in 1690. By the late 18th century, the site developed into a small self-sufficient industrial village containing more than 40 buildings including homesteads, workers' cottages, a paper mill complex, a church, a school, and a firehouse. Today, seven buildings, including a barn housing a papermaking studio, the original Rittenhouse Family Homestead, and the original Rittenhouse Homestead Bakehouse, remain and are open to the public for tours.

More than 10 generations of the Rittenhouse family lived on-site and operated the mill for more than 150 years, among them William's grandson, David Rittenhouse. Born at the mill in 1732, David went on to become a mathematician, astronomer, statesman, and first president of the U.S. Mint. In the late 1870s, the family sold the 30 acres, which are maintained by Historic Rittenhouse, Inc., a member-supported organization dedicated to preserving its history. In 1992, it was named a National Historic Landmark.

🌙 LAUREL HILL CEMETERY

3822 Ridge Ave., 215/228-8200,
www.thelaurelhillcemetery.org
HOURS: Mon.-Fri. 8 A.M.-4:30 P.M., Sat.-Sun.
9:30 A.M.-5 P.M., closed major holidays
COST: Free admission, $5 self-guided tour and map,
$10-20 most guided tours
Until the 1830s, city cemeteries were as crowded and unsanitary as the streets they butted up

against. Bodies filled small churchyards in packed residential and commercial areas, and when space ran out, additional layers of graves were often added. A picturesque, rural burial ground was a revolutionary idea at the time. Envisioned as a dignified resting place for the departed as well as a country retreat for the living, Laurel Hill Cemetery was situated several miles northwest of Philadelphia's urban bustle on a large estate overlooking the Schuylkill River. Notable people interred in the grounds include almost 40 Civil War–era generals, six *Titanic* survivors, and many members of the prominent Rittenhouse, Elkins, Widener, and Strawbridge families. More than 170 years later, Laurel Hill Cemetery remains a lovely respite from urban life adjacent to Fairmount Park. Walk around and read the names and dates in the ancient mausoleums and stones and try to piece together the stories of those buried. Even better, take a self-guided tour or one of the special themed tours offered several times a month. You'll hear fascinating stories about the lives—and deaths—of some of the city's most prominent early residents. The facility attracts joggers and horticulturalists as much as architecture and history buffs. Its vast archives of contracts, maps, photographs, and documents are a resource for historians, genealogists, and scholars.

◖ PHILADELPHIA ZOO

400 W. Girard Ave., 215/243-1100, www.phillyzoo.org
HOURS: Daily 9:30 A.M.-5 P.M. Mar.-Nov.,
9:30 A.M.-4:30 P.M. Dec.-Feb.
COST: $17 adult, $14 child Mar.-Nov.; $13 adult and child, free under 2, Dec.-Feb.

Founded in 1874, the oldest zoo in the country has only recently joined the ranks of the very best. In the past decade, each year has brought new and increasingly exotic animals along with updated exhibits and attractions. The latest and greatest is the **Channel 6 Zooballoon** (Apr.–Oct. weather permitting, $10 weekends and holidays, $8 weekdays). It takes visitors on an exhilarating 15-minute trip 400 feet above the ground for a 360-degree view of the city skyline and Fairmount Park. In addition to being a fun ride, the balloon offers a historical

tribute to the first North American passenger balloon flight taken by Philadelphia pilot Jean-Pierre Blanchard in 1785; President George Washington was among the onlookers.

You could easily spend a whole day here, with highlights that include watching the carnivores feed (11 A.M. and 3 P.M.) in Carnivore Kingdom, walking among flying birds in the Jungle Bird Walk, and hanging out with the primates in the interactive PECO Primate Center. Kids love to feed the animals in the Children's Zoo and climb and play in the giant Treehouse ($1 admission).

The site encompasses 42 acres in West Fairmount Park, complete with winding landscaped paths and historic architecture, including the country home of William Penn's grandson. The botanical collections include more than 500 plant species and animal sculptures include Heinz Warneke's giant *Cow Elephant and Calf* and Henry Mitchell's popular *Impala Fountain and Hippo Mother and Baby.* The long history of the zoo includes the first orangutan and chimp births in a U.S. zoo (1928), the world's first Children's Zoo (1957), and the first U.S. exhibit of white lions (1993).

SMITH CIVIL WAR MEMORIAL
N. Concourse Dr., W. Fairmount Park

Framing the street in two separate sections on the way to Memorial Hall from Center City stands the large bronze Smith Civil War Memorial. It was erected 1897–1912 with funds provided by its wealthy namesake, Richard Smith. There is a bronze statue of Smith himself, along with accomplished war heroes Generals Hancock and McClellan, and others. At the base of each tower is a curved wall with a bench, known as the whispering benches; if you sit at one end and whisper, someone at the other end can hear you.

HISTORIC MANSIONS OF FAIRMOUNT PARK

In the 18th and early 19th century, many of the city's wealthy class built retreat homes along the elevated, picturesque banks of the Schuylkill River in Fairmount Park. They

© DAMIAN KOHUT

Smith Civil War Memorial

offered a quick escape from some of the ills of urban life, including the summer heat and epidemics like typhoid and yellow fever. A number of these historic houses have been preserved and are open to the public for tours. The homes all offer a glimpse into the lives of early Philadelphians, along with a variety of early architectural styles and period furnishings. Cedar Grove, Sweetbriar, and Belmont are on the west side of the river, while all the others are on the east side. All are operated by various civic groups and have various hours. With the exception of Belmont Mansion, which is its own separate entity, **admission** for each is $5 adult, $3 senior, $2 child 6–12, and free under the age of 6. For information about the seasonal guided trolley tours in summer and during the winter holiday, call **Park House Information** (215/684-7926) or the individual house numbers included in the listings.

BELMONT MANSION

2000 Belmont Mansion Dr., 215/878-8844, www.belmontmansion.org

HOURS: Tues.-Sun. 11 A.M.-5 P.M., weekends in winter noon-5 P.M.

COST: $7 adult, $5 student, senior, child, free under 6

Built in the late 18th century, Belmont Mansion is one of the finest examples of palladian architecture in the United States standing today, with an original decorative plaster ceiling that is considered one of the oldest in America. The land was bought in 1742 by William Peters, an English lawyer and land agent for the William Penn family. He designed the mansion and formal gardens, and later passed it on to his son, Richard. In the turbulent times of the Revolution, Richard served as Secretary of the Board of War for the Revolutionary Army and Pennsylvania Delegate to Congress under the Articles of Confederation. George Washington, John Adams, Thomas Jefferson, and James Madison all stayed at the house at times. After the Revolution, Richard became Speaker of the Pennsylvania Assembly, Pennsylvania State Senator, and Judge of the United States District Court, and an environmental scientist and prominent abolitionist.

In 2007 after a long restoration project, the American Women's Heritage Society opened the house as an interpretive and educational center and **Underground Railroad Museum.** On a tour, you'll learn about the role of the home and its owners and slaves in history and in the abolitionist movement.

CEDAR GROVE
1 Cedar Grove Dr., 215/878-2123,
www.fairmountparkhouses.org
HOURS: Tues.-Sun. 10 A.M.-5 P.M.

Unlike the other historic houses of Fairmount Park, Cedar Grove originated in a different part of the city. In 1746, wealthy widow Elizabeth Coates Paschall acquired land in the Frankford section of the city, where she built a large house for herself and her three children. Over subsequent generations, Cedar Grove grew with multiple additions and renovations, most notably when Elizabeth's granddaughter Sarah and her husband, Isaac Wistar Morris, doubled its size around 1800. They added a formal parlor, a new kitchen, and a 3rd floor. The house was in Frankford until the 1920s, when it was moved brick by brick to Fairmount Park. Today, tourists and history buffs can stroll through the mansion and take in the fine mix of federal, baroque, and rococo architectural styles, including notable features like the large kitchen with original utensils and a two-sided wall of closets on the 2nd floor.

LAUREL HILL MANSION
7201 N. Randolph Dr., 215/235-1776,
www.fairmountparkhouses.org
HOURS: Wed.-Sun. 10 A.M.-4 P.M. July-mid-Dec.,
Sat.-Sun. 10 A.M.-4 P.M. Apr.-June

Laurel Hill Mansion was built by Rebecca Rawle around 1767, after she lost her first husband. During the Revolutionary War the house was seized from her and her second husband, Philadelphia Mayor Samuel Shoemaker, because they were considered British sympathizers. It was later returned to the family and occupied by Rebecca's son William Rawle, who became a noted lawyer and founded the Philadelphia Bar Association. The elegant Georgian structure was augmented with wings on the southern and northern sides, and its position on a bluff overlooking the Schuylkill River makes it particularly notable.

LEMON HILL
Sedgeley and Lemon Hill Drives, 215/232-4337,
www.lemonhill.org
HOURS: Wed.-Sun. 10 A.M.-4 P.M. Apr. 1-mid-Dec. except major holidays, by appt. Jan.-Mar. 31

One of the many stately manors that dot the green banks of the Schuylkill River, Lemon Hill was built in 1800 by wealthy merchant Henry Pratt on land formerly owned by Declaration of Independence signatory Robert Morris. Of particular architectural note are the curved doors, windows, and fireplaces in the two oval rooms that look out over the lush gardens. The property was the first purchased by the city for the creation of its magnificent Fairmount Park system, and holds a special place in local, mercantile, and horticultural histories.

MOUNT PLEASANT
3800 Mount Pleasant Dr., 215/763-2719,
www.fairmountparkhouses.org
HOURS: Tues.-Sun. 10 A.M.-5 P.M.

When future president John Adams once declared Mount Pleasant to be "the most elegant seat in Pennsylvania," he was validating its owners' ambitions. Built 1762–1765 by Scottish ship captain John Macphearson and his wife, Margaret, the house was intended to make a grand statement with its exquisite architecture and its site high above the Schuylkill River. Architect Thomas Neville, a protégé of Independence Hall architect Edmund Woolley, designed Mount Pleasant in an interesting Scottish interpretation of the then-current Georgian style. Among its many noteworthy owners were national traitor Benedict Arnold and Jonathan Williams, a great nephew of Benjamin Franklin and the first superintendent of West Point. Later, after becoming part of Fairmount Park, it served as a dairy farm. It is currently displayed unfurnished, so visitors can see the materials and architecture of the house directly, but no period furniture.

© KARRIE GAVIN

Lemon Hill is open for tours.

STRAWBERRY MANSION

2450 Strawberry Mansion Bridge Dr., 215/228-8364,
www.fairmountparkhouses.org

HOURS: Wed.-Sun. 10 A.M.-4 P.M. July-mid-Dec.

Although Strawberry Mansion shares a name with a nearby section of the city that has been long distressed by poverty and crime, the largest of Fairmount Park's historic houses knew nothing of urban decay. During its heyday the mansion occupied a rural setting. Dating to around 1790, it was built for renowned lawyer Judge William Lewis, who's now best remembered for drafting the United States' first law abolishing slavery. Lewis built the middle section of the house and the Greek revival–styled wings were added by the next owner, Judge Joseph Hemphill. It provides visitors with a unique window into the past, with two floors of furniture and decorative arts from the federal, regency, and empire styles, and an attic stuffed with antique toys and a large doll collection. The name Strawberry Mansion comes from Mrs. Grimes, a resident who sold strawberries and cream from the house in the mid-19th century.

SWEETBRIAR

1 Sweetbriar Dr., 215/222-1333,
www.fairmountparkhouses.org

HOURS: Wed.-Sun. 10 A.M.-4 P.M. July-mid-Dec.

Samuel Breck, a Boston-born merchant, built his country estate overlooking the Schuylkill in 1797. He chose the neoclassical style, rather than the then-dominant Georgian, for its design and furniture, installing an entryway colonnade, large Italianate windows, and a stairway with a balcony. Breck hosted fabulous salons and dinners, and entertained such luminaries as Lafayette and Tallyrand. He also kept thorough diaries detailing the life of Philadelphia in the post-Revolutionary period. Though Sweetbriar, along with other "country estates," was built in part for its owners to escape the epidemics sweeping the city proper, Breck's own daughter died of typhoid. Today, as part of Fairmount Park, the house holds arts and crafts, a significant library, and architectural and artistic details like the elegant "Etruscan" room.

WOODFORD

33rd and Dauphin Sts., 215/229-6115,
www.fairmountparkhouses.org
HOURS: Tues.-Sun. 10 A.M.-4 P.M.

Woodford is a classic example of Philadelphia Georgian architecture for the elite. Furnished with 18th- and 19th-century furnishings, it also contains a large collection of English, Continental, and American decorative arts. In 1756, William Coleman bought this tract of land along the Schuylkill River. He built the home, which was originally one story. The second story and back wing was added later by David Franks, but the house was confiscated from him during the Revolution due to his British sympathies. It was later acquired by Isaac Wharton, whose mother, Rebecca Rawle, built nearby Laurel Hill Mansion, and it stayed in that family until it was acquired by the city in 1868.

Northwest Philadelphia   Map 9

CLIVEDEN AND UPSALA

6401 Germantown Ave., 215/848-1777,
www.cliveden.org
HOURS: Thurs.-Sun. noon-4 P.M. Apr.-Dec.,
and by appt. all year
COST: $8 adult, $6 student, 2-for-1 with AAA

Georgian-style Cliveden was built 1764–1767 as the summer home for Benjamin Chew. He sought relief from the summer heat in a slightly cooler area that was then a suburb. A marker at the corner of Cliveden Street and Germantown Avenue reads "6 to P," meaning six miles to Philadelphia; before railroad or automobiles, that was a significant journey.

One of the first English-speaking residents in the predominantly German neighborhood, Chew was an attorney who represented William Penn's family. Appointed Chief Justice of the Colony of Pennsylvania by King George, he was often in opposition to Ben Franklin because of his British ties. He was naturally distrusted when the war began, and was moved to New Jersey and placed under house arrest. This was lucky for him, since it meant he was absent during the bloody battle that took place on the grounds of his home, the Battle of Germantown. In October 1777, British troops were passing through on their way to Philadelphia when they got word of an impending attack by the Continental Army. They broke into Cliveden for protection and hid behind the thick stone walls for several hours while American troops fired muskets and cannons from Upsala across the street. Backup eventually arrived and the British ultimately won the battle.

After the war, Chew was accepted into American society and led a life of public service. He sold his devastated house but bought it back again near the end of his life. Descendants of his family lived in Cliveden until 1972, when it was donated to the National Trust for Historic Preservation. Inside, you can see the family's extraordinary collection of 18th- and 19th-century furnishings, decorative arts, and artifacts.

Upsala remains one of Germantown's finest examples of classic federal architecture. John Johnson Jr., a descendant of Dirk Jansen, one of the area's first settlers, built the home in 1798 on land that was in his family for four generations and lived here through the 19th century. In 1944, a group of Germantown citizens led by preservationist Frances Anne Wister raised money to purchase and restore Upsala. In 2004, the foundation merged with Cliveden, but Upsala is currently closed to the public.

DESHLER-MORRIS HOUSE

5442 Germantown Ave., 215/597-7130,
www.nps.gov/demo
HOURS: Fri.-Sun. 1-4 P.M. Apr.-Dec. and by appt.
COST: Free

George Washington lived in the Deshler-Morris House, also called the "Germantown

White House," on two occasions. In October 1793, he came to escape the Yellow Fever epidemic ravaging Philadelphia, and the following summer, he came again on vacation. Ironically, his enemy British General Howe was also one of the house's former residents. Howe stayed here after he and his troops defeated the Continental Army in the Battle of Germantown.

Originally a simple four-room cottage, a nine-room addition later transformed it into an elegant manor befitting a presidential address. The interior offers a glimpse into the lifestyles of Washington and other residents. Most of the furnishings belonged to the Deshler and Morris families, and one red sofa is thought to have belonged to George Washington. The house is now operated and maintained by the Independence National Historical Park Services. While you're here, stop to check out the Civil War Monument in Market Square across the street, installed in 1883.

EBENEZER MAXWELL MANSION

200 W. Tulpehocken St., 215/438-1861, www.ebenezermaxwellmansion.org
HOURS: Hours vary, call ahead
COST: Free

Built in 1859 by clothing merchant Ebenezer Maxwell, this elaborate stone mansion is a classic example of the Victorian architecture that became popular in the mid-19th-century. At the time, a new railroad made it possible to quickly commute from Germantown to Center City, establishing Germantown as a fashionable residence for wealthy Philadelphians. When Germantown officially became part of the city as a result of Consolidation in 1854, buildings like this were springing up all over the rapidly developing neighborhood. The tower, long windows, landscaped gardens, and hand-painted ceilings were typical of the expensive Victorian homes of the day. While many of the homes on this very block were probably equally impressive in their heyday, the Maxwell Mansion is the only one open to the public. It contains a small exhibit space highlighting its history.

GERMANTOWN HISTORICAL SOCIETY

5501 Germantown Ave., 215/844-0514, www.germantownhistory.org
HOURS: Tues. 9 A.M.-1 P.M., Thurs. and Sun. 1-5 P.M., and by appt., call to confirm
COST: $5 adult, $4 senior and student, $2 child

Founded in 1901 as the Site and Relic Society of Germantown, the Germantown Historical Society offers a wealth of information about the history of German Township (which now consists of the neighborhoods of Germantown, Mt. Airy, and Chestnut Hill). It serves as a good starting point for visits to the area's historic sites and also contains a small museum and extensive library and archive collections. Many of the more than 50,000 historical objects, documents, and photographs are on display and available to the public.

GRUMBLETHORPE

5267 Germantown Ave., 215/843-4820, www.philalandmarks.org
HOURS: Tues., Thurs., and Sun. 1-4 P.M., last tour 3 P.M. Apr.-Dec.
COST: $5 adult, $4 student and senior, $3 pp for groups of 10 or more, $12 for family, free under 6

With a name straight out of a Harry Potter book, Grumblethrope was originally called "John Wister's Big House" because it had multiple stories. Built as a summer home in 1744 for wine importer John Wister, the stone and oak structure is a classic example of 18th-century Pennsylvania German architecture. Until the 1950s, generations of notable Wisters lived here, during which time they made various contributions to American literature, horticulture, historic preservation, and astronomy. Owen Wister, author of a novel about the American West, *The Virginian,* spent many summers in the home. Sally Wister, a teenager living in the house during the Revolution, kept a fascinating diary that has since been published. Charles Jones Wister, who is credited with naming the house Grumblethorpe after a place in the humorous 19th-century book *Thinks I to Myself,* was known for his scientific knowledge and for crafting intricate scientific tools. For decades, Charles kept a weather record, which is still used by forecasters to mark record-setting temperatures in Philadelphia. Period furnishings and many of the Wisters' belongings are on display in the home, now maintained by the Philadelphia Society for the Preservation of Landmarks.

The home even played a role in the Battle of Germantown while the Wisters were out of town. General James Agnew was staying in the house, and after being wounded in battle, he died in the front parlor. His blood stains can still be seen on the floor—providing great fodder for ghost stories.

JOHNSON HOUSE

6306 Germantown Ave., 215/438-1768,
www.johnsonhouse.org
HOURS: Thurs.-Fri. 10 A.M.-4 P.M., Sat. 1-4 P.M. with tours at 1:15, 2:15, and 3:15 P.M.
COST: $5 adult, $3 senior and child over 12, $2 child 12 and under

This National Historic Landmark was built for John Johnson 1765–1768 by Jacob Knorr, also responsible for many other Germantown area landmarks, including Cliveden. The Johnson House was home to three generations of a Quaker family of abolitionists. In the 1850s, the main house and smaller properties on the grounds became an important station on the Underground Railroad. The Johnsons also participated in the boycott of produce grown with slave labor and supported the Home for Infirmed and Aged Colored Persons, the Association of Friends for the Free Instruction of Adult Colored Persons, and the Emlen Institute for the Benefit of Children of African and Indian Descent. They were well connected with other prominent abolitionists including William Lloyd Garrison, Oliver Johnson, William Still, Lucretia Mott, Harriet Tubman, and John Greenleaf Whittier. On the 45-minute tour, you will learn about the history of the house and its inhabitants.

STENTON

4601 N. 18th St., 215/329-7312, www.stenton.org
HOURS: Tues.-Sat. 1-4 P.M. Apr.-Dec. and by appt. all year
COST: $5 adult, $4 student and senior

Stenton is one of the best-preserved Georgian mansions in Philadelphia, built in 1730 by James Logan, secretary to William Penn and one of the major players in the growth of early Pennsylvania. Logan lived here during his final 20 years of life, during the period that he became a distinguished scholar and accumulated an extensive library, which is now housed at the Library Company of Philadelphia. The home stands on three acres of the original 500-acre plantation. Tour the mansion, grounds, and the 1787 barn, which contains an exhibit of agricultural tools dating from the 18th and early 19th centuries. For the past 100 years, it has been maintained by the National Society of the Colonial Dames of America; tours, educational programs, and special events are offered.

WYCK

6026 Germantown Ave., 215/848-1612, www.wyck.org
HOURS: Tues. and Thurs. noon-4 P.M., Sat. 1-4 P.M. Apr.-Dec.
COST: $5 adult, $4 student and senior, $10 family

Wyck offers a glimpse into the lives of nine generations of a Quaker family in early Philadelphia. The home was used by British troops as a field hospital during the Battle of Germantown, but its real interest lies in the history of the people that lived here—as seen through the home, gardens, and more than 100,000 artifacts accumulated over 300 years. Hans Milan, a Quaker from Germany and descendant of a Swiss Mennonite family, was the home's earliest owner. His daughter Margaret married well-known Dutch Quaker Dirk Jansen. The house served as a summer home and retreat for the family who primarily lived in the center of Philadelphia until the yellow fever epidemic took the lives of several family members and scared the rest of the family into settling permanently in Germantown, outside of the close quarters of the city—an early example of suburban flight. The family's fascinating history is too long to report here, but a visit to the home reveals some of the marks they left on Philadelphia.

The grounds include a nationally known rose garden dating from the 1820s. The hall is the oldest part of the home, dating 1700–1720. Various additions and renovations took place throughout the 18th century, but the decor has changed little since 1824 when William Strickland rearranged the interior to create an open, light-filled space.

Greater Philadelphia   Map 10

ADVENTURE AQUARIUM
1 Aquarium Dr., Camden, NJ, 856/521-5176,
www.adventureaquarium.com
HOURS: Daily 9:30 A.M.-5 P.M.
COST: $18 adult, $15 child

During its first 10 years, the New Jersey State Aquarium at Camden played perpetual second fiddle to larger, fancier facilities in Baltimore and Washington, D.C., but after a full renovation and expansion, it reopened in 2005 as the new and much-improved Adventure Aquarium. Anchoring the steadily developing Camden waterfront, the aquarium holds over 8,000 animals in a variety of aqueous and semi-aqueous habitats. Besides the countless varieties of fish, seals and penguins are also on display. Exhibits include the humongous Ocean Realm featuring native Atlantic fish, the Amazon-themed Irazu River Falls, the Touch-a-Shark interactive tank, the West African River Experience with huge Nile hippos and exotic river fish, and much more. Adventure Aquarium also features a 150-seat "4D" theater that shows nature documentaries and commercial-run movies in addition to kid-friendly interactive shows.

BATTLESHIP *NEW JERSEY*
62 Battleship Pl., Camden, NJ, 866/877-6262,
www.battleshipnewjersey.org
HOURS: Fri.-Mon. 10 A.M.-3 P.M. Jan.-Feb., daily 9:30 A.M.-3 P.M. Mar.-Apr., daily 9:30 A.M.-5 P.M. May-Sept. 1, daily 9:30 A.M.-3 P.M. Sept. 2-Dec. 31
COST: self-guided tour: $15 adult, $10.50 senior, veteran, and child 6-11, free child under 6 and active military; guided tour: $17 adult, $12 senior, veteran, and child 6-11, free child under 6 and active military

Considered "America's most decorated battleship," the *New Jersey* earned 19 battle and campaign stars for outstanding service throughout World War II, the Korean War, Vietnam, and the Gulf War. It was built in the Philadelphia Naval Yard and launched on December 7, 1942, and today is docked in nearby Camden and open to the public for tours, events, and overnight trips. At 887 feet and 45,000 tons, the longest battleship ever built is the length of nearly three football fields and more than 11 stories high. On a tour, you'll see exhibits detailing the ship's history and you'll be free to explore hands-on. You can climb up ladders and into the 16-inch gun turret; a 4-D flight simulator, "Seahawk," re-creates a WWII-era dogfight over Iwo Jima. For a $2 surcharge, you can take the expanded Firepower Tour, which highlights the ship's weapon systems and includes areas not seen on the regular tour (offered four times daily, 10 A.M., noon, 1 P.M., and 3 P.M.).

BETH SHOLOM SYNAGOGUE
8231 Old York Rd., Elkins Park, 215/887-1342,
www.bethsholomcongregation.org
HOURS: Call ahead to see when services are held
COST: Free

While Jewish synagogues in the Philly region are plentiful, especially in the near northern suburbs, only one was designed by legendary architect Frank Lloyd Wright. Beth Sholom Synagogue, which means "House of Peace" in Hebrew, was built to house the congregation when it moved from North Philadelphia to Elkins Park in the 1950s. It was the only synagogue Wright ever designed and it was the last project he completed before his death. The design is heavy with sacred imagery. A large glass pyramid calls to mind both a mountain and a tent, and Wright himself referred to it as a "luminous Mount Sinai." The congregation itself is of the Conservative doctrine, with a membership of about 1,000 families.

HIGHLANDS MANSION AND GARDENS

7001 Sheaff La., Fort Washington, 215/641-2687, www.highlandshistorical.org

HOURS: Mon.-Fri. tours at 1:30 and 3 P.M., and by appt.

COST: $5 adult, $4 senior, $3 student, free under 6

About 17 miles north of Philadelphia in Fort Washington, the Highlands Mansion and Gardens is the 44-acre historic site of a late 18th-century Georgian mansion and formal gardens. Construction of the Highlands was completed by 1796 for Anthony Morris (1766–1860), a wealthy politician and merchant seeking an escape from yellow fever epidemics in the city. It was acquired by Philadelphia wine merchant George Sheaff in 1813. There are nine outbuildings and the walled gardens offer a beautiful example of early 20th-century gardens. It has had a series of owners and parts have deteriorated, but in 1975, the Highlands Historical Society was formed to preserve, restore, and interpret the site. Many improvements have been made since, and tours tell the history of the property and the people who lived there for more than 200 years.

RODEPH SHALOM

615 N. Broad St., 215/627-6747, www.rodephshalom.org

HOURS: Mon.-Fri. 10 A.M.-3 P.M., Sun. 10 A.M.-noon

COST: Free

The oldest Ashkenazic congregation in the Western Hemisphere, Rodeph Shalom was founded in 1795. The current structure was completed in 1928 and stands as one of the only synagogues in the country in the Byzantine-Moorish style, designed by Simon and Simon. A large dome, starburst skylights, stained-glass windows, an ark supported on marble columns, and bronze-and-enamel doors are just a few of the architectural highlights. The Broad Street Foyer houses the Leon J. and Julia S. Obermayer Collection of Jewish ritual art, containing more than 500 ceremonial objects dating to the 1700s. Call in advance to schedule a tour at this active congregation.

VALLEY FORGE NATIONAL HISTORICAL PARK

1400 Outer Line Dr., King of Prussia, 610/783-1077, www.nps.gov/vafo

HOURS: 8 A.M.-6 P.M. June-Sept., 9 A.M.-5 P.M. Oct.-May

COST: Free

While no battles were fought here, the lush fields of Valley Forge were the site of the most challenging and one of the most critical periods of the Revolutionary War for the Continental Army. During the six months they were encamped here in the winter of 1777–1778, around 2,000 men were lost to sickness and disease. The army was lacking food and medical supplies and was ill-equipped to deal with the weather. Despite their extreme suffering, this is known as a time when the army came together, survived, and got stronger, and by sheer force of will went on to win the war.

A renovated visitors center and interactive displays and tours have made the site more interesting than ever. The Historical Society Museum houses a collection of 4,000 artifacts and memorabilia and exhibits that include "Determined to Persevere" and "Forging a Nation," which tell the story of the troops. You can tour Washington's original stone headquarters, restored and furnished, and other replicated structures. There are statues and monuments throughout the park commemorating the army and costumed interpreters help bring the period to life. Once Upon a Nation, the same group responsible for the storytelling benches throughout Independence Park, have costumed storytellers at Valley Forge and they offer guided trolley tours and an after-hours tour from April/May to October.

Connected to Philadelphia by the Schuylkill River Trail and adjacent to Valley Creek, Mount Joy, and Mount Misery, Valley Forge National Historical Park offers miles of hiking trails, with connections to other parks via the Perkiomen Trail. Some of the trails expose hikers to Revolutionary War history and equipment, colonial architecture, and fascinating stories from the 18th century. The Joseph Plumb Martin Trail links key historical sites in the park to one another, and Horseshoe Trail connects George Washington's campsite to the Appalachian Trail.

WAYNESBOROUGH

2049 Waynesborough Rd., Paoli, 610/647-1779, www.philalandmarks.org

HOURS: Tours Wed.-Sun. 1–4 P.M., last tour 3 P.M. mid-Mar.-Dec.

COST: $5 adult, $4 student and senior, $3 pp for groups of 10 or more, $12 family, free child 6 and under

Approximately 20 miles from Center City and five miles from Valley Forge in Chester County, Waynesborough was the 18th-century home of Revolutionary War hero General Anthony Wayne. Wayne was the only commander in chief of the American military who never served as president of the United States, but his contributions to the war were momentous. He led the Pennsylvania Line in the battles of Brandywine and Germantown, and survived the Valley Forge encampment. The national hero was nicknamed "Mad Anthony" as a result of his bravery and mercilessness. Wayne spent ten years at this classic Pennsylvania farm manor house, but left in 1792 when President Washington asked him to serve as major general and commander in chief of the Legions of America. The Georgian-style home was built using stone quarried on the property, and has been restored and furnished to reflect the Wayne family's life here over seven generations from 1724 to 1965.

RESTAURANTS

Philadelphia has always had a healthy dose of reliably good cuisine. But, beginning with the "restaurant renaissance" of the 1990s, the food scene evolved into one of the best, and most talked-about, in the country, with new and exciting eateries continuing to pop up in Center City and beyond.

Centuries-old mom-and-pop eateries share the streets with stylish bistros and fine-dining restaurants by world-renowned restaurateurs, including Georges Perrier, Susanna Foo, and Morimoto. Cozy neighborhood BYOBs have loyal followings, offering locals an inexpensive way to dine out. And dining in the many gastro-pubs—bars offering high-quality cuisine rather than deep-fried frozen apps—is more appealing than ever thanks to the smoking ban passed in 2007.

With some exceptions at the very high end, mostly around Rittenhouse, and the trendy end, mostly in Old City, anything goes as far as dress, including jeans and sneakers. There are always a few fashionistas in the house, but the dining scene is generally laid-back and casual, and jackets and ties are a rarity.

It goes without saying that the Philadelphia food scene extends far beyond cheesesteaks. That said, unless you're a strict vegetarian, there is no excuse for not sampling at least one of the greasy delights while you're in town. They're just not the same anywhere else. Philly's other culinary trademarks include hoagies, soft pretzels, and water ice, which are also requirements for any food lover to try. And no visit to Philadelphia is complete without a stop at the Reading Terminal Market or Italian

PHOTO BY K. CIAPPA FOR GPTMC

HIGHLIGHTS

LOOK FOR ☾ TO FIND
RECOMMENDED RESTAURANTS.

☾ Best Special Occasion Restaurant:
Take the elevator up to **XIX,** or Nineteen, named for its location on the 19th floor of the Park Hyatt at the Bellevue. You'll be treated to panoramic views of the city along with unique, perfectly prepared cuisine in one of the city's most elegant settings (page 67).

☾ Best Coffee: For true strong-coffee lovers, **La Colombe** is the spot. This is the coffee served by many of the city's other great coffee shops, so why not go straight to the source (page 70)?

☾ Best Neighborhood Restaurant: The Fairmount neighborhood has a sprinkling of great restaurants and bars, and **Bridgid's** is a shining star among them, with a stellar beer selection and a small but high-quality lunch and dinner menu. The prices and friendly atmosphere are top-notch (page 74).

☾ Best Brunch: Sabrina's Café offers heaping portions of delicious omelettes and stuffed French toast to eager locals. Be prepared to wait for a table on weekends – but it's worth it (page 76).

☾ Best Vegan Restaurant: Just off South Street, the creative and unexpected flavors of the "New Vegan" cuisine at **Horizons** work so well that even carnivores won't miss the meat (page 82).

☾ Most Socially Conscious Restaurant: A University City mainstay, **White Dog Café** is a place where you can feel good about what you're eating and who you're supporting. The focus is on locally sourced ingredients and progressive business practices; the result is ultra-fresh, delicious food (page 84).

☾ Best Bar Food: The **Standard Tap** is a Northern Liberties staple offering excellent burgers, fries, and other fare in a lively, young atmosphere. Go for dinner, and stay for drinks to make a night out of it (page 85).

© PARK HYATT

XIX

☾ Most Romantic Waterfront Dining: Two of the city's most romantic restaurants just happen to be on the waterfront. You'll find the elegant **Water Works Restaurant** overlooking the Schuylkill River, and if that's not close enough to the water, the *Moshulu* is an actual ship converted to a restaurant on the Delaware River at Penn's Landing (pages 87, 63).

☾ Best Delivery: While most places only deliver within a short range of their shop, **Tiffin** offers service to all of Center City and beyond, with plans to expand to the entire city. They also happen to serve the best affordable Indian food in town (page 90).

☾ Best Old World Pizzeria: For an authentic Philly experience and the city's best pizza, you'll have to get off the beaten path. The family-owned **Tacconelli's Pizzeria,** in its fifth generation in the Port Richmond neighborhood, still serves up the best thin-crust pizza around (page 91).

RESTAURANTS

PRICE KEY

💲   Most entrées less than $10

💲💲   Most entrées between $10-20

💲💲💲   Most entrées more than $20

2000 Philadelphia was named the "fattest city in America" by *Men's Fitness* magazine. Just seven years later, *Cooking Light* magazine named it one of the 10 healthiest U.S. cities, citing the number of highly rated restaurants, the wealth of farmers markets, and the city's prime walkability.

Speaking of national media attention, in 2004, national foodie magazine *Saveur* named Philadelphia "America's most underrated food town." Philly has since received much overdue attention for its unique cuisine. But don't take anyone else's word for it—go out and see for yourself. Beyond the select sampling I've included to help get you started, there are approximately 4,000 others for you to discover on your own.

Market, for a vast variety of affordable ethnic cuisine and a unique atmosphere.

The amount of healthy options has also increased, with many restaurants focusing on fresh, locally grown ingredients—which isn't hard considering the many nearby farms in Pennsylvania and New Jersey. As an example of how far the city has come in this department, in

Old City

Map 1

For as many historic sites as there are in Old City, there are at least as many restaurants. With stylish bistros, fine dining, gastro-pubs, pizza joints, and practically every ethnic specialty, there is something for every taste and budget. A variety of options line Market and Chestnut Streets, between Front and 5th Streets, as well as nearby side streets.

ASIAN
BUDDAKAN 💲💲💲
325 Chestnut St., 215/574-9440, www.buddakan.com
HOURS: Mon.-Thurs. 11:30 A.M.-2 P.M. and 5-11 P.M., Fri. 11:30 A.M.-2 P.M. and 5 P.M.-midnight, Sat. 5 P.M.-midnight, Sun. 5-11 P.M.

Perhaps the most famous member of Stephen Starr's renowned restaurant empire, Buddakan has a modern Asian-themed atmosphere complete with a massive statue of Buddha. The over-the-top, if borderline cheesy, decor contributes to an unforgettable experience in the low-lit dining room. The large menu features fusion dishes like wasabi-crusted filet mignon, raw tuna on flatbread, and whole sizzling fish with sweet black-bean chili. There is certainly more authentic Asian cuisine in the city, but Buddakan offers a fun night-on-the-

town atmosphere, delicious but pricey drinks, and undeniably tasty, creative dishes.

MORIMOTO 💲💲💲
723 Chestnut St., 215/413-9070, www.morimotorestaurant.com
HOURS: Mon.-Thurs. 11:30 A.M.-2 P.M. and 5-11 P.M., Fri. 11:30 A.M.-2 P.M. and 5 P.M.-midnight, Sat. 5 P.M.-midnight, Sun. 4-10 P.M.

Though the Iron Chef himself now spends most of his time in the New York location, his original eponymous restaurant, also a Stephen Starr spectacle, is still a jewel. The space will wow you before you even sit down, with its ultra-modern dining room dimly lit with alternating multicolor lights and a cutting-edge design with lots of curved edges. It only gets better from there, with amazing sushi, sashimi, seafood, steak, salads, and several eat-till-you-die *omakase* (chef's tasting) options. Though your wallet will suffer for it, Morimoto is a must for any real restaurant lover—it's an experience.

CAFÉS
OLD CITY COFFEE 💲
221 Church St., 215/592-1897, www.oldcitycoffee.com
HOURS: Mon.-Wed. 6:30 A.M.-6 P.M., Thurs.-Fri.

6:30 A.M.–7 P.M., Sat. 7 A.M.–7 P.M., Sun. 7 A.M.–6 P.M.
Since 1984, this popular Old City coffeehouse has been roasting and brewing what many locals consider the city's best java. Sit inside the warm and cozy shop or snag a seat outside for great people-watching. A small but tasty selection of bagels, scones, muffins, and cookies is served along with a few breakfast and lunch options such as salads, soups, and breakfast sandwiches. Free WiFi is available, so get comfortable and stay awhile. Old City Coffee also has a booth in Reading Terminal Market, offering take-away and very limited seating.

COLONIAL AMERICAN
CITY TAVERN ❸❸❸

138 S. 2nd St., 215/413-1443, www.citytavern.com
HOURS: Mon.–Thurs. 11:30 A.M.–9 P.M., Fri.–Sun. 11:30 A.M.–10 P.M.

The previous regulars at this historic tavern and restaurant include some guys you may have heard of, including George Washington, Benjamin Franklin, John Adams, and Thomas Jefferson. The original tavern, completed in 1773, was much the same as the current restored replica completed in 1976. In its early incarnation, the tavern was more than just a bar and eatery as we know it today. Without modern office buildings, this was where people met to discuss important business. The colonial-garbed waiters and period furnishings are true to the era, as is the menu inspired by foods popular in colonial times. Chef Staib turns out West Indies Pepper Pot Soup, Martha Washington–Style Colonial Turkey Pot Pie, Braised Rabbit, and Pan-Seared Brook Trout. A place like this is in real danger of being kitschy, but with the food and atmosphere as good as they are, no one seems to mind. Don't miss the sweet-potato-and-pecan biscuits, supposedly a favorite of Thomas Jefferson.

FOOD COURT
THE BOURSE FOOD COURT ❸

111 S. Independence Mall East (5th St. btwn. Market and Chestnut Sts.), 215/625-0300, www.bourse-pa.com
HOURS: Mon.–Sat. 10 A.M.–6 P.M. year-round, Sun. 11 A.M.–5 P.M. Mar.–Nov.

If you're looking for a quick bite in the

© KARRIE GAVIN

food court and shops at the Bourse

middle of sightseeing or need to feed a big, choosy family, the Bourse is a cheap, convenient option. Just across the street from the Liberty Bell, Independence Hall, and the Constitution Center, you'll find a mall-like food court offering the standards: fast food, pizza, cheesesteaks, and Chinese food. Several touristy knick-knack and memento shops can also be found inside the grand old building. Built in 1895, the Bourse (meaning "place of exchange" in Middle French) was the brainchild of George E. Bartol. He got the idea during a visit to Hamburg and decided that Philadelphia needed one of its own. It once housed Philadelphia's stock, grain, and maritime exchanges and was renovated into its current form in the 1980s.

FRENCH
PATOU ❸❸

312 Market St., 215/928-2987,
www.patourestaurant.com
HOURS: Tues.–Thurs. 5–11:30 P.M., Fri.–Sat. 5 P.M.–2 A.M.

Part stylish bar, part upscale French

restaurant, Patou is good in both departments. The back dining room has ultra-high ceilings and a modern Mediterranean-inspired decor of bright white and blue lines. The open kitchen serves as the centerpiece. French classics include pâté escargots, coq au vin, cassoulet, and *pommes frites,* and other dishes are French with a Mediterranean or African flair. The bar in front offers great deals on its small-plate menu; choose three for $14 or $7 each from tasty options like spicy hanger-steak brochette, citrus lobster ceviche, and bluepoint oysters.

INDIAN
CAFÉ SPICE ⑤⑤
35 S. 2nd St., 215/627-6273, www.cafespice.com
HOURS: Mon.-Thurs. 11 A.M.-3 P.M. and 5-10:30 P.M., Fri. 11 A.M.-3 P.M. and 5-11:30 P.M., Sat. 11:30 A.M.-4 P.M. and 5-11:30 P.M., Sun. 11:30 A.M.-4 P.M. and 5-10:30 P.M.

Part of a small and relatively upscale chain of restaurants in New York, New Jersey, and Pennsylvania, Café Spice offers well-prepared Indian fare in a trendy lounge atmosphere. It has been quite a hit in Old City, attracting a mix of tourists, business people, and the young, beautiful people overflowing from the nearby Continental. The large menu features Indian favorites and, this being Old City, a large selection of cocktails and martinis. It also offers Sunday brunch and delivery. There is a Café Spice Express in the food court at the Shops at Liberty Place (1625 Chestnut St.), offering lower-priced versions of many of the same Indian specialties.

ITALIAN
GIANFRANCO PIZZA RUSTICA ⑤
6 N. Third St., 215/592-0048
HOURS: Mon.-Thurs. 10 A.M.-10 P.M., Fri. 10 A.M.-11 P.M., Sat. 10 A.M.-10 P.M., Sun. 1-9 P.M.

Serving up the best pizza in Old City, this is a great place to grab a quick slice in the middle of sightseeing or bar-hopping. The thin crust, fresh tomato sauce, and a vast variety of standard and interesting toppings (including pesto, artichokes, broccoli rabe, potatoes, and prosciutto) keep customers coming back.

Calzones, stromboli, and sandwiches round out the tasty offerings. You may have to wait a bit for your order at lunch time on weekdays, but it's worth it.

LA FAMIGLIA ⑤⑤⑤
8 S. Front St., 215/922-2803, www.lafamiglia.com
HOURS: Mon. 5:30-9:30 P.M., Tues.-Thurs. noon-2:30 P.M. and 5:30-9:30 P.M., Fri.-Sat. 5:30-10 P.M.

Luxurious and elegant, La Famiglia pampers guests with old-school Italian charm, classic decor, and tuxedoed waitstaff. The Sena family serves an authentic taste of traditional Naples, with offerings such as antipasti and Vitello con Fontina (medallions of veal topped with fontina cheese in a white-wine demi-glace). Choose a glass or bottle of wine from the expansive selection dating from the 1940s. Save room to sample from the dessert cart, or enjoy a cheese course, sorbet, ice cream, or traditional biscotti. Considering the steep price, this is a place best reserved for special occasions, but this Italian indulgence makes for an unforgettable evening.

POSITANO COAST
BY ALDO LAMBERTI ⑤⑤
212 Walnut St., 215/238-0499, www.lambertis.com
HOURS: Mon.-Thurs. 11:30 A.M.-10:30 P.M., Fri. 11:30 A.M.-midnight, Sat. noon-midnight, Sun. 1-10 P.M.

Just one block from the wildest of Old City's revelry, Positano Coast by Aldo Lamberti offers a refined take on contemporary southern Italian cuisine, with dishes like lamb and leeks, lobster truffle, pan-seared skate, chicken rolatini, pesto crab cakes, and more. The menu is big on *crudo* (seafood and meat served raw) and small plates for sharing. An ample outdoor covered seating area on the 2nd floor allows patrons to feel the summer breeze and observe the passersby, or snag one of the comfy couches or a table in the back in the Sopra lounge. Fine wines and cocktails are available, but Positano Coast also offers diners a BYOB option on Sunday and Monday. Happy hour Monday–Friday 5–7 P.M. includes $3 glasses of wine, along with food and other drink specials.

JAPANESE
HARU ❸❸❸

241 Chestnut St., 215/861-8990, www.harusushi.com

HOURS: Mon.-Tues. 11:30 A.M.-3 P.M. and 5-11 P.M., Wed. 11:30 A.M.-3 P.M. and 5 P.M.-midnight, Thurs.-Fri. 11:30 A.M.-3 P.M. and 5 P.M.-1 A.M.

This elite sushi chain has seven New York locations, one in Philadelphia, and one in Boston. Housed on a busy Old City corner in a former bank, the Philly outpost has a grand bi-level space with soaring ceilings, massive arched windows, and comfortable, squishy booths that look deceivingly like bamboo. In addition to the dramatic main area, there is additional seating near the sushi bar and a 2nd-floor bar area. From traditional miso to lobster miso soup, and from classic, fresh sashimi to modern, inventive rolls and hot fusion entrées, the menu is diverse and delicious. A full drink menu includes a variety of sake cocktails.

NEW AMERICAN
FARMICIA AND METRO CAFÉ ❸❸

15 S. 3rd St., 215/627-6274, www.farmiciarestaurant.com

HOURS: Farmicia: Tues.-Thurs. 11:30 A.M.-3 P.M. and 5:30-10 P.M., Fri. 11:30 A.M.-3 P.M. and 5:30-11 P.M., Sat. 11 A.M.-3 P.M. and 5:30-11 P.M., Sun. 11 A.M.-3 P.M. and 5-9 P.M.; Metro: Tues.-Fri. 8 A.M.-4 P.M., Sat.-Sun. 8:30 A.M.-4 P.M.

Farmicia and Metro Café, an expanded version of Metropolitan Bakery that also offers breakfast and lunch, operate out of the same great Old City space. One of the least typical "Old City" spots in Old City, the simple, fresh flavors of the food and drinks and the friendly, casual atmosphere is a refreshing change from the sometimes over-prepared, trendy offerings at some nearby establishments. Between the café and restaurant, you can get snacks, breakfast, coffee, lunch, brunch, dinner, or a bar menu practically any time of day. The focus of the food is organic, locally grown, and artisan ingredients, and of course, using only the best breads from Metropolitan. Best of all, at no additional charge, you can BYOB any time. An excellent happy hour is offered at the bar Tuesday–Friday 5–7 P.M., with reduced-price food and drinks.

FORK ❸❸❸

306 Market St., 215/625-9425, www.forkrestaurant.com

HOURS: Mon.-Thurs. 11:30 A.M.-10:30 P.M., Fri. 11:30 A.M.-11:30 P.M., Sat. 5-11:30 P.M., Sun. 11 A.M.-3 P.M. and 5-10:30 P.M.

Hip, sophisticated bistros come and go like the breeze in trendy Old City, but Fork has remained a hit for more than a decade. High ceilings, velvet curtains, wrought-iron chandeliers and pendant lighting create an elegant yet cozy atmosphere. Owner Ellen Yin and Chef Ngo offer a seasonal menu that changes daily and focuses on locally sourced ingredients. Don't miss the extensive and generous fruit-and-cheese platter or the strong specialty cocktails. You can watch the action in the open kitchen, or really be part of it by coming to the bistro dinner at 8 P.M. on Wednesday nights—it's an excellent way to experience the best Fork has to offer at a lower pricewith two starters, an entrée, dessert, and wine served at a large communal table for $40. And be sure to check out **Fork, Etc.** (308 Market St., 215/625-9425) around the corner for gourmet take-out lunch and snacks.

JONES ❸❸

700 Chestnut St., 215/223-5663, www.jones-restaurant.com

HOURS: Mon.-Thurs. 11 A.M.-midnight, Fri. 11 A.M.-1 A.M., Sat. 10 A.M.-1 A.M., Sun. 10 A.M.-11 P.M.

With its Brady Bunch–inspired decor, Jones is the homiest outpost in local restauranteur Stephen Starr's vast and trendy gastronomic empire. Shag carpeting and stone fireplaces set the tone, but while the interior takes its cues from '70s suburbia, it didn't have anything like this in the way of food or friendly waitstaff. The reasonably priced comfort food includes some decidedly contemporary twists. Alongside mashed potatoes, meatloaf, and fried chicken and waffles, you can find pistachio-crusted tilapia and Seared Tuna Tacos. There's also a good selection of tasty if overpriced drinks, including the Happy, the Hound Dog, and the Morning Glory.

SEAFOOD
PHILADELPHIA FISH & CO. $$$

207 Chestnut St., 215/625-8605,
www.philadelphiafish.com

HOURS: Mon.-Thurs. 11:30 A.M.-10:30 P.M., Fri.
11:30 A.M.-4 P.M. and 5 P.M.-midnight, Sat. noon-3 P.M.
and 4:30 P.M.-midnight, Sun. 4-10:30 P.M.

Since 1983, Philadelphia Fish & Co. has been
an Old City favorite for simple, fresh quality
seafood. Choose between the simply prepared
dishes, like grilled or pan-seared salmon,
tuna, butterfish, swordfish, or shrimp, or
have one of Chef Rambo-Garwood's unique
creations like rare yellowfin tuna served with
chickpea puree and red pepper sauce. While
seafood is the major draw, meat lovers will not
be disappointed with the delectable strip steak
served with bacon, mushroom, pearl onion,
and scotch butter sauce. Come for lunch to
try variations of many of the dinner entrées
at lower prices or the absolute steal of a bar
menu, where for $6 you can enjoy seared
catfish, steamed mussels, or one of the best
burgers in town, any time of day. Happy hour

specials are offered from 9 P.M. until closing
with $5 cocktails.

SNACKS AND SWEETS
FRANKLIN FOUNTAIN $

116 Market St., 215/627-1899,
www.franklinfountain.com

HOURS: Sun.-Thurs. noon-11 P.M., Fri.-Sat.
noon-midnight

The perfect addition to historic Old City,
Franklin Fountain has the feel of an authentic old-school ice cream and soda shop, even
though it's only been around for a few years.
Sit at the marble countertop and enjoy a banana split or sundae made with creamy homemade ice cream. Or try a classic egg cream,
made with milk, flavored syrup, and club soda.
Servers dressed in traditional soda-jerk gear and
the building's early details, including tin walls
and ceiling and a mosaic tile floor, help set the
mood. If you haven't satisfied your sweet tooth
with the ice cream, candy, or homemade fudge,
stop into **Shane Handcrafted Candies** (110
Market St., 215/922-1048) a few doors down;

Find fresh seafood in Old City.

the oldest candy shop in Philadelphia has been owned and operated by the same family for nearly 100 years.

SPANISH
AMADA $$$

217-219 Chestnut St., 215/625-2450,
www.amadarestaurant.com
HOURS: Mon.-Wed. 11:30 A.M.-2:30 P.M. and 5-11 P.M., Thurs.-Fri. 11:30 A.M.-2:30 P.M. and 5 P.M.-midnight, Sat. 5 P.M.-midnight, Sun. 4-11 P.M.

Upon opening in 2007, Amada quickly became one of the hottest restaurants in the city, which is saying a lot. The vibe is always stylish, fun, and energetic, but even more so on Wednesday and Friday with live flamenco dancers. But the main reason it's so hard to get a table here at times is the food—delectable, authentic Spanish tapas created by internationally acclaimed chef Jose Garces. Watch through the open kitchen as chefs prepare cured meats, artisan cheeses, and traditional and creative inventions in beautiful preparations. Whether you want savory, salty, or sweet, the robust flavors on the menu are sure to please. A full bar offers an extensive wine list, as well as red and white sangria, the perfect accompaniment to any dish.

Society Hill   Map 1

Society Hill is primarily residential, except for the areas that border Old City, Washington Square, and South Street. Headhouse Square, encompassing several blocks of 2nd Street just north of South Street, is packed with bars and restaurants. Penn's Landing, the waterfront strip along the Delaware, has a few good offerings, and is just a short walk across a foot bridge from Society Hill.

MEXICAN
XOCHITL $$$

408 S. Second St., 215/238-7280,
www.xochitlphilly.com
HOURS: Tues.-Sun. 5-10 P.M.

This Headhouse Square restaurant offers upscale, authentic Mexican cuisine in a cozy setting. Start with the delicious guacamole made tableside and sample one of several mouth-watering fresh ceviches. Other menu highlights include the Sopa Axteca (a soup made with pasilla pepper, *crema,* avocado, and chihuahua cheese) poured tableside over fried tortillas, Barbacoa de Borrego (slow-cooked lamb), and Camarones al Mojo de Ajo (sautéed shrimp with garlic and cilantro). An extensive tequila list can be served by the shot or flight or made into a margarita or other specialty drink. Save room for dessert; the *churros y chocolate* is just divine. The tequila bar downstairs is a good alternative for tequila lovers who would rather drink and hear a DJ spin than eat a full dinner. Go for happy hour: half-priced house margaritas, $2 select beers, and a $6 Guero Special (shot of Sauza Blanco and a can of Tecate) at the upstairs bar Tuesday–Sunday 5–7 P.M. or in the lounge Thursday, Friday, and Saturday 10 P.M.–midnight.

NEW AMERICAN
🄲 MOSHULU $$$

401 S. Columbus Blvd., 215/923-2500,
www.moshulu.com
HOURS: Mon.-Sat. 11:30 A.M.-3 P.M. and 5:30-10:30 P.M., Sun. 11 A.M.-2 P.M. and 5:30-10:30 P.M.

Dining on a docked ship offers the romantic experience of being surrounded by water without the seasickness that comes with a typical dinner cruise. Built in 1904, the *Moshulu* had been used for shipping goods; it served as a warehouse on water; and it was confiscated twice during wars over the course of its long life. But interesting as its history is, the real reason to come is for quality food in the heart of Penn's Landing. What could have easily become a cheesy tourist trap is instead an elegant restaurant offering classics like filet mignon, crab cakes, and salmon in updated, tasteful variations. On Sunday, an upscale buffet brunch is offered for $30 per person, and while prices are a bit steep, the experience is memorable. To experience the boat for less money, visit the Bongo Bar on the upper deck for drinks and a lower-priced, tasty bar menu, with live music at times.

SEAFOOD
OCEANAIRE $$$

700 Walnut St., 215/628-8862, www.theoceanaire.com
HOURS: Mon.-Thurs. 11:30 A.M.-10 P.M., Fri.
11:30 A.M.-11 P.M., Sat. 5-11 P.M.
The selective upscale chain came to a historic building in Society Hill on the edge of Old City in 2007. Overlooking Washington Square, the restaurant has a unique decor designed to resemble ocean liners from the 1920s and '30s. The menu changes daily to offer the freshest seafood available. An extensive raw bar offers fresh oysters galore, along with other fish and shellfish. The professional staff prides itself on pairing each dish with the perfect wine, so be sure to get a recommendation from your waiter. Family-style sides and desserts are enormous and delicious, so try to save some room, and be sure to share with the table.

Center City East   Map 2

This large area is packed with restaurants, with the majority concentrated in Chinatown, Washington Square West, and along the Avenue of the Arts. Chinatown has more than just Chinese restaurants, but also Cambodian, Vietnamese, Burmese, and more. Wash West, also known as the Gayborhood, offers plenty of BYOBs and bars serving great food, especially along Pine Street, Spruce Street, and 13th Street south of Market. Avenue of the Arts has mostly large, upscale chains.

ASIAN
1225 RAW SUSHI
AND SAKE LOUNGE $$

1225 Sansom St., 215/238-1903, www.rawlounge.net
HOURS: Mon.-Wed. 11:30 A.M.-2:30 P.M. and
5-10 P.M., Thurs. 11:30 A.M.-2:30 P.M. and 5-11 P.M.,
Fri. 11:30 A.M.-2:30 P.M. and 5 P.M.-midnight, Sat.
5 P.M.-midnight, Sun. 5-10 P.M.
The sleek, modern lounge-like decor comes complete with red walls, a bamboo ceiling, and high-backed booths, with a welcoming outdoor courtyard with additional seating. An array of creative salads, meat dishes, and cooked plates does not disappoint, but the highlight of the menu is definitely the sushi. The chef turns out generous and beautiful portions of fresh sashimi, maki, and nigiri in inventive combinations. The full bar serves beer, wine, and specialty drinks, many made with sake from the extensive selection. Try a flight of four different types of sake, or the *omakase* (chef's tasting menu) offered Monday–Thursday.

CAFÉS
RAY'S CAFÉ AND TEA HOUSE $

141 N. 9th St., 215/922-5122, www.rayscafe.com
HOURS: Mon.-Thurs. 9 A.M.-9 P.M., Fri. 9 A.M.-10 P.M., Sat.
11:30 A.M.-10 P.M.
Ray's serves the best, and most expensive, coffee in Chinatown, along with a wide selection of teas and a small Thai food menu. Coffee is made to order from exotic ground beans and brewed with spring water. Some brews are rather pricey ($8.50—ouch), but true coffee connoisseurs will find it worth it. Coffee and tea drinks are all served in an elegant display with a fruit tart or homemade cookie.

CHINESE
LAKESIDE CHINESE DELI $

207 N. 9th St., 215/925-3288
HOURS: Mon.-Wed. and Fri.-Sun. 11 A.M.-8 P.M.
A Chinatown favorite for cheap and delicious dim sum, Lakeside is not a deli, but it is a

© KARRIE GAVIN

Soft pretzels are a Philly favorite.

great place to grab a snack, a quick lunch, or dinner. Noodle soups and other entrées are also good, but less popular than dim sum (which costs a quarter more per item at dinner). At prices of around $1 for most, it's still a great deal, plus you can BYOB. Unlike some places where you choose pre-made dim sum from the cart, they bring it out of the kitchen made to order, but if you can't decide what to order, the servers will usually make excellent suggestions.

SINGAPORE CHINESE VEGETARIAN $
1006 Race St, 215/922-3288
HOURS: Sun.-Thurs. 11:30 A.M.-10 P.M., Fri.-Sat. 11:30 A.M.-11 P.M.
Singapore Chinese Vegetarian offers a delicious range of vegetarian options. Besides standards like steamed or sautéed vegetables with rice, Singapore makes some of the most delicious soy/wheat/gluten/seitan fake meats you'll ever have the pleasure to taste. Mock beef and chicken in every flavor permutation populates the menu.

SZECHUAN TASTY HOUSE $
902 Arch St., 215/925-2839
HOURS: Tues.-Sun. 11 A.M.-midnight
Feelin' hot, hot hot? Szechuan Tasty House has some of the most flavorful, spicy food in Chinatown. Tell your server if you want more or less spice; they sometimes discourage their American guests from the super-spicy because they don't believe you can take it, so be clear about what you want. Most dishes are not just hot, but also wonderfully flavored. Don't miss the dumplings in hot-pepper oil as an appetizer and the three-pepper chicken or classic Sczechuan beef as entrées. A variety of noodle dishes and vegetarian dishes, including well-prepared tofu, are also excellent.

ITALIAN
MERCATO $$
1216 Spruce St., 215/985-2962,
www.mercatobyob.com
HOURS: Mon.-Thurs. 5-10:30 P.M., Fri.-Sat. 5-11 P.M., Sun. 5-10 P.M.
This tiny cash-only BYOB is always noisy

BRING YOUR OWN BOTTLE

While it's easy to spend a few hundred bucks on dinner for two at Philadelphia's top restaurants, it's just as easy to spend under $50 by bringing your own bottle to one of the city's many BYOBs – many of which rival their liquor-serving counterparts in quality. While locals have long complained about Pennsylvania's strict liquor licensing laws and high taxes on liquor sales, the fringe benefits are out of this world. The law makes it so hard for a new business to serve liquor, that as a result Philly has one of the largest and best BYOB scenes in the country. The wide variety offers something for every taste and budget, and BYOBs have to maintain very high food standards to compete. Most maintain a casual, comfortable neighborhood vibe, and few have corkage fees – this added charge for bringing your own is more likely at a place that has a bar of its own but also allows the BYO option. In this case, the fee should be clearly noted on the menu.

There are plenty of BYOBs listed throughout this chapter, but a few local favorites not to miss include Center City's **Mercato, Audrey Claire,** and **Pumpkin;** University City's **Marigold Kitchen** and **Vientiane Café;** and **Dmitri's** South Philly location. Some restaurants, like **Farmicia** in Old City, offer a full bar but also let you bring your own bottle if you prefer, without a fee.

In addition to those places where wine is the drink of choice for most BYOB-ers, there are also spots where other drinks are commonly brought to the table. Beer is common at causal spots like the **Jamaican Jerk Hut, Tacconelli's Pizzeria,** and **Plaza Garibaldi.** And people love to bring their own tequila to **Lolita** or **Molcajete Mixto,** Mexican spots where they will mix your booze into their own margarita mixes.

Purchasing alcohol in Pennsylvania is not always simple. There are beer distributors and state-run Wine & Spirits shops in every neighborhood, but beer cannot be sold at the same store as wine and booze. Hours are limited, with the latest spirits shops closing at 9 P.M., but most closing at 7 or 8 P.M. Beer distributors stay open somewhat later, but very few of either type of store are open on Sunday, so plan ahead. Many bars sell six-packs to go, but expect to pay higher premiums for the convenience. Visit www.pawineandspirits.com for the state store locations, or ask a local to point you in the right direction.

and crowded—partly due to the close tables and its immense popularity, and also perhaps because most guests here like to drink (it's not abnormal to see a 1:1 ratio of guests to wine bottles at a table). Chef Evan Turney (also of Valanni across the street) serves excellent modern Italian dishes at reasonable prices from his open kitchen. Start with a plate of bread and artisan cheese paired with an olive oil tasting. Then choose from an array of pasta, fish, and meat dishes that combine traditional and updated flavors and preparations. A molten chocolate lava cake and a mascarpone cheesecake are just two of the excellent desserts. Reservations are not taken, so you'll often have to wait for a table—especially on weekends—but it's well worth it.

MEDITERRANEAN-LATIN
VALANNI $$

1229 Spruce St., 215/790-9494, www.valanni.com

HOURS: Mon.-Fri. 5 P.M.-1 A.M., Sat.-Sun. 11 A.M.-3 P.M. and 5 P.M.-1 A.M.

This stylish Mediterranean-Latin restaurant and bar is credited to the same owner-chef, R. Evan Turney, as the popular BYOB Mercato across the street. With one wall of exposed brick, dim pendant lighting, and lots of candlelight, the mood is romantic yet fun. The bar is often filled with regulars who come for the strong, delicious award-winning specialty cocktails like the Ecstasy, White Cosmo, and Chuck's Cosmo (which substitutes tequila for vodka). Dishes are hard to peg into one style, but there are plenty of Mediterranean and Latin influences. Small plates, which can be eaten as appetizers or alone as a tapas-style meal, include lobster-and-crab macaroni and cheese, spicy chicken empanadas, and grilled beef kabobs. Some dishes are served with lighter sides, sauces, and garnishes in summertime to match the mood. Desserts are enormous and delicious, especially the deep-fried oreo beignets and the carmelized rum bananas. Happy hour Monday–Friday from 5 to 6 P.M. offers great drink specials.

MEXICAN
LOLITA 💲💲
106 S. 13th St., 215/546-7100,
www.lolitabyob.com
HOURS: Sun.-Tues. 5-10 P.M., Wed.-Thurs. 5-10:30 P.M., Fri.-Sat. 5-11 P.M.

Exposed brick walls, a bright open kitchen, and just-right lighting set the mood in this popular BYOB owned by Valerie Safran and Chef Marcie Turney. There is a high level of quality and savory flavor in each and every contemporary Mexican dish—from the grilled sugarcane-morita marinated pork chop to the shitake and lancaster jack cheese enchiladas. The Fundido Con Rajas—homemade tortillas served with a generous portion of melted oaxaca and chihuahua cheeses, roasted poblano, smoked brandied chorizo, and mexican oregano for dipping—is a delicious but filling appetizer meant to be shared. Bring wine or bring your own tequila to mix with their homemade fresh margarita mix in flavors including original, watermelon, and mint.

NEW AMERICAN
🄲 XIX 💲💲💲
Broad and Walnut Sts. (19th fl. in the Park Hyatt Philadelphia at the Bellevue), 215/790-1919,
www.hyatt.com/gallery/nineteen
HOURS: Daily 6:30 A.M.-11 P.M., afternoon tea 2-4 P.M.

The 19th floor of the Park Hyatt at the Bellevue is dripping with elegance befitting a restaurant occupying one of the city's finest and oldest hotels. Perfect for a celebration or romantic dinner, XIX (pronounced "nineteen") offers outstanding new American cuisine, and the knowledgeable sommelier makes excellent pairing recommendations from the extensive wine list. Innovative chef Marc Plessis takes full advantage of seasonal and local ingredients, and his creative flavor combinations always seem to hit the mark. A raw bar occupies the center of the main dining room under the high domed ceiling. But the most alluring aspect of the room is the spectacular view of the city through the expansive windows. If you don't have a few hundred dollars to drop on dinner for two, you can still enjoy the elegant atmosphere with breakfast, lunch, or brunch or a visit to the bar, which offers an ample, delicious menu at much lower prices. A classic afternoon tea is served by reservation only.

SNACKS AND SWEETS
CAPOGIRO 💲
119 S. 13th St., 215/636-9250,
www.capogirogelato.com
HOURS: Mon.-Thurs. 7:30 A.M.-10 P.M., Fri. 7:30 A.M.-midnight, Sat. 9 A.M.-midnight, Sun. 10 A.M.-10 P.M.

Another upscale addition to this now-trendy section of 13th Street, Capogiro Gelato Artisans provides customers with deliciously dense, creamy, traditional Italian ice creams in countless fruity and savory flavors that change with the seasons. In additional to the traditional flavors like hazelnut and strawberry, there are innovative ones like rosemary/honey/goats milk and mascarpone fig. Ideal for a sweet ending to a date or a break in the middle of a day of shopping, Capogiro has expanded to a second location (Map 3, 117 S. 20th St.) near Rittenhouse and distributes through several local markets. Not your grandmother's ice cream cone, a small will cost you close to $5, but it is worth every cent.

NAKED CHOCOLATE CAFÉ 💲
1317 Walnut St., 215/735-7310,
www.nakedchocolatecafe.com
HOURS: Mon.-Sat. 10 A.M.-11 P.M., Sun. 11 A.M.-9 P.M.

The sumptuous Naked Chocolate Café has been expanding waistlines and lightening wallets for a few years now. A chocolate lover's dream, the father/daughter-owned café offers endless varieties of chocolates, truffles, and other baked and confectionery treats, almost all made on-premises. One of the most popular items is drinking chocolate like you've never imagined: hot, thick, impossibly rich, and spiced with flavors like chili powder and cinnamon. The well-coiffed clientele comes for people-watching as much as the decadent sugar fix, ensuring a bustling atmosphere until closing time on most nights.

SOUL FOOD
MS. TOOTSIE'S SOUL FOOD CAFÉ $
1314 South St., 215/731-9045
HOURS: Mon.-Thurs. 5-10 P.M., Fri. noon-1 A.M., Sat. 5 P.M.-1 A.M., Sun. noon-8 P.M.

Philadelphia is definitely an eating town, but it's not generally known for its soul food; Ms. Tootsie's wants to change that. Combining a cozy yet upscale setting with affordable comfort food, the charming staff dishes out healthy portions of Southern favorites like fried chicken, smothered pork chops, and catfish. Sides are where the kitchen especially shines, with candied yams, collared greens, and mouth-watering macaroni and cheese that all hit the spot. The restaurant is BYOB, but the adjacent **Ms. Tootsie's Lounge,** has a full-service bar (open Wed.–Sun. 5 P.M.–2 A.M.). The mood next door is more stylish and modern, and the menu offers small plates in contrast to the heaping portions at the café.

VIETNAMESE
VIETNAM $$
221 N. 11th St., 215/592-1163, www.eatatvietnam.com
HOURS: Sun.-Thurs. 11 A.M.-9:30 P.M., Fri.-Sat. 11 A.M.-10:30 P.M.

One of the city's most popular Vietnamese restaurants occupies a warm, inviting space in the heart of Chinatown. It's hard to go wrong with anything on the reasonably priced menu. Crispy spring rolls and tender summer rolls are top-notch, as is the grilled BBQ platter that lets you sample a range of appetizers. For entrées, catfish cooked in a clay pot and a variety of vermicelli and *pho* dishes do not disappoint. You may have to wait for a table on weekends, but you can order a strong specialty drink from the full bar to pass the time. Vietnam's main competitor is **Vietnam Palace** (222 N. 11th St., 215/592-9596), just across the street. It's also a local favorite, so try both if you have time.

Center City West   Map 3

This area is home to many of the most elegant restaurants in the city, but you can also find anything in this area. Walnut Street is lined with restaurants between Broad and 18th Streets, with additional options on the surrounding side streets, including several directly on Rittenhouse Square and a few good options on 20th Street.

ASIAN
FUJI MOUNTAIN $$
2030 Chestnut St, 215/751-0939, www.fujimt.com
HOURS: Mon.-Fri. 11:30 A.M.-1:45 P.M. and daily 5 P.M.-1:30 A.M.

This sushi bar and karaoke lounge is one more attraction signaling the rebirth of this section of Chestnut Street west of Broad, which used to shut down once the happy hour crowds left for the day. Besides serving up some of the city's best sushi and sashimi, the four-floor restaurant boasts a karaoke room for up to 30 people where you can belt out the best Japanese and American pop favorites while enjoying a full bar and food menu. Other rooms in the complex offer traditional Japanese dining, with delicious entrées, appetizers, bottle service, and cocktails. Fuji Mountain takes online orders and delivers to nearby addresses.

SUSANNA FOO $$$
1512 Walnut St., 215/545-2666, www.susannafoo.com
HOURS: Mon.-Thurs. 11:30 A.M.-2:30 P.M. and 5-10 P.M.,

FOOD TRUCK FARE

Those small, sparkling-metal mini-kitchens-on-wheels throughout the city often serve surprisingly good food – and at prices that cannot be beat. Frequented by everyone from students to white-collar elite, food trucks can be found in the downtown business district and near the universities.

A good rule of thumb is to join the longest lines. These trucks not only serve the best-tasting fare, but you can rest assured that the hygiene levels are satisfactory since the locals keep coming back. With seasoned professionals and impossibly hot grills, the food trucks churn out meals in a jiffy, so even the longest lines usually move fast. Choose from bagels, egg-and-cheese sandwiches, cheesesteaks, and hoagies to practically every ethnic food under the sun – even sushi. Aside from the greasy fare, heaping portions of affordable fresh fruit are on hand at many trucks. The **Magic Carpet**, a University City favorite at 34th and Walnut Streets, serves up delicious vegetarian and vegan cuisine.

Fri. 11:30 A.M.-2:30 P.M. and 5-11 P.M., Sat. 5-10 P.M., Sun. 5-9 P.M.

The only truly "fine-dining" Chinese restaurant in the city is also one of the city's most well-regarded restaurants overall. Nationally acclaimed chef-owner Susanna Foo has received much attention for her spectacular upscale cuisine (and also for her arrest for a questionable run-in/assault on a parking attendant). The dining room is elegant, with its high ceilings, white tablecloths, and subtle ethnic touches like silk lanterns. A sampler plate of four appetizers is an excellent starter, followed by tea-smoked Peking duck breast or seared diver scallops with emulsified truffle sauce. But really, everything on the menu is divine, and at these prices, it better be. Tasty specialty cocktails and the wine list

are excellent but will run your check through the roof if you're not careful.

VIC $

2035 Sansom St., 215/564-4339
HOURS: Mon.-Fri. 11 A.M.-10 P.M., Sat. 5-10 P.M.

Could it really be that Philly finally has a top-quality, take-out sushi joint so affordable that you can go several times a week? The friendly staff welcome you to sit at one of the six bar seats if they're not taken, but with the options of delivery or take-out, it doesn't matter. The specialty rolls are loaded with multiple types of fish, avocado, and more, and one (around $9) is filling enough to eat for lunch. And don't miss the sashimi appetizer, with two perfect pieces each of everyone's favorites: yellowtail, tuna, and salmon. But it's hard to resist the unbeatable deal of three simple eight-piece rolls for $9.95. Choose from the basics like spicy tuna, yellowtail with scallion, or shrimp tempura and you have yourself a sushi dinner for under $10. With Vic, Philadelphians no longer have to spend all their money at Morimoto or cross the bridge into New Jersey to go to Sagami to enjoy excellent sushi, at an even more excellent price.

CAFÉS

ANTS PANTS $

2212 South St., 215/875-8002,
www.antspantscafe.com
HOURS: Mon.-Fri. 7 A.M.-4 P.M., Sat.-Sun. 8 A.M.-3 P.M.

As the website of this seemingly odd-named café explains, "ants' pants" is an Australian colloquial term meaning "the best" or "height of fashion." Well, if I were Australian I would say that the coffee, food, and atmosphere at this small local haunt are "the ants' pants." They serve breakfast, lunch, and brunch, and while snagging a seat on the weekend is often challenging, at most other times, this is a place where you can sit for hours over your coffee, book, or laptop (free WiFi is provided). Don't miss the crème brûlée–battered French toast, the Salmon BLAT (smoked salmon, bacon, lettuce and tomato), or the delicious spinach salads. When the weather is nice, sit outside in the small back patio area.

RESTAURANTS

DARLING'S CAFÉ $

401 S. 20th St., 215/545-5745,
www.darlingscheesecake.com
HOURS: Mon.-Fri. 7 A.M.-7 P.M., Sat. 8 A.M.-7 P.M., Sun.
9 A.M.-3 P.M.

Darling's proudly claims to be purveyors of the "Original Philly Cheesecake"—yes, you heard right, cheesecake, not cheesesteak. I didn't know there was such a thing, but apparently it's lighter in color and creamier in texture than the New York variety. Regardless, they make one damn good cheesecake. There are a selection of other delicious desserts as well, all of which you can order by the slice or a whole pie in advance. Try the award-winning Bananas Foster cheesecake, the Forbidden Fruit, or the peanut butter silk. You're not going to be able to come in without trying the desserts, but the café also serves good breakfast and lunch fare, including soup, salad, and hot and cold sandwiches along with a full coffee bar. There is also WiFi here and at the café's second location behind the Franklin Institute (Map 4, 2100 Spring St., 215/496-9611).

◖ LA COLOMBE $

130 S. 19th St., 215/563-0860, www.lacolombe.com
HOURS: Mon.-Fri. 7:30 A.M.-6:30 P.M., Sat.-Sun.
8:30 A.M.-6:30 P.M.

The most popular Center City coffee shop caters to one type only—coffee lovers. Just off Rittenhouse Square, it's filled with the Rittenhouse elite, hipsters, bohemians, and regulars that look like they might be homeless—basically, everyone comes to La Colombe. One of the few coffee shops where the coffee is so good that they don't need to offer WiFi or a large food menu to keep customers happy, La Colombe keeps it simple with strong fresh-roasted gourmet coffee and espresso drinks and just a tiny case of croissants and scones at the counter. A medium-sized roaster, La Colombe proves that not everyone is looking for Starbucks.

CARIBBEAN
JAMAICAN JERK HUT $$

1436 South St., 215/545-8644
HOURS: Mon.-Thurs. 11 A.M.-10 P.M., Fri.-Sat.
11 A.M.-11 P.M., Sun. 5-10 P.M.

When the weather is nice, continue past the somewhat cramped interior to the choice seating area—the large backyard patio filled with tables for dining al fresco. You might wait awhile for your food, but if you've got sunshine, friends, and a few Red Stripes to pass the time at this unique BYOB, time will fly. Flaky patties stuffed with beef, chicken, or vegetables are a great starter, and the menu features something for meat lovers and vegetarians alike. Spice-sensitive diners should avoid the jerked dishes—they pack a punch. Curried dishes, while still flavorful, are more manageable, and all the homemade juices are worth sampling. While the place is a bit run-down, and the outdoor space is surrounded by a chain fence and the sides of houses, the place has got character—so much in fact that this is where the wedding was held in the last scene of *In Her Shoes*. Remember that movie, girls?

CHEESESTEAKS AND SANDWICHES
TONY JR.'S $

118 S. 18th St., 215/568-4630, www.tonylukes.com
HOURS: Mon.-Fri. 8 A.M.-9 P.M., Sat. 9 A.M.-9 P.M., Sun.
11 A.M.-7 P.M.

You no longer have to go to deep South Philly to get a perfect Tony Luke's cheesesteak. The Rittenhouse branch offers the same sandwiches on perfect rolls, in classic form or dressed with Italian ingredients of your choosing like broccoli rabe or roasted peppers. In addition to cheesesteaks, the roasted pork, sausage and pepper, breakfast, and veggie sandwich are all popular, but if you've never had one, stick with the cheesesteak. If you get a chance, you should still check out the original **Tony Luke's in South Philly** (39 E. Oregon Ave., 215/551-5725), which not only has the awesome food but also the traditional atmosphere. **Tony Luke's Beef and Beer Sports Bar** (26 E. Oregon Ave.) is also just down the street.

FRENCH
BRASSERIE PERRIER $$$

1619 Walnut St., 215/568-3000,
www.brasserieperrier.com

HOURS: Main dining room: Mon.-Thurs. 11:30 A.M.-2:30 P.M. and 5:30-10 P.M., Fri.-Sat. 11:30 A.M.-2:30 P.M. and 5:30 -10:30 P.M., Sun. 5-9:30 P.M.; Lounge: Mon.-Thurs. 11:30 A.M.-4 P.M. and 5:30-11 P.M., Fri.-Sat. 11:30 A.M.-4 P.M. and 5:30-11:30 P.M., Sun. 5-9:30 P.M.

If, like most people in the world, you're priced out of Philly's legendary Le Bec-Fin, you can still get a taste of restaurateur Georges Perrier at his bistro, Brasserie Perrier. Still not cheap by any stretch, the poshly appointed restaurant caters mostly to a hip, young professional crowd. High-end, French-influenced fare like frisée salad, *pommes frites*, potato gnocchi, chicken spanakopita, gazpacho, and more are quite good, and for dessert, chocolate beignets, crème brûlée, and chocolate lava cake are spectacular. Sunny days allow patrons to take advantage of the outdoor seating, where they can watch the scene on Walnut Street.

LE BEC-FIN ❸❸❸

1523 Walnut St., 215/567-1000, www.lebecfin.com
HOURS: Mon.-Sat. lunch starting at 11:30 A.M., two dinner seatings at 6 P.M. and 9:30 P.M.

If you are very wealthy or working with an extremely liberal expense account, a trip to Philadelphia isn't complete without a visit to the city's ultimate fine-dining restaurant. Since it opened in the 1970s, George Perrier's famous restaurant has been accepted by many as the city's best, and it has consistently received the coveted Mobil Five Star and AAA's Five Diamond awards, the highest honors in the hospitality industry. It oozes elegance and sophistication—from the high ceilings and grand chandeliers to the attentive, well-coordinated tuxedo-clad servers. The French cuisine is fresh, elegant, and perfectly prepared. The dessert cart and the cheese cart will make you feel that you've died and gone to heaven; you are encouraged to have as many as you like from the dozens of selections. The reduced-price prix fixe dinner available Monday–Thursday is still a whopping $90 per person, not including drinks from the book-length list, but this is a substantial discount from the regular six-course menu. Jacket and tie are required. Alas, if you're not a trust-fund baby or a CEO, you can visit **Le Bar Lyonnais** lounge on the lower floor to enjoy delicious drinks and food from a far less expensive menu prepared in the same kitchen as the rich upstairs neighbor.

IRISH
THE BLACK SHEEP ❸

247 S. 17th St., 215/545-9473, www.theblacksheeppub.com
HOURS: Mon.-Sun. 11:30 A.M.-2 A.M.

A block from always-jumping Rittenhouse Square, The Black Sheep is a multi-dimensional Irish pub. It has three levels where you can drink, watch a game, play darts, or sample traditional Irish dishes. Shepherd's Pie and Guinness Stew are flavorful versions of the Gaelic classics, while Sunday brunch offers staples like Bangers and Mash and Eggs Benedict. The menu is not strictly limited to traditional Irish fare, as green-curry mussels and a decent pulled-pork sandwich are also pleasing options. Wednesday nights feature Quizzo, a group trivia game that goes well with a perfect pint of Guinness.

MARKET
DIBRUNO BROS. ❸

1730 Chestnut St, 215/665-9220, www.dibruno.com
HOURS: Mon.-Fri. 9 A.M.-8 P.M., Sat. 9 A.M.-7 P.M., Sun. 9 A.M.-6 P.M.

Philadelphia's answer to Dean & Deluca began as a small family-run cheese shop in the Italian Market in 1940. Two smaller shops still exist in the market—each offering a modest sampling of the massive array of cheeses, stuffed olives, flavored oils, spreads, charcuterie, produce, and prepared foods offered in this mega-store. The two-floor DiBruno Bros. on Chestnut Street has all this times ten, along with a separate fish and meat market, a coffee, baked goods, and gelato bar, and an upstairs café with full salad bar, deli, cooked entrées, and sushi bar. Whether you're looking for a quick bite for lunch, want to take home a fully prepared meal, need all the ingredients to throw a big party, or you're looking for a perfect gift basket for your food-loving friend, DiBruno Bros. has it all. It can get expensive, but both stores are stocked with enough free samples of breads, oils, and cheeses that you just may find you're no longer hungry for lunch by the time you make it to the cash register.

MEXICAN
LOS CATRINES RESTAURANT & TEQUILA'S BAR ⑤⑤⑤

1602 Locust St., 215/546-0181, www.tequilasphilly.com
HOURS: Mon.-Thurs. 11:30 A.M.-2 P.M. and 5-10 P.M., Fri. 11:30 A.M.-2 P.M. and 5-11 P.M., Sat. 5-11 P.M., Sun. 5-10 P.M.

Upscale authentic Mexican cuisine is served in an eclectic yet elegant setting in a converted old brownstone. High ceilings and dim lighting welcome you into the front room featuring a grand, mirrored bar offering more than 90 different tequilas. Partitioned into three separate additional dining areas, the large restaurant maintains a cozy feel. But the reason locals and visitors keep coming back is the food. Choose from the excellent meat and seafood entrées, and do not miss the fresh, limey ceviche or the divine guacamole. Sangria and margaritas can be ordered by the glass, pitcher, or a full carafe. Oh, and be sure to mention if it's your birthday: The staff will sing to you in Spanish and bring out a free shot of tasty, sweet tequila mixed with cinnamon and more.

NEW AMERICAN
AUDREY CLAIRE ⑤⑤

276 S. 20th St., 215/731-1222, www.audreyclaire.com
HOURS: Sun.-Thurs. 5-10 P.M., Fri.-Sat. 5-10:30 P.M.

Audrey Claire was at the forefront of Philadelphia's popular BYOB onslaught, and the cash-only restaurant named after her continues to pack guests into its small but airy location near Rittenhouse Square. The menu is divided into smaller and larger plates, and each section offers standouts. Seared brussels sprouts with parmesan are unlike anything your mother tried to feed you, while the pear-and-gorgonzola flatbread blends sweet and tart to perfection. If you opt for larger

dishes, grilled rack of lamb and a hearty pork chop are both stellar, and make sure to inquire about the specials. By the same owner, **Twenty Manning** (261 S. 20th St., 215/731-0900) is another local favorite located a block north across 20th Street. A stylish bistro feel and a full bar menu of specialty drinks make this a popular date restaurant. Both offer sidewalk seating.

MONK'S ⑤⑤

16th and Spruce Sts., 215/545-7005, www.monkscafe.com
HOURS: Mon.-Sat. 11:30 A.M.-2 A.M., Sun. 11 A.M.-2 A.M.

You'll often have to wait for a table while crammed into the front entrance like sardines at this extremely popular spot, but it's worth it. If you're lucky, you'll nab a bar seat while you wait and drink from their extensive Belgian beer collection. Avoid weekends, or go at an off time unless you can stand crowds and the smells of delicious food wafting past your empty stomach for up to an hour while you wait. Well-known for its farm-raised mussels in delicious sauce made with beer, garlic, and more; *pommes frites* with Bourbon mayonnaise dipping sauce; and excellent selection of quality beer, it's hard to go wrong with anything on the reasonably priced menu. The salads, burgers with a variety of toppings, and sandwiches are as delicious as the entrées.

PUMPKIN ⑤⑤⑤

1713 South St., 215/545-4448
HOURS: Tues.-Thurs. 6-10 P.M., Fri.-Sun. 5:30-10 P.M.

A relative newcomer to Philadelphia's vibrant BYOB scene, Pumpkin's orange-accented storefront exterior and small—some might say cramped—interior do not do justice to the work of its kitchen. The revolving menu features seasonal, mostly local ingredients. Scallops make frequent appearances on the appetizer list, and are a great starter. In fact, seafood in general is a smart choice. The husband-and-wife owners (he is the chef, she runs the front of the house) accept cash only, and reservations are recommended, so plan ahead.

ROUGE ⑤⑤⑤

205 S. 18th St., 215/732-6622
HOURS: Mon.-Fri. 11:30 A.M.-2 A.M., Sat.-Sun.
10 A.M.-2 A.M.

One of the few establishments occupying the prime location directly on Rittenhouse Sqaure, Rouge is always packed. Snagging a table from happy hour onwards can be difficult, especially on weekends, but you can enjoy a drink at the elegant bar while you wait for a table or go in the middle of the day when it's not too busy. The scene is dominated by beautiful and wealthy yuppies letting their highlighted hair down after work. Despite that, the view of the square from the elegant bar—or better yet, a sidewalk table—is excellent, and may just make you forget about the steep prices for the tasty drinks and upscale food (try $15 for a hamburger and $10 or more for a martini). And despite the fact that you pay the premium for the location, the food—American with a French flair—is really quite good, especially the generous fresh-tuna sashimi appetizer.

SNACKBAR ⑤⑤⑤

252 S. 20th St., 215/545-5655,
www.phillysnackbar.com
HOURS: Daily 4 P.M.-2 A.M. and brunch 11 A.M.-3 P.M. on weekends

You'll find big flavors in small portions in this stylish eight-table corner restaurant just off Rittenhouse Square. In the colder months, an inviting fireplace against the back wall beckons diners to enter the draped entrance. In the warmer months, it's a popular spot for outdoor dining. Talented chef Jonathan McDonald creates delightful dishes out of unexpected ingredients, like brussels sprouts with truffles and marcona almonds or caramel apples encrusted with miso and wasabi peas. Have one as a true snack or a light lunch, but if you go in for a meal, you'll need to order about three per person. A selective wine, beer, and cheese list and several divine desserts round out the diverse offerings. The small bar is a nice place to stop for a good, but not cheap at $8–14, glass of wine. Food served until 1 A.M. and bar open until 2 A.M.

SEAFOOD

SANSOM ST. OYSTER HOUSE ⑤⑤

1516 Sansom St., 215/567-7683
HOURS: Mon.-Sat. 11 A.M.-10 P.M., Sun. 3-9 P.M.

This longtime establishment is well known for its fresh oysters, snapper soup, and a fried-oyster-and-chicken-salad sandwich that is an all-but-forgotten old Philly tradition. The bar area in the front draws a big happy hour crowd that comes in to knock back a few drinks along with oysters shucked in front of them at the bar. The back dining areas cater to the sit-down lunch and dinner crowd, who come for the oyster po' boys, crab cakes, and fresh catches of the day. Chef-owner Cary Neff has incorporated a few creative items into the mostly traditional seafood menu, but many regulars prefer to stick to the basics in this classic spot. Don't miss the divine key lime pie for dessert.

SEAFOOD UNLIMITED ⑤⑤

270 S. 20th St., 215/732-3663,
www.seafoodunlimited.com
HOURS: Mon.-Thurs. 11:30 A.M.-2:30 P.M. and 5-9:30 P.M., Fri.-Sat. 11:30 A.M.-2:30 P.M. and 5-10:30 P.M., Sun. 5-9 P.M.

This casual, friendly Rittenhouse Square seafood restaurant serves perfectly fresh fish that ranges from simple and classic to exotic and creative. Each is done just right, and at prices that are low—especially for this area—it is a local favorite with many return customers. The New England and Manhattan clam chowders are excellent; fresh oysters on the half shell never disappoint; and the steamed lobster stuffed with crabmeat can't lose. But the best way to go is to ask which fish is best on any given day or check out the fish case up front and see for yourself. You can have any of it broiled, grilled, fried, or pan seared, all with herb butter, or choose from the more exotic items on the menu. An excellent happy hour is offered every day from 5 P.M. to close with $5 wines, $2.50 Yuengling lager drafts, and a few great small plates including steamed mussels, buffalo shrimp, and portabella salad, all for $5 each. If you're staying somewhere with a kitchen, buy fresh fish or perfect scallops to cook at home.

RESTAURANTS

SNACKS, SWEETS, AND BREAD

LEBUS ❸

135 S. 18th St., 215/569-8299, www.lebusbakery.com

HOURS: Mon.-Fri. 7 A.M.-7 P.M., Sat. 8 A.M.-6 P.M., Sun. 9 A.M.-5:30 P.M.

A classic grassroots independent-business success story, LeBus started serving food to University of Pennsylvania students out of a school bus more than 25 years ago. Today, in addition to several retail locations, it supplies wholesome artisan breads to more than 500 clients, including the Four Seasons, Saladworks, and US Airways. Using ancient European recipes and natural ingredients, LeBus breads are known for their full flavors, from the signature French baguette and raisin walnut bread to croissants, muffins, and bagels. The Rittenhouse store is a popular morning stop for coffee, baked goods, and sweet treats and for lunch for its homemade soups, quiche, and sandwiches. Be warned: Snagging croissants or bagels after noon can be difficult. Take out only, no inside seating. Winnie's LeBus, a full restaurant in Manayunk, uses all LeBus bread products and serves delicious and hearty lunch and dinner.

REMEDY TEA BAR ❸

1628 Sansom St., 215/557-6688, www.remedytea.com

HOURS: Mon.-Fri. 7:30 A.M.-7 P.M., Sat. 9 A.M.-7 P.M.

A tea shop with all the perks of your favorite coffee shop (but without the coffee), Remedy's awesome variety of premium hot and cold teas make it a little easier to cut back on the java. Owned and run by two friendly sisters, recent college grads and tea lovers Kristen and Courtney, the atmosphere is laid-back and comfortable and they never pressure you to order or leave. Remedy also serves tea lattes and blended tea drinks they call mar-tea-nis. A detailed descriptive menu explains the health benefits and caffeine levels of each tea; it's so convincing you might just become a tea convert. A small but tasty selection of lunch fare from other vendors is available, along with delicious muffins, bagels, and other tempting sweet treats. Free WiFi is available.

VEGETARIAN

MAMA'S VEGETARIAN ❸

18 S. 20th St., 215/751-0477, www.mamasvegetarian.com

HOURS: Sun. noon-7 P.M., Mon.-Thurs. 11 A.M.-9 P.M., Fri. 11 A.M.-3 P.M., closed on Jewish holidays

If you find yourself in need of a quick bite in Center City, you could do a lot worse than Mama's, whether you're a vegetarian or not. This no-frills kosher eatery stars hefty portions of falafel on freshly baked pita. The sandwich is filling; the platter, which comes with hummus and vegetables, is almost enough for two. The menu is limited, but standouts include the eggplant and the crisp french fries. The small, packed eatery is not the best place to linger, especially during the lunch rush, but it is a cheap, tasty place to refuel.

Benjamin Franklin Parkway/Fairmount   Map 4

There isn't much to eat directly on the Parkway, but there is plenty within a short walk to Center City or Fairmount. The Art Museum has its own café if you find yourself hungry while inside; Darling's Café can be found behind the Franklin Institute; and the Four Seasons is right there if you want to spend a lot of money. Otherwise head south to Center City West or a few blocks north into Fairmount.

AMERICAN

❪ BRIDGID'S ❸❸

726 N. 24th St., 215/232-3232, www.bridgids.com

HOURS: Mon.-Fri. 11:30 A.M.-3 P.M. and 4:30-11 P.M., Sat. 4:30-11 P.M., Sun. 11:30 A.M.-3 P.M. and 4-9 P.M.

This neighborhood restaurant and bar has all the right ingredients: affordable, delicious food, an impressive beer list, and a cozy, friendly atmosphere complete with a fireplace.

It's no wonder it's such a popular local favorite. The first but not the last Philadelphia establishment to specialize in Belgian beers, Bridgid's offers excellent brews from around the world. The menu changes daily. You can expect to find fresh, perfectly prepared dishes like Salmon Dijon, Chicken with Pineapple Curry, and Filet Roquefort. Stop in for lunch to sample delicious entrées like vegetable lasagna and honey-fried chicken for around $8 per generous plate.

CAFÉS
MUGSHOTS COFFEEHOUSE AND CAFÉ $

2100 Fairmount Ave., 267/514-7145,
www.mugshotscoffeehouse.com
HOURS: Mon.-Thurs. 6:30 A.M.-9 P.M., Fri.
6:30 A.M.-6 P.M., Sat.-Sun. 7:30 A.M.-6 P.M.

Just across from the Eastern State Penitentiary, Mugshots is a classic neighborhood coffeehouse. It's a great place to stop for coffee, lunch, or a snack from the tasty menu of salads, sandwiches, wraps, and baked goods. It's the perfect spot to read, study, chat, or go online (they have WiFi and one computer available to the public with a 15-minute suggested time limit). In addition, the environmentally and socially conscious business only serves fair-trade, organic coffees, supports local farms, and recycles absolutely everything they can. Check out the additional location in Manayunk just off Main Street (110 Cotton St., 215/482-3964, Mon.–Fri. 6:30 A.M.–4 P.M., Sat.–Sun. 8 A.M.–4 P.M.).

NEW AMERICAN
FOUNTAIN AT THE FOUR SEASONS $$$

18th St. and the Benjamin Franklin Parkway,
215/963-1500,
www.fourseasons.com/philadelphia/dining
HOURS: Mon.-Fri. 6:30 A.M.-10 P.M., Sat.-Sun.
7 A.M.-10 P.M.

For anyone who is independently wealthy or celebrating a rare and special occasion, indulge in this idyllic dining experience. Continuously ranked among the nation's best, it was ranked

RESTAURANTS

© KARRIE GAVIN

Mugshots is a great place to stop for lunch or coffee after visiting Eastern State Penitentiary.

#1 restaurant in Philadelphia by Zagat, among others. The Fountain's kitchen creates perfect, inventive dishes and the staff provides impeccable service, giving each guest the royal treatment in a comfortable, quiet, and classic setting. A jacket and tie should be worn for dinner, and smart casual dress is suggested for breakfast, brunch, and lunch. The Sunday brunch is exquisite, as it should be at $65. The Swann Lounge and Café, also in the Four Seasons, offers a more relaxed but still elegant dining and drinking option.

LONDON GRILL 💲💲

2301 Fairmount Ave., 215/978-4545,
www.londongrill.com
HOURS: Mon.-Fri. 11:30 A.M.-3 P.M. and 5:30-10:30 P.M., Sat. 11 A.M.-3:30 P.M. and 5:30-10:30 P.M., Sun. 11 A.M.-3:30 P.M. and 4:30-9:30 P.M.

Since 1991, London Grill has been a staple in the mostly residential Fairmount neighborhood. Situated along Fairmont Avenue along with the majority of the other nearby businesses, the front room draws a bar crowd and those looking for a casual, lively atmosphere. For a more formal sit-down dinner, try the back dining room; surrounded by glass, it resembles a greenhouse. When the weather is nice, sidewalk tables are popular. The menu has evolved since its early days, with plenty of Asian, Latin American, and Mediterranean twists on the diverse and tasty menu. Don't miss the happy hour with $3 drinks and food from 4 to 7 P.M. on weekdays.

JACK'S FIREHOUSE 💲💲

2130 Fairmount Ave., 215/232-9000,
www.jacksfirehouse.com
HOURS: Mon.-Fri. 11:30 A.M.-4 P.M. and 5-10:30 P.M., Sat. 11 A.M.-3 P.M. and 5-10:30 P.M., Sun. 11 A.M.-3 P.M. and 4-9 P.M.; bar menu Mon.-Sat. 11:30 A.M.-10:30 P.M., Sun. 1-9 P.M.

Occupying a 19th-century firehouse that still features the original mahogany interior and brass fire pole, Jack's Firehouse is one of the most unique dinning experiences in Philadelphia, inside and out. The stellar outdoor dinning area offers views of the historic Eastern State Penitentiary across the street. Nationally renowned chef Jack McDavid serves hearty portions of flavorful cuisine that showcases locally grown, farm-fresh ingredients. His North Carolina–style crab cakes with corn-chipotle sauce and the grilled pork tenderloin with sweet-potato mash and pineapple sauce melt in your mouth. Or try the Chef's Special, a hearty four-course meal for $40 per person. Lunch and weekend brunch menus are also big hits with locals as well as with visitors to the Eastern State Penitentiary.

South Street/South Philadelphia   Map 5

South Philly is many locals' favorite place to eat, with an abundance of both traditional and contemporary Italian restaurants in and around the Italian Market, and affordable Asian and Mexican eateries on nearby Washington Avenue. South Street and Queen Village, the neighborhood just south of it, are filled with restaurants, gastro-pubs, and BYOBs. Further south, a continually developing stretch of Passyunk Avenue has another sprinkling of excellent old and modern dining options side by side. South Philly is also home to an abundance of cheesesteaks, including the dueling Pat's and Geno's on opposing corners at 9th Street and Passyunk Avenue.

BRUNCH
🅒 SABRINA'S CAFÉ 💲

910 Christian St., 215/574-1599, www.sabrinascafe.com
HOURS: Mon.-Sat. 8 A.M.-10 P.M., Sun. 8 A.M.-4 P.M.

Oh Sabrina's … Just the thought of your delicious food and ridiculously oversized portions is enough to lift many a hungover local from bed to come and wait an hour to be seated for brunch. Quite simply the best brunch spot in Philadelphia, Sabrina's offers every configuration of standard breakfast fare, as well as proprietary specialties like its famous challah French toast stuffed with farmer's cheese (which, for those with smaller stomachs, comes by the half-order as well). It's best known for its exquisite all-day brunch menu, which you will have to wait for on weekends, but lunch and dinner at Sabrina's are also quite good, with a nice variety of soups, sandwiches, wraps, and entrées like shrimp puttanesca and goat-cheese ravioli. The cozy eatery stretches by twists and turns across several former row houses and offers outdoor seating that's great for people-watching on the Italian Market on sunny days. It has been such a success that in 2007, the owners opened **Sabrina's Café and Spencer's Too** at 18th and Callowhill, skirting the Fairmount neighborhood.

SAM'S MORNING GLORY DINER $

10th and Fitzwater Sts., 215/413-3999, www.morningglorydiner.com
HOURS: Mon.-Fri. 7 A.M.-4 P.M., Sat.-Sun. 8 A.M.-3 P.M.

There is something indescribably cozy about drinking your morning coffee from a metal mug. The home-cooked meals have a flair that makes them more upscale than your average greasy-spoon diner, but still a little grittier than its nearby famous counterpart, Sabrina's, around the corner. Brunch is the house specialty here, too, and it's all made with plenty of fresh, local ingredients. Check your diet at the door and sink your teeth into the amazingly warm and oozy chocolate cherry bread dusted with confectioners' sugar, the gigantic breakfast burrito, or one of the frittatas. The wait for weekend brunch can be brutal, so go early and enjoy the strong, free coffee while you wait. Oh, and the only other negative is the homemade ketchup; it simply does not compare to good old Heinz in my opinion.

CAFÉS
ANTHONY'S ITALIAN COFFEE HOUSE $

903 S. 9th St., 215/627-2586, www.italiancoffeehouse.com
HOURS: Mon.-Thurs. 7:30 A.M.-6 P.M., Fri.-Sat. 7:30 A.M.-10 P.M., Sun. 7:30 A.M.-5 P.M.

Enjoy a perfectly brewed espresso, cappuccino, or a regular cup of joe in this authentic old-school Italian Market coffee house where dark-wood paneling and pictures of the Italian Market's early days set the mood. Delicious paninis, cannolis, cookies, and other sweets are also served. If you need a little more to satisfy your sweet tooth, visit **Anthony's Chocolate House** (915 South St.) a few doors down for a wide array of delicious homemade chocolates and sweets.

CHAPTER HOUSE CAFÉ $

620 S. 9th St., 215/238-2626, www.chapterhousecafe.org
HOURS: Daily 7 A.M.-10 P.M.

One of the city's best coffee shops, the Chapter House Café is barely a block from the bustling concrete jungle of South Street, but it might as well be on a different planet. The minimalist white walls, dark-wood floors, and spare but comfortable black-and-silver seating are brightened by rotating installations of paintings and mobiles by local artists hanging on the walls. You're likely to see multiple people with Mac laptops and square-frame glasses sipping lattes and being creative, or at least looking like they are. Besides great coffee, Chapter House serves sandwiches, cocoa, Italian sodas, and teas. And though it's always out of bagels, there's a good selection of pastries and muffins.

CHEESESTEAKS AND SANDWICHES
FAMOUS 4TH ST. DELICATESSEN $

700 S. 4th St., 215/922-3274
HOURS: Daily 8 A.M.-9 P.M.

Simple, bright, and cheery, this corner sandwich shop may not look like much, but it has a long list of notable clientele. City politicians, public officials, and prominent (and occasionally notorious) business folk find their way to this Jewish deli in Queen Village. The sandwiches are stacked high and packed so full, they're a challenge for even the biggest mouth. The prices are a little steep for corned beef or pastrami on rye (each sandwich over $10), but they're large enough to split and still have leftovers.

RESTAURANTS

CHEESESTEAKS 101

As much as I'd love to give you a definitive answer to the question of where to get the best cheesesteak in Philly, there just isn't one. The argument will never be settled, because it's truly a matter of personal preference. Some like the rolls toasted and crispy, while others prefer them soft and chewy. Some like it dripping with grease, while others complain that too much grease makes the roll soggy. Some like the meat diced as thinly as possible, while others prefer slightly larger chunks. Some love fake, yellow Cheez Whiz, while many prefer American or provolone cheese. Regardless, the one undisputable fact is that cheesesteaks are just not the same anywhere else. The closest I've come is New Jersey, and it turned out the guy making them was originally from Philly. Another fact is that most locals eat them regularly, but we try to keep our consumption in check. Let's be honest, they're not exactly health food.

WHAT MAKES A GREAT CHEESESTEAK

All good cheesesteaks start with a solid roll that is chewy – not airy or tough – and many of the best spots in town use Amoroso's brand, a Philly tradition since 1904. The meat should always generously fill the roll. Skimping or leaving an inch of meatless roll is a definite no-no. Fried onions and hot or sweet peppers are common additions, but beyond that, you're getting into fancy-schmancy territory. Some like to add pizza sauce, making it a pizza steak, or tomato, lettuce, onion, and mayo, making it a cheesesteak hoagie. Others opt for the only slightly healthier chicken cheesesteak, with chicken substituted for the beef. While all are great, cheesesteak virgins should keep it simple and go for beef with fried onions and the cheese of your choice – I like American.

HOW TO ORDER

While not everyone is hard-core about ordering correctly, if there is a long line, it's best to know what you're doing and keep things moving. First, don't *ever* order a "Philly cheesesteak" – you're in Philly, so that part goes without saying. The basic rule of thumb is to minimize the words you need to convey what you want, so don't bother saying the word "cheesesteak" if that is the main thing they serve. It's implied, so you can just give the specs: "Whiz wit," means Cheez Whiz with fried onions, and "prov without" means – yes, you guessed it – provolone cheese without fried onions. These rules are most strictly observed at Pat's and Geno's, the famous dueling spots on 9th Street and Passyunk Avenue in South Philly. Don't make the mistake John Kerry did and order Swiss cheese; that is blasphemous in cheesesteak land. Of the two superstars, I have a slight preference for Pat's, the less neon-decked of the two, but there are far better cheesesteaks in the city. That said, this corner offers a worthwhile cultural experience, and it's open 24 hours a day. While you wait in line it's fun to check out the autographed photos of celebs that have come through; everyone from Justin Timberlake to Oprah has been here.

WHERE TO GET THE BEST

You're never far from a great cheesesteak in Philly. They're served in every neighborhood, at diners, out of food trucks and store windows, and in restaurants serving upscale twists on the classics, but here are a few of my faves. **Jim's** on South Street is open until 3 A.M. on weekends, and is also frequented by celebs. It's **Pat's** and **Geno's** other biggest rival, and in my opinion, the far superior of the big three. Others to try are: **Sonny's Famous Steaks** in Old City; **Tony Luke's** in South Philly or **Tony Jr.'s** in Rittenhouse; **Jon's Roast Pork** in South Philly; **Dalessandro's** or **Chubby's** in Roxborough; and **McNally's** in Chestnut Hill.

JIM'S STEAKS $

400 South St., 215/928-1911, www.jimssteaks.com

HOURS: Mon.-Fri. 10 A.M.-1 A.M., Sat. 10 A.M.-3 A.M., Sun. 10 A.M.-10 P.M.

The original still sits at 431 N. 62nd St., but it's the South Street location that brings the crowds, with a line that wraps around the corner on weekend nights. Jim's Steaks is a Philadelphia landmark, serving a mean cheesesteak that is rarely left out of any "great cheesesteak" debate. Signed photographs of famous people who have eaten at Jim's line the walls on two floors. The menu offers more options than famous competitors Pat's and Geno's a few blocks to the south, with more fixins' and hoagies, soups, Italian sausage, and vegetarian steaks among the choices. Bright fluorescent lights can be tough during late-night visits, but if you're passing after a night out on the town, you will not be able to resist the smell wafting out onto the street.

SHANK'S AND EVELYN'S $

932 S. 10th St., 215/629-1093

HOURS: Tues.-Sat. 8 A.M.-10:30 P.M.

Run out of a small storefront just a block from the Italian Market, this classic South Philly luncheonette has a unique old-school charm and some of the city's best lunch fare. In addition to the cheesesteaks and hot and cold hoagies, try the chicken cutlet or pork sandwich—either one with the signature broccoli rabe or sharp provolone on top. A classic roast beef sandwich drenched in gravy, spicy sausage-and-pepper sandwich, hearty soups, traditional breakfast fare, and egg-and-cheese sandwiches are also favorites. At this family-run business the service is quick and there isn't a lot of small talk unless you're a regular, but they're perfectly friendly as long as you are. As of late 2007, the restaurant started serving dinners, as it did in its early years. The verdict is not yet out, but if the dinner fare in any way compares to the breakfast and lunch menu, it is sure to be a hit. Cash only.

FRENCH
BEAU MONDE $

624 S. 6th St., 215/592-0656, www.creperie-beaumonde.com

HOURS: Tues.-Fri. noon-11 P.M., Sat. 10 A.M.-11 P.M., Sun. 10 A.M.-10 P.M.

At this French crêperie, the elegant interior—with its foil prints and bright windows—perfectly complements its delicious food. Though it offers certain small dishes like a cheese plate and chicken satay, it is primarily a place to enjoy perfect, thin crepes, which come in a variety of sweet and savory combinations. Fillings include apricot compote, cheese, flavored butter, chicken, nutella, grilled vegetables, baked pear, ham, seasonal berries. Any combination your heart desires can be yours, whether you're looking for dinner, lunch, brunch, or just dessert. And, to top it all off, L'Etage, a kickin' little lounge, is located just upstairs from the dining room.

COQUETTE $$

700 S. 5th St., 215/238-9000, www.coquettebistro.com

HOURS: Tues.-Thurs. 5 P.M.-midnight, Fri. 5 P.M.-1 A.M., Sat. 10 A.M.-3 P.M. and 5 P.M.-1 A.M., Sun 10 A.M.-3 P.M. and 5 P.M.-midnight

This small French bistro occupies a prime corner just off South Street in the Queen Village neighborhood. Large windows, an attractive bar, and a hexagonal-pattered tile floor create a casual but stylish mood. Opened in 2007 by the same chef-owner as Center City's long-established Sansom St. Oyster House, it offers a fresh raw bar packed with, yes, oysters—one of owner Neff's obvious specialties. It also serves excellent French classics like onion soup, Niçoise salad, and cassoulet. Brunch features classic breakfast fare with French influences like quiche and omelettes with caramelized onions, and a late-night menu is served until 1 A.M. on weekends; dinner ends at 10:30 P.M.

ITALIAN
RALPH'S $$

760 S. 9th St., 215/627-6011, www.ralphsrestaurant.com

HOURS: Sun.-Thurs. noon-9:45 P.M., Fri.-Sat. noon-10:45 P.M.

Ralph's opened in 1900, laying claim as the country's oldest family-owned Italian restaurant in the United States. While the food might

ITALIAN MARKET

One of the oldest and largest outdoor markets in the United States dates back more than a century. An influx of Italian immigrants arrived in Philadelphia in the early 20th century and the market developed to cater to the new community. It has been bustling ever since, and many of the vendors and shops have remained the same. A living, breathing historic site, the market offers a glimpse into a time before supermarkets, when eating was a community effort. It spans about nine blocks, with the bulk of the action centering on 9th Street between Christian Street and Washington Avenue. The numerous stalls and shops include baked goods, fish, meat, and cheese shops, cafés, and even ones selling books or household goods. Though parts of it are a little dilapidated, and the street is often in dire need of a good scrub, it holds all the delicacies of Italy: paper-thin slices of prosciutto, juicy mounds of mozzarella, succulent olives, and some of the freshest bread, pasta, and produce in Philadelphia.

Locals, tourists, and gourmands alike can explore and discover the myriad of unique goodies and shops in the Italian Market while soaking in the unique atmosphere. Notice the giant mural of Frank Rizzo, the controversial, polarizing 1970s Philadelphia mayor whose likeness occupies a full wall at 9th and Montrose Streets, and recall Rocky Balboa's famous jog down the street, burned into the local collective consciousness. If you visit in winter, you may really see old men warming their hands over giant barrels of fire. The area continues to attract immigrants of many origins, and a significant number of Vietnamese, Korean, Chinese, and Mexican business owners have set up shop alongside the Italian ones − enriching the culinary and cultural experience for everyone.

no longer be the best Southern Italian fare in the city, it is still reliably very good, and more than that, this traditional two-floor eatery has unbeatable, authentic old-school ambience. It transports you to a more Mafioso-inspired time, which, minus the killing and espionage, makes for a fun, classy atmosphere and offers glimpse into a piece of history. Your first bite of the stellar eggplant parm or spaghetti and meatballs make the debate over whether you're eating sauce or gravy immediately irrelevant; it's delicious either way. And don't forget to order mussels in garlicky red sauce and sop it all up with your bread. The service can be patchy and credit cards are not accepted, so bring your easy-going attitude and some cash.

MEXICAN
MOLCAJETE MIXTO ❸❸
746 Christian St., 215/413-0171,
www.molcajetemixto.com
HOURS: Mon.-Fri. 5-10 P.M., Sat.-Sun. 11 A.M.-3 P.M.

At the edge of the famed Italian Market, Molcajete Mixto reflects the area's burgeoning Mexican population. With impeccable service and space for large groups, it's ideal for kicking off a night on the town. Perfectly crisp chips and homemade salsas are complimentary. Corn mushroom quesadillas are a unique appetizer, while every salad is worthy. Braised pork and chicken with mole sauce are standouts, or try the restaurant's namesake dish, which offers sizzling steak, chicken, and cactus. Billed as a BYOB, it's really best to BYOT (tequila). They make their own mixes, offering watermelon as a smooth alternative to the traditional lime.

PLAZA GARIBALDI ❸
935 Washington Ave., 215/922-2370
HOURS: 11 A.M.-11 P.M.

Some of the best laid-back, authentic Mexican in the city can be found on Washington Avenue. With its colorful, cozy decor, the atmosphere is nice enough to bring your own bottle and dine in, but with burritos at around $6 and only a few entrées topping $10, it is also cheap enough to order pick-up or delivery on an ordinary weeknight. Try the moist, slightly sweet chicken mole burrito or the enchiladas suizas swimming in a tart, creamy green sauce. The nachos are a meal in and of themselves, covered with meat galore. For a quicker, order-at-the counter burrito experience, try the fluorescent-lit **Taqueria Veracruzana** (908 Washington Ave.) across the street.

MOROCCAN
MARRAKESH ❸❸❸

517 S. Leithgow St, 215/925-5929
HOURS: Sun.-Thurs. 5:30-11 P.M., Fri.-Sat. 5:30 P.M.-midnight

Tucked away in a small alley just off South Street, accessible by a nearly unmarked door that you may have to knock on to enter, Marrakesh is a hidden gem for those who can find it. Its mazelike interior is dimly lit and lots of comfortable seating strewn with cushions create a romantic atmosphere. Waiters in traditional Moroccan garb serve a lovely, lengthy seven-course meal (around $30 pp) that you eat with your hands. My advice: Go hungry, allow yourself at least two hours, and pace yourself. Each course is delicious, from the stuffed phyllo pastry to the moist chicken to the tender lamb, to baklava and mint tea at the end. Allow yourself to drown in the waves of food, but don't try to finish everything or you'll never make it to the seventh course. It's BYOB, but they also have a small wine list you can order from.

NEW AMERICAN
ANSILL ❸❸❸

627 S. 3rd St., 215/627-2485,
www.ansillfoodandwine.com
HOURS: Mon.-Thurs. 5:30-10 P.M., Fri.-Sat. 5:30 P.M.-midnight

Ansill Food + Wine is a sampler's paradise, offering small plates of amazing food concoctions paired with a variety of world wines and European cheeses. Each dish is beautifully plated and exotic and inventive in taste. For adventurous foodies, lamb's tongue, boar, duck eggs, and octopus make appearances on the menu. Plates are meant to be shared: Bring friends to explore Ansill's wild, tasty menu and the large selection of wines, beers, ports, and aperitifs.

SEAFOOD
DMITRI'S ❸❸

795 S. 3rd St., 215/625-0556
HOURS: Mon.-Sat. 5:30-10 P.M., Sun. 5-11 P.M.

It's not easy to get a table at this tiny corner BYOB that doesn't accept reservations, but it's well worth the wait. Be sure to come at least an hour before you're hungry, and don't even bother trying on weekends during prime dinner hours. You can wait outside, or have a drink across the street at the great bar **New Wave Café** and wait for the hostess to come get you. Once seated, you will be treated to an affordable menu of fresh, grilled Mediterranean-inspired seafood like shrimp, scallops, bluefish, and octopus. Most dishes are sautéed and marinated with fresh, simple flavors like olive oil, garlic, lemon, and red-wine vinegar. Don't miss the perfect hummus and baba ghanoush served with grilled pita wedges or the avocado citrus salad for starters. For a similar menu without as long of a wait, visit the Center City West location (2227 Pine St., 215/985-3680). While it doesn't have as much character as the original, the second location still turns out excellent food from a very similar menu, and has a full bar. Both have cool open kitchens so you can watch the action.

SNACKS AND SWEETS
ISGRO PATICCERIA ❸

1009 Christian St., 215/923-3092,
www.isgropastries.com
HOURS: Mon.-Thurs. 8:30 A.M.-6 P.M., Fri.-Sat. 8:30 A.M.-8 P.M., Sun. 8:30 A.M.-4 P.M.

Opened in 1904 by Mario Isgro, who studied culinary arts in Vienna and Messina before coming to Philadelphia, this popular old-school South Philly bakery has been owned and operated by members of his family for over 100 years. Recipes for the award-winning cannolis (my personal fave), cookies, and cakes have been passed down through generations, and have garnered a loyal following in generations of Philadelphians. The sweet aromas fill the street outside the row-house storefront, and inside, traditional Italian ricotta baba au rhum, *fogliatella,* jelly-filled croissants, hazelnut genoise, and chocolate cake with layers of ganache and raspberry jam fill the glass cases. Be warned, the line often wraps well around the block during the holidays.

JOHN'S WATER ICE $

701 Christian St., 215/925-6955

HOURS: Open in summertime, hours vary

Who needs a $5 cup of Capogiro gelato when you can have a John's water ice for $1? OK, both are wonderful, but just make sure you get to John's at least once. On a hot summer day or night, there is nothing better than a cool, light water ice, and there is no place better to get one than John's. The corner storefront serves perfectly smooth water ice with no ice chunks and just the right amount of sweetness. There are only four regular flavors—cherry, lemon, chocolate, and pineapple—and sometimes one or two special flavors on weekends. Vanilla, chocolate, or butter pecan ice cream can be mixed with any water ice flavor for a gelati, which is also delicious, but if you're a water-ice virgin, stick with the straight stuff.

VEGAN

❿ HORIZONS $$

611 S. 7th St., 215/923-6117,

www.horizonsphiladelphia.com

HOURS: Tues.-Thurs. 6-10 P.M., Fri.-Sat. 6-11 P.M.

Owned and operated by vegan husband-and-wife team Rich Landau (chef) and Kate Jacoby (pastry chef), Horizons moved into the city from the suburbs in 2006, much to the delight of many locals. The kitchen serves colorful combinations of seitan, tofu, tempeh, and vegetables, arranged in delightful presentations with flavors that do not disappoint. Avocado, mango, tomato, and veggie mixtures brighten most plates, and creative "New Vegan" items include hits like deviled oyster mushroom fritters and garbanzo-crusted tempeh. The bar features tropical margaritas and mojitos along with a nice wine list, or try a caipirinha, a signature spirit that finishes the Jamaican BBQ seitan well. The chic upstairs dining room has a breezy, island decor, with pretty colors and a bamboo fan in the high wooden ceilings. It is small and popular, so try to make reservations about a week in advance, or for those eating on a whim, the lounge downstairs is an option. The lounge hosts a happy hour Tuesday–Thursday, 5:30–7:30 P.M.

VIETNAMESE

NAM PHUONG $

1110-1120 Washington Ave., 215/468-0410,

www.namphuongphilly.com

HOURS: Daily 10 A.M.-10 P.M.

A great location for hungry groups on a budget, Nam Phuong is renowned for its extensive menu, heaping portions, and economical prices. The fact that the food is actually stellar is an additional bonus. With over 200 dishes to choose from, it's easy for a diner to become a little overwhelmed. Fortunately, the attentive waitstaff will guide you in the right direction. *pho* (soup) and *bun* (a rice-noodle dish offered with a variety of meats) are common crowd favorites, and the papaya salad and summer rolls with a thick, perfect peanut sauce are not to be missed.

West Philadelphia/University City   Map 6

Many people rarely venture across the bridge into West Philly for dinner. Even though it's just a hop away, there is something about the area being separated from Center City by a body of water that creates a mental block. When they do cross the water, many wonder why they don't do it more often. With so many affordable restaurants, many serving a variety of ethnic cuisine, it is well worth "the trip." There are a few great options directly on and around Penn's campus, including Sansom Street off 34th, the Baltimore Avenue corridor, and the area around the Bridge movie theater at 40th and Walnut Streets.

CAFÉS
THE GREEN LINE CAFE $

4239 Baltimore Ave., 215/222-3431,
www.greenlinecafe.com

HOURS: Mon.-Sat. 7 A.M.-11 P.M., Sun. 8 A.M.-7 P.M.

When it opened in 2003, the Green Line Cafe complemented its University City/West Philly

neighborhood so perfectly that it seemed to have been there forever. Named for the #34 trolley that runs right outside on Baltimore Avenue, the coffee shop quickly became a vital gathering place for the community. It serves Penn and Drexel students, professors, families, punk anarchists, kids, and just about everyone else in the neighborhood. Standard coffee shop pastries and lunch fare are offered, and the café hosts a variety of events and artist exhibits. The concept proved so successful that several other locations opened not too far away: **The Other Green Line** (4305 Locust St., 215/222-0799, Mon.–Fri. 7 A.M.–9 P.M., Sat.–Sun. 8 A.M.–8 P.M.), and **Green Line-Powelton Village** (3649 Lancaster Ave., 215/382-2143, Mon.–Fri. 7 A.M.–9 P.M., Sat.–Sun. 8 A.M.–8 P.M.).

ETHIOPIAN
DAHLAK $

4708 Baltimore Ave, 215/726-6464,
www.dahlakrestaurant.com

HOURS: Daily 4-10:30 P.M.

Dahlak is a local gem a bit beyond the environs of the universities offering delicious and authentic Ethiopian/Eritrean fare, which there isn't a lot of in Philly. For those who don't know, East African food usually comes in the form of flavorful stews, eaten by hand with moist, spongy *injera* bread rather than utensils. The stews are often delicately spiced, though some can be pretty hot, so be clear on the level of spice you're looking for. For the veggies among us, Dahlak offers a good selection of meat-free dishes. Oh, and there's also a bar around back that's popular with the local hipsters. Another location in Germantown (5547 Germantown Ave., 215/849-0788, noon–4 P.M. and 5–11 P.M.) is also quite good if you're in the neighborhood.

MEDITERRANEAN
LA TERRASSE $$$

3432 Sansom St., 215/386-5000,
www.laterrasserestaurant.com

Nestled on a narrow side street near the heart

Green Line Cafe, a favorite U. City hangout

of Penn's bustling campus, La Terrasse offers an alternative to the post-adolescent energy of the college scene that dominates many nearby bars and restaurants. Instead, it caters more to the faculty, staff, grad students, and locals, with a mature selection of wines and food. It opened in 1966 and began as a French bistro, one of the first in the city, but its menu has evolved and diversified into what they now call Mediterranean. Popular for lunch, post-work drinks, and dinner, the menu includes offerings like littleneck clams, apple-and-brie salad, seared tuna, and seared duck breast. The lunch menu features well-constructed sandwiches with a variety of tasty spreads and ingredients.

NEW AMERICAN
MARIGOLD KITCHEN $$$
501 S. 45th St., 215/222-3699,
www.marigoldkitchenbyob.com
HOURS: Tues.-Sat. 5:30-10 P.M.

The oldest continually operating BYOB in the city (which says a lot in a city as old as Philadelphia), Marigold Kitchen is a local favorite. The tiny kitchen of the converted University City row home on a tree-lined residential street turns out unique, flavorful dishes. While the head chef and style of the cuisine has seen many incarnations throughout the restaurant's history, the menu and cozy atmosphere keeps fans coming back. Chef Erin O'Shea offers interesting renditions of classic Southern cooking.

RAE $$$
2929 Arch St., 215/922-3839, www.raerestaurant.com
HOURS: Mon.-Thurs. 7 A.M.-10 A.M., 11 A.M.-2:30 P.M.
and 5:30-10 P.M.; Fri. 7 A.M.-10 A.M., 11 A.M.-2:30 P.M., and
5:30-11 P.M.; Sat. 5:30-11:30 P.M.; Sun. 10:30 A.M.-2:30 P.M.

No longer is the food court of the 30th Street train station the area's only dining option. Acclaimed restaurateur Daniel Stern's wildly successful Rae offers a convenient, upscale dining option just across the street, serving breakfast, lunch, dinner, and weekend brunch. The stylish restaurant opened in 2007 on the ground floor of the shiny new Cira Center, and was soon named Philadelphia's best new restaurant by *Philadelphia*

magazine. Rae attracts everyone from the downtown business set on power lunches to stylish youngsters at the bar. An open kitchen turns out American classics, called "Standards," and Stern's inventive variations called "Renditions." All are quite tasty, but the Renditions are truly something to talk about. An impressive wine list offers more than 200 selections. Visit for the popular happy hour Monday–Thursday 4:30–7 P.M. for reduced drink prices and an array of free snacks. You can also order from the well-priced all-day bar menu.

WHITE DOG CAFÉ $$$
3420 Sansom St., 215/386-9224, www.whitedog.com
HOURS: Mon.-Thurs. 11:30 A.M.-2:30 P.M. and
5:30-10 P.M., Fri.-Sat. 11:30 A.M.-2:30 P.M. and 5:30-11 P.M.,
Sun. 10:30 A.M.-2:30 P.M. and 5-10 P.M.

The success of this one-of-a-kind Philly gem can be credited to owner and longtime community activist Judy Wicks, who lives in the upper floors of the White Dog's University City brownstone. The restaurant opened in 1983, proving that progressive and socially conscious business models can work. Wicks' goal was not based purely on profit maximizing, but also on maintaining a positive relationship with the environment and the community—which unfortunately remains a novel concept in the business world today. An advanced, first-of-its-kind in the city composting system in the backyard helps reduce and efficiently dispose of the restaurant's waste. Local farmers deliver organic, humanely treated, hormone- and pesticide-free ingredients each week, so the menu changes regularly with the seasons. Many classic American dishes have an interesting international flair. Visit for lunch, dinner, weekend brunch, or drinks and some of the best burgers in town at the bar. Check the website to find out more about the many events at the restaurant.

LAOTIAN-VIETNAMESE-THAI
VIENTIANE CAFÉ $
4728 Baltimore Ave., 215/726-1095
HOURS: Mon.-Sat. 11 A.M.-3 P.M. and 5-10 P.M.

At its opening, Vientiane Café made news for being the city's only restaurant serving

Laotian and Vietnamese cuisine. Today, it also serves Thai dishes, but its acclaim stands on the merits of its excellent food and great prices. Inside the small, tastefully appointed interior, patrons enjoy beef and chicken *lab,* Pad Thai, soups, skewers, rolls, and well-spiced dishes. With most entrées under $10, it has become a favorite of local students and residents, and it's even become something of a date spot among those with a taste for exotic cuisine. The fact that it's a BYOB puts it in the very affordable category. Vegetarians will also find plenty of choices on the menu.

Northern Liberties
Map 7

Northern Liberties has plenty of bars serving great food at great prices within a few blocks. There are also a few excellent BYOBs and a fantastic tapas joint. In general, the prices are lower, the vibe more laid-back, and the scene a bit more bohemian than in trendy nearby Old City.

AMERICAN
NORTH 3RD ⑤

801 N. 3rd St., 215/413-3666, www.norththird.com

HOURS: Mon.-Tues. 5 P.M.-midnight, Wed.-Fri. 5 P.M.-1 A.M., Sat. 11 A.M.-3:30 P.M. and 5 P.M.-1 A.M., Sun. 11 A.M.-3:30 P.M. and 5 P.M.-midnight; bar open daily until 2 A.M.

The entrées at North 3rd are of the traditional stick-to-your-ribs variety, but the preparation is surprisingly light and fresh. The simple roasted chicken breast and mashed potatoes is supremely satisfying. The chorizo and chicken quesadilla with salsa fresca is another standout, and it's a great place for groups to order several small plates to share. Every square inch of the dimly lit bar and restaurant is covered with conversation pieces, from tribal masks and oil paintings by local artists to artifacts and even some tasteful taxidermy (believe it or not!).

🍴 STANDARD TAP ⑤

2nd and Poplar Sts., 215/238-0630

HOURS: Daily 4 P.M.-2 A.M.

One of the most popular bar/restaurants not just in Northern Liberties, but in the whole city, Standard Tap is always busy. Both floors of the large, converted corner house are filled with tables and cozy booths in various rooms and cozy nooks. Regulars and newcomers come to enjoy the great beer selection (including many local brews), upscale but affordable bar food, and cool but unpretentious vibe. The burgers and fries are considered some of the city's best. Check out the chalkboard wall menus to see what other sandwiches, salads, and entrées are offered on any given night.

JEWISH AND SOUTHERN
HONEY'S SIT N' EAT ⑤

800 N. 4th St., 215/925-1150

HOURS: Mon.-Fri. 8 A.M.-10 P.M., Sat.-Sun. 8 A.M.-4 P.M.

On a quiet corner, Honey's doles out Southern/Jewish comfort food. The bustling café blends hearty, down-home flavors with a hipster crowd. Breakfast is served all day, drawing the big crowds for the challah French toast, Frisbee-sized pancakes, and homemade biscuits and gravy. Lunch is also delicious; don't overlook the long list of specials, which may include such winners as fried green tomatoes and lobster macaroni and cheese. A wide array of vegetarian and vegan options make Honey's a satisfying and affordable destination for anyone.

SPANISH
BAR FERDINAND ⑤⑤

1030 N. 2nd St., 215/923-1313, www.barferdinand.com

HOURS: Sun.-Mon. 5-11 P.M., Tues.-Thurs. 5 P.M.-midnight, Fri.-Sat. 5 P.M.-1 A.M.

A pedestrian path called Liberties Walk is home to a sprinkling of appealing eateries and shops. The cute enclave raised the bar with the addition of this authentic tapas bar. Affordable,

EAT AT A BAR

A relatively new breed of bars that some are referring to as "gastro-pubs" has become a mainstay in the Philly dining scene, and eating in a bar is more popular than ever since the ban on smoking passed in 2007. In gastro-pubs the food is at least as big a draw as the drinks – as opposed to places where chicken fingers and wings are par for the course and jalapeño poppers are gourmet cuisine. Many still serve burgers, but those burgers just may be stuffed with Roquefort cheese, and you just may be able to choose a well-made salad to accompany it in lieu of fries. And if you do go with the tried-and-true fries, they may be sweet-potato fries, or they may come with a bourbon-mayo dipping sauce instead of ketchup. Serving everything from lobster spring rolls to seared tuna to colorful salads, these pubs are generally affordable and casual places to eat and drink, and they are many locals' choice for dinner on an average night. To get you started, some of the best are: **Standard Tap** and **North 3rd** in Northern Liberties; **Eulogy Belgian Tavern,** and **The Plough and the Stars** in Old City; **Nodding Head, Monk's,** and **Good Dog** in Center City; and **Royal Tavern** in South Philly. With so much crossover between quality dining and the bar scene in Philly, it isn't always easy to classify a place as either a restaurant or a bar, so don't forget to check out the bars in the *Nightlife* chapter for still more dining options.

delicious hot and cold tapas range from $4 to $9. Choose from the quieter, more romantic dining areas with tables and booths, or sit at the fun, sociable bar—especially happening on weekends. Owner Owen Kamihara emphasizes the importance of the authentic tapas experience, so feel free to come for dinner or just have a few bites while you drink, as is customary in Spain. Try the cured meats and cheeses, and the interesting configurations like tuna confit, roasted eggplant empanadas, or sautéed mussels with chorizo and fried capellini. About half of the 50-plus bottles of Spanish wine are available by the glass, along with beers and specialty cocktails. Each week a different wine is offered for just $2 a glass.

Fairmount Park Map 8

While it is primarily green space, Fairmount is also home to two restaurants that both happen to be wonderful. They stand alone, and aren't places you'd typically pass on your travels, but manage to draw crowds because of their uniqueness. Water Works is on the very edge of the park behind the Philadelphia Museum of Art. And to really feel like you're dining in a woodsy setting, Valley Green is in a more remote location in the Wissahickon section of the Park.

NEW AMERICAN
VALLEY GREEN INN $$$
Valley Green Rd. at Wissahickon, 215/247-1730, www.valleygreeninn.com

HOURS: Mon.-Thurs. noon-4 P.M. and 5-9 P.M., Fri. noon-4 P.M. and 5-10 P.M., Sat. 11 A.M.-4 P.M. and 5-10 P.M., Sun. 10 A.M.-3 P.M. and 5-9 P.M.

Built in 1850, the building once served as the Valley Green Hotel, but the restored building on the Wissahickon Creek in Fairmount Park has since been converted into a lovely restaurant. Brunch, lunch, and dinner are served and menus change seasonally. Offerings include classics like New Zealand rack of lamb and more modern touches like lobster spring rolls. Brunch is a very popular time to go, especially for the Brie-stuffed French toast. While the food is very good, the real draw is the idyllic setting along the creek surrounded by towering trees. With no other houses in sight, you'll feel like you're visiting a remote colonial-era farmhouse. The interior matches the feel, with period furnishing and unfinished hardwood floors. Additional seating on the wooden front porch gives you an up-close view of the creek when the weather is nice.

◖ WATER WORKS RESTAURANT ❸❸❸

640 Water Works Dr. (at Kelly Dr.), 215/236-9000, www.thewaterworksrestaurant.com

HOURS: Tues.-Thurs. 11:30 A.M.-3 P.M. and 5-10 P.M., Fri. 11:30 A.M.-3 P.M. and 5-11 P.M., Sat. 11 A.M.-2 P.M. and 5-11 P.M., Sun. 11 A.M.-2 P.M. and 4:30-9 P.M.

After major renovations of the architecturally-magnificent building, Water Works Restaurant opened in 2006 to much local and national acclaim. Part of the Fairmount Water Works National Historic site complex that once supplied water to the entire city, the restaurant occupies a lovely spot steps from the Philadelphia Museum of Art and Boathouse Row on the edge of the Schuylkill River. The restaurant serves delicious New American cuisine with Mediterranean influences, and several different seating areas offer different vibes: there's a dramatic, main dining room; a romantic glassed-in porch offering views of the River; and a stylish bar area.

RESTAURANTS

Water Works Restaurant offers fine dining on a historic site.

When the weather is nice, you can dine al fresco on the River. The prices are fairly steep for dinner, but brunch offers another way to experience the unique atmosphere without breaking your budget.

Northwest Philadelphia   Map 9

The majority of restaurants in this part of the city are located on or near Germantown Avenue in Chestnut Hill or Main Street in Manayunk—both bustling business strips in otherwise residential neighborhoods. Both areas have excellent cafés, gourmet markets, and a variety of restaurants, including a few standouts. Chestnut Hill is also home to a farmers market that is open Thursday–Saturday. Germantown Avenue in Mt. Airy, just down the hill from Chestnut Hill near the intersection of Mt. Pleasant Avenue, also has a few neighborhood gems.

CHESTNUT HILL
Asian
OSAKA ❸❸❸

8605 Germantown Ave., 215/242-5900, www.osakachestnuthill.com

HOURS: Mon.-Wed. 11:30 A.M.-2:30 P.M. and 5-10:30 P.M., Thurs.-Fri. 11:30 A.M.-2:30 P.M. and 5 P.M.-1 A.M., Sat. 5 P.M.-1 A.M., Sun. 5-10:30 P.M.

This contemporary Japanese restaurant with a full sushi bar is a popular Chestnut Hill favorite. The traditional decor includes a Tatami room, but the kitchen turns out modern Asian fusion offerings like lobster ravioli and Carribean snapper. While it's all tasty, it's hard to beat the classic sushi, sashimi, and ni-giri—always fresh and delicious. The specialty rolls are inventive; try the Hong Kong Dragon and North Shore Rolls. Osaka has in the past received "Best of" awards from Citysearch, Zagat, and even the *Wall Street Journal* for their sushi.

Cheesesteaks and Sandwiches
MCNALLY'S TAVERN $

8634 Germantown Ave., 215/247-9736,
www.mcnallystavern.com

HOURS: Mon.-Sat. 11:15 A.M.-11 P.M., Sun. noon-8 P.M.

Just when you thought you couldn't get any more artery-clogging than the cheesesteak, along comes the Schmitter. In addition to beef, onions, and extra cheese, the Schmitter comes with tomatoes, salami, and a special se-cret mayonnaise-y sauce. The sandwich has be-come a widely known Philly phenomenon, and is now also sold at Citizens Bank Park during Phillies' games. McNally's also offer plenty of other less intimidating house specialties, soups, salads, and, of course, regular cheesesteaks and hoagies. A casual spot in the refined Chestnut Hill neighborhood, it also has a long history. An early incarnation of the restaurant was es-tablished in 1921 by Rose McNally to provide lunch for the trolley operators, including her husband. Her great-granddaughters operate the business today out of the same house the family bought to accommodate the growing business in 1927.

Sweets and Breads
METROPOLITAN BAKERY $

8607 Germantown Ave., 215/753-9001,
www.metropolitanbakery.com

HOURS: Mon.-Fri. 7:30 A.M.-7 P.M., Sat. 8 A.M.-6 P.M., Sun. 8 A.M.-5 P.M.

With five locations throughout the city, you're never far from the delicious breads, bagels, pastries, and coffee of Metropolitan Bakery. More than 30 varieties of bread are sold at the shops and also served and sold at many other local restaurants and markets. Well known for their signature French berry rolls, homemade granola, and croissants, Metropolitan offers an array of single rolls as well as whole loaves along with other gourmet treats like olive oils, coffees, teas, jams, cheeses, and spreads. Each shop is a little different, but all offer amazing gourmet treats. Locations: Old City, Metro Café (15 S. 3rd St., Mon.–Fri. 8 A.M.–4 P.M., Sat.–Sun. 8:30 A.M.–4 P.M.), University City (4013 Walnut St., daily 7:30 A.M.–8 P.M.), Rittenhouse Square (262 S. 19th St., Mon.–Fri. 7:30 A.M.–7:00 P.M., Sat.–Sun. 8 A.M.–6 P.M.), and Reading Terminal Market (12th and Arch Sts., Mon.–Sat. 8 A.M.–6 P.M., Sun. 9 A.M.–4 P.M.).

Vegetarian and Seafood
CITRUS $$

8136 Germantown Ave., 215/247-8188,
www.citrusbyob.com

HOURS: Tues.-Thurs. 5-9:30 P.M., Fri. 5-10:30 P.M., Sat. 11:30 A.M.-2:30 P.M. and 5-10:30 P.M.

You'll find reasonably priced vegetarian dishes and seafood at this cozy neighborhood BYOB. Filled with fresh and organic ingredients, the menu includes several vegan options and an array of seafood, including renditions of salmon, tuna, scallops, and more. The ani-mal-loving owners request that diners do not wear fur or shearling into the restaurant, in keeping with the vegetarian, animal-loving theme, which is a nice touch if a bit unneces-sary with the veggie crowd. It only seats about 20 people and reservations are not accepted, so be prepared to wait on weekends and other busy times.

MANAYUNK
Cajun and American
BAYOU BAR & GRILL $

4245 Main St., 215/482-2560, www.thebayoubar.com

With most items under $10, this is an afford-able place to eat on Main Street, with a lively atmosphere. Cajun and Creole classics like gumbo, jambalaya, and Creole chili are served along with standard but good pub fare like burgers, appetizers, and award-winning buffalo wings. The hard-shell crabs are also a big hit. In existence for more than 15 years, it's a local favorite that draws a regular crowd for dining and an even more regular crowd for the bar scene—the friendly atmosphere, nightly drink and happy hour specials, football games, and to party on the covered outdoor deck when the weather is nice. In search of a bit more upscale Cajun-inspired cuisine? Check out Bourbon Blue at Main and Rector Streets.

Pizza
COUCH TOMATO $

102 Rector St., 215/483-2233,
www.thecouchtomato.com
HOURS: Daily 11 A.M.–9 P.M.

University of Delaware graduates promise quick service of "Manayunk cuisine without the Manayunk prices" at their cozy, laid-back café. In addition to the extravagantly topped 20-inch gourmet pizzas cooked to perfection over pizza stones, they offer salads, soups, wraps, calzones, and desserts. Indoor and outdoor seating are available, but convenient curb-side pick-up and a wide delivery make takeout a popular option.

New American
JAKE'S $$$

4365 Main St., 215/483-0444,
www.jakesrestaurant.com
HOURS: Mon.–Thurs. 11:30 A.M.–2:30 P.M. and 5:30–9:30 P.M., Fri. 11:30 A.M.–2:30 P.M. and 5:30–10:30 P.M., Sat. 11:30 A.M.–2:30 P.M. and 5–10:30 P.M., Sun. 10:30 A.M.–2:30 P.M. and 5–9 P.M.

The only truly fine-dining restaurant in Manayunk is the acclaimed contemporary American Jake's. The food has always been top-quality, and the restaurant has been fully renovated with a space to match. It has earned the coveted four stars from *Mobil Travel Guide* and has received high praises from Zagat, *Gourmet*, *Wine Spectator*, the *Philadelphia Inquirer*, and others, attracting customers from both Center City and the nearby Main Line. The menu consists of many of the typical upscale restaurant offerings, like surf-and-turf, crab cakes, and duck breast, but each is prepared to perfection, and most have an interesting flair.

MANAYUNK BREWERY AND RESTAURANT $$

4120 Main St., 215/482-8220,
www.manayunkbrewery.com
HOURS: Mon.–Thurs. 11 A.M.–10 P.M., Fri.–Sat. 11 A.M.–11 P.M., Sun. 1–9 P.M.; late-night menu served until 11 P.M. weekdays, 2 A.M. weekends, 10 P.M. Sun.

A former textile factory, the restaurant and brewery is now a staple of Manayunk's Main Street. In addition to their classic menu offerings, there is also a sushi bar, stone pizza oven, and a rotisserie. From burgers to crab cakes to raw tuna, there is something for every taste and budget on the extensive menu. Sushi fiends be warned; there is no sushi on Sunday or Monday. Several different bars offer a large selection of beer, wine, and drinks, including the popular in-house brews. With one of the nicest and largest al fresco dining areas in the city, be sure to sit on the back deck overlooking the Schuylkill River if you visit when the weather is nice. There are often events and live entertainment, including a live jazz brunch on Sundays, 10:30 A.M.–2:30 P.M.

RESTAURANTS

Greater Philadelphia
Map 10

RESTAURANTS

The following are a select number of restaurants that fall outside the major neighborhoods outlined in this book. They're all within Philadelphia proper and are included here because they are well worth the short trip.

CHEESESTEAKS AND SANDWICHES
CHUBBY'S STEAKS $
5826 Henry Ave., 215/487-2575
HOURS: Thurs. 11 A.M.–1 A.M., Fri.–Sat. 11 A.M.–2 A.M., Sun. 11 A.M.–11 P.M.

This seemingly unimpressive sandwich stop is regarded as one of the best in the city, making the trip to Roxborough, next-door neighbor to Manayunk, well worth it. Each sandwich is loaded with greasy beef—or chicken, which is also highly recommended. With steaks this filling, side dishes won't be necessary, but fries (mmm, cheese fries) or onion rings are a good addition if you've got a really big appetite. Have a beer or drink with your cheesesteak at the bar or in the back booths, or you can grab a six-pack to go. Just across the street, you'll see **Dalessandro's** (600 Wendover St. at Henry Ave., 215/428-5407), another local favorite. Like the Pat's-and-Geno's rivalry in South Philly, locals have their favorite on this Roxborough corner. Personally, I prefer Chubby's cheesesetaks, but Dalessandro's is top-notch for hoagies.

JOHN'S ROAST PORK $
14 E. Snyder Ave., 215/463-1951,
www.johnsroastpork.com
HOURS: Mon.–Fri. 6:45 A.M.–3 P.M., Sat. 9 A.M.–4 P.M.

Pat's and Geno's get all the publicity, followed by Jim's, but ask a real Philly eater who serves the best sandwich in town and your answer very well may be John's. On the same South Philadelphia corner since 1930, John's is a no-frills joint, with little more than a counter and an outdoor table for accommodations. The cheesesteaks—greasy, oozing cheese on perfect rolls—are simply delicious. The roast pork sandwiches, it should go without saying, are also exceptional. John's closes by mid-afternoon, so get there early if you want to taste some of the best sandwiches in Philadelphia.

INDIAN
TIFFIN $
710 W. Girard Ave., 215/922-1297, www.tiffinstore.com
HOURS: Mon.–Fri. 11:30 A.M.–10 P.M., Sat.–Sun. noon–10 P.M.

What started as a takeout and delivery service expanded into a small sit-in restaurant due to popular demand for what many consider to be the best, most affordable Indian food in the city. The menu is filled with simple, classic dishes with a few more creative specials offered daily as well. The flavors hit right on the mark each time. Delivery service is available in many areas of the city, including Center City, Old City, Northern Liberties, Washington Square, University City, Fishtown, Queen Village, Bella Vista, Temple University campus, Fairmount, with limited service to Mt. Airy and Chestnut Hill, and the service area is always expanding. Three different meal packages are offered for delivery every weekday, each including two entrées, rice, dal, chutney, and pickles and at least one package is vegetarian. Best of all, the packages, called "tiffins," cost only $7.50 each. The options change and are always reliably good, but you have to place an order by 10 A.M. for lunch delivery and 2 P.M. for dinner. Your lunch will arrive 11 A.M.–1 P.M. and dinner 5–7 P.M. Place an order online or by phone, or just go to eat in or take out from the full menu.

PIZZA
MARRA'S PIZZA $
1734 E. Passyunk Ave., 215/463-9249
HOURS: Tues.–Sat. 11:30 A.M.–11:30 P.M., Sun. 2–10 P.M.

It's worth the trip into deep South Philly to taste what is arguably the best pizza in the city. On a rapidly developing stretch of Passyunk Avenue that now also has a sprinkling of many good but in some cases upscale, trendy restaurants, this is a taste of the old neighborhood. Sit in a red-vinyl booth, sip from a carafe of wine, and eat huge portions of homemade pasta, mussels, calamari, and antipasti. While the other food is generally good, standard hearty Italian, the best reason to come is for the delicious thin-crust pizza with a variety of standard and exotic toppings.

◖ TACCONELLI'S PIZZERIA ⑤

2604 E. Somerset St., 215/425-4983,
www.tacconellispizzeria.com
HOURS: Wed.-Thurs. 4:30-9 P.M., Fri.-Sat. 4:30-10 P.M., Sun. 4-9 P.M.

Giovanni Tacconelli came to Philly in 1918 and with the help of some friends built a massive 20-square-foot brick oven. For years, he baked bread in it, until the 1940s when he started making pizza. Now, five generations later, Tacconelli's ultra-thin-crust pies—still baked in that same handcrafted oven—remain a Philly staple. People travel from all over the city and beyond to the Port Richmond neighborhood, which is not by any stretch a typical stop on the tourist or even local dining circuit. The cash-only BYOB offers all the toppings, and in addition to the excellent tomato-sauce pies, the white pizza is a popular choice. Call a day ahead to reserve the dough for your pizza; if you show up unannounced, you could wait over an hour and they may not have enough for you. Grab a seat near the oven if you can, and watch the expert pizza makers whip out pizzas almost as fast as you can eat them.

RESTAURANTS

NIGHTLIFE

Nightlife in Philly spans cheesy, swank, hip, and divey—along with everything in between. Though there are plenty of exceptions to this, the scenes can be classified by area. Old City bars and clubs tend to be stylish and trendy, catering to a decked-out, bar-hopping crowd often on the prowl. The somewhat more subdued, sophisticated lounges and bars of Rittenhouse cater to anyone with money. The grittier Northern Liberties is known as the hip, artsy part of town, but is fast becoming the destination of choice for youngsters of all types.

While there is no shortage of upscale martini spots and velvet-lined lounges, Philly is by and large a casual city, where many locals hang out at the corner bar on an average night. Visiting a neighborhood bar can reveal much about local culture, and won't cost you more than $3 for a Yuengling lager, the local brew of choice. Gamers can find heated karaoke competitions, team trivia games (known locally as Quizzo), or pool tournaments throughout the city. There is also plenty of high-quality bar food, so when deciding where to eat dinner, bars should be considered—especially since the smoking ban was passed in 2007. Happy hour specials abound from 5 to 7 P.M. on weekdays.

Fans of live music will be happy to know that every major and minor act comes through Philly, and on any given night—especially on weekends—you can find national headliners, up-and-comers, and open-mike stages in diverse venues across the city. From intimate jazz clubs like Ortlieb's, to hipster bars like Johnny Brenda's and Starlight Ballroom, to acoustically

HIGHLIGHTS

LOOK FOR 🎧 TO FIND RECOMMENDED NIGHTLIFE.

🎧 **Best Jazz Club:** Jazz enthusiasts come from far and wide to experience **Ortlieb's Jazzhaus,** an intimate Northern Liberties venue that has hosted some of the top names in jazz on its small stage (page 95).

🎧 **Best Live Music Venue:** An intimate venue with spectacular acoustics, **World Café Live** hosts a diverse lineup of small- and bigger-name acts (page 97).

🎧 **Best Dance Club and Diner All in One:** One of the hottest dance clubs in Northern Liberties, **Silk City** also has an adjoining upscale diner and second bar area (page 98).

🎧 **Best Dive Bar:** More than just a dive bar, **Bob & Barbara's** is a local institution. The $3 special – a shot of whiskey and a can of PBR – can't be beat, and a wide array of events throughout the week attract a diverse clientele (page 99).

🎧 **Best Quizzo Game:** In a city where competitive bar sports are all the rage, there is no shortage of intense Quizzo (team trivia) games. **Fergie's** has the best – with big prizes and fierce competition (page 100).

🎧 **Best Bar Burger:** Locals come to **Good Dog** as often for the eponymous burger as they do for the chill bar scene (page 100).

🎧 **Best Wine Bar:** The food, microbrews, and of course, the wine are spectacular at **Tria.** Now with two locations, you're never far from delicious cheese and a perfect Riesling (page 104).

🎧 **Best Gay Nightlife: Woody's,** the center of gay nightlife in Philly for nearly 30 years, boasts a variety of spaces, moods, and themed nights that appeal to a wide variety of gay men, and also some women. The alley behind it is home to **Sisters,** the only club in town specifically devoted to lesbians, complete with a lively upstairs dance floor (page 105).

superb mid-size stages like World Café Live, Philly has the perfect stage for every act.

Unless otherwise stated, most bars and clubs in Philly close at 2 A.M. sharp, and most don't have a dress code. That said, there is always a major concert, deejay, or late-night party happening somewhere around town; just ask a friendly local, or check out the weekly papers, *PW* and *City Paper,* for extensive listings of nightlife events.

Live Music

ELECTRIC FACTORY

421 N. 7th St., www.livenation.com

Map 7

Founded in 1968 and housed in an actual converted electric factory, this archetypal Philly venue has two floors, each equipped with a full bar and seating area, ensuring ample visibility and elbow room from every section. With a performance roster ranging from mainstream radio's premiere rock bands to the newest hip-hop crazes, the Factory has become a rite of passage for bands graduating from the smaller local venues and the fans willing to follow them.

FILLMORE AT THE TLA

334 South St., 215/922-1010, www.livenation.com

Map 5

Formerly the Theater of Living Arts, this South Street staple provides an intimate setting for performances by bands ranging from the independent to the infamous. Often an alternative-rock showcase, the venue has hosted the likes of Echo & the Bunnymen, Patti Smith, and Gang of Four, along with many of today's most beloved indie darlings. Patrons can enjoy a great view from anywhere inside with two floors of space and plenty of room to dance. The newly renovated decor promises a trip down memory lane with walls adorned with vintage concert posters.

FIRST UNITARIAN CHURCH

2125 Chestnut St., www.r5productions.com

Map 3

One of the flagship venues for R5 Productions, this local church has become a renowned house of a different kind of worship for the local punk rock scene. Many of independent rock music's best up-and-coming acts make their Philly debuts in the Church's small basement. A tiny stage offers an intimate perspective that larger venues don't allow, while the loud acts and hyped attendees create an atmosphere worthy of a much larger arena.

JOHNNY BRENDA'S

1201 N. Frankford Ave., 215/739-9684, www.johnnybrendas.com

Map 7

Not content with merely being a bar and restaurant, this Fishtown favorite has quickly made a name for itself as a hip little hot spot for the indie set, and has become one of R5 Productions' premiere venues. Located on the 2nd floor of the bar/restaurant, the performance space boasts spectacular sound quality and a bar and balcony worthy of a much larger arena. The list and stature of performers grows by the week, but the venue still makes time for local bands and even the occasional private party, which—thanks to its size and setting—is essentially what every concert at Johnny Brenda's feels like.

KHYBER PASS

56 S. 2nd St., 215/238-5888, www.thekhyber.com

Map 1

Bring your ear plugs, because the bands that play here come to rock. The Khyber offers a very different experience depending on which room you choose. The long, dark main bar area is a chill space where young hipsters and musicians sit and talk. Just off the main bar, the live stage hosts a consistently solid

Johnny Brenda's is an intimate Fishtown bar that hosts a variety of live music acts.

PHILLY'S MUSIC ROOTS

Modern-day chart-toppers like Pink, Eve, and Will Smith are familiar names, but Philadelphia's musical history goes back much further and covers many genres. Classical composers like Alexander Reinagle, Rayner Taylor, and Susannah Haswell Rowson made their names in the 18th century, while the 19th century was given over to English opera, religious orchestrals, and gospel. In the 20th century, Philly was at the center of the national musical consciousness with vibrant jazz musicians like John Coltrane, Dizzy Gillespie, Eddie Lang, and Joe Venuti.

In the 1950s, Dick Clark took center stage with *American Bandstand*, drawing attention to local acts like Bobby Rydell and Frankie Avalon as well as the nascent phenomenon known as rock 'n' roll. The '60s and '70s were most notably marked by contributions of African American musicians, including girl groups like Brenda & the Tabulations, Barbara Mason, Claudine Clarke, and the LaBelle Sisters. As they fired up the charts, the production team of Gamble and Huff created the unique "Sound of Philadelphia." TSOP, for short, is a rich, funk-driven sound created with large ensembles of string and horn instruments – a break from the blues-oriented sound of earlier rhythm and blues. The TSOP studio, Philadelphia International Records, still stands at Broad and Spruce Streets.

More-recent Philly musicians include Boyz II Men, Lisa Lopes (the "crazy one" in TLC), Eve, Beanie Sigal, the Roots, Jill Scott, Jedi Mind Tricks, and Musiq Soulchild. Local DJ and producer Diplo is a star of the electronic music world, while Dieselboy is one of the most popular drum and bass producers in the world.

line-up of indie and small-label rock bands. The 2nd-floor lounge usually features a local deejay spinning a diverse mix of danceable favorites.

NORTH BY NORTHWEST

7165 Germantown Ave., 215/248-1000, www.nxnwphl.com

Map 9

It is difficult to categorize this venue as just one thing since it excels as a bar, a restaurant, and as a live music venue. It's also the only live venue of its stature in this part of the city and probably the only venue in Mt. Airy that draws so many people from outside the neighborhood. There are a wide variety of small to mid-name musical acts that come through, as well as salsa dancing nights, comedy acts, and dance parties. Under the same ownership as North Star Bar, it's no surprise that it has been such a success. The music offerings cater to a diverse and often more mature crowd than many of the other small bars/live music venues in the city, and the reasonably priced menu offers good, hearty American food.

NORTH STAR BAR

2639 Poplar St., 215/787-0488, www.northstarrocks.com

Map 4

Just four long blocks from the Philadelphia Museum of Art, the North Star Bar offers a full bar menu and pool tables in the front area, but is cherished for its eclectic line-up of reasonably priced live shows several nights a week. Nothing to look at from the outside, the stage area offers great acoustics and a 2nd-story balcony that practically overhangs the stage. Catching a cab after the show can be tough at this somewhat isolated corner in the Fairmount neighborhood; ask the bartenders to call one for you.

☾ ORTLIEB'S JAZZHAUS

847 N. 3rd St., 215/922-1035, www.ortliebsjazzhaus.com

Map 7

Considered by many to be the city's best live jazz venue, this intimate space is in the former cafeteria of a 19th-century brewery. The bar/restaurant has attracted jazz enthusiasts from

NIGHTLIFE

THE BEST IN INDIE MUSIC: R5 PRODUCTIONS

Born in 1996, this local do-it-yourself promotion company (named for the SEPTA regional rail that connects the Main Line to Center City) was founded by Ardmore native Sean Agnew with the express purpose of bringing back quality indie rock to a city that was often skipped over by touring bands due to lack of suitable venues. The idea was to give audiences big shows in small spaces, for a more intimate live music experience. With no alcohol served and generally low prices, the shows cater to all ages, but especially the younger set. Over a mere decade, Agnew's baby has become synonymous with Philadelphia's independent music scene.

Organizing and promoting shows at a variety of small-but-mighty venues, including the staple, The First Unitarian Church, and up-and-coming joints like Johnny Brenda's and the Starlight Ballroom, R5 has hosted many of today's best names in indie music. Hot acts like Arcade Fire and the Yeah Yeah Yeahs played some of their first shows in Philly thanks to R5, while other cult favorites like Xiu Xiu and Mirah now make regular stops.

Philly's punk and indie crowds no longer need to travel to New York or D.C. to see their new favorite acts play, nor do they have to pay double the admission price to see old favorites play larger, overcrowded clubs and arenas. Likewise, bands can now come to this city and play to the whole audience and not just the people standing in the front row. And the fact that many of them come at all, as opposed to a decade ago, can be gratefully attributed to R5.

As more venues are used and bigger bands come to play, Agnew's philosophy holds true: "For the kids, by the kids." No self-respecting music lover in Philly would have it any other way. Check out www.r5productions.com for lineup and venue information.

© DAMIAN KOHUT

An active church, the First Unitarian Church also serves as a unique venue for R5 Productions' indie and punk shows.

the city and beyond for more than 20 years, making it one of the first and longest-standing entertainment venues in the now-happening Northern Liberties neighborhood. While the music is certainly the establishment's chief draw, tasty, reasonably priced Cajun American food is also served.

ROTUNDA

4014 Walnut St., 215/573-3234,
www.foundationarts.org

`Map 6`

Straddling the fuzzy line where University City becomes the grittier part of West Philly, the Rotunda offers an excellent reason to cross over. An old church transformed into a community and artistic space now hosts live music and events about 250 nights a year, including rock, jazz, hip-hop, theater, spoken word, film, deejays, panels, art installations, flea markets, and more. The alcohol- and smoke-free venue welcomes all ages and best of all, most events are free. Audiences are diverse but tend toward the eager undergrad and activist types. Many attendees enjoy drinks at one of the nearby bars before stumbling in for a free show.

STARLIGHT BALLROOM

460 N. 9th St., 215/769-1530,
www.r5productions.com

`Map 7`

A frequent host to R5 Productions' shows, the Starlight Ballroom has expanded beyond its dance-club roots to become a formidable live music venue. The dancehall layout makes for a perfect forum for smaller acts with very loyal followings like TV on the Radio, Arctic Monkeys, and the dearly departed Sleater-Kinney. There are tables, bars, and concessions available for patrons occasionally coming off the dance floor for air. As more bands and audiences discover it, the Ballroom could very well eclipse the neighboring Electric Factory as the area's premiere concert spot.

TOWER THEATER

69th and Ludlow Sts., Upper Darby, 215/568-3222,
www.tower-theatre.com

`Map 10`

Built a year before the Great Depression, the Tower retains its classic, lavish marble decor while hosting some of music's most prestigious modern-day acts. The seated venue consists of an orchestra, loge, and two balconies, making it one of the city's largest venues. The lineup of performers is even bigger, as the theater has evolved from its days as a vaudeville mainstay into the perfect forum for intimate performers like Tori Amos and Sufjan Stevens as well as larger-arena-worthy acts like Radiohead.

TROCADERO THEATRE

1003 Arch St., 215/922-5483, www.thetroc.com

`Map 2`

A landmark on the outskirts of Chinatown, this former burlesque theater is one of the city's busiest and most versatile venues. The main roster most frequently consists of up-and-coming punk rockers, metal enthusiasts, and the occasional indie-rock stalwart courtesy of R5 Productions, while the "Balcony Bar" on the 2nd floor provides the pre-gaming and after-parties with deejays and a smaller yet just as mighty stage. On Monday nights, the venue even doubles as a movie theater, showing both new releases and cult classics to a packed house.

◖ WORLD CAFÉ LIVE

3025 Walnut St., 215/222-1400, www.worldcafelive.com

`Map 6`

World Café Live represents another big step in making University City worth the trip across the river from Center City. Two truly lovely performances spaces, Upstairs Live and Downstairs Live, have been carved out of an old factory, hosting independent, contemporary, and folk artists several nights a week. Its diverse performance lineup isn't the only draw; it serves delicious food and drinks from tasty lunch specials to a more upscale yet affordable dinner menu. Also housed in the building are the studios for WXPN, the non-commercial radio station whose nationally syndicated *World Café* program gave the venue its name, though the station and venue have no relationship beyond that.

NIGHTLIFE

Dance Clubs

FLUID

613 S. 4th St., 215/629-3686, www.fluidnightclub.com

`Map 5`

Since it opened in 1997, Fluid has become a staple of the underground music scene. Its diverse deejay lineup includes electronica, funk, house, soul, trip-hop, trance, progressive, drum and bass, jungle, break beat, hip-hop, rock, punk, and everything in between. Regular deejays include Philadelphia's own ?uestlove of the Roots along with countless other top national and international guests. The cave-like 2nd-floor space is dark enough to get lost in anonymous dancing for hours, but just light enough to check out the other fine dancers. Cover varies but is usually $5 and can often be avoided by arriving before 10 P.M.

L'ETAGE

624 S. 6th St., 215/592-0656,
www.creperie-beaumonde.com

`Map 5`

Just off South Street above the delicious crêperie Beau Monde lies a decadent little dance club that regularly packs the house. The French-themed lounge has a beautiful dark-wood bar, comfy leather banquettes, and a cozy dance floor that is packed on weekends. Examples of the nightly entertainment include deejays, a Cabaret, an 80s night, and gay dance parties. The danceable tunes promise a great night for anyone who'd like to shake it like a Polaroid picture. Come before 10 P.M. on weekends to avoid the $5 cover.

LOIE

128 S. 19th St., 215/568-0808, www.loie215.com

`Map 3`

By day and into the early evening, Loie serves up tasty food, but by night—especially on weekends—the small dance floor in the back turns into a sweaty, pulsating dance party. Boys and girls grope and grind to mostly popular hip-hop, and some even slink into corners to take the dirty dancing to the next level. The crowd is filled with pretty people dressed to kill, and most are ready for some action. If this sounds like you, check out Loie on a weekend night. For all others, stay far, far away.

700 CLUB

700 N. 2nd St., 215/413-3181

`Map 7`

On other days, the 700 Club is just a local watering hole and casual neighborhood hangout, but on Thursday–Saturday nights, the small 2nd-floor dance floor becomes a sweaty free-for-all as the deejay spins hip-hop, indie rock, and '80s for the mostly 20-something crowd. It looks and feels like Grandma's house—complete with old, musty furniture and a psuedo kitchenette as a bar. The lights are low enough to hide the stains on the upholstery and to encourage you to dance like no one is watching. The 700 Club takes you back to the days of high school parties when your parents were out of town and drinking was an exhilarating, illicit event.

SHAMPOO

418 N. 8th St., 215/922-7500, www.shampooonline.com

`Map 7`

One of the last behemoth clubs still shaping the Philly scene, Shampoo has succeeded by being many things to many different people, depending on the night. The cavernous warehouse features a multitude of rooms of various sizes, so hip-hop heads, reggaeton rovers, pop lovers, and dance drones can peacefully coexist. And the schedule features Shaft Fridays, the weekly gay night; Spoiled Saturdays, a teen night for the 14–18 set, most Saturdays; a 17-and-over night on Sundays; and an industrial/goth night on Wednesdays.

◖ SILK CITY

435 Spring Garden St., 215/592-8838,
www.myspace.com/phillysilkcity

`Map 7`

Part diner and part dance club, Silk City is your one-stop shop for Saturday night. Formerly a truck stop called DeeDee's Diner, a hole-in-the-wall serving cheap booze and beer out of questionable taps, it's now one of the most popular spots in Northern Liberties, with one side a chic restaurant where you're more likely to order tuna tartare than eggs and toast. An adjoining club/lounge hosts popular deejays on weekend nights and sometimes live bands.

TRANSIT

600 Spring Garden St., 267/258-1321,
www.transitnightclub.com
Map 7

Like a beautiful old mansion taken over by squatters, Transit is both a little run down and a little posh. Resembling an Eastern European super-club, it's massive and full of sin. The cavernous former bank has three floors, three bars, and quite a few nooks and crannies to get lost in. The scene varies drastically depending on the night, from goth to gangsta to indie to pop. When parties are good here, like the legendary Making Time events held every few months, Transit epitomizes "going out dancing." It's also open late, sometimes very, very late, like 6 A.M. Cover varies, but is usually $10.

Bars

THE BARDS

2013 Walnut St., 215/569-9585, www.bardsirishbar.com
Map 3

In a sea of Irish pub imposters, The Bards is the real thing. Any Guinness aficionado (except for the ones who swear by The Plough and the Stars in Old City) will tell you that this is the best place in Philly to grab a pint of the dark stuff. Outfitted in an Irish literary theme, The Bards is a good place to read or write while you sip a pint and have fish-and-chips on a quiet afternoon in the middle of the week. Weekend nights, including live traditional Irish music on Sunday evenings, and Quizzo nights (Thurs. 10 P.M.) tend to get a bit rowdier. Sometimes The Bards even turns a little more Greek than Irish when the Penn frat boys cross the river to play darts and blast Bon Jovi and Journey on the electronic jukebox.

◖ BOB & BARBARA'S

1509 South St., 215/545-4511
Map 3

While others try so hard, B & B's is simply cool without having to try. A distinguished jazz band of mature men decked in tuxes plays on weekends and on Monday nights, so despite the dirt-cheap prices and dirty floors, the place has an air of class. The relaxed vibe and varied events draw a diverse crowd all week: a table-tennis tournament on Tuesday, bingo on Wednesday, a drag show on Thursday, and even a drunken spelling bee on the second Monday of the month. The "Special" is a shot of whiskey and a can of Pabst Blue Ribbon for the irresistible price of $3; even if you think you don't like PBR, you'll find yourself craving one after a few minutes surrounded by wall-to-wall vintage posters advertising it. If you have time, stop at **Tritone** (1508 South St., www.tritonebar.com) across the street for more good vibes, decent bar food, a live music stage, and the same irresistible "Special."

ORDER A LAGER

Yuengling lager, that is. In Philly – in most of Pennsylvania, in fact – lager is synonymous with the Yuengling brand. The first Yuengling beer was brewed in 1829 in Pottsville, Pennsylvania, making the brewery America's oldest. While the brewery makes other beers, including a porter, the traditional golden lager is the most popular. Considered better than other domestic brews at about the same price, it is many locals' drink of choice. So if you want to fit in, saddle up to the bar and order a "lager." The minute you say "Yuengling lager," it's obvious you're not from around here.

NIGHTLIFE

CAVANAUGH'S

119 S. 39th St., 215/386-4889,
www.cavanaughsrestaurant.com

Map 6

Cavanaugh's is University City's premier sports bar. Hosting a rowdy crowd for professional and college games—especially when the Eagles or one of the "Big 5" local college basketball games are on—it is a good place to be part of the action. Specials abound, and the local favorite, College Night, draws the coeds by the masses with 75-cent drinks and free pizza.

DIRTY FRANK'S

347 S. 13th St., 215/732-5010

Map 2

Dirty Frank's is a total and complete dive, not one of those pseudo-dives that is actually kind of hip and only dive-y in an intentional way, but a real, true dive. The bartenders are aloof; the beer is cheap ($8 pitchers, and $2.50 bottles), and the crowd is down-to-earth. The booths are torn; the walls are covered in graffiti; and the bathrooms—well, just avoid them if you can. But if you're looking for a place to sit in a booth and kick a few back without going broke, this is a perfectly good place to do so. The only touch of class is the mural on the outside consisting of famous Franks, including Frankie Avalon, Aretha Franklin, Franklin Delano Roosevelt, Frank Zappa, Frankenstein, St. Francis of Assisi, and Frank Sinatra.

EULOGY BELGIAN TAVERN

136 Chestnut St., 215/413-1918, www.eulogybar.com

Map 1

Just three blocks from Independence Hall, this two-story row-house bar immediately feels like home. But with over 300 international and domestic craft-brewed bottled beers and over 20 on draft, it's just that much better. Try a pint of Eulogy's Busty Blonde, brewed in Belgium especially for this Philly gem, and don't miss the highlight of the stellar pub fare, the Belgian *frietjes* served with a delicious dipping sauce. In typical Old City form, it's packed on weekend nights and getting a seat can be very difficult.

◖ FERGIE'S

1214 Sansom St., 215/928-8118, www.fergies.com

Map 2

The great thrill of Fergie's Pub—aside from the well-priced and varied selection of good beer and pub grub—is seeing Philly's favorite red-bearded Irish bartender in the flesh. A big name on the local scene, Fergie even has his own advice column in the local weekly newspaper, *PW*. The Irish bar has the attitude of a neighborhood dive bar with zero pretentiousness, even though it's in the heart of Center City and offers a much nicer setting and better food. Fergie's has entertainment and events on most nights, from various live music acts to the popular Open Mike Night (Monday at 9:30 P.M.) which draws a regular, talented crowd. On Tuesday or Thursday night, go upstairs to play or watch the most competitive Quizzo game in the city. Regulars come every week to reserve their favorite table, so come by 8:30 P.M. for the 9:30 game and bring your smartest friends. It's free to play; first-place winner gets a $50 credit off the night's bill, and second place gets $25 off.

GIGI

319 Market St., 215/574-8880, www.gigiphilly.com

Map 1

Gigi has great outdoor seating on the sidewalk in front and on a side patio. Add to that great happy hour drink specials and close proximity to Independence Park, and you've got the perfect stop for a few drinks or food after or during a long day of sightseeing. The menu offers a variety of tasty small plates to share at reasonable prices. On Tuesday nights, go for Cocktail Crush, where $30 will get you lessons on how to make three different drink concoctions (which you get to drink), a shaker, and complimentary appetizers.

◖ GOOD DOG

224 S. 15th St., 215/985-9600, www.gooddogbar.com

Map 3

This unassuming bar in the heart of Center City has the feel of a casual neighborhood spot. Featuring a canine-themed decor, it's popular with locals for its great food, great location, and great vibe, and is sometimes short on seating. If you can't score a booth downstairs or a table upstairs during high-traffic times, pull up a seat at the bar and order one of the many regionally brewed beers on draft, or head up to the 3rd floor for standing room only. Many people come for the Good Dog signature burger stuffed with Roquefort cheese (voted one of the best burgers in Philly by the premier local food critic) and a side of mixed traditional and sweet-potato fries.

LAS VEGAS LOUNGE
704 Chestnut St., 215/592-9533,
www.lasvegaslounge.com
Map 1

Despite its name and worn-out red-pleather booths, the Las Vegas Lounge is more of a cheap neighborhood bar than a lounge. Those wanting to get away from the trendier Old City spots venture a few blocks west to this local hangout. Nightly drink specials offer reduced prices on the already cheap drinks. The large space has plenty of seating, as well as pool tables and a Ms. Pac-Man game. Food consists of typical greasy bar apps and sandwiches.

MCGLINCHEY'S
259 S. 15th St., 215/735-1259
Map 3

Somewhat of an urban enigma, this quintessential dive bar is in the heart of the Center City action. Waitresses are charmingly informal and prices are dirt cheap, especially for pitchers of domestic draft classics like Yuengling, Yards, and Rolling Rock, with Guinness not much more. The bar is dark, dingy, and lined with booths. You can order a hot dog with all the fixins', listen to a rock 'n' roll–packed jukebox, or play Ms. Pac-Man at an old-school sit-down-style game.

MCMENAMIN'S TAVERN
7170 Germantown Ave., 215/247-9920
Map 9

This classic Mt. Airy neighborhood bar is like Cheers to its faithful regulars. The friendly atmosphere, excellent beer selection, and good,

affordable bar food makes it a popular local hangout for all ages and types. Young hotties and old men sit side-by-side at the long wooden bar and an outdoor patio in the back offers additional seating. This stretch of Germantown Avenue in Mt. Airy between Chestnut Hill and Germantown is seeing increasing development, with a few great bars and restaurants now available in an otherwise residential part of town.

NEW DECK TAVERN
3408 Sansom St., 215/386-4800,
www.newdecktavern.com
Map 6

Always bustling, New Deck Tavern is a worthwhile stop on the University City circuit even if you're not a college student. This Irish pub has been delighting the Penn and Drexel crowds for over two decades with giant portions of tasty bar food and a good selection of beer. Burgers and cheesesteaks are popular with students looking to soak up some of the booze. Quizzo, live acoustic music sessions, and karaoke are regular events.

NODDING HEAD BREWERY
1516 Sansom St., 2nd fl., 215/569-9525,
www.noddinghead.com
Map 3

A medal-winning microbrewery, Nodding Head provides the thirsty with eight of its own delicious beers along with an excellent selection of foreign brews. An English-style pub, it turns a bit rowdy during soccer games and heated Sunday-night Quizzo tournaments, but at other times is a chill spot for dinner and conversation. An extensive bobblehead collection greets patrons at the top of the stairs and a dark-wood bar area has booth dining or a red velvet lounge environment; the main dining area has more traditional table seating. This little-menu-that-could offers far-flung variety, from a full rack of baby-back ribs to polenta topped with puttanesca sauce. The appetizer menu is just as diverse; try the white beans and sage served with warm pita bread. High-quality bar fare is reasonably priced, and the same burgers, fries, and mussels served at the popular nearby Monk's (of the same owners) can be enjoyed here with a much shorter wait.

THE PLOUGH AND THE STARS
123 Chestnut St., 215/733-0300, www.ploughstars.com
Map 1

This restaurant/bar has two faces. By day, The Plough and the Stars is a respectable place to grab a nice sit-down lunch on the main floor or on the balcony of the high-ceilinged space. By night, it lives up to its prime Old City location and hosts some of the loudest partying, drinking, and dancing in town. Though ostensibly Irish, the Plough's menu has a decidedly contemporary flair, with Mahi Fillet, avocado mousse, and a fairly extensive wine and drinks list alongside the bangers and mash, and fish-and-chips. There's also a decent brunch and bar menu and what many claim is the best pint of Guinness in the city.

ROYAL TAVERN
937 E. Passyunk Ave., 215/389-6694,
www.royaltavern.com
Map 5

A gorgeous antique wooden bar is the centerpiece of this neighborhood bar in South Philadelphia's Bella Vista neighborhood. A long row-home space is filled with regulars, chatting and drinking at the bar or dining at the small tables that fill the space. There is a good beer selection and reasonably priced tasty sandwiches along with more dinner-style entrées. Don't miss the summer rolls, fresh salads, and delightful roast pork sandwiches. While some people come just to drink, the majority of people eat while they're here as well.

SUGAR MOM'S
225 Church St., 215/925-8219
Map 1

Dive bars are harder to come by in swanky Old City than in the rest of the city, but Sugar Mom's fits the bill. Offering dirt-cheap drinks, pool tables, and debauchery, the basement space is filled with a casual crowd as well as a few of the fancier Old City bar-hoppers who've spent all their money at nearby establishments and need one last nightcap. A few retired bumper cars on the floor provide additional seating for the drunken masses. Typical bar fare is served.

TATTOOED MOM
530 South St., 215/238-9880
Map 5

This South Street gem's cheap prices and casual, grungy atmosphere make it a popular hangout. The somewhat cleaner and nicer 1st floor is painted an odd shade of green, and has strange sculptures perched just outside its windows but could be considered upscale compared to the funky 2nd floor. The walls are covered in graffiti from floor to ceiling, and two pool tables occupy the entire front room. Standard pub fare—poppers and mozzarella sticks—are available on both floors.

TEN STONE
2063 South St., 215/735-9939,
www.tenstone.com
Map 3

Just on the edge of Center City, Ten Stone is a popular spot—perhaps because it is one of the only bars in this rapidly growing stretch of South Street. Wooden booths line the warm, orange walls and an attractive full wooden bar sits at the center of the room. The scene is mostly 20- and 30-somethings from the neighborhood who come for the menu of great salads and sandwiches and a good beer selection. It's a bit on the pricey side for a neighborhood hangout, but that doesn't seem to stop it from filling up. A room off to the side has a pool table and a dart game, and a cozy room with a few tables is in the back behind the bar.

Lounges

BLEU MARTINI
24 S. 2nd St., 215/940-7900,
www.bleumartinionline.com
Map 1

A typical swanky lounge in the heart of Old City, Bleu Martini specializes in—you guessed it—martinis. Offering more than 30 different martinis, you can have anything from the classic to a fruity, alcoholic dessert in a glass. The food menu is also popular, offering Asian, American, and fusion cuisine, including elaborate sushi creations. There is music nightly, and the small dance floor gets packed on weekends. A VIP lounge and waitress-only table service is also available if you're willing to pay the price.

DENIM
1712 Walnut St., 215/735-6700,
denimlounge.com
Map 3

Denim is more like the expensive pair of jeans you squeeze into than the old comfortable ones you save for a lazy Sunday. This Rittenhouse spot requires its patrons be as stylish as it is, so be prepared to dress up. Its plush interior will make you think you've been teleported 15 blocks to trendy Old City. Like other high-end lounges around Philly, Denim offers a selection of specialty cocktails and bottle service. So if you see people queuing up on Walnut Street, this is probably where they're going.

32°
16 S. 2nd St., 215/627-3132, www.32lounge.com
Map 1

32°, or 32 degrees when you say it aloud, is a lavish, trendy lounge where people come to see and be seen. In a part of the city known for nightlife excess, it features a dimly lit interior, with bottles highlighted on elaborately lighted display cases. A well-coiffed waitstaff serves an impressive choice of imported and domestic liquors and a selection of interesting cocktails, and clubby, pulsating music rocks the house. European-style bottle service is available for those with more money than they know what to do with, making this a popular spot with ballers and hip-hoppers in town. Close to the Ben Franklin and Walt Whitman Bridges, and just a few blocks from the PATCO train to Jersey, it is popular with New Jersey youngsters looking for a hot club scene.

WALNUT ROOM
1709 Walnut St., 2nd fl., 215/751-0201,
www.walnut-room.com
Map 3

Walnut Room has a loungey atmosphere and a diverse clientele. Punks chat with trendies while young professionals take shots with hip-hop ballers. But best of all, there is danceable music every night of the week in this 2nd-floor space in the heart of Rittenhouse Row. The delicious cocktails can get pricey and the bottle service is a tad frivolous, but overall, Walnut Room is a good place for serious dancing in a small bar/lounge rather than a massive nightclub.

NIGHTLIFE

Wine Bars

TINTO
114 S. 20th St., 215/665-9150,
www.tintorestaurant.com
Map 3

Spanish for red wine, Tinto—Philadelphia's hottest new restaurant and wine bar—lives up to its name. More than 100 varieties of Spanish and French wines fill the handcrafted wooden grids that completely surround the intimate space. Reminiscent of an elegant yet rustic wine cellar, the dining area is complete with high tasting tables and a 22-foot bar covered in black-and-white Spanish tiles. Acclaimed chef and owner Jose Garces's inventive Basque menu features *pinxtos* (the Basque equivalent of tapas), charcuterie, cheeses, *mariscos* (shellfish), brochettes, and *bocadillos* (sandwiches).

◖ TRIA

123 S. 18th St., 215/972-8742,
www.triacafe.com
Map 3

The three stars at Tria are wine, cheese, and beer. Whether you prefer a bold cabernet, a full-bodied Riesling, an earthy Raclette, or a buttery Nevat, the wine list is long and leaves nothing to be desired, but a selection of microbrewed beers from around the world offers an alternative. Artisan cheeses, cured meats, bruschetta, salads, and sandwiches are offered, and while it's possible to order a relatively simple chicken sandwich, only food virgins leave without sampling the numerous other sensuous delights. A cheese tasting,

paired with exotic accompaniments, is an essential part of the experience. A second Tria in Washington West (Map 2, 1137 Spruce St., 215/629-9200) was added in 2007 due to the enormous popularity of the first location near Rittenhouse Square.

VINTAGE

129 S. 13th St., 215/922-3095,
www.vintage-philadelphia.com
Map 2

At least 60 wines are available by the glass and more than 100 by the bottle at this relatively new hot spot. An excellent selection, small and large food plates, and an appealing atmosphere complete with large windows and high ceilings have made it an instant success. Or maybe it's the ridiculously great happy hour specials; on weekdays from 5 to 7 P.M., you can choose from a generous list of good wines for a measly $3 a glass, far cheaper than you'd pay for a glass of lesser wine at most bars.

Queer

THE BIKE STOP

206 S. Quince St., 215/627-1662, www.thebikestop.com
Map 2

Philly's leather bar is a chill neighborhood watering hole to gather with friends and enjoy cheap pitchers—and the occasional spanking. Depending on the night, patrons can see either sitcom reruns on the flat-panel TVs or watch a leather-clad man getting whipped on stage; it's the luck of the draw. The little-used 3rd floor offers a small dance floor, but it's the downstairs Pit Stop room that draws a crowd for its underwear-only Wednesdays and cruise-y weekend nights.

BUMP

1234 Locust St., 215/732-1800, www.bumplounge.com
Map 2

Whether you're looking for a pick-me-up after a rough day, a good start to a big night out, or an easy Sunday brunch, Bump never disappoints. Center City's most fabulous luxe lounge

is the place for trendy gay men and their best girlfriends to grab a drink and be seen, either in the main lounge or the outdoor garden. Bump is famous for its menu of flavored martinis, including the Viagra, the Windex, the Gorgeous Geisha, and the Sex and the City. Even better is the 5–7 P.M. happy hour special, when said drinks are priced at just $3, drawing a large mixed crowd of mostly gay men, but a good few lesbians and straight men and women as well. Large black-and-white photos of hot, almost-nude men adorn the walls.

PURE

1221 St. James St., 215/735-5772, www.purephilly.com
Map 2

Pure is the Gayborhood's only after-hours club, so while the main floor is sparsely populated for most of the night, it picks up around 2 A.M. for another hour and a half of dancing and debauchery (some of which notoriously happens in the bathroom stalls). It has a large mezzanine that offers amazing wraparound views of the main floor below, and the more intimate Pink Lounge is the place for karaoke, bingo, and Quizzo. The $2 "pink drinks" served nightly from 9 to 11 P.M. ensures that patrons are both exhausted and hungover for work the next day.

◖ SISTERS

1320 Chancellor St., 215/735-0735,
www.sistersnightclub.com
Map 2

Sisters, Philadelphia's only dedicated lesbian bar, is tucked away in the alley behind Woody's. The bartenders know how to keep the liquor flowing on both floors of the large two-level space. Tables off the main bar offer a place to sit and chat, while the upstairs has a rowdier dance-club atmosphere. Thursday offers what is possibly Philadelphia's most economical invitation for public drunkenness, where a $10 cover gets you eight (yes, eight!) drink tickets, a buffet, karaoke, and dancing. While the wait for drinks can be long, and they are served in small plastic cups, it is still an unbeatable deal. Gay or straight, this is one of the most happening dance floors in the city on Thursday night.

TAVERN ON CAMAC

243 S. Camac St., 215/545-0900,
www.tavernoncamac.com
Map 2

Something of a schizophrenic, Tavern on Camac is an "only in Philly" type of place. The downstairs is an old-fashioned piano bar while the upstairs has one of the city's best dance floors. It's always packed and pumping with great music. Patrons of all ages switch between high-energy house music and melodic show tunes several times throughout the night. Both gays and lesbians come to Tavern to play and drink. The drinks are strong, and the people are pretty.

12TH AIR COMMAND

254 S. 12th St., 215/545-8088, www.12thair.com
Map 2

The largest gay venue in Philly, 12th Air Command has five bars on three levels and a large roof deck with panoramic views of the downtown skyline. It also offers pub food and dancing, and since it's rarely full, it usually ends up being more of a chill hangout to shoot pool than the throbbing dance palace it thrives to be. However, 12th Air is more adventurous in its programming than other clubs, offering Roman gladiators and Asian-themed parties. And a renovated dance floor offers hope that it may one day bring on the club atmosphere the space is capable of, at full force.

UNCLES

1220 Locust St., 215/546-6660
Map 2

Despite the common perception, which can be partly attributed to its name, a good number of younger guys, and even the rare girl, frequents Uncles in additional to the more, ahem, mature gay men. The friendly neighborhood bar has a decent jukebox and welcoming bartenders, and the crowd typically includes businessmen, old friends, and the occasional college student. On warmer days, the large picture windows are open to the street for great people-watching. As a plus, if you are a young, cute guy, you can often get drinks bought for you.

◖ WOODY'S

202 S. 13th St., 215/545-1893,
www.woodysbar.com
Map 2

Even with a change in ownership and a new dance floor, Woody's is still the same place it's been for a long time—the epicenter of gay nightlife in Philadelphia. The huge venue has a half-dozen bars spread out on two floors, an upstairs dance floor, and a restaurant on the street level. The decor is nothing to write home about—think early-'80s dive with flourishes of ski lodge—but the bartenders are friendly and they have a heavy hand with the booze. Monday offers karaoke, Wednesday hosts the always-riotous all-ages night, and Saturday is usually wall-to-wall men on the prowl in the upstairs bar and dance floor.

NIGHTLIFE

ARTS AND LEISURE

From world-class museums, theaters, and art galleries to practically every type of recreation, arts and leisure opportunities abound in Philadelphia. And while there is plenty to do throughout the year, the city kicks into turbo gear during spring and summer, with a multitude of festivals and musical and cultural events.

The city's wealth of museums honor practically every slice of its rich history and culture, from world-class art, science, and history to museums focusing on many different ethnic groups. Art galleries display a variety of traditional and cutting-edge art forms, and ongoing events and open houses make them accessible to everyone.

The Avenue of the Arts, the section of Broad Street that extends south from City Hall, is home to most of the city's first-run theater and classical concert venues, from the grand old Academy of Music to the stunningly modern Kimmel Center. Additional concert venues are spread throughout the city, ranging from the huge Wachovia Center, hosting top national acts, to casual, open-air stadiums like the Mann Center for the Performing Arts.

Outdoor lovers will be thrilled to discover that Philadelphia is home to the largest urban municipal park system in the world. Fairmount Park's more than 9,200 acres offer endless recreational opportunities, including hundreds of miles of hiking, biking, and jogging trails, and water sports along the two rivers that straddle Center City. The city's many green spaces are home to gardens, arboretums, dog parks, playgrounds, and sports' fields, and sometimes serve as outdoor venues for events, markets, and festivals—especially in the summer.

HIGHLIGHTS

LOOK FOR ◖ TO FIND RECOMMENDED ARTS AND ACTIVITIES.

◖ **Best Interactive Museum:** The **Franklin Institute Science Museum** showcases the best scientific advancements in history. The interactive museum is a giant playground for adults and children alike (page 113).

◖ **Best Kids' Museum:** The hands-on exhibits at the **Please Touch Museum** are so much fun that kids don't realize they're learning (page 114).

◖ **Best Concert Halls:** It's a tie. The **Academy of Music,** built in 1857, and the **Kimmel Center,** built in 2001, are Philly's most esteemed, world-class venues. The two superstars of the Avenue of the Arts represent the best of old and new architecture (page 119).

◖ **Best Art House Cinema:** Between the three **Ritz Theatres** in Old City, you can always find that foreign, indie, or artsy movie you've been dying to see. Each theater offers excellent titles in comfortable spaces, without the glitz of the mainstream theaters (page 121).

◖ **Best Festival:** Usually held during the first two weeks of September, the **Philadelphia Live Arts Festival and Philly Fringe** presents cutting-edge theater, dance, music, and other events. There is no limit to the quantity and diversity of events, since the "fringe" element means any artist can self-produce and become part of the festivities (page 124).

◖ **Best Gardens:** **Morris Arboretum** boasts 92 acres of beautifully landscaped Victorian gardens, streams, and sculptures in Chestnut Hill. Originally part of a wealthy Quaker family estate, the historic gardens were planted in 1887 (page 126).

◖ **Best Walking, Jogging, and Biking Trail:** The scenic 25-mile **Schuylkill River**

PHOTO BY K. CIAPPA FOR GPTMC

Franklin Institute Science Museum

Trail winds around both sides of the river. The easily accessible and popular 8.4-mile paved stretch known as "the loop" extends out behind the Art Museum (page 128).

◖ **Best Place to Get Away from it All:** In the Northwest section of the city, **Wissahickon Park** offers 1,800 acres of towering trees and scenic trails. It's easy to get lost in the woods and completely forget you're in the city (page 129).

◖ **Best Bowling Alley:** If you've never thought of bowling as particularly hip, then you've never been to **North Bowl.** This popular Northern Liberties spot offers a latenight lounge along with two levels of lanes (page 132).

◖ **Nation's Oldest Boxing Ring:** The **Legendary Blue Horizon** is well-known in the boxing world as one of the last remaining oldschool boxing venues in the country. The historic ring has hosted many of the sport's greats and continues to hold matches (page 141).

ARTS AND LEISURE

Any sports fan should try to catch at least one professional game while in town. Despite the inability of any of those teams to bring home a championship in more than two decades, there is simply no city more impassioned and committed to all four of its major professional teams than Philadelphia. Even former mayor Ed Rendell, now governor of Pennsylvania, is a huge sports fan. He hosts the Eagles postgame show every Sunday. Rooting for—and talking trash about—our teams brings the city together, perhaps more than anything else.

The Arts

A vast array of museums, theaters, galleries, concert venues, and cinema of all kinds can be found in Philadelphia. The weekly papers *PW* and *City Paper* both offer extensive listings of events. Note that the Philadelphia Museum of Art, the city's grandest museum, is listed in the *Sights* chapter rather than here, because it is a sight to behold both inside and out.

MUSEUMS
Art
BARNES FOUNDATION
300 N. Latches Ln., Merion, 610/667-0290, www.barnesfoundation.org
HOURS: Fri.-Sun. 9:30 A.M.-5 P.M. Sept.-June, Wed.-Fri. 9:30 A.M.-5 P.M. July-Aug.
COST: $10, audio guide additional $7
Map 10

Eccentric art collector Albert C. Barnes never could have imagined his little art collection would cause such trouble. His legacy, the Barnes Foundation, is an awesome multibillion-dollar collection of Impressionist and Expressionist works by Cézanne, Gauguin, El Greco, Goya, Manet, Matisse, Modigliani, Monet, Picasso, Renoir, and Van Gogh, along with impressive African sculpture and more. Cosseted away in the suburbs since the 1920s, it has been embroiled in a lengthy battle to move the collection into a more accessible Philadelphia location. The same neighbors who hated its visitors' traffic now screech for it to stay. It has been decided that it will move to the Benjamin Franklin Parkway to join the city's other top museums, but a date has not been set as of this printing. Call ahead to make sure you're going to the right place; whether it's still in the 'burbs or conveniently in the city, all art lovers will want to make it to this world-class collection. Currently, advanced reservations are required and can be made by phone, fax, or email. Because of its popularity and limited hours, it is recommended that you make reservations at least a month in advance for your choice date and time.

INSTITUTE OF CONTEMPORARY ART
118 S. 36th St., 215/898-7108, www.icaphila.org
HOURS: Wed.-Fri. noon-8 P.M., Sat.-Sun. 11 A.M.-5 P.M.
COST: $6 adult, $3 student and senior, free member, child under 12, Penn staff, and students
Map 6

One day, the lay public will understand the difference between modern, postmodern, and contemporary art, but until then, the Institute of Contemporary Art is keeping its name direct and to the point. The ICA, nestled away on Penn's campus in University City, hosts exhibitions, commissions works, produces publications, and holds educational programs. Hopefully, those classes will be able to explain why a gallery showing Rothko would never put up a piece by Duchamp. The museum is free on Sunday 11 A.M.–1 P.M.

PENNSYLVANIA ACADEMY OF THE FINE ARTS
118 N. Broad St., 215/972-7600, www.pafa.org
HOURS: Tues.-Sat. 10 A.M.-5 P.M., Sun. 11 A.M.-5 P.M.
COST: $7 adult, $6 senior and student, $5 child 5-18, free member and child under 5
Map 2

Having recently celebrated its 200th anniversary—take that, Guggenheim!—the Pennsylvania Academy of the Fine Arts is the oldest art school and oldest museum in the country. Inside the National Historic Landmark building, holdings include paintings and other works by many of the masters, including Cecilia Beaux, William Merritt Chase, Frank Duveneck, Thomas Eakins, Winslow Homer, Childe Hassam, and Edmund Tarbell. Eakins is particularly associated with PAFA, as its most controversial and paradigm-shifting director. Now, the academy he led is one of the most prestigious art schools in America, and is a must-see for any art-loving visitor. Guided tours are included with admission, at 11:30 and 12:30 P.M. on weekdays, and noon and 1 P.M. on weekends. The **Morris Gallery** exhibitions on the ground floor are free and open to the public.

RODIN MUSEUM

22nd St. and Benjamin Franklin Pkwy.,
215/568-6026, www.rodinmuseum.org
HOURS: Tues.-Sun. 10 A.M.-5 P.M.
COST: $3 donation suggested
Map 4

Many will recognize Auguste Rodin's famous sculpture *The Thinker* that welcomes all into the small museum dedicated entirely to the French artist's work. Walk past the garden and fountain to see many of his other masterpieces, including *The Gates of Hell* framing the main entrance of the impressive building. Wander through the high-ceilinged, marble-floored rooms and you'll be amazed by the endless true-to-life sculptures of the human body— he was especially skilled and obsessed at creating human hands—that Rodin created in his lifetime. Exhibiting one of the largest Rodin collections in the world, the museum provides an in-depth look at not only his work, but also his thought processes and his life while he created the works. Some of his original tools, early sketches, and journals are on display.

History and Culture
AFRICAN AMERICAN MUSEUM IN PHILADELPHIA

701 Arch St., 215/574-0380, www.aampmuseum.org
HOURS: Tues.-Sat. 10 A.M.-5 P.M., Sun. noon-5 P.M.
COST: $8 adult, $6 senior, child, and physically challenged
Map 1

Founded in 1976 for the bicentennial, the African American Museum in Philadelphia was the first museum in a major U.S. city dedicated to celebrating African American culture and history. The museum holds over 750,000 objects including arts, artifacts, clothing, furniture, weapons, documents, photographs, records, and diaries. There are three dominant themes: the African Diaspora, the Philadelphia Story, and the Contemporary Narrative, but the museum is continually adding new, permanent, and rotating exhibits, like one dedicated to female African American artists. The museum also hosts a variety of lectures and other educational programming.

The Thinker, by August Rodin, welcomes visitors to the museum displaying his work.

ARTS AND LEISURE

© KARRIE GAVIN

AMERICAN SWEDISH HISTORY MUSEUM
1900 Pattison Ave., 215/389-1776,
www.americanswedish.org
HOURS: Tues.-Fri. 10 A.M.-4 P.M., Sat.-Sun. noon-4 P.M.
COST: $6 adult, $5 senior and student, free child under 12 and member
Map 10

Swedish colonists settled in the Delaware Valley in the mid-1600s—long before William Penn arrived—and this museum aims to preserve their history. The nation's oldest Swedish museum was founded in 1926 on the 150th anniversary of the drafting of the Declaration of Independence. Built on land given to colonist Sven Skute by Sweden's Queen Christina in 1653, the building was modeled after a 17th-century Swedish manor. Numerous artifacts fill the 12 galleries showcasing the history of the colonists, including collections of early Swedish furniture and handmade peasant dolls. Other exhibits honor famous Swedes including author Carl Sandberg, inventor/seaman John Ericsson, and Alfred Nobel, who invented dynamite and established the Nobel Prizes. It's a bit out of the way in deep South Philly, but worth a trip for history buffs or anyone interested in Swedish culture.

ATWATER KENT MUSEUM
15 S. 7th St., 215/685-4830,
www.philadelphiahistory.org
HOURS: Wed.-Sun. 1-5 P.M.
COST: $5 adult, $3 senior and child
Map 1

This Greek-revival style building on the edge of Old City originally housed the Franklin Institute until it was relocated to its current large space on the Benjamin Franklin Parkway. A. Atwater Kent then purchased the space to create a museum that would honor Philadelphia's history. Today, the museum showcases local inventions in manufacturing and technology, toys and tools from the colonial era, and local artwork. While not nearly as widely appreciated as many of the major Old City sights, this museum is a must for those who want an in-depth look at Philadelphia's past. A large map of the city on the floor allows

© KARRIE GAVIN

Atwater Kent Museum

you to literally walk on top of Philadelphia's many colorful neighborhoods, and serves as a good orientation to the city.

CIVIL WAR AND UNDERGROUND RAILROAD MUSEUM

1805 Pine St., 215/735-8196, www.cwurmuseum.org
HOURS: Thurs.-Sat. 11 A.M.-4:30 P.M.
COST: $5 adult, $4 senior and AAA member, $3 student, free child under 3
Map 3

Another Philly first, the Civil War and Underground Railroad Museum was founded in 1888 as the first chartered institution in the United States created to preserve the history of the Civil War and antislavery movement. Its nine galleries are filled with artifacts, photographs, artworks, and archival materials. You can see weapons, uniforms, paintings, photographs, flags, receipts for the purchases of slaves, and memoirs and autobiographies of abolitionists. The library has the largest collections of Civil War material in the United States outside of government institutions. By 2010, it will move into the First Bank of the U.S. building in the heart of Independence National Historical Park. The impressive structure and prime location is fitting of the museum's importance in local and national history, and is sure to make it one of the major stops on most visitors' travels.

FIREMAN'S HALL MUSEUM

147 N. 2nd St., 215/925-1438, www.firemanshall.org
HOURS: Tues.-Fri. 9 A.M.-5 P.M.
COST: Free
Map 1

Benjamin Franklin had the unprecedented idea of starting the first fire insurance company in Philadelphia in the 1730s, and he is just one of many people and advancements that are honored at the Fireman's Hall Museum. Housed in a 19th-century firehouse, the museum pays tribute to the brave men and women who fought fire and risked their lives for public safety. The collection of firefighting history and memorabilia includes an array of axes, hoses, tools, fire trucks, and parade badges from the 1800s.

INDEPENDENCE SEAPORT MUSEUM

Penn's Landing, 211 South Columbus Blvd. and Walnut St., 215/413-8655, www.phillyseaport.org
HOURS: Daily 10 A.M.-5 P.M.
COST: $9 adult, $6 child 3-12, $8 senior and student, free Sat.-Sun. 10 A.M.-noon.
Map 1

Independence Seaport Museum explores the city's rich maritime history in a fitting location on Penn's Landing overlooking the Delaware River. The exhibits "Bound for Philadelphia" and "Coming to America" highlight the city's immigration history and its importance in the growth of the nation's population. It also explains the hardships and hazards often faced by the many immigrants who crossed the Atlantic in search of a new life. Exhibits on small crafts, industrial shipping, and deep-diving technology give the museum a modern aspect. Enjoy excellent views of the Delaware River throughout many of the exhibit spaces, making it easy to imagine the hordes of people landing on that very shore in centuries past. While you're here, you can also explore the USS *Olympia,* which served as a flagship in the Spanish-American War, and the USS *Becuna,* a World War II submarine. Both National Historic Landmarks are open during museum hours, and noon-4 P.M. on the first Saturday of each month you can get a behind-the-scenes guided tour of additional areas that are normally closed to the public.

MUMMERS MUSEUM

1100 S. 2nd St., 215/336-3050, www.mummersmuseum.com
HOURS: Tues.-Sat. 9:30 A.M.-4:30 P.M., Sun. noon-4:30 P.M.
COST: $3.50 adult, $2.50 child, senior, and student
Map 5

"What is a Mummer?" you may ask. He or she is a lavishly costumed, dancing, marching, instrument-playing, feather-and-sequin covered Philadelphian who brings the city's unique brand of celebration to fever pitch. The purest example of Philadelphia's spirit, the Mummers celebrate every occasion, but none more so than the New Year, which they usher in with a parade on Broad Street. If you haven't seen a

PHOTO BY EDWARD SAVARIA, JR. FOR PCVB

A costumed Mummer celebrates at the annual New Year's Day Mummers Parade on Broad Street.

Mummers parade before, it is a sight not to be missed. While the earliest Mummers date back to ancient Egypt, the tradition of Mummers in Philadelphia began in the late 17th century and has held strong every since. The joyous group is passionate and proud, and their traditions have become an important part of Philadelphia's history. The Mummers Museum in South Philadelphia has exhibits that pay homage to their unique history.

NATIONAL LIBERTY MUSEUM

321 Chestnut St., 215/925-2800,
www.libertymuseum.org
HOURS: Tues.-Sun. 10 A.M.-5 P.M., also Mon. Memorial
Day–Labor Day
COST: $7 adult, $6 senior, $5 student, $2 child 5-17,
free child under 5
Map 1

Just two blocks from the Liberty Bell and Independence Hall, the National Liberty Museum pays tribute to the profound accomplishment of creating a free society. The museum's

varied galleries explore topics of heroism, freedom, diversity, faith and more, and pay homage to people who have contributed to the creation of a free country. The fine art gallery features an array of sculptures, paintings, and an impressive collection of delicate glass works that explore the idea of the beauty and fragility of freedom.

NATIONAL MUSEUM OF AMERICAN JEWISH HISTORY

44 N. 4th St., 215/922-5446, www.mikvehisrael.org
HOURS: Mon.-Thurs. 10 A.M.-5 P.M., Fri. 10 A.M.-3 P.M.,
Sun. noon-5 P.M.
COST: $4 adult and senior, $3 student and child 6 and
over, free child under 6 and member
Map 1

The National Museum of American Jewish History aims to encapsulate the experience of Jews in America. Exhibits and artifacts celebrate and explore Jewish culture, negotiating immigrant identity in a new country, and the experience of Philadelphia Jews. The small museum attached to the Mikveh Israel Cemetery has been one of the more obscure stops on the Philly tourist circuit, but that is all likely to change soon. It is moving into a new, modern facility in a prominent location on Independence Mall (55 N. 5th St., 215/923-3811, www.nmajh.org) just across the street from the Liberty Bell. The opening is slated for Independence Day 2010, and the new space will feature five floors of interactive exhibition space and the nation's largest collection of Jewish American memorabilia.

POLISH AMERICAN CULTURAL CENTER AND MUSEUM

308 Walnut St., 215/922-1700,
www.polishamericancenter.org
HOURS: Mon.-Fri. 10 A.M.-4 P.M. Jan.-Apr., Mon.-Sat.
10 A.M.-4 P.M. May-Dec.
COST: Free
Map 1

This small museum in the heart of Old City honors Polish culture and heritage and celebrates the contributions of its citizens to the United States and the world. The center was founded in February 1981 and offers a small display of memorabilia and biographical materials about famous Poles, including religious leader John Cardinal Krol, Revolutionary War heroes Thaddeus Kosciuszko and Casimir Pulaski, composers Fryderyk Chopin and Ignacy Jan Paderewski, and scientists Marie Curie and Nicholas Copernicus. There is a prominent display on Pope John Paul II. Exhibits highlight Polish traditions that immigrants brought to the states, including Pisanki (painted Easter eggs) and decorative wooden plates.

UNIVERSITY MUSEUM OF ARCHAEOLOGY AND ANTHROPOLOGY

3260 South St., 215/898-4000,
www.museum.upenn.edu

HOURS: Tues.-Sat. 10 A.M.-4:30 P.M., Sun. hours vary depending on season

COST: $8 adult, $5 child, senior, and student, free member and child under 6, free Sun. Memorial Day–Labor Day

Map 6

A paradise for the Indiana Jones at heart, the University of Pennsylvania's museum houses a magnificent chest of archaeological treasures. It opened in 1899 and today there are more than 100 unique displays and one million artifacts representing practically every corner of history and prehistory. Trace the earliest Homo sapiens' routes through time as you walk the long artifact-lined corridors and wander through rooms that offer glimpses into centuries and civilizations past. Decipher North America's earliest hieroglyphics in the Mesoamerica Exhibit; walk before the enormous sphinx at the Palace of the Pharaoh Merenptah; and advance through the technology, art, politics, and religion of the Etruscans, Greeks, Canaanites, and Romans.

Science
ACADEMY OF NATURAL SCIENCES

1900 Benjamin Franklin Pkwy., 215/299-1000,
www.ansp.org

HOURS: Mon.-Fri. 10 A.M.-4:30 P.M., Sat.-Sun. 10 A.M.-5 P.M.

COST: $10 adult, $8 child, senior, military, and student

Map 4

Over 40 feet long and smiling with hundreds

of razor-sharp teeth, a replica of an extinct giganotosaurus greets guests as they enter the Academy of Natural Sciences, where exhibits follow evolutionary history from the Mesozoic era to present-day animal habitats. From the *Tyrannosaurus* to tigers, the Academy captures animal life across the planet and through time in glass-enclosed realistic-looking displays. While the place is undeniably interesting, some animal lovers may find the still-lifes a little bit creepy. Children love to take part in real archaeological digs and the live animal exhibit.

◀ FRANKLIN INSTITUTE SCIENCE MUSEUM

222 N. 20th St., 215/448-1200, www2.fi.edu

HOURS: Daily 9:30 A.M.-5 P.M.

COST: $14.25 adult, $13.25 senior, military and student, $11.50 child (4-11), free child under 4, additional fees for IMAX theater, planetarium, and special exhibits

Map 4

Scientist and inventor Benjamin Franklin would be proud of the impressive museum named for him and dedicated to one of the major focuses of his life's work—expanding knowledge of the universe through science. A larger-than-life statue of Ben himself welcomes guests into the grand high-ceilinged lobby. The large museum showcases many of Franklin's inventions, along with countless technological and scientific advances throughout history. The fun, interactive exhibits are as interesting and educational for adults as they are for children. Visitors can explore the engine room of a real 19th-century locomotive, walk through a massive replica of a human heart, and take in the vast expanse of the cosmos in the "Space Command" exhibit. The Institute hosts the world's best traveling science exhibits in addition to the ever-expanding permanent displays. A planetarium and one of the best surround-style IMAX theaters in the country round out the museum's offerings, and can be visited separately or in coordination with the museum for a separate fee.

ARTS AND LEISURE

PHOTO BY K. CIAPPA FOR GPTMC

The Franklin Institute, named for Ben Franklin, is a world-class science museum.

ARTS AND LEISURE

MUTTER MUSEUM
19 S. 22nd St., 267/563-3737,
www.collphyphil.org/mutter.asp
HOURS: Daily 10 A.M.–5 P.M.
COST: $12 adult, $8 child, senior, and student
Map 3

Gross or cool? The fascinating Mutter Museum is a little bit of both. This showcase of medical oddities was founded in 1858 by the College of Physicians of Philadelphia. Exhibits include a wall of real eyeballs, President Grover Cleveland's tumor, the tallest skeleton in the country, and the world's largest colon. Portraits and pieces by Philadelphia artists Thomas Eakins and John Singer Sargent are on display alongside the body parts in jars. With such a weird array of science and medicine guests are bound to learn something—if they can stomach it.

PLEASE TOUCH MUSEUM
Memorial Hall, West Fairmount Park, 4231 N.
Concourse Dr., 215/963-0667,
www.pleasetouchmuseum.org
HOURS: Daily 9 A.M.–4:30 P.M.
COST: $9.95 adult and child, $1 under the age of 1
Map 8

With a name like Please Touch, it's obvious that this giant playground is meant to be enjoyed hands-on. Children love to dress up in costume, have tea with Alice and the Mad Hatter, operate flying machines, and drive the SEPTA bus. Exhibits aim to motivate learning, development, and imaginations, but are also lots of fun. A long-time favorite for families with children, the museum is better than ever, with new and improved exhibits in its three-times-larger, gorgeous new location in Memorial Hall in Fairmount Park.

GALLERIES
There is a wealth of art galleries throughout the city, spanning every type of traditional and cutting-edge art form. Items for sale range from the reasonably priced to limited-edition nationally known gems. The galleries around Rittenhouse tend to be of the high-end variety, while Northern Liberties and Chinatown have

more of the thriving artists and artists' co-ops. Old City has the greatest concentration of galleries of all kinds. Listed below are a few of the best and most unique galleries, but visit www .phillygalleryguide.com for more comprehensive listings. Unless otherwise noted, they are all free.

ART STAR
1030 N. 2nd St., 215/238-1557, www.artstarphilly.com
HOURS: Tues.-Sat. 10 A.M.-7 P.M., Sun. noon-6 P.M.
Map 7

This quirky little Northern Liberties boutique/gallery is committed to providing local budding artists an opportunity to be seen and hopefully make a buck. One-of-a-kind and limited-edition ceramics, prints, clothing, dolls, and jewelry are sold on a consignment basis. Exhibitions rotate every six weeks and range from cartoon paintings to unusual stuffed animals and other household items. Named "the city's first cutting-edge craft shop" by *Philadelphia* magazine, Art Star offers an eclectic mix that reflects the diverse Northern Liberties arts community.

CLAY STUDIO
139 N. 2nd St., 215/925-3453, www.theclaystudio.org
HOURS: Tues.-Sat. 11 A.M.-7 P.M., Sun. noon-6 P.M.
Map 1

For more than 30 years, the Clay Studio has been a veritable fixture in Philadelphia's urban art community. As you walk down the hallway leading to the gallery, which features funky mosaic tile work by local artist-celeb Isaiah Zagar, you'll know you're in for a treat. The gallery displays juried solo exhibits, work from local emerging ceramists, and artists from its highly competitive studio-run residency and fellowship programs. The Clay Studio offers a little something for every taste, ranging from functional vessels like coffee mugs and vases to more conceptual work like sculptures and installations.

FABRIC WORKSHOP AND MUSEUM
1222 Arch St., 215/568-1111, www.fabricworkshop.org
HOURS: Mon.-Fri. 10 A.M.-6 P.M., Sat. noon-4 P.M.

COST: suggested donation $5 adult, $2 child
Map 2

The Fabric Workshop and Museum is the only museum of its kind in the country, and is a must for those interested in creating art using fabric. It sets out to support the development of "new work in new materials." The museum and shop is a successful collaboration between both emerging and famous artists experimenting with unfamiliar mediums—often, but not solely, fabric. Founded in 1977, the museum displays permanent and rotating exhibits. Located in a former industrial building near the convention center, it contains three exhibition galleries, a video lounge, a shop, and artist studios.

FLEISHER ART MEMORIAL
719 Catharine St., 215/922-3456, www.fleisher.org
HOURS: Mon.-Thurs. 11 A.M.-5 P.M., and 6:30-9:30 P.M., Fri. 11 A.M.-5 P.M., Sat. 10 A.M.-3 P.M.
Map 5

This Bella Vista neighborhood gem is home to a small rotating gallery of drawings, paintings, sculpture, and photography by mostly local artists. But the coolest thing about Fleisher is the low-priced and free art classes offered on an ongoing basis. This is a great opportunity for everyone from beginners to advanced artists to hone their skills in a supportive and affordable environment. Advanced workshops and classes, including photography, sculpture, art history, and many types of drawing and painting, are offered for a fee.

F.U.E.L. COLLECTION
249 Arch St., 215/592-8400, www.fuelcollection.com
HOURS: Tues.-Fri. 11 A.M.-6 P.M., Sat.-Sun. noon-4 P.M.
Map 1

F.U.E.L. is an acronym for Fostering Undergraduate Exposure on Location. The mission of this progressive gallery is to "expose the unexposed, promote the next generation of artists, encourage creative collaboration, and aid the launch of successful artistic careers by creating a truly unique and singular forum for the display of art." F.U.E.L. is more than just a gallery displaying interesting and diverse

ARTS AND LEISURE

ART FOR ALL: FIRST FRIDAYS AND SECOND THURSDAYS

First Friday has become the most popular on-going event in the city since its start in 1991. On the first Friday evening of each month, the art galleries of Old City open their doors to the public, and many offer free wine, beer, and snacks, creating a festive atmosphere. The bulk of the action is concentrated within a few square blocks between Market and Vine and Front and Third Streets, although additional art events are often held outside of Old City as well.

A much more recent addition to the local art scene, **Second Thursdays** is the Northern Liberties/Fishtown neighborhoods' counterpart. The area has become a haven for artists over the past decade, and the second Thursday of each month, a group of galleries holds open houses. Many artists display their work out of Crane Arts (1400 N. American St., 215/232-3203, www.cranearts.com), an art complex with studios and a cool display area and project space. A smaller and less-known event, at least for now, the art here is generally a bit more off-beat.

At both events, the art spans practically every form of classic and contemporary art, including painting, drawing, photography, designer furniture, crafts, glass, and more. Some of it is even relatively affordable for purchase, although many people just come to look. Most galleries at both events are open from 6 to 9 P.M.

up-and-coming artists' work; it is also a community haven and support system for budding artists. As such, the work does not fall into any specific genre, but the gallery offers a wide variety of interesting and affordable pieces.

SNYDERMAN GALLERY AND THE WORKS GALLERY

303 Cherry St., 215/238-9576 (Snyderman), 215/922-7775 (The Works), www.snyderman-works.com
HOURS: Tues.-Sat. 10 A.M.-6 P.M.
Map 1

These two very different but complementary galleries share an expansive 6,000-square-foot space in Old City. The Snyderman Gallery focuses primarily on the continually evolving areas of studio furniture and sculptural glass. A must-see on the national art circuit, it hosted one of the first exhibits of Dale Chihuly's renowned botanical glass work and architect Robert Venturi's furniture designs for Knoll. The Works Gallery is dedicated to ceramics, jewelry, textiles, and fiber. Since 1965, its owners have organized landmark exhibits of artists from around the world, showcasing

work that spans from figurative to functional. Stark white walls, two-story rooms, and delicate work atop a series of pillars offer a lovely setting for the display of intricate handiwork in a variety of materials.

SPACE 1026

1026 Arch St., 2nd fl., 215/574-7630, www.space1026.com
Map 2

This well-known collaborative art space/gallery hosts quirky events and sometimes even doubles as a venue for indie bands, performances, and film screenings. It occupies two floors of space used by a community of local artists and art enthusiasts. It often displays work that has roots in pop surrealism and comic books, and also specializes in screen printing. Unique shows such as a flipbook festival are not uncommon. There are no official hours, but you can stop by anytime and ring the bell or call ahead to make sure someone is there to let you in.

TEMPLE GALLERY

259 N. 3rd St., 215/925-7379, www.temple.edu/tyler/exhibitions

HOURS: Wed.-Sat. 11 A.M.-6 P.M.

Map 1

The exhibition arm of Temple University's renowned Tyler School of Art, the Temple Gallery is known in the Old City gallery scene for its cutting-edge contemporary artwork. As part of an institution of higher education, the gallery aims to inspire and support students, local artists, and the general public through a diverse body of work. Created by both emerging and established local and international artists in a wide array of mediums, the work is often displayed in group shows with unique themes and plenty of installations to explore.

VOX POPULI AND KHMER GALLERY

319 N. 11th St., Vox: 3rd fl., 215/238-1253,
www.voxpopuligallery.org,
Khmer: basement, 215/922-5600,
www.khmerartgallery.com,
HOURS: Vox: Wed.-Sun. noon-6 P.M.; Khmer: Wed., Fri., and Sat. 11 A.M.-4 P.M., first Fri. of the month 5-9 P.M.

Map 7

These two unique galleries are not related, other than by nature of being housed in the same large warehouse just north of Chinatown. Vox Populi hosts contemporary exhibitions including experimental film, cutting-edge installations, and a wide range of work by mostly Philadelphia-based artists. It is also host to numerous indie and experimental musical performances, and has a sophisticated feel while remaining a true DIY artist collective.

Khmer, in the basement level, is very different. Featuring original and reproduction Cambodian sculpture, artwork, jewelry, and photography collected by the friendly Cambodian-born owner Bonna and her husband, Bob, it is an interesting stop for anyone interested in Asian art. Most of the pieces are large and way out of the price range of the average person—try upwards of $50,000 for a marble garden statue—but there are some modestly priced items like jewelry and small artwork. The museum-like space is fun to wander around even if you're not looking to outfit a large Asian-themed estate or restaurant.

THEATER
ADRIENNE THEATRE
2030 Sansom St., 215/568-8077

Map 3

Just a quick walk from Rittenhouse Square, but worlds away from the big theater houses on the Avenue of the Arts, the Adrienne Theatre offers an intimate space for small theater companies. Actually, it offers three different great spaces of varying sizes. Named for theater professional Adrienne Neye, the theater hosts resident companies including the comedy troupe 1812 Productions, Theater Catalyst, ComedySportz. The largest resident company is the socially-minded InterAct Theatre, whose mission is to produce plays that explore the cultural, social, and political issues of the day. The intention is admirable, so we'll look the other way if InterAct's sometimes heavy-handed productions are a touch didactic. Still, when good, these shows hit a real nerve, whether they're examining America's appetite for war, complex racial questions, or the role of the outsider in society. One thing's certain: You'll find works here that broach topics no other company will touch, and the mission is admirable and necessary.

ARDEN THEATRE COMPANY
40 N. 2nd St., 215/922-1122, www.ardentheatre.org

Map 1

When it moved from Center City to Old City in 1995, the Arden Theatre helped reinvigorate the old industrial neighborhood and injected the Philly theater scene with new energy. Since 1988, Arden has been producing top-quality productions of plays, musicals, and children's shows. On its 360-seat main stage and 175-seat blackbox, shows range from reinterpretations of Shakespeare and Shaw to works by emerging playwrights like Pamela Gien and David Auburn.

FORREST THEATRE
1114 Walnut St., 215/923-1515,
www.forrest-theatre.org

Map 2

Built in the late 1920s by the Shubert

ARTS AND LEISURE

Organization and named for legendary 19th-century actor Edwin Forrest, the Forrest Theatre has no resident company but hosts a variety of traveling shows. With most Broadway fare setting up shop at the nearby Academy of Music, it is frequently empty, which is unfortunate since the building is lovely. However, a partnership with the Kimmel Center holds out hope that the Forrest will once again become a necessary stop for theater-loving Philadelphians in search of a good show.

MUM PUPPETTHEATRE

115 Arch St., 215/925-7686,
www.mumpuppet.org
Map 1

It takes a certain level of mastery to use puppets to tell the story of, say, the Holocaust. But trust Mum Puppettheatre to appropriate the quintessentially childhood medium to tell sophisticated, adult stories—like *Animal Farm,* for example. The talented 20-year-old company stages shows specifically for kids as well, with almost-yearly productions of *The Velveteen Rabbit* and *A Christmas Carol,* as well as a series of original plays starring the curiously named Fantocci Brothers.

NEW FREEDOM THEATRE

1346 N. Broad St., 215/765-2793,
www.freedomtheatre.org
Map 10

Most of the action on the Avenue of the Arts goes on below Market Street, but Freedom Theatre is struggling to keep North Broad Street hopping. The oldest African American theater in Pennsylvania, Freedom is currently in a state of limbo, with no regular season and a severely slashed employment roster. In the past, it has showcased fine plays based on African American stories, like Toni Morrison's *The Bluest Eye.* Its operations today consist primarily of conducting theater and dance classes for kids and adults. Here is hoping that it may find new life again as a venue for professional shows, as North Philly could use the positive energy of a thriving theater.

PAINTED BRIDE ART CENTER

230 Vine St., 215/925-9914, www.paintedbride.org
Map 1

The Painted Bride Art Center was a flower child in 1969, when it moved from South Street to Old City—long before the former warehouse neighborhood was the hot spot it is today. Stepping past the colorful mirror-and-tile mosaic exterior, you'll enter a large gallery space showcasing the works of daring young artists. The theater features dance, world music, performance, jazz, and more, with a focus on works that make social and political statements as well as advocacy for excluded communities. The Bride features both local faves and international stars, and is responsible for Philadelphia's longest-running jazz series.

PHILADELPHIA THEATRE COMPANY/ SUZANNE ROBERTS THEATRE

480 S. Broad St., 215/985-0420,
www.phillytheatreco.org
Map 2

The first of several eager young theater companies to take 1970s Philly by storm, the Philadelphia Theatre Company has evolved into one of the most respected arts organizations in the region. Not content to merely rehash classics or safely import successful traveling shows, it has held over 100 world and Philadelphia premiers by playwrights including Terrance McNally, Christopher Durang, and Naomi Wallace. But the plays aren't the only new and exciting thing for the company; after a long residency at the small Plays & Players theater in the Rittenhouse neighborhood, the company moved into its stunning new home, named the Suzanne Roberts Theatre for its benefactor, in the fall of 2007. The $25 million 370-seat theater occupies a deserved location among the city's top theaters on the Avenue of the Arts.

PRINCE MUSIC THEATER

1412 Chestnut St., 215/569-9700,
www.princemusictheater.org
Map 2

Hollywood may just be rediscovering the

musical, but the old razzle-dazzle never left the stage. Here in Philly, that stage belongs to the Prince Music Theater. Though founded in 1984 as the American Music Theater Festival, it was reinvented in 1999 with a new name and a new venue on Chestnut Street just off the Avenue of the Arts. A typical season includes classics like *Cole Porter, Annie Get Your Gun,* and *Hair,* as well as new musicals by emerging artists. In addition to its regular season, the Prince hosts a cabaret series and is a venue for Philadelphia's film festivals.

WALNUT STREET THEATRE
825 Walnut St., 215/574-3550,
www.walnutstreettheatre.org
Map 2

The official State Theater of Pennsylvania is the Walnut Street Theatre, the oldest continually operating theater in the English-speaking world. It opened in 1809 as a circus house, but it is now known for more high-minded fare. Luminaries who have graced its stage include Edwin Booth, Marlon Brando, Henry and Jane Fonda, Audrey Hepburn, and Sidney Poitier. Besides the 1,000-plus-seat main theater, it also holds Studio 3 and Studio 5, smaller houses for second-stage productions and rentals to outside theater companies.

WILMA THEATER
265 S. Broad St., 215/893-5496,
www.wilmatheater.org
Map 2

We may never get to see David Mamet in drag, but the Wilma Theater is named after Shakespeare's fictional female alter-ego. Since the early 1970s, the company has been staging daring, tradition-defying productions of both new plays and classics, including works by Tom Stoppard, Sophocles, Arthur Miller, Tennessee Williams, Bertolt Brecht, and yes, Mamet. Even in its beautiful and spacious home on the Avenue of the Arts, it hasn't lost the feeling of intimacy that makes small theaters so appealing.

CONCERT VENUES
◖ ACADEMY OF MUSIC
Broad and Locust Sts., 215/893-1999,
www.academyofmusic.org
Map 2

Nobly dubbed "The Grand Old Lady of Broad Street," the Academy of Music has been a proud institution since 1857. It is the oldest grand opera house in the United States still functioning as an opera house today. The regal Renaissance-style theater is adorned with wood carvings, ceiling murals, and an impressive crystal chandelier hanging elegantly overhead. Home to the Opera Company of Philadelphia and the Pennsylvania Ballet, the Academy of Music is no stranger to the most gifted musicians that come through the city. Over the years it has hosted Igor Stravinsky, Richard Strauss, Pyotr Tchaikovsky, Joan Sutherland, and a myriad of other world-renowned artists and composers.

CURTIS INSTITUTE OF MUSIC
1726 Locust St., 215/893-5252, www.curtis.edu
Map 3

One of the most prestigious music conservatories in the world occupies a prestigious spot in the heart of Rittenhouse Square. While its foremost goal is teaching gifted students classical music, its founder has always believed in the philosophy of learning by doing. Lucky for us, the institute offers more than 100 public performances a year, including orchestra, operas, and solo and chamber music recitals. While some performances are held at other nearby theaters, others are held on-site at Field Concert Hall. Prices vary greatly, and many student recitals or practices are free to the public. They are generally held on Monday, Wednesday and Friday at 8 P.M., but call the student hotline at 215/893-5261 to double check.

◖ KIMMEL CENTER
260 S. Broad St., 215/790-5800,
www.kimmelcenter.org
Map 2

After a decade of planning, fundraising,

PHOTO BY G. WIDMAN FOR GPTMC

Kimmel Center on the Avenue of the Arts

litigating, and building, the Kimmel Center opened its doors in 2001, providing the city with a venue that deserves that bold label: world-class. Architect Rafael Viñoly and acoustics company Artec Consultants combined efforts in creating the magnificent crowning jewel of the Avenue of the Arts. With two posh theaters, imported exotic wood finishes, and a soaring vaulted glass ceiling rising 150 feet above the lobby, the Kimmel is truly breathtaking. Its resident companies include the renowned Philadelphia Orchestra, Opera Company of Philadelphia, and Pennsylvania Ballet, but it's much more than just a venue for ladies who lunch. It also programs international musicians, local dance company PhilaDanco, all-night rock shows, and a variety of free shows. Performances are held in the innovatively designed music halls, offering incredible acoustics and aesthetics. The expansive Verizon Hall seats over 2,500 on red-velvet chairs, and the more intimate Perelman Theater holds 650. Before or after a performance, you can stroll through the Dorrance H. Hamilton Roof Garden to enjoy the great views. Or take a free tour, offered on a first-come, first-served basis daily except Monday, beginning at the information desk in Commonwealth Plaza at noon, 1 P.M., and 2 P.M.

MANN CENTER FOR THE PERFORMING ARTS
5201 Parkside St., 215/546-7900,
www.manncenter.org
Map 8

Located in leafy Fairmount Park, the Mann Center provides a large open-air venue for a diverse range of performances. Originally a summer home for the Philadelphia Orchestra, today the Mann hosts instrumental music, jazz, opera, pop, dance, drumming, and ballet. It has hosted many of the biggest-name pop and rock musicians, though many now perform at the larger Susquehana Bank Center in Camden instead. It holds up to 4,000 under the pavilion and up to 10,000 on the lawn and terrace.

WACHOVIA CENTER

3601 S. Broad St., 215/336-3600,
www.comcastspectacor.com

Map 10

Philly provides venues aplenty for all kinds of spectator activities, but for major music acts, professional basketball and hockey, and the 2000 Republican National Convention, only the Wachovia Center will do. The state-of-the-art indoor arena began as the Corestates Center, then became the First Union Center (or locally, the FU Center), until Wachovia acquired naming rights. It has a capacity topping 20,000 and hosts the Philadelphia Fliers, 76ers, Wings, and Soul. Big stars who have performed in the space include Billy Joel, Madonna, Ray Charles, KISS, and just about everyone else.

CINEMA
THE BRIDGE: CINEMA DE LUX

40th & Walnut Sts., 215/386-3300,
www.thebridgecinema.com

Map 6

The year 2002 was a great one for moviegoers in Philly, because The Bridge: Cinema de Lux opened its doors in University City. No longer did we have to brave the sticky floors and stinky bathrooms of the Riverview on Columbus Boulevard or drive out to a megamall in the suburbs or, heaven forbid, Cherry Hill, New Jersey, to see a first-run blockbuster. The clean, spacious Bridge offers plush stadium seating, a specialty coffee bar, and a lounge where you can grab a salad, sandwich, pizza, or even a martini before the screening. Conveniently located near plenty of dining options, it's ideal for a dinner-and-a-movie date. It's good that movies require silence, because, frankly, we're speechless.

INTERNATIONAL HOUSE

3701 Chestnut St., 215/387-5125, www.ihousephilly.org

Map 6

Possibly the strangest and coolest dorm ever, International House of Philadelphia is home to over 400 international students studying at area colleges and universities. It's also a nexus of cultural and artistic programming for University City and Philly as a whole. Given its mission, I-House focuses on world culture, and offers an extensive and jaw-droppingly diverse series of film screenings, art shows, installations, live music, food festivals, dance performances, speakers, and more. The auditorium has a large projection screen, and while not quite up to par with a typical movie theater as far as quality, the place is much cooler than anything typical.

(RITZ THEATRES

Ritz 5 (214 Walnut St.), Ritz at the Bourse (400 Ranstead St.), and Ritz East (125 S. 2nd St.), 215/925-7900, www.ritztheatres.com

Map 1

When Philadelphians want to see movies that don't feature explosions, dude-hit-in-the-balls gags, or boobs (at least not American boobs), they usually head to one of the Ritz Theatres in Old City. A total of 12 screens are spread out over the three different Ritz theaters, all offering clean, enjoyable places to watch good films. Concessions include the standards—Jujubes and Raisinets—along with more upscale offerings that vary by theater but may include Toblerone and Lindt chocolates, yogurt-covered pretzels, coffee, and tea. The art-house chain was recently acquired by Landmark Theaters, but will keep the Ritz name as well as its mix of independent, international, and all-around good artsy-fartsy programming. There is a parking lot at the Bourse and Ritz East, and you can have your ticket validated for a reduced rate at any of the theaters.

UNITED ARTISTS RIVERVIEW STADIUM 17

1400 S. Columbus Blvd., 215/755-2353

Map 5

You can count on the Riverview to run all the top blockbusters in this large, adequate, but unremarkable and sometimes not entirely well-kempt megaplex. You certainly won't be getting the Ritz experience here, but if you need to catch the latest natural disaster summer blockbuster and it isn't playing at the Bridge, this is your place.

ARTS AND LEISURE

Festivals and Events

Philly has many festivals throughout the year, especially during the spring and summer. There are also events during the holidays, which are typically celebrated with a parade and/or fireworks. The winter holiday is kicked off with a Thanksgiving Day parade, and soon after, signs of Christmas light up Center City. The last hurrah of the year is the New Year's Eve fireworks display. There are often cultural celebrations in honor of Chinese New Year and Black History Month, as well as a St. Patrick's Day parade. Here is a sampling of some of the best and biggest annual events; be sure to visit www.gophila .com/Phila/EventsCalendar, www.phillyfunguide.org, and the festivals' websites for more comprehensive listings and exact dates.

WINTER
WING BOWL
Wachovia Center, 800/298-4200, www.610wip.com
Map 10

Fans of chicken wings, drinking, and scantily clad women will find their own strange heaven at this popular event. The Wing Bowl was founded by AM radio staple WIP 610 as a promotion to compensate for the Philadelphia Eagles' losing ways. The city needed something to get excited about since the team kept losing, and somehow the Wing Bowl has partially lived up to that strange expectation, garnering much local fanaticism in its own right. Traditionally held the Friday before the Super Bowl at the Wachovia Center, crowds form outside well before dawn, enjoying beer and wings for breakfast. Over 150 contestants compete in the wing-eating contest and more than 20,000 attend to watch the intensely competitive gorge-fest. Tickets are required and the event often sells out within 24 hours.

SPRING
DAD VAIL REGATTA
Schuylkill River along Kelly Dr., 215/542-1443, www.dadvail.org
Map 8

Over 100 universities from North America participate in this rowing classic on the Schuylkill. The Dad Vail Regatta, one of the nation's most historic student athletic events, brings thousands of students and families to Philadelphia each year. The weekend of activities begins in early May, and hordes of locals and visitors come out to be part of the festivities. The 6,000-foot race winds along the Schuylkill River; the best seats are at the Grand Stand finish line, along Kelly Drive beyond Boathouse Row coming from the Art Museum. The packed bleachers afford a great view, and the atmosphere is bustling with cheering onlookers.

EQUALITY FORUM
Various locations in the Gayborhood, 215/732-3378, www.equalityforum.org

It's fitting that Equality Forum, which bills itself as the country's largest gay-lesbian-bisexual-transgendered civil rights organization, hails from the city where American democracy began. The group, which began as the weekend-long PrideFest Philadelphia in 1993, hosts a full week of programs, panels, colloquies, screenings, and social events every April. It is capped off by SundayOUT, which is certainly Philly's, but also one of the country's, largest and most fabulous gay pride events. During its off-season, the Equality Forum organization keeps busy by producing gay-themed documentaries, advocating for same-sex marriage, and lobbying Fortune 500 corporations for non-discrimination policies and domestic-partner benefits.

ITALIAN MARKET FESTIVAL
9th St. btwn. Fitzwater and Federal Sts., www.9thstreetitalianmarketfestival.com
Map 5

The Italian Market feels a bit like a festival on most Saturday afternoons, but one weekend each May, it closes to car traffic and an all-out party ensues. As if the market wasn't tempting enough on a regular day with its delicious smells and tastes, vendors set up shop outside their businesses with prepared foods that are simply irresistible. Stroll while you eat and sample goodies along the way, and don't miss the stage featuring live music and chef demonstrations.

JAM ON THE RIVER

The Great Plaza at Penn's Landing, Columbus Blvd. btwn. Chestnut and Walnut Sts., 215/922-2386, www.jamontheriver.com

Map 1

Memorial Day weekend kicks off with Jam on the River at Penn's Landing. For more than 20 years, the festival has hosted musical acts in genres including rock, blues, soul, jazz, and pop. The festival started as a Louisiana-themed event but has expanded to encompass a diverse weekend with all kinds of great music and food.

PENN RELAYS

235 S. 33rd St., Franklin Field, 215/898-6145, www.thepennrelays.com

Map 6

Penn Relays dates back more than 100 years, making it the oldest recognized relay meet in the world. Each year in late April, massive crowds come to the University of Pennsylvania's Franklin Field to watch the world's top track athletes compete. The highlight and most popular event is usually the USA vs. World races on Saturday. In addition to the action on the field, there is a carnival atmosphere around the entire campus with food, crafts, and entertainment.

PHILADELPHIA FILM FESTIVALS

Various theaters, 267/765-9700, www.phillyfests.com

If you see a lot of bleary eyes in Center City in March or July, it's not because a new after-hours club just opened. Movie lovers have probably been taking advantage of the **Philadelphia Film Festival** or its midsummer sibling, the **Philadelphia International Gay and Lesbian Film Festival.** Programmed by TLA Entertainment Group and its independent nonprofit Philadelphia Film Society, both fests are huge affairs with hundreds of screenings across multiple venues, guest stars, VIP meet-and-greets, and of course, loads of parties and events. In case of back-to-back screenings, don't forget the Visine.

RITTENHOUSE ROW FESTIVAL

Walnut St. btwn. Broad and 19th Sts.

Map 3

Center City celebrates spring in style by bringing together this affluent neighborhood's best cuisine and shops to kick off springtime. The first Saturday of May is reserved rain-or-shine for the festivities. Vendors set up in and around Rittenhouse Square and several blocks of Walnut Street, which is closed to car traffic. Enjoy samples of five-star dining at great prices in front of the restaurants along with other special offers from many local businesses. There is music and people galore, and when the weather is nice, the event is that much better.

SUBARU CHERRY BLOSSOM FESTIVAL

Various locations, 215/790-3810, www.jasgp.org/sakura

Map 8

Named for *sakura,* the pretty pink cherry blossoms that come out in spring and hold deep significance in Japanese culture, this two-week festival celebrates Japanese culture and welcomes spring. Watch Taiko drumming or martial arts demonstrations, learn to make origami or sushi, or take part in a traditional tea ceremony. Sakura Sunday is the highlight, with a festival at the Japanese House and Gardens in Fairmount Park. Even if you miss the organized events, be sure to take a moment to take in the cherry blossoms throughout the city and especially in Fairmount Park.

SUMMER
CONCERTS IN THE PARK

Rittenhouse Square, 18th and Walnut Sts., www.philadelphiaweekly.com

Map 3

On a series of Wednesdays from 7 to 9 P.M., usually during the month of August,

ARTS AND LEISURE

Philadelphia Weekly sponsors concerts in Rittenhouse Square. Everyone comes out with blankets, food, and drinks to sit on the grass and listen to live music. The acts are varied and generally good, but often take second stage to the socializing happening around them.

ODUNDE AFRICAN AMERICAN STREET FESTIVAL

23rd and South Sts., 215/732-8510,
www.odundeinc.org

Map 3

The Odunde Street Festival takes place the second weekend in June in one of Philadelphia's oldest, historically African American neighborhoods just south of Center City. In existence for more than 30 years, it has become a three-day event filled with festivities and cultural events, culminating with a large street festival on Sunday. The festival day kicks off with a procession to the nearby Schuylkill River for prayers and blessings and returns to 23rd and South Streets for traditional African music, food, and crafts. Around the same time, mid-June, there are often other events throughout the city in honor of Juneteenth, the holiday which celebrates the official end to slavery. Visit www.pennsylvaniajuneteenth.com to find out what else is happening.

PRO CYCLING TOUR

Kelly Dr. and other locations,
www.procyclingtour.com

Known locally as the Bike Race, one of the biggest sporting events in the United States is, for most Philadelphians, just another excuse to party. On a Saturday in June, cyclists complete 10 laps of a scenic 14.4-mile circuit, passing over the Benjamin Franklin Parkway, Kelly Drive, through Fairmount Park, and up the infamously steep Manayunk Wall. Watch from the Benjamin Franklin Parkway, the steps of the Philadelphia Museum of Art, or head to Main Street in Manayunk or near the Manayunk Wall. Many neighborhood households along the route hold parties on their front porches to cheer the athletes on and drink the day away.

SUNOCO WELCOME AMERICA FESTIVAL

Various locations,
www.americasbirthday.com

It's fitting that Independence Day is a huge deal in the city where it all began. You might wonder why a petroleum company has its name on this summer festival, and the answer is quite simple: The people behind the Philly-headquartered megacorp paid millions for naming rights so they can pour gas all over the fires of patriotism, pump up tourist spending, and fuel a sense of city-wide camaraderie—and it actually works quite well. The week is filled with fun, family-friendly concerts, museum events, outdoor screenings, street festivals, fireworks, and a big parade and concert on the Parkway, which has recently featured Hall and Oates, Elton John, and other somewhat-faded but still-entertaining stars. While some locals try to escape the mayhem and the heat by heading to the Jersey shore, others embrace the revelry and join the throngs of tourists in the action.

FALL

◖ PHILADELPHIA LIVE ARTS FESTIVAL AND PHILLY FRINGE

Various locations, 215/413-1318,
www.livearts-fringe.org

Unnecessarily confusing name aside, there's a lot to love about the Philadelphia Live Arts Festival and Philly Fringe. The early fall extravaganza is a tribute to theater, dance, music, spoken word, and other arts and performance mediums. The Live Arts part is developed by festival organizers, bringing the best performers from around the world to Philly. However, it's the Fringe part that gets really wild, since anyone with a venue and a dream can include their show in the program. And yes, "venue" occasionally means the sidewalk. It's a thrilling and unpredictable artistic ride and the no-cover fringe cabaret promises good times, and often hungover mornings, for all involved.

PHOTO BY R. KENNEDY FOR GPTMC

a breakdancer at an outdoor stage at Philly Fringe

TERROR BEHIND THE WALLS AT EASTERN STATE PENITENTIARY

2124 Fairmount Ave., 215/236-5111, www.easternstate.org/halloween

COST: $20

Map 4

The place is creepy enough on a regular tour, but every October, the former prison hosts Philadelphia's most frightening tradition. Terror Behind the Walls is Eastern State Penitentiary's haunted-house tour, where guests walk through long, shadowy corridors and past dark, seemingly empty cells. Enhanced by realistic cosmetics and incredible acting, deformed and decaying monsters are everywhere and eager to greet you. Tours begin at 7 P.M. every night and continue every 30 minutes. Be warned: There is often a line around the block to get into this popular event. Ask about the more subdued "Family Night," which offers a somewhat less terrifying alternative for the easily frightened and younger crowds.

Recreation

Most of the city's recreational opportunities take place in Fairmount Park. In addition to the large areas of the park that straddle the Schuylkill River—East and West Parks—it also encompasses 63 distinct neighborhood parks and gardens, including hundreds of miles of hiking, biking, and jogging trails, including the popular Schuylkill River Bike Path. Those in search of less-trafficked areas head to the Wissahickon in the northwest section of the city or to one of the many nearby suburban parks and nature reserves. Beyond the endless recreational opportunities on land, Philadelphia's two major rivers—the Delaware and Schuylkill—offer water enthusiasts a place to enjoy kayaking, rowing, boating, and water tours. Visit www.phila.gov/recreation for more information about public recreation indoors and out.

PARKS AND GARDENS

The majority of Philadelphia's parks and gardens are maintained by the Fairmount Park system even if they are not physically connected to the major areas of East and West Parks. You're never very far from a park bench to sit and take a break and read your newspaper (or Moon guidebook) anywhere in Philadelphia. Several impressive arboretums, children's playgrounds, and historic gardens can also be found.

BARTRAM'S GARDEN

54th St. and Lindbergh Blvd., 215/729-5281, www.bartramsgarden.org

HOURS: Garden: daily 10 A.M.–5 P.M., Museum Shop and House Tours: daily except Mon. noon–4 P.M. Mar.–mid-Dec.

ARTS AND LEISURE

COST: Gardens free, tours of house and gardens $5 adult, $4 senior and student, free child under 12

Map 10

The nation's earliest botanical garden is alive and well in southwest Philadelphia. Founded in 1728 by John Bartram, a devout Quaker, the gardens and the adjacent Bartram family home are both National Historic Landmarks. The 44-acre area straddling the Schuylkill River features native plants and flower gardens, ancient trees, a water garden and a river trail. The oldest gingko tree in the country and the *Franklinia alatamaha,* a tree named for John Bartram's friend Benjamin Franklin, are just two of the notable flora found here. Explore the garden for free on your own or pay for a 45-minute guided tour of the home and garden. History, science, and nature programs are also often offered. The Schuylkill Banks River Tours offer scenic guided boat tours from the Schuylkill River Bike Path to the garden.

CLARK PARK

4400 Baltimore Ave., 215/555-8186,
www.clarkpark.info

Map 6

Established in 1895, this nine-acre park in West Philadelphia is a treasured community asset for students, families, and community members. The park is home to the Gettysburg Stone, a Civil War battlefield monolith, and a life-size bronze statue of Charles Dickens and Little Nell of his novel *The Old Curiosity Shop*; a literary celebration is held in the park each February to honor Dickens's birthday. There are plenty of places to sit and relax in the bench-lined park on any given day, but a host of events and concerts bring people in hordes. They come for fresh, affordable, produce at the **farmers market** held Saturday 10 A.M.–2 P.M. from May until Thanksgiving and Thursday 3–7 P.M. from June–Thanksgiving, and on Saturday 10 A.M.–1 P.M. the rest of the year. There is also a monthly **Clark Park People's Flea Market** on select Saturdays, offering food, antiques, and crafts at great prices (call 215/387-0919 for dates).

JAPANESE HOUSE AND GARDENS (SHOFUSO)

N. Horticultural and Montgomery Aves., 215/878-5097, www.shofuso.com

HOURS: Tues.-Fri. 10 A.M.-4 P.M., Sat.-Sun. 11 A.M.-5 P.M. May-Oct.

COST: $5 adult, $3 student and senior

Map 8

In 1876, the Japanese Bazaar and Garden came to the area for the Centennial Exposition, and while the site has changed shape several times, there has been some form of Japanese landscaping here ever since. Today, it offers a glimpse into the home and gardens of a 17th-century Japanese scholar. Originally designed by Yoshimura Junzoo and built in 1953 in Nagoya, Japan, the house was reassembled at the current site in 1958. Enjoy the tranquil setting, take part in a traditional tea ceremony, and learn about the structure and culture of an authentic Japanese *shofuso*.

◖ MORRIS ARBORETUM

100 E. Northwestern Ave., 215/247-5777,
www.upenn.edu/arboretum

HOURS: Mon.-Fri. 10 A.M.-4 P.M., Sat.-Sun. 10 A.M.-5 P.M. Apr.-Oct., Thurs. in summer until 8:30 P.M., Daily 10 A.M.-4 P.M. Nov.-Mar.

COST: $10 adult, $8 senior, $5 child 3-18 years, free child under 3 and member

Map 9

In the late 1800s this was home to "Compton," the summer estate of the Morrises. They built a lovely garden and plant and sculpture collection and made plans to add a school and laboratory of horticulture and botany. This dream was ultimately realized in 1932 when the University of Pennsylvania purchased it and transformed the Morris Arboretum into an interdisciplinary resource center. It is now the official arboretum of the Commonwealth of Pennsylvania and is listed on the National Register of Historic Places. Stroll through the 92-acre Victorian landscape and take in the sights and scents of the beautifully landscaped gardens, streams, and sculptures. A summer concert series features mostly jazz and classical music and an on-site café serves food.

PHILADELPHIA HORTICULTURE CENTER

100 N. Horticultural Dr. (near Belmont and Montgomery Dr.), 215/685-0096, www.fairmountpark.org/HortCenter.asp

HOURS: Display House: daily 9 A.M.-3 P.M. except holidays, Grounds: daily 9 A.M.-5 P.M. Oct.-June, 9 A.M.-6 P.M. July-Sept.

COST: Free

Map 8

Fairmount Park's Horticulture Center includes an arboretum that dates to 1876, an expansive greenhouse that was built for the bicentennial celebration in 1976, and more than 20 acres of lush landscape. Paths wind through gardens, also home to a butterfly garden, a large reflecting pool, and various sculptures of poets, musicians, and animals. The inside display area contains colorful tropical plants, flowers, perennials, herbs, everlastings, and rare trees. Picnic areas are available on the grounds.

RITTENHOUSE SQUARE

Btwn. 18th and 19th Sts. and Walnut and Locust Sts.

Map 3

When the weather is nice, it can be difficult to find a bench during lunchtime in Rittenhouse Square. Despite the crowds that fill the pretty tree-lined park in the swankiest part of town, it remains a peaceful respite from the bustle of the city. A convenient break from the skyscrapers and upscale shops just outside, the square is filled with suits on lunch break, families, dogs, artists, and musicians. Rittenhouse was called Southwest Square until 1825 when it was renamed for famous Philadelphia astronomer and clockmaker David Rittenhouse (1732–1796), descendant of William Rittenhouse of paper-mill fame. Architect Paul Cret, also responsible for the Benjamin Franklin Parkway and many of its buildings, designed the entrances, the central plaza, stone railings, the pool, and the fountain in 1913. If you can't snag a bench, there is always space to sit along the walls surrounding the center fountain—great for people-watching.

ROSE GARDEN AND MAGNOLIA GARDEN

Locust St. btwn. 4th and 5th Sts.

Map 1

While touring the sights of Old City and Society Hill, take a minute to stop and smell the roses. A cobblestone path leads through the Rose Garden, a tribute to the signers of the Declaration of Independence and the Constitution. The buds reach their peak in June. It was planted by the Daughters of the American Revolution, a volunteer women's service organization dedicated to promoting patriotism and preserving American history. Just across the street, the smaller Magnolia Garden was built in honor of George Washington, who apparently loved the magnolia tree. The 13 magnolia trees bordering the garden represent the 13 original colonies.

SMITH MEMORIAL PLAYGROUND AND PLAYHOUSE

33rd and Oxford Sts., East Fairmount Park, 215/765-4325, www.smithplayhouse.org

HOURS: Playground: Tues.-Sun. 10 A.M.-4 P.M. Apr.-June and Sept.-Oct., daily 10 A.M.-7 P.M. second Tues. in June-Aug.; Playhouse: 10 A.M.-4 P.M. Tues.-Sun. year-round

Map 8

The historic building and grounds were opened in 1899 by Richard Smith, a wealthy Philadelphian who made his fortune in the typesetting business. He and his wife Sarah lived in North Philadelphia and wanted to create a safe, free place for children to play, and that's what it still is today, more than a century later. The highlight is the giant enclosed wooden slide. Built in 1905, it is large enough to accommodate about 10 kids across at one time. But there is plenty for kids to play with both outside and inside the unique toy-filled playhouse. Open only to supervised children 10 years and younger, Smith Playground is a popular spot for kids' birthday parties.

WASHINGTON SQUARE PARK

Btwn. Walnut and Locust Sts. and 6th and 7th Sts.

Map 1

A quieter counterpart to Rittenhouse Square,

ARTS AND LEISURE

Washington Square serves a similar purpose for the Old City, Society Hill, and Washington Square West neighborhoods it borders. People stop to eat, read, or take a break from it all in the leafy respite. Originally called Southeast Square in 1682, it was renamed as a tribute to George Washington in 1825. Used as a burial ground for troops during the Revolutionary War and for victims of the yellow fever epidemics that followed, it wasn't until the surrounding neighborhoods developed that the square transformed into its current shape. In 1952, a major renovation included the creation of a monument to the soldiers and sailors of the Revolutionary War. Designed by architect G. Edwin Brumbaugh, the Tomb of the Unknown Soldier occupies an area near the center, memorializing the bodies buried below with a constant flame burning at the site.

HIKING, BIKING, AND JOGGING TRAILS

With more than 215 miles of scenic trails winding through Fairmount Park, there is a place for everyone to jog, hike, blade, bike, or ride horses. Paths range from paved to rocky terrain, flat to steep, and crowded to desolate. Some trails are only open to hikers or bikers, so be aware of the markers. You can also grab a map of Fairmount Park at the visitors center or visit www.fairmountpark.org/trailsintro.asp for more information. Valley Forge, Fort Washington, and Ridley Creek offer additional trails just outside the city.

PENNYPACK PARK
8500 Pine Rd., 215/685-0470,
www.fairmountpark.org/pennypackpark.asp
Map 10

This 1,300-acre portion of Fairmount Park in Northeast Philadelphia may be the least utilized area of the park, but restoration projects over the past decade are finally bringing it to the attention of residents and visitors. Pennypack, named after the Lenni Lenape Indian word for slow-moving water, follows Pennypack Creek southeast for nine miles

from Montgomery County to the Delaware River. Miles of paved and unpaved trails offer hikers, bikers, and horseback riders a variety of paths for recreation. Visit www .pennypackpark.com for a schedule of the free summer concert series, which features mostly tributes to big-name entertainers like the Beatles and Elvis. The on-site Pennypack Environmental Center offers programs at nearby Fox Chase Farm, a city-owned 112-acre working livestock farm.

RIDLEY CREEK STATE PARK
1023 Sycamore Mills Rd., Media, 610/892-3900,
www.friendsofrcsp.org
Map 10

Just 16 miles from Center City Philadelphia, Ridley Creek State Park offers more than 2,600 acres of woodlands and meadows, along with several seasonal attractions. There are 12 miles of biking and hiking trails, along with fishing, horseback riding, camping, cross-country skiing, and tobogganing, and the park is open for archery deer hunting in season. A National Historic Landmark, it is also home to the **Colonial Pennsylvania Plantation** (610/566-1725), a 300-year-old farming mainstay and small re-created 18th-century village where interpreters in period costume bake bread, mend fences, and card wool. The village, open on weekends April–November, aims to re-create the lives of members of the Pratt family who lived on the Quaker plantation for three generations as early as 1710.

◖ SCHUYLKILL RIVER TRAIL
Access along both sides of the Schuylkill River,
including behind the Art Museum, 484/945-0200,
www.schuylkillriver.org
Map 8

The area's most popular trail is 25 miles long and follows the Schuylkill River from Center City all the way to Oaks in Montgomery County, and connects with Valley Forge, which has additional trails. Whether you want a short ride or an all-day outing, there is a section of this trial to suit most needs. It is mostly flat, and practically all of it is

PHOTO BY EDWARD SAVARIA JR. FOR PCVB

A spring day brings joggers, rowers, and bladers to the Schuylkill River and adjacent trail.

paved. It consists of several Fairmount Park trails and the Manayunk Canal Tow Path, so terrain varies somewhat along the way, but is constantly improving and expanding to connect an even greater area. The trail can be accessed in Center City via stairs or ramps on Market, Chestnut, or Walnut Streets, or on the street level on Locust Street or just behind the Art Museum. The busiest portion is the River Drive Recreational Loop, commonly referred to as just "the loop." This 8.4-mile paved stretch begins and ends near the Art Museum, winds around both sides of the river, and crosses the East Falls Bridge. Exercise caution when walking or riding here, especially with children or on weekends, as it gets very crowded on nice days. There are a few vendors selling water, soft pretzels, water ice, and candy nearby when the weather is pleasant. **Lloyd Hall** (1 Boathouse Row, 215/695-3936) has a café, bathrooms, and a rental facility for bicycles and inline skates. On sunny weekends, unofficial but entertaining disco roller-skating exhibitions take place out front.

◖ WISSAHICKON PARK

Main entrance to Forbidden Drive: Valley Green Rd. at Wissahickon; Friends of the Wissahickon located at 8708 Germantown Ave., 215/247-0417, www.fow.org
Map 9

Those seeking an escape will be thrilled to learn that dense forests, lush greens, and a gentle creek exist within the city limits. The part of Fairmount Park that occupies the northwest section of Philadelphia is known as "the Wissahickon." It surrounds Wissahickon Creek, which runs along the length of its seven miles. There are around 57 miles of trails snaking through the park and the Wissahickon Gorge, crossing bridges, climbing high ridges, and offering ample views. Some are rugged and hilly and others are flat with gravel. The Friends of the Wissahickon publishes a detailed map for $6, available at FOW office and several other locations listed on their website. It includes roads, trails, buildings, bridges, dams, and statues, and is well worth it for anyone looking for an in-depth exploration of the park. Easy access and parking can be found near

ARTS AND LEISURE

PHOTO BY R. KENNEDY FOR GPTMC

The Wissahickon is a large part of Fairmount Park in Northwest Philadelphia.

Forbidden Drive, the 11-mile well-traversed gravel stretch. There are no restrooms along the trails, so be sure to use the public restrooms at the entrance near the Valley Green Inn restaurant and parking area. There are multiple entry points throughout the neighborhoods of Mt. Airy, Roxborough, and Chestnut Hill.

BIKE RENTALS AND REPAIRS

Bicycling is an excellent way to see the city, eliminating the worry about pesky parking, traffic, or waiting for public transportation. Since Philadelphia is mostly flat, especially Center City, it's an easy bike ride. While somewhat limited, there is an increasing network of bike-friendly streets with wide bike-only lanes. A map of bike routes can be found at the Independence Visitor Center or at www.phila.gov/streets; for your safety and comfort, use these routes whenever possible. The bike rental shops that follow are all conveniently located on or near the Schuylkill River Bike Path. **The Bicycle Club of Philadelphia** (www.phillybikeclub.org) is also a great resource for bike enthusiasts. Founded in 1979, the club sponsors recreational cycling activities open to the public for a small fee and promotes bicyclists' rights and safe biking practices.

DRIVE SPORTS 2

1 Boathouse Row (hut next to Lloyd Hall), 215/232-7900
Map 8

You can rent hybrid and mountain bikes, child carriers, and inline skates from a hut on Kelly Drive. It is located behind the Art Museum near Lloyd Hall, the first large building at the start of Boathouse Row. Hours are somewhat limited, but it is always open on weekends in summer. It's wise to call ahead at all other times. You can't beat it for convenience if you're staying in Center City and looking to get out on the Schuylkill River Bike Path.

HUMAN ZOOM

4151 Main St., Manayunk, 215/487-7433,
www.humanzoom.com
HOURS: Mon.-Thurs. 11 A.M.-7 P.M., Fri. 11 A.M.-8 P.M.,
Sat. 10 A.M.-6 P.M., Sun. 11 A.M.-4 P.M., sometimes later
in summer

COST: Hybrids $8 per hour, $25 per 24 hours, $45 weekend (48 hours), $100 weekly; road bikes $40 for 24 hours

Map 9

A seller of top-quality bikes, Human Zoom also rents out bikes and is the only place in the city that offers road bikes in addition to hybrids. It's located close to the Schuylkill River Trail in the Manayunk neighborhood. A credit card and driver's license is required for rentals, and no reservations are accepted for hybrids. The store also offers free bike repair classes on select Mondays, but space is limited, so call ahead.

NEIGHBORHOOD BIKE WORKS

3916 Locust Walk (Penn campus btwn. Walnut and Locust Sts. near 40th St.), 215/386-0316
HOURS: Sun., Tues., and Thurs. 6:30-9 P.M.

Map 6

Neighborhood Bike Works is a bike co-op known locally as "the bike church." Located in the basement of the rear building of St. Mary's Church, visiting is literally and figuratively an underground experience. The gritty warehouse offers used and salvaged bike parts at a minimal price—normally ranging from just $1–10—and there is no service charge since you do the work yourself. The veteran volunteer bike mechanics that facilitate repairs are generally friendly, but often busy and understaffed. If you stick it out and have patience, they are always willing to help. They can even assist you in building a custom bike from scratch. Tools and some parts are provided.

PHILADELPHIA BIKE TOURS

Most tours begin behind the Atwater Kent Museum on Ranstead St. btwn. 7th and 6th Sts., 215/514-3124 or 866/667-3395, www.philadelphiabiketour.com

Map 1

Bikes ($36 half day, $57 full day) and mopeds ($69 half day, $87 full day) are available for rental and can even be delivered directly to your hotel. Or take a guided two-hour moped tour, three-hour bike tour, or customized tour of your choosing for a group of four or more. Tours stop at the Atwater Kent Museum,

Old Swedes Church, the Italian Market, Independence Square, the Edgar Allan Poe House, Water Works, and the Philadelphia Museum of Art, among other sites. The pace is relaxed, allowing time to stop and take in the attractions. Call 24 hours in advance to book tours and rentals. A valid ID and a credit card are required and minors must be accompanied by a parent or guardian. Tours are generally on weekends only, but weekday tours can sometimes be arranged with advance notice.

TROPHY BIKES

3131 Walnut St., 215/222-2020, www.trophybikes.com
HOURS: Store: daily 10 A.M.-6 P.M.; rentals Mar.-Oct.
COST: $20 for 4 hours, $25 for 24 hours

Map 6

First and foremost a bike store, Trophy Bikes also has affordable rentals including a selection of hybrids, one tandem, and one folding bike, available for full- and half-day rentals, with helmet, lock, and map included. You must be 18 or older and a major credit card is required. They don't take reservations, so bikes are rented on a first-come, first-served basis. They will, however, let you pick up a bike at the end of the day Friday for a Saturday rental at no extra charge—a good idea to ensure you snag one at busy times.

GUIDED TOURS

In addition to the many sightseeing tours of Independence National Historical Park listed in the *Sights* chapter, the following tours are available for those looking to get off the beaten path and explore other areas.

I-GLIDE TOURS AND RENTALS

Depart from Eakins Oval, 215/735-1700, www.iglidetours.com

Map 4

The latest and arguably the greatest way to tour the city is on a Segway, a two-wheeled, self-balancing electric scooter from I-Glide Tours. Tours start with a half-hour instructional period so you can get used to get the machine, but just in case, you also wear a helmet and a dorky bright-orange vest for safety.

Your guide will offer unique facts about Philadelphia as you ride through Fairmount Park, Boathouse Row, along the Benjamin Franklin Parkway, and elsewhere, depending on the length of your tour. Daytime tours are 2.5 hours long and evening tours are 1.5 hours. Participants must be 13 years old and weigh 100–285 pounds, and all minors must be accompanied by a parent or guardian. All tours begin at Eakins Oval across the street from the Philadelphia Museum of Art, and are offered daily at 10 A.M., 1:30 P.M., and 7 P.M.; cost is $49 for evening tours and $69 for daytime. Reservations are required.

PHILADELPHIA SOCIETY FOR THE PRESERVATION OF LANDMARKS

1616 Walnut St., 215/546-1146,
www.preservationalliance.com

These tours are popular with locals who are particularly interested in architecture and history. The mission of the Philadelphia Society for the Preservation of Landmarks is to promote the appreciation of Philadelphia's historic buildings, communities, and landscapes, so tours are just a small part of what they do. On a tour, you'll learn about the in-depth history and significance of the buildings and landmarks you visit from extremely knowledgeable guides. You'll often see off-the-beaten places that most visitors and many locals never see in and around Philadelphia. They hold special events and workshops, and many tours take place one time only, so check the website to see what is currently offered. Prices and times vary by tour.

POOR RICHARD'S WALKING TOURS

Various locations, 215/206-1682

Named for Ben Franklin's famous almanac, the majority of Poor Richard's Walking Tours are led by professional scholars, history teachers, and graduate students from the University of Pennsylvania. They range from general three-hour history tours to themed tours, including: human rights struggles in the city; Colonial Philadelphia, the 19th-Century City; Ethnic Philadelphia;

Chinatown to South Philadelphia; West Philadelphia: Past & Present; The University of Pennsylvania & Environs; and The Streetcar Suburb. With highly knowledgeable and insightful guides, these tours are far more educational than most. Customized tours are available for groups, and prices and times vary.

OTHER RECREATION
Bowling
LUCKY STRIKE LANES

1336 Chestnut St., 215/545-2471,
www.bowlluckystrike.com

HOURS: Sun.-Thurs. noon-midnight, Fri.-Sat. noon-2 A.M.

COST: $4.95 or $5.95 per game, depending on day and time, $3.95 shoe rental

Map 2

Lucky Strike Lanes is the Beverly Hills of bowling, bringing a slice of Los Angeles—where the swank chain originated—to Philadelphia. You'll pay a high price for the tasty cuisine, modern technology, and posh scene. The concept is based on the circa-1960 Hollywood Star Lanes, so there is a faux-vintage element to the decor. A strictly enforced dress code forbids sweats, jerseys, headgear, construction boots, sleeveless or "excessively baggy T-shirts," making Lucky Strikes the most exclusive—ok, only exclusive—alley in town. Lanes can get crowded on Friday and Saturday nights, but many come in just for the scene or to play pool. Lanes can be reserved by the hour for a maximum of two hours, for $45–65 per hour depending on day and time. No reservations accepted to pay per game. You must be 21 to enter after 8 P.M.

◀ NORTH BOWL

909 N. 2nd St., 215/238-2695,
www.northbowlphilly.com

HOURS: Mon.-Fri. 5 P.M.-2 A.M., Sat.-Sun. 11 A.M.-2 A.M.

COST: $4.95 before 9 P.M., $5.95 after, $3 shoe rental

Map 7

Housed in a former mechanics garage, North Bowl's 21,000 square feet of space spread over two floors is a popular pre- or post-

THE PAST AND FUTURE OF LOCAL SKATE CULTURE

Philly has long been a hot spot for skateboarding. For many years, skaters from New York, Boston, Los Angeles, and even overseas made the journey to Philadelphia's landmark **Love Park** (officially JFK Plaza). They came to thrash on its ramps, ledges, and stairs in a prime setting smack in the center of urban Philadelphia. Featured in practically every skate magazine there is and frequented by many pro and semi-pro skaters, Love Park was internationally recognized, and Philly was chosen to host the 2001–2002 ESPN X-Games as a result.

And then the city government stepped in and ruined everything. In response to damage complaints and other alleged nuisances, one of Philadelphia's major recreational assets and one of the things that made it so popular with youth came to an end. Despite many protests, the city closed Love Park to skaters in 2002 so that the suits on lunch breaks could eat in peace.

Since then, the skaters have been relegated to the only remaining large-scale skateboarding area in the city, **FDR Park.** Located on Pattison Avenue and Tuscany Drives at the park's south end, it's within walking (or rolling) distance to the Broad Street Subway Line. Philly's skate culture lives on in the shade of the raised highway, I-95, above. Fishbowls, ramps, innovative skate structures, and a 30-foot half pipe make this skate park perfectly nice, but the location leaves something to be desired. It's completely separate from the rest of the city, unlike prominent Love Park.

There is a (hopefully) happy ending to this story. Plans are underway for a brand-new, better-than-ever skate park in another outstanding location. The proposed **Paine's Park** has found a 2.5-acre home on a picturesque stretch along the Schuylkill River next to the Art Museum. The designs incorporate interesting skate-friendly surfaces with art and green space, in the hopes that it will attract the general public to share the space with the skateboarders. Momentum is building, funds are being raised, and the city is closer to having the world-class skate park that skaters have been waiting for since the loss of Love.

bar-hopping hangout in Northern Liberties. People come almost as much to hang out in the stylish yet comfortable setting, as they do for the lanes. The restaurant serves much better food than you'd expect at a bowling alley, and pool tables and games offer additional entertainment. Happy hour specials Monday–Friday 5–7 P.M. promise discounts and a lively after-work scene. There is often a wait for lanes on weekends, so call ahead to reserve, or snag a seat on one of the leather benches while you wait.

STRIKES BOWLING LOUNGE
4040 Locust St., 215/387-2695,
www.strikesbowlinglounge.com
HOURS: Mon.-Fri. 3 P.M.-2 A.M., Sat.-Sun. 10 A.M.-2 A.M.
Map 6

Strikes Bowling Lounge in University City offers bowling, billiards, and beverages to its mostly collegiate crowd. With a lively atmosphere on weekends and decent bar food to snack on between frames, it's easy to spend an entire night here. Lanes, food, and drinks can add up to a fat bill at the end of the night, but daily drink specials, happy hours, and lane discounts for students help keep prices in check.

Fitness Centers
There are plenty of local and international chain fitness clubs with multiple locations all over the city, including Bally's, Sweat, and Philadelphia Sports Club. There is an extensive network of YMCAs that differ in amenities and cost, but tend to be cheaper than private clubs. The two listed here are unique offerings in a sea of perfectly nice, if sometimes pricey, well-equipped and easy-to-find chain establishments.

ARTS AND LEISURE

RITTENHOUSE FITNESS CLUB

2002 Rittenhouse Sq., 215/985-4095,
www.ritfit.com

HOURS: Mon.-Thurs. 6 A.M.-10 P.M., Fri. 6 A.M.-8 P.M.,
Sat.-Sun. 9 A.M.-5 P.M.

COST: $449 year membership, $75 month, $10 day
pass, with discounts for students and couples joining
together

Map 3

Despite the ritzy association with the name "Rittenhouse," this no-frills health club is one of the best deals in town. It has all the standard equipment, but lacks most of the lavish amenities and high prices of other Center City gyms. Many members have been coming forever, so it's a place where everybody knows your name but no one is likely to hit on you while you exercise. All the standard classes are held, including yoga, pilates, aerobics, and spinning. If you get a chance, take a spinning class with Mario, where the jokes and conversation among his loyal following are as much a part of the experience as the sweaty workout.

12TH STREET GYM

204 S. 12th St., 215/985-4092,
www.12streetgym.com

HOURS: Mon.-Thurs. 5:30 A.M.-11 P.M., Fri.
5:30 A.M.-10 P.M., Sat. 8 A.M.-8 P.M., Sun. 8 A.M.-7 P.M.

Map 2

The 12th Street Gym is in the heart of the city's Gayborhood. The facility is one the largest in the city, with a 22-station strength training circuit, cardio machines galore, a roof deck, pool, sauna, juice bar, and full-size basketball and racquetball courts. More than 60 weekly group fitness classes include the old standbys like cardio, abs, and several varieties of yoga and pilates, as well as innovative concepts like the self-explanatory Broadway Dance Workshop and Zumba Dance Fitness, a Latin dance workout. Besides the ever-present gay population, 12th Street Gym's clientele also has plenty of patrons from all over the city. One of the better deals among the first-rate gyms with all the bells and whistles, there is a $99 start-up fee to join, but then you can pay $49 a month for a 12-month commitment or $59 a

month for a month-to-month pass. A one-day pass costs $20, or you can stay and use the gym for free after a tour if you're considering joining. Many members also frequent the **Soleil Tanning Center** next door; it's owned by the gym but you don't have to be a gym member to use it.

Frisbee

SEDGELEY WOODS DISC GOLF COURSE

East Park, 33rd and Oxford Sts.,
www.fairmountpark.org/discgolf.asp

Map 8

Established in 1977, the second-oldest disc golf course in the country occupies a lovely setting in East Fairmount Park. As its name implies, the sport is a combination of Frisbee (the only equipment used) and golf (the object is to hit specific targets in the least amount of attempts). The course and parking are free and open to the public. A doubles league is held every Thursday year-round and can get quite competitive. Considered a great course by disc golf aficionados, the woods provide many natural obstacles. It's BYOD: Bring your own discs.

Horseback Riding

Fairmount Park has excellent trails for equestrians from beginner to advanced levels. There is nowhere to rent a horse in Fairmount Park but there are a few places where you can take lessons, ride with a group, or board your horse.

CHAMOUNIX EQUESTRIAN CENTER

98 Chamounix Dr., 215/877-4199,
www.worktoride.net

Map 8

With 35 stalls and access to more than 1,300 acres of Fairmount Park trails, the Chamounix Equestrian Center offers group and individual lessons for children and adults at all levels April–November. Each year the center holds a polo program and summer camp. Work to Ride, Inc., the nonprofit dedicated to teaching disadvantaged children equine sports and horsemanship, also runs programs out of the Chamounix Equestrian Center.

NORTHWESTERN STABLES

120 Northwestern Ave., 215/242-8892,
www.nwefonline.org

Map 9

Surrounded by open fields at the north end of Wissahickon Creek's Forbidden Drive in Fairmount Park, Northwestern Stables provide a sophisticated horseback riding experience that brings English-style riding to Philadelphia. The experienced staff leads a summer camp for young riders and a schooling show that specializes in flat riding and jumps. A six-week riding lesson costs $250 and sessions are held throughout the year except when summer camp is in session.

Ice Skating
BLUE CROSS RIVER RINK
AT PENN'S LANDING

Market St. and Columbus Blvd., 215/925-7465,
www.riverrink.com

HOURS: Mon.-Thurs. 6-9 P.M., Fri. 6 P.M.-1 A.M., Sat. 12:30 P.M.-1 A.M., Sun. 9:30 A.M.-9 P.M. Nov.-Feb.

COST: $6 admission, $3 rental

Map 1

When the temperature drops, the city becomes a scenic backdrop for skaters gliding on ice at the Blue Cross River Rink. Alongside the Delaware River at Penn's Landing, the River Rink is a nice way to start a winter day with kids or spend an evening with a romantic date. Holiday parties, New Year's Eve countdowns, and St. Valentine's soirees are just a few of the special events that take place throughout the season. The River Rink also offers rentals, lessons, games, activities, and group packages.

UNIVERSITY OF
PENNSYLVANIA ARENA

3130 Walnut St., 215/898-1923,
www.business-services.upenn.edu/icerink

HOURS: Mon., Wed., and Fri. 11:30 A.M.-1 P.M. Sept.-Mar.

COST: $9

Map 6

An impressive donation by the University of Pennsylvania's Class of 1923 funded this facility. Built in 1972, it is located in University City just across the Walnut Street bridge from Center City and is frequented by Penn students. Home to collegiate events for more than 30 years, ice hockey, figure skating, and speed games are common practice at the rink. The arena boasts 18,000 square feet of skating surface, six locker rooms, and 2,900 seats, and is open to the public for skating when other events are not taking place.

WISSAHICKON ICE SKATING RINK

550 W. Willow Grove Ave., 215/247-1759,
www.wissskating.com

COST: $6 admission, $3 rental

Map 9

Chestnut Hill's indoor year-round ice rink is popular with families, and with pre-teens looking for a fun night out on a weekend. Also home to youth and adult hockey leagues, skating lessons, figure skating, and a pro-skating club, many people on the ice are members, but the general public is also welcome. Session times vary by season, but the rink is open Friday and Saturday evenings year-round.

Water Activities
PA ROWING CAMPS

East Park Canoe Club on Kelly Dr., 267/971-9073,
www.parowing.com

COST: $250 basic sessions, $595 competitive sessions

Map 8

The Schuylkill River is one of the nation's most popular rivers for rowing—which also happens to be a very expensive and exclusive sport. Paul Coomes and Amy Giddings opened PA Rowing Camps in 2000 to provide a (somewhat) more affordable experience. PA Rowing Camps teaches youths and adults rowing techniques, and a series of four classes (held during summertime) begin at $250. Courses cater to all different ages and skill levels. If you can't afford or aren't up for rowing yourself, you can still hang out by Boathouse Row and watch the collegiate and professional rowers glide by.

PHILADELPHIA CITY SAIL

Penn's Landing, 215/413-0451, www.citysail.org

Map 1

Through sailing and maritime education, this

ARTS AND LEISURE

PHOTO BY EDWARD SAVARIA JR. FOR PCVB

rowers on the Schuylkill River

nonprofit aims to teach children the value of the environment, science, mathematics, and maritime arts. For adults, Philadelphia City Sail provides excitement as well, with public sails, chartered trips, and special events on the Delaware River aboard the *North Wind*, Philadelphia City Sail's 75-foot schooner.

SCHUYLKILL BANKS RIVER TOURS

Schuylkill Riverfront at Walnut St., 215/222-6030 or 888/748-7445, www.schuylkillbanks.org

Map 3

You can choose between three different seasonal tours on the RiverLoop that glide you along the Schuylkill River. One offers a general tour of the River; another will take you to Bartram's Garden where you'll have time to get off and explore; and another offers the chance to hear jazz music while cruising. Kayak tours are also available, departing from the same spot, offering trips to the Fairmount Water Works in one direction or to Bartram's Garden in the other. A certified instructor offers brief lessons before the tour, and trips require participants to be

moderately fit, but you don't need to have kayaking experience. Participants must be at least 8 years old; anyone under 14 needs to be accompanied by a guardian, and anyone under 18 needs parental permission.

Yoga and Meditation
DHYANA YOGA STUDIO

1737 Chestnut St., 2nd fl., 215/496-0770, www.dhyana-yoga.com

Map 3

This lovely little studio is a bright and airy oasis in the middle of metropolitan Philadelphia. Hardwood floors, two full walls of windows, and a few Buddha sculptures create a simple, soothing atmosphere. There are five classes a day in a variety of yoga styles, from free meditation classes to advanced Vinyasa and even Kundalini. Most classes begin with a Sanskrit chant and end in *shivasana* (final relaxation pose). Check the website for the frequent workshop offerings in areas like Thai massage and partner yoga. A single class costs $15 and several packages are offered for repeat visits.

WAKE UP YOGA

2329 Parrish St., 215/235-1228, www.wakeupyoga.com

Map 4

Wake Up's original Vinyasa yoga studio is in Fairmount; they later opened a second in West Philly (4916 Baltimore Ave.). Each studio offers two to four 90-minute classes a day varying in level of difficulty; all levels are welcome. Wake Up emphasizes the physical, spiritual, and philosophical aspects of yoga as much if not more than the physical workout. Sanskrit (along with English) is used in classes. Wake Up seeks to provide a nurturing, supportive atmosphere for students. Most single classes costs $13, but some are offered at the bargain price of $5.

YOGA SCHELTER

3502 Scotts Lane, Building 3, Suite 1, 215/991-9642, http://yogaschelter.com

Map 10

Tucked away in a unique living and artist studio complex of Sherman Mills in East Falls, Yoga Schelter is a little hard to find, but it's the perfect place to find yourself. A cozy check-in area welcomes you into the bright, high-ceilinged studio named for founder and owner Jennifer Schelter. A highly skilled yoga practitioner and instructor, she offers commentary and guidance through the poses that makes each one feel relevant to life. You'll leave ready to face the world—more peaceful and flexible than you were when you came in.

Spectator Sports

In addition to the four major professional teams—the Eagles, the Phillies, the Flyers, and the 76ers—the city has several minor league teams that play entertaining if somewhat less heated games at lower prices. The area is also home to an unparalleled five college basketball teams, in the Big 5: Temple, University of Pennsylvania, St. Joe's, Villanova, and LaSalle. Penn's arena, the Palestra, has a storied history, and while somewhat run-down, it remains a favorite place for b-ball enthusiasts to watch a game.

BASKETBALL

76ERS

Wachovia Complex, 3601 S. Broad St., www.nba.com/sixers

Map 10

Providing the city with countless highlights, lowlights, and players of legendary and infamous status, the 76ers, or the "Sixers," has been Philadelphia's pro basketball team since 1963. The 1967 and 1983 teams won the NBA Championship, and both teams are often included in discussions of the NBA's all-time greatest. The 1983 team remains the last professional team in Philadelphia to bring home a title.

Beginning in the 1960s with Wilt Chamberlain, the Sixers have always boasted star power if not always a stellar record. The fortunes of the franchise have coincided with the comings and goings of some of the greatest superstars in NBA history, including Julius "Dr. J" Erving, Moses Malone, Charles Barkley, and Allen Iverson. Unfortunately for Sixers fans, most of these stars were ultimately traded in bad deals for the team. These trades, beginning with Wilt going to Los Angeles, followed by Moses Malone to Washington, and Charles Barkley to Phoenix, have resulted in prolonged periods of ineptitude and frustration for players and fans alike. Allen Iverson was sent to Denver in 2006 after 10 successful years with the team and fans can only hope the pattern of the past will soon change.

Among the enduring legacies of the Sixers is the championship titles, the fierce, bitter, and often personal battles waged against division rival Boston in the 1960s–1990s, the fast-breaking teams of Dr. J and George McGinnis in the mid to late '70s, the sustained excellence of the team from the late '70s–mid-'80s, the explosiveness and candor of Charles Barkley, and the singular talent and heart of Allen

ARTS AND LEISURE

LEGENDARY SPORTS FIGURES

Philadelphia has been home to some of the most legendary sports figures of all time, and remembering them is a bittersweet endeavor, since the teams have seen less than their share of success. Perhaps that is why the most famous Philadelphia sports figure of all is a fictional character – Rocky Balboa, a gritty fighter who did not fall short against the odds. But any true sports fan should read on to understand the impact that some of the most colorful athletes of all time had on the game – and the city.

BASKETBALL

Wilt Chamberlain was the towering center who grew up in West Philly and played for the Philadelphia Warriors and the 76ers. Combining size, strength, and agility, Wilt destroyed opponents and records. His impressive credits include 100 points in a game, 55 rebounds in a single contest, and averaging 50 points a game for an entire season. His off-court records include his famous claim of going to bed with 20,000 women.

Julius "Dr. J" Irving was a showman who joined the 76ers in 1976 and rejuvenated the sport. With his massive afro and debonair goatee, Dr. J had an in-your-face elegance that brought style and flair to the NBA. His ability to float in the air created the standard by which all high-flyers – from Michael Jordan to Vince Carter – are judged today. One of the most popular players in franchise history, he led the 1983 team to a world championship, cementing his iconic status forever.

Charles Barkley was considered short (at 6'6") and fat (his weight sometimes topped 300 lbs.) when he entered the NBA in 1984. With explosive strength and intensity, he became the face of the franchise when Dr. J

retired in 1986. Arguably the greatest pure rebounder of his era, he became the shortest player to lead the league in rebounds in 1987. His emotions and relationship with fans and media were tumultuous, but today he is remembered for his honesty and self-deprecating humor, remaining hugely popular in Philly.

A six-foot shooting guard who scores more points than anyone and throws his body around like a football player, **Allen Iverson** was the number one overall pick in the 1996 draft when he came to Philly. His astonishing scoring ability was matched by his passion and willingness to play through injury. This, along with his frenetic style, endeared him to fans and carried him through numerous off-court distractions and tabloid headlines. There was never a dull moment with A.I., and while many bristled at his contempt for authority, the city was mesmerized by his toughness and electric abilities. He played every game like it was his last – a favorite line of his – and for that he'll always be loved.

FOOTBALL

Chuck Bednarik, known as "Concrete Charlie," was a linebacker and center for the Eagles in the 1950s and '60s. One of the last "two-way" players, Bednarik had mangled hands and a nasty attitude that Philly fans loved. He is fondly remembered as the face of the only championship team in Eagles history, the 1960 NFL Champions (pre-Super Bowl, which came into existence in 1966).

Dick Vermeil was the coach of the 1980 Eagles team that went to the Super Bowl – the team's first title game since 1960. The team played above expectations for a coach known for his intensity and 20-hour work days. A high point for the team was a victory over its hated rival, the Dallas Cowboys – a team that otherwise had its way with the Eagles throughout the 1970s. Unfortunately, the Eagles were routed by an Oakland Raiders team that spent their nights on Bourbon Street while the Eagles studied plays in their hotel rooms to no avail.

Reggie White, who played for the Eagles 1985-1992, is arguably the best defensive lineman in team history. With legendary strength, he routinely tossed huge offensive lineman out the way en route to the quarterback. A devout Christian and ordained minister, "the Minister of Defense" was a rare combination of athlete and leader who headed one of the best defenses in NFL history.

HOCKEY

Ask anyone about the Flyers and they're sure to mention **Bobby Clarke.** Captain of the Stanley Cup-winning teams of 1973-1974 and 1974-1975, "Clarkie" embodied the blood-and-guts effort of the hockey team and the town. A diabetic, he was never even supposed to play hockey, but his work ethic and talent were an unstoppable combination.

Bernie Parent was the goalie of those Stanley Cup-winning teams, and many knowledgeable fans agree he was the biggest part of those championships. Arguably the best goalie of his era, his record for most games won in a single season was not broken by any goalie until 2007.

Eric Lindros came to the NHL as highly touted as any player in history, and the Flyers landed him after a bitter legal proceeding with the New York Rangers. Despite his talent, his time with the team was marked by injury, bitter disputes, and disappointingly, no Stanley Cup. He was tagged the next Wayne Gretzky or Mario Lemieux, perhaps unfairly, and he never delivered.

BASEBALL

Richie Ashburn, one of the few men around town who could pull off the nickname "Whitey," was beloved in Philadelphia first as the centerfielder for the Phillies in the 1950s and later as a radio commentator. His understated style and easy humor connected with fans, who adopted him as a native son. His signature line, "Hard to believe, Harry," (directed to his radio partner, Harry Kalas), often followed a goofy blooper or awkward moment for the Phillies.

Perhaps the greatest third baseman of all time, **Mike Schmidt** played his entire career with the Phils. The cornerstone of the team that won the only World Championship in franchise history in 1980, he made it look easy with great power at the plate and superior glovework at the hot corner. Despite his talent, he had a perplexingly embattled relationship with the home crowd and often heard boos. He has since become more appreciated, and a statue of him is featured prominently outside Citizens Bank Park.

Hall of Fame pitcher **Steve Carlton** was responsible as much as anyone for leading the Phils to their only World Series Championship in the modern era. Known as "Lefty" for obvious reasons, he was virtually unhittable during his prime in the mid-1970s and early 1980s. Known for his surly nature, he refused to speak to reporters and was not subtle in discouraging the team manager or catcher from "disturbing" him while he was on the mound. He also was known for his large wine collection.

PHILLY SPORTS FANATICS

The stereotype of Philadelphia sports' fans is that they are a boorish, negative collection of boo-birds who revel in the collective misery of a decades-long championship drought. And while I can't completely dispute this stereotype, it isn't the full picture. The unique passion for sports in Philadelphia means that all four major sports have a fan base that is ravenous, persistent, and incredibly loyal. Being a Philadelphia sports fan means expecting to lose but watching anyway – year after year. It means getting pumped every season and saying to each other "this is the year," and at the end of the season when the team loses, shaking our heads and saying "that's Philly for you."

The signature call of the Philly fan is the much used, oft-discussed, and never ambiguous boo. Booing is done in nearly every city in America, but in Philly, booing is more an act of protest, a fight for inclusion into the happenings on the field or court – our own way of participating. People boo for good reasons, like when a referee makes a bad call, and for poor ones, like a fan answering a question wrong during a time-out game. In the equal opportunity nature of booing, kids get booed when they drop a foul ball, cheerleaders get booed if they don't dance well enough, officials get booed, coaches get booed, and players, obviously, get booed. And it's easy to see why the fans are booing: No other city with four professional teams has gone longer than Philadelphia since its last championship – since 1983, when the Sixers won the NBA Championship. We take the losses hard and personally, and the longer the championship drought continues, the more the pressure mounts and clamoring for a title builds.

But the boos are merely a small chapter in a complex relationship between the fans and the teams. As tough as the city is on its teams, a good team will always be supported by big crowds in Philadelphia – especially a good team that plays hard and has character. For all these reasons, Philadelphia is one of the few true sports towns in the country.

But remember, the relationship between the teams and the fans is like a family: You can insult your own family all you want, but if somebody else does, watch out. Check out a game and see for yourself what a Philly crowd is all about.

Iverson—who in 2001 led the team to its first finals appearance since 1983.

The low points include many poor trades and dubious drafting, but the team's all-time low was its 9–73 record in 1972–1973, which to this day remains the record for fewest wins in a season by a professional basketball team. Several draft-day decisions crippled the team in the 1980s and early '90s, including disappointments Shawn Bradley and Sharone Wright—top picks that never delivered.

Games are played at the fan-friendly Wachovia Center. A hard-core fan could complain of too many songs, promotions, and distractions from the actual game, but this is not specific to Philadelphia but more of a general trend in stadiums across the league. The crowd at a Sixers game is the most diverse in age and ethnicity of any of the pro teams and on a good night, it is an electrifying experience. Tickets are generally not difficult to get and range from $15 in advance to well over $100 on game day, available online or at the stadium.

BASEBALL
PHILLIES

Citizens Bank Park, 1 Citizens Bank Way,
215/463-1000, www.phillies.com
Map 10

No team has lost more games for more years and in more torturous ways and circumstances than the Philadelphia Phillies. The oldest pro team in the city, the Phillies have been instilling cynicism into the hearts of baseball fans since 1883. They've won a grand total of one championship—the World Series of 1980. In 2007, they lost their 10,000th game, setting a record for most losses of any professional team in any sport in American history. Their one World Series victory shines bright as a lonely reminder of one of the few periods of success and optimism in the franchise's history.

Before this starts to sound totally depressing, I will add that many superb ballplayers have worn the Phillies uniform, and every so often a great team takes form and gives the fans a wild and unexpected run. The Whiz Kids of 1950 and the ragamuffin squad of 1993 gave the city thrilling rides to the World Series before losing—both remain etched in the memories of fans. The 1964 team was 6.5 games in front with just 12 games to play when they lost 10 in a row and missed the playoffs, becoming forever the gold standard of choking in baseball.

In 2007, the Phils led the biggest comeback in MLB history to beat the Mets and become the National League East Division champs. It was their first playoff run in 14 years, and the city rejoiced, if only briefly. The team was swept by the Colorado Rockies in the next series—the first time since 1976 they were swept in a series.

But despite long stretches without a playoff appearance and a multitude of bad free-agent signings, bungled trades, and unfortunate injuries, the fans keep wearing their Phillies shirts and caps and trudging to the ballpark every summer. The current team shows much promise and fans hope that the trio of Ryan Howard, Chase Utley, and Jimmy Rollins (2007 National league MVP) will someday join the Philly legends class.

Citizens Bank Park opened in 2004, replacing the cavernous relic of Veterans Stadium. While many die-hard fans were resistant to the change, the bright, clean, modern stadium has been a big hit with fans and a major marketing tool for the franchise. Always a great spectator sport with its unique rhythm and laid-back atmosphere, baseball in Philadelphia is, more than ever, a fun night out. Crowds are a mix of families, couples, college kids, and rowdy fanatics, all united in the mostly fruitless endeavor of cheering the Phillies

© KARRIE GAVIN

Philadelphia Phillies scoreboard

towards victory. It should also be noted that the one member of the organization who always does his job is the mascot, the Phillies Fanatic—hands down the greatest mascot in all of sports. He alone is worth the price of admission. Tickets, relative to the other sports, are affordable and easy to snag, ranging $14–100. Tickets are usually available on game day. And, though it's illegal, it's also not uncommon to encounter scalpers before the game.

BOXING
[THE LEGENDARY BLUE HORIZON
1314 N. Broad St., 215/763-0500,
www.legendarybluehorizon.com
`Map 10`

The building dates back to 1865, but it wasn't until 1961 that it opened as a boxing venue. The Legendary Blue Horizon became one of the country's finest and most famous boxing institutions. The oldest boxing ring operating today, it has earned the "Legendary" in its title by housing many of the greatest Philadelphia fights in history. It has become a landmark center for training, education, and community participation, and the best boxers and teachers from the city and beyond train, fight, and teach here throughout the year. Come out for "fight night" to see the purest showcase of boxing available anywhere today. The Blue Horizon has been voted the "#1 Boxing Venue in the World" by *Ring* magazine and the "last boxing venue in the country" by *Sports Illustrated Magazine*.

EVOLVED FIGHTING
NEW ALHAMBRA

7 Ritter St., 215/520-9682, www.evolvedfighting.com
COST: $30 general, $45 ringside, $55 VIP
Map 10

As Mixed Martial Arts asserts its place in the sports world, Evolved Fighting brings MMA fanatics something to cheer for in Philadelphia. Evolved Fighting organizes some of the East Coast's most exhilarating Muay Thai and kickboxing events, with lightning kicks, hard hits, and amazing speed. Most events take place in South Philly's New Alhambra Arena. It's considered a very violent, barbaric sport by many people—blood will be shed. True fight fans won't want to miss the action.

FOOTBALL
EAGLES

Lincoln Financial Field, 1 Lincoln Financial Field Way, 215/336-2000, www.philadelphiaeagles.com
Map 10

In a crowded and passionate sports town, no team draws more attention than the Eagles. The combination of being a perennial contender, playing in a new stadium, and the national obsession with football, has positioned the Eagles as the number one sports draw in the city and surrounding area—a standing that shows no sign of changing soon. The popularity of the club far outpaces the success of the franchise. The Eagles are still looking for their first Super Bowl Championship (before the Super Bowl existed, they won the Championship in 1960),

a quest that riles the fan base into a fever every autumn, and so far has left them heartbroken every January.

When Andy Reid became head coach in 1998, the team was following a depressing 3–13 season. What has taken place since is the franchise's most consistently competitive streak in 50 years. A Super Bowl appearance in 2004 capped a streak of five consecutive trips to the playoffs and four straight NFC Championship Games, three of which were lost. Despite competitive and exciting teams, frequent trips to the playoffs, and a roster stocked with high-profile names, the lack of a Super Bowl trophy looms large over the team and the city. Nothing short of a championship will satisfy the embattled Eagles fans, who with each passing year become more vociferous and cranky, turning Lincoln Financial Field into a notorious cauldron of noise, emotion, and the occasional drunken brawl.

The party inside the stadium is an extension of the tailgate scene that begins early on Sundays and continues until kickoff. And even beyond the stadium scene, football and Sunday go hand-in-hand in Philadelphia, as the Eagles' faithful use the entire day to drink and yell away the previous week of work and responsibility. Possessing a bad reputation that is not entirely unwarranted, Eagles' fans don't often waste a chance to yell at opposing teams and their fans, and sometimes even each other, in and outside of the stadium. Be warned: If you show up at a game wearing a jersey of the other team, you *will* catch heat and may be putting yourself at real risk.

Eagles tickets have become the most expensive and elusive in the city with a long and implacable waiting list. Individual tickets go on sale before the season's start and get snapped up in a matter of minutes. The best bet for tickets is online at the team website (www.philadelphiaeagles.com), or on eBay or Craigslist (www.craigslist.org), either way you will pay hundreds of dollars to see a game. Scalpers sell tickets at the stadium; those tickets come with a high price and the risk of arrest for the illegal purchase.

ARTS AND LEISURE

THE PHILADELPHIA SOUL
Wachovia Center, 3601 S. Broad St., 888/744-5235,
www.philadelphiasoul.com
Map 10

Named for the distinct sounds of soul music that originated in Philly, the Soul is Philadelphia's team in the Arena Football League. Under the direction of New Jersey–born rock star Jon Bon Jovi, who founded the team in 2004, Soul games are family-friendly events at the Wachovia Center. With alcohol-free seating zones and games and activities for children, fans can get close to the action. The season begins in March, and ticket packages are available. This version of Philly football is a far cry from the Eagles, but with low-end tickets available for as little as $15, it offers an alternative to satisfy a football fix.

HOCKEY
FLYERS
Wachovia Center, 3601 S. Broad St.,
http://flyers.nhl.com
Map 10

The Orange and Black. The Broad Street Bullies. The Philadelphia Flyers, the youngest of the professional teams in Philly, lacks for nothing when it comes to owning a secure place in the mythology of the sports scene. With arguably the most loyal and fervent fans in the city, Flyers hockey has always meant big hits, wild punches, and sold-out stadiums.

Created in 1967 as part of hockey's expansion, the Flyers have been a perennial contender year in and year out, coming close many times but still looking for their first championship since winning back-to-back Stanley Cups in 1973–1974 and 1974–1975. The bruising style and reputation they developed in the early '70s, which earned them the "Bullies" nickname, made them Flyers local heroes in Philly and one of the most hated teams in the league. The championship teams and its players forged a strong connection to the city that remains strong and partially accounts for their intense and loyal following. Fans still clamor for the style of play that was successful in the '70s and often a crunching check or violent confrontation between two enforcers gets the Philly crowd more juiced than a nice pass or a pretty goal. Hockey tends to takes a back seat to the other three major sports in terms of its overall impact on the city, but when the Flyers are doing well, additional fans come out in droves.

Tickets can be purchased online at the team website and at the stadium. Even during down years the Flyers remain a tough ticket to nab—and an expensive one. Individual tickets cost $25–105.

PHANTOMS
Wachovia Spectrum, 3601 S. Broad St., 215/465-4522,
www.phantomshockey.com
Map 10

Philadelphia's other hockey team, the Phantoms, is the AHL minor-league affiliate of the Flyers. With players destined for the Flyers roster, the Phantoms serve as a pipeline of talent to the NHL and an alternate source of hockey at a more reasonable price for hungry hockey fans. Half-time entertainment, games, free giveaways, and regular meet-the-players sessions make games especially popular with families. With one of the strongest followings in the league and a history of success including winning the Calder Cup in 2005, games sometimes sell out.

HORSE RACING
PHILADELPHIA PARK
3001 Street Rd., Bensalem, 215/639-9000,
www.philadelphiapark.com
Map 10

Live thoroughbred racing draws visitors to bet on horses at Philadelphia Park in Bensalem, a 10-minute ride from the city just past Northeast Philadelphia. Avoid the sad casino packed with two floors of slot machines, and instead take a picnic lunch and enjoy the grounds while watching the races. The annual **Devon Horse Show and Country Fair,** the largest and oldest horse show in the Unites States, is held here for 10 days late May–early June.

ARTS AND LEISURE

LACROSSE
THE PHILADELPHIA WINGS

Wachovia Center, 3601 S. Broad St., 215/389-9464, www.wingslax.com

`Map 10`

Lacrosse fans will find a rowdy crowd in the Wachovia Center when the Philadelphia Wings take to the turf. With constant chants, inescapable heckling, and the team's unofficial anthem, Guns & Roses' "Welcome to the Jungle," playing at every game, it's difficult to leave without a hoarse throat. The season begins in January, with NLS play-offs following in the spring.

SOCCER
THE PHILADELPHIA KIXX

Wachovia Spectrum, 3601 S. Broad St., 888/888-5499, www.kixxonline.com

`Map 10`

A team unaware of any Philly sports curse, the Philadelphia KiXX have won two championships since the turn of the century and show no signs of slowing down. One of the Major Indoor Soccer League's powerhouse teams, the KiXX have missed the playoffs only once since 2000. The season runs Nov.–Mar. and tickets are very reasonably priced.

SHOPPING

There was a time when the most fashionable Philadelphians regularly made the two-hour trip to New York for all their serious shopping needs. Fortunately, as with most things in Philadelphia, the shopping scene has come into its own, especially in the past decade. The major shopping districts have expanded while increasing numbers of unique, independent shops have sprung up in neighborhoods throughout the city. With no shortage of mega-chains, small boutiques, art galleries, vintage shops, and much more, you will have no problem finding everything your consumer heart desires.

Philadelphia's shops have a flavor all their own. While the latest trends make their marks here as they do everywhere else, many of the city's independent, local designers and buyers remain true to their tastes regardless of what is on the runway. And while Philly cannot compare to New York in its quantity of offerings, shopping in Philly is more manageable, more affordable, and, dare I say, often more fun.

In addition to the major downtown shopping areas, including Old City, Rittenhouse, South Street, and Washington Square West, there are the artsy boutiques of Northern Liberties, the college-dominated shops in University City, and South Philadelphia's eclectic Passyunk Avenue. The three shopping rows—Jeweler's Row, Fabric Row, and Antique Row—offer unparalleled selections. Head to Chinatown for all things Asian, or Reading Terminal Market and the Italian Market for kitchenwares, gourmet treats, and other specialty items. Chestnut Hill and Manayunk offer a small-town shopping

© KARRIE GAVIN

HIGHLIGHTS

◖ **Best Independent Bookstore:** The small, inconspicuous **Joseph Fox Bookshop** offers a selection of excellent titles, and the friendly, helpful staff will help you find your next favorite (page 149).

◖ **Best Vinyl Selection:** The **Philadelphia Record Exchange** is a must for all record lovers. Three full floors in a row house just off South Street are stocked with rock, jazz, soul, punk, R&B, and more (page 152).

◖ **Best Sports Gear:** For more than a century, **Mitchell & Ness** has been providing quality sporting gear to Philadelphia teams and locals. Today, it draws crowds from far beyond the city for its classic throwback jerseys (page 153).

◖ **Best Shoe Store: Benjamin Lovell Shoes** proves that you don't have to sacrifice comfort for style. Offering men's and women's shoes in three different locations, the store carries the top brands in the world of high-comfort shoes (page 156).

◖ **Most Unique Home Store: PHAG** (an acronym for Philadelphia Home Art Garden) offers a wide array of unusual home, garden, and gay-themed specialty items. From stylish home accessories to bachelor-party kitsch, it has a little bit of everything (page 160).

◖ **Best Gift Store: AIA Bookstore and Design Center** is run by the American Institute of Architects, so it makes sense that it carries an excellent selection of architecture and design books. However, you'll also be impressed by the unique gifts, cards, and other diverse specialty items (page 162).

LOOK FOR ◖ TO FIND RECOMMENDED SHOPS.

◖ **Prettiest Paper Shop:** For gorgeous stationary, journals, and other paper products, **Details** is top-notch. Embossing, calligraphy, and all types of paper services are provided along with a wide variety of elegant paper designs (page 162).

◖ **Best Place to Get a Handmade Messenger Bag: R.E. Load Baggage, Inc.** is the place to go for durable custom-designed bags. This grassroots company is 100 percent Philly (page 162).

◖ **Best Bath and Body Shop: Duross & Langel** offers soaps and all sorts of body, face, and hair lotions and potions in every delicious scent you can imagine. Made using natural ingredients crafted on location, the items at this independent shop are lower-priced than at most of the upscale cosmetic chains (page 166).

◖ **Best Place to Take a Break: Terme Di Aroma** offers a calm, soothing haven in the heart of bustling Old City. Take a break from sightseeing to be pampered with an aromatherapy massage or facial (page 166).

COURTESY OF TERME DI AROMA

Terme Di Aroma

feel just a short drive from Center City, and in case you want malls or big-box stores, they're nearby too.

Weekends are bustling in all the major shopping areas, so go during the week to avoid crowds. Many stores in Center City stay open later on Wednesday evenings, closing at 8 or 9 P.M. rather than 5 or 6 P.M. Most Center City shops are open seven days a week, but in some neighborhoods, many shops are closed on Monday. And remember, there is no sales tax on clothing in Pennsylvania, so take full advantage if you're looking for any big-ticket items.

SHOPPING DISTRICTS

Several major shopping districts that contain a wealth of shops in a concentrated area make excellent starting points. Center City is one big shopping district, with stores lining Broad Street and spreading out to the east and west. And don't miss Chestnut Hill and Manayunk, the two shopping areas in the northwest section of the city unique enough to attract even the downtown crowd. In addition to being home to lots of shops, all of these districts are characterized by their own distinctive style and atmosphere, making them an enjoyable place to stroll.

Old City

Old City is not only home to the city's largest concentration of historic attractions; it is also a shopper's paradise. Tourists and locals alike flock to the clothing boutiques and art galleries. Whether you're looking for books and music, vintage jeans, or furniture that doubles as artwork, Old City has it all. With great restaurants, bars, coffee shops, and an attractive, manageable several square blocks to navigate, it is also one of the most pleasant areas for shopping. The best time to shop for art is during the first Friday of each month, when the galleries open their doors to the public to display and sell their wares.

Rittenhouse Row

If you have a deep wallet and a love of shopping, you'll find paradise in the sophisticated Rittenhouse Square area. The abundance of

shopping on Germantown Avenue in Chestnut Hill

PHOTO BY R. KENNEDY FOR GPTMC

retail opportunities is unparalleled, with unique boutiques and high-end luxury chain stores sharing Walnut and Chestnut Streets and the blocks all around. Two urban malls, the Shops at Liberty Place and the Shops at the Bellevue, are packed with mainstream and high-end retailers respectively. In fact, all the chain staples can be found in this area, including the Gap, J. Crew, Victoria's Secret, Ann Taylor, Borders, Zara, H&M, Loehmann's, and American Apparel, along with the somewhat hipper, harder-to-find chains like Puma, Lucky Jeans, and Nicole Miller, and high-end chains like Kenneth Cole, Brooks Brothers, BCBG, Tiffany, and Williams-Sonoma. The latest major chains to call Rittenhouse home are Barney's Co-Op and Sephora, raising the status of the Philadelphia shopping scene yet again to a level befitting one of the largest cities in the country.

South Street

Concentrated primarily on the blocks and side streets between Front and 8th Streets, South

Street offers an eclectic mix of more than 300 shops. Most are independently owned and cater to a mix of, well, just about everyone. Head shops, tattoo parlors, hip-hop clothing stores, independent record stores, whimsical home and gift shops, and kinky lingerie and sex shops coexist on the street. From the ridiculously comfortable options at Benjamin Lovell Shoes to the cheap and trendy fashions at Bare Feet to athletic wear at Reebok and Foot Locker, South Street is the place for shoes of all kinds.

Chestnut Hill

One of two shopping areas in the northwest section of the city (Main Street in Manayunk is the other one), Germantown Avenue in Chestnut Hill is referred to as "the Avenue" by locals. The only business district in a largely residential area, it feels like Main Street in a small town with its quaint storefronts, Victorian lampposts, cobblestone streets, and shoppers who stop to chat with one another. While selections are varied, you can find a good dose of antiques, upscale home goods, several art galleries, spas, and clothing and jewelry shops. More people from the surrounding neighborhoods and suburbs than from Center City frequent these shops, although a few of the unique art, antiques, and furniture stores draw the downtown sect.

Manayunk

The Manayunk shopping scene has blossomed

South Street storefronts

in the past decade as the area transformed from a run-down mill town into one of the city's major business districts. Occupying a stretch of Main Street and spilling into the side streets, it offers upscale and vintage boutiques, jewelry, accessories, stylish eyeglasses, and independent music and art galleries. Main Street also claims to hold the largest concentration of furniture and home-goods stores on one street on the entire East Coast.

Books and Music

You can find a Borders, Barnes & Noble, and f.y.e. at every turn, and while there is nothing wrong with a place where you can buy the bestsellers or the greatest Top 40 hits, why not take advantage of Philly's underground book and music scene? Independent book and music stores are spread across the city, with the South Street area home to a wealth of record stores.

BOOKS

BIG JAR BOOKS

55 N. 2nd St., 215/574-1650,
www.balancingman.org
HOURS: Daily 10 A.M.–9 P.M.
Map 1

Whether it's the sound of the creaking wooden slats beneath your feet or the permeating smell of espresso and baked goods from the front, the vibe inside this cozy Old City café and used bookstore is worn-in and homey. With a substantive collection of literary fiction, mysteries, children's books, and art and photography tomes, there is something for everyone to buy—or to just peruse while you hang in the store. The owners have recently opened another equally lovely little book shop, **Brickbat Books** (Map 5, 709 S. 4th St., 215/592-1207, www.balancingman.org, daily 11 A.M.–7 P.M.), on Fabric Row in South Philly.

BOOK TRADER

7 N. 2nd St., 215/925-0511
HOURS: Daily 10 A.M.-10 P.M.
`Map 1`

The cash-strapped can find creative ways to acquire new reading materials at this one-of-a-kind Old City bookstore. Barter with a box of your own used books, or contribute your labor by sorting and organizing piles of books in exchange for store credit. The laid-back staff wants every customer to leave with something to read, one way or another. While the store is cluttered and there are often cats wandering through the aisles, it is the perfect place to relax and hunt for great reading material. The antithesis of the overpriced, squeaky-clean chains taking over the world, this is a place to enjoy while it lasts.

GIOVANNI'S ROOM

345 S. 12th St., 215/923-2960,
www.giovannisroom.com
HOURS: Mon.-Sat. 11:30 A.M.-7 P.M., Sun. 1-7 P.M.
`Map 2`

A Gayborhood mainstay since 1973, Giovanni's Room has grown into one of the largest bookstores in the world that specializes in gay, lesbian, bisexual, and transgender literature. In addition to shelves stocked with queer-oriented novels, magazines, videos, calendars, self-help books, travel guides, and art books, the store contains enough rainbow paraphernalia to stock a *Queer as Folk* reunion tour. It also hosts speakers and readings, and serves as a de facto community

PHOTO BY R. WIDMAN FOR GPTMC

Giovanni's Room specializes in gay and lesbian themes.

resource center. The enthusiastic staff can help you find what you need and will track down hard-to-find titles if they're not in stock. Both the staff and materials serve as a great resource for gay visitors who are getting oriented to the city.

◆ JOSEPH FOX BOOKSHOP

1724 Sansom St., 215/563-4184,
www.foxbookshop.com
HOURS: Mon.-Sat. 9:30 A.M.-6 P.M., Wed. until 7 P.M.
`Map 3`

It's cramped. It's overcrowded with books. It's in the basement. There's no Internet and no coffee. And those are just some of the reasons we love it. Established in 1951, Joseph Fox Bookshop has always been independently owned and operated by passionate lovers of the written word. It is committed to supporting and showcasing talented local authors. And it may not have every book, but it has a carefully chosen selection of what the owners consider to be the best, and additional items can be special ordered. Take a step back in

ROWS AND ROWS

Philadelphia is home to Antique Row, Fabric Row, and Jewelers' Row, offering endless selections and a one-of-a-kind shopping experience. And like most things in Philly, each row has its own long and unique history.

ANTIQUE ROW

The tree-lined stretch of Pine Street concentrated between 9th and Broad Streets is a treasure trove of antiques stores and boutiques known as Antique Row. The oldest continuously operating antiques district in the entire country has continually evolved. While there are at least 15 antiques stores to choose from today, the area is now also home to a wide variety of furniture, home accessories, jewelry, stained glass, clothing, and collectibles representing a diverse mix of the old and the new. Just steps from one another on Pine Street, shops range from **Kohn and Kohn** (1112 Pine St., 215/923-0432, www.kohnandkohnantiques.com), specializing in antique furniture, glass, and collectibles, to **Twist** (1134 Pine St., 215/925-1242, www.twisthome.com), filled with vibrant, colorful, ultra-modern housewares and luxurious 600-thread-count linens. Many shops offer both antique and modern items, like **Halloween** (1329 Pine St., 215/732-7711), an impressive jewelry shop packed tight with vintage and estate pieces, and unique modern and handcrafted gems. Antique Row is part of the Washington Square West shopping area, with plenty of additional stores along the streets to the north, especially 13th Street – home to everything from books, records, and cosmetics to gay-themed specialty stores.

FABRIC ROW

At the turn of the 20th century, scores of Jewish immigrants settled in the southern outskirts of Center City – now South Philadelphia. The many skilled tailors and seamstresses among them were often forced to take jobs in sweatshops creating fine clothes for the upper class. Many sold goods in pushcarts on several blocks of South 4th Street between South and Catherine Streets; some eventually opened their own shops, and the area became known as Fabric Row. What remains is a vibrant and eclectic (if a bit run-down on the outside) community of fabric shops, along with a sprinkling of clothing and shoe boutiques, a

---

time to when having quality at your fingertips mattered more than having everything at your fingertips.

ROBIN'S BOOKSTORE

108 S. 13th St., 215/735-9600,
www.robinsbookstore.com
HOURS: Mon.-Sat. 10 A.M.-8 P.M., Sun. noon-8 P.M.
Map 2

The oldest independent bookstore in Philadelphia, Robin's opened in 1936 and is still the place to go for rare poetry as well as psychology, political, and new-age books. Jazz and classical music typically provide the background soundtrack as you browse the ample fiction and children's sections. With hundreds of in-store author readings through the years from greats like Sonia Sanchez, Walter Mosley, and Maya Angelou, the history of this liberal and counter-cultural literary outpost is palpable. The 2nd floor is filled with magazines and discounted books, and a smaller second store (1837 Chestnut St.) is fully devoted to discounted books and magazines.

MUSIC
AKA MUSIC

27 N. 2nd St., 215/922-3855,
www.myspace.com/aka_music
HOURS: Mon.-Wed. 11 A.M.-11 P.M., Thurs.-Sat.
10 A.M.-11 P.M., Sun. 11 A.M.-6 P.M.
Map 1

The musical times, they are a-changin'. Luckily for old-school music enthusiasts, AKA is a welcome aberration in the age of digital downloads. Catering mostly to the indie crowd, the large, bright, meticulously organized warehouse

gourmet market, and a café. While most of the stores appear the same on the outside, locals have their favorites. Those who like to create clothing or home wares love **Kincus Fabrics** (754 S. 4th St., 215/923-8836), with its vast selection of cotton, spandex, Lycra, rayon, silk, draperies, and faux fur. **Marmelstein's** (760 S. 4th St., 215/925-9862) offers the most comprehensive selection of decorative trimmings and drapery hardware in the country. And the basement of **Maxie's Daughter** (724 S. 4th St., 215/829-2226) offers a veritable fabric history of Philadelphia, with vintage textiles that haven't seen the light of day for the better half of a century. If you don't work with fabric already, the fabulous finds just may inspire you to sew your own curtains or reupholster that old, comfy chair.

JEWELERS' ROW

Satisfy all your bling needs on Jewelers' Row — the oldest and the second-largest (after New York) diamond district in the country. Concentrated on a brick-paved stretch of Sansom Street between 7th and 8th Streets and continuing along 8th Street between Chestnut and Walnut Streets, Jewelers' Row is home to more than 300 jewelry specialists, retailers, wholesalers, craftsmen, and traders. A staggering variety of diamonds, precious and semiprecious stones, platinum, pearls, watches, and more can be found. And while the sky is the limit on prices, with so much competition in such a small area, discounts are often available. There are plenty of big-name chain retailers like **Robbins Diamonds** (801 Walnut St., 215/925-1877) and **Steven Singer Jewelers** (739 Walnut St., 215/627-3242), sharing the intersection of 8th and Walnut Streets, along with plenty of smaller stores, like the **I. Gansky & Co.** (718 Sansom St., 215/922-0505), a wholesaler that opened in 1851.

The row was established as a center for jewelers in the years 1860-1880, but its historical significance dates back even earlier. Originally named Carstairs Row for builder and architect Thomas Carstairs, the row was home to 22 look-alike dwellings built 1799-1820. The first row homes in the country, they provided affordable housing and initiated a widespread housing trend that remains prevalent throughout downtown Philadelphia today.

space is stocked with rare originals and reissues, as well as many current titles. Can't find what you're looking for? The incredibly fine-tuned ears of the savant-like staff will be glad to turn you on to a similar artist you've probably never heard of.

HIDEAWAY MUSIC

8612 Germantown Ave., 215/248-4434

HOURS: Mon.-Fri. 11 A.M.-6 P.M., Sat. 10 A.M.-6 P.M., Sun. noon-5 P.M.

Map 9

Chestnut Hill's independent music store is a popular local stop for its excellent selection of CDs, DVDs, LPs, vintage concert posters, rock 'n' roll memorabilia and used CDs. The CD selection offers contemporary and classic selections, and the vinyl collection is dominated by good old rock 'n' roll. The friendly staff in the small shop will be glad to help you find that Stones album you somehow lost track of over the years.

MAIN STREET MUSIC

4444 Main St., 215/487-7732

HOURS: Mon.-Thurs. 11 A.M.-7 P.M., Fri.-Sat. 11 A.M.-9 P.M., Sun. noon-6 P.M.

Map 9

The only record store in Manayunk, this independent-music mainstay has a faithful following. Listen to new and used CDs at listening stations and if you like what you hear, buy it or trade for some of your own old music. For a small space, it's well stocked with plenty of indie, local bands, new releases, and random oldies of whatever other people traded. The helpful and well-versed staff will order anything you want at no extra charge.

◖ PHILADELPHIA RECORD EXCHANGE

618 S. 5th St., 215/925-7892, www.philarecx.com

HOURS: Daily noon-8 P.M.

Map 5

The Philadelphia Record Exchange is a vinyl lover's dream, with the largest selection in the city. Unless you're being watched over by a higher power, you're not likely to find a sought-after hidden classic amid the stacks, since music diehards and deejays regularly troll the shelves. But if your taste is eclectic and you have the time to browse, you'll probably get lucky and find a few gems. Record Exchange also buys music, but they are choosy and at times a bit snobby, so go in with a thick skin if you're looking to sell your childhood memories.

REPO RECORDS

538 South St., 215/627-3775, www.reporecords.com

HOURS: Mon.-Thurs. noon-9 P.M., Fri.-Sat. noon-11 P.M., Sun. noon-8 P.M.

Map 5

Specializing in punk/hard-core and dance/electronic, this South Street record store has a wealth of new and used records and CDs, boxed sets, imports, hard-to-find indie singles, and B-sides. Out of-print finds from the U.K. and beyond can also be found here. The downstairs is home to plenty of seven-inch vinyl, used CDs, and bargain bins with dirt-cheap offerings. A second location in Bryn Mawr is worth a trip for hard-core indie fans.

SOUND OF MARKET STREET (JAZSOUND)

15 S. 11th St., 2nd floor, 215/925-3150, www.jazsound.com

HOURS: Mon.-Sat 9:30 A.M.-7 P.M.

Map 2

With more than 80,00 titles in stock, Sound of Market is Philadelphia's largest independent music store, boasting one of the most extensive selections of R&B, jazz, and gospel on the East Coast. The wide array of genres represented includes old-school and current rap and hip-hop, disco, dance, reggae, funk, doo-wop, Afro-Cuban, big band/swing, country, electronic, experimental, and folk. The large space is packed with music, spanning the 2nd and 3rd floors of the building.

Clothing, Accessories, and Shoes

With so many independently owned boutiques and shops in Philadelphia, many owners stock the shelves with a little bit of all their favorites, so there is often crossover between stores offering clothes, shoes, and accessories, and even home and gift items. Many offer items for both men and women, and in some cases children as well. In order to help point you in the right direction more quickly, they are grouped here into what they are best known for, but keep in mind that these categories are not strictly bound.

CHILDREN'S STORES
BORN YESTERDAY

1901 Walnut St., 215/568-6556

HOURS: Mon.-Fri. 10 A.M.-6 P.M., Sat. 10 A.M.-5:30 P.M.

Map 3

If adults ask for Walnut Street designer shops for the latest fashions, then why wouldn't babies cry for the same? High-fashion, European-style clothing lines the aisles at this Rittenhouse destination, and it's all in sizes of up to 8 for boys and 10 for girls. Born Yesterday carries the newest designs and latest trends in infant clothing as well, so your newborn can be posh before crawling. Modern and vintage toys are available for babies up to about two years.

CHILDREN'S BOUTIQUE

1702 Walnut St., 215/732-2661, www.echildrensboutique.com

HOURS: Mon.-Tues. 10 A.M.-6 P.M., Wed. 10 A.M.-7 P.M., Thurs.-Sat. 10 A.M.-6 P.M., Sun. noon-5 P.M.

Map 3

In business since 1966, the family-owned store carries all the big brand names, including

Lacoste, Polo Ralph Lauren, Amiana, and Joan Calabrese, as well as special designs available only here. Domestic and European designs for children of all ages are on hand, along with shoes, toys, gifts, and select items for infants. The Children's Boutique offers plenty of formal clothing for children and orders can be placed online.

MEN'S CLOTHING AND ACCESSORIES

BOYD'S
1818 Chestnut St., 215/564-9000,
www.boydsphila.com
HOURS: Mon.-Sat. 9:30 A.M.-6 P.M., Wed. until 9 P.M.
Map 3

Finely tailored men's slacks, dress shirts, jackets, and suits are the specialty of this word-class retailer. The climate is set by extravagant marble and mahogany fixtures, while a bountiful array of doting salespeople help you navigate through the fine European import fabrics. Browse the ready-to-wear sportswear and formal attire by luxury-lifestyle purveyors like Hugo Boss, Burberry, Ferragamo, Gucci, and Zegna. A smaller selection of women's wear can also be found, with highlights including coveted designers Badgley Mischka, Narciso Rodriguez, Piazza Sempione, and Zac Posen. Stop at the in-store café for a shot of espresso or even better, a martini, in between fittings, or if you're not fully loaded, just stroll through the store to see how the other half lives.

I. GOLDBERG
1300 Chestnut St., 215/925-9393,
www.igoco.com
HOURS: Mon., Tues., Thurs., and Sat. 9 A.M.-5:45 P.M., Wed. and Fri. 9 A.M.-6:45 P.M.
Map 2

You won't be awarded the purple heart for shopping at I. Goldberg, the Philadelphia Army Navy store that outfits the rugged urban soldier, but you will be awarded some fashion brownie points. Stocked with standard surplus gear like wool pea coats, bright-orange hunting vests, and water canteens, along with brands like Carhartt, Timberland, Levi's, Wrangler, North Face, and Dickies, these clothes, shoes, and accessories are designed to get you ready for the trenches, but they also make good understated-yet-stylish city wear.

◖ MITCHELL & NESS
1318 Chestnut St., 267/765-0613,
www.mitchellandness.com
HOURS: Mon.-Sat. 9:30 A.M.-7 P.M.
Map 2

If sportswear-makers are allowed to have a storied history, then Mitchell & Ness is the stuff of legends. Starting out in a modest downtown storefront in 1904, the two-person outfitter started crafting and retailing tennis racquets, golf clubs, and other items before moving on to specialize in team uniforms. The Phillies, Athletics (pre-Oakland, of course), and Eagles all wore their clothes. Flash forward to the present, when the team jersey has become a high-priced fashion item, and Mitchell & Ness is the supplier of choice for urban and suburban high-schoolers, middle-aged men recapturing their youth, hip-hop heads, and ballers. A destination shop, it is a must for anyone interested in classic sports gear. It's so popular with a national and even international crowd that a branch recently opened in Japan. Items can also be ordered through their website.

PEDESTRIAN
252 South St., 215/592-7510,
www.pedestrian215.com
HOURS: Sun.-Thurs. noon-9 P.M., Fri.-Sat. noon-10 P.M.
Map 5

If you're scratching your chin wondering where that dude came from—you know, the one who just rode by on that killer Cinelli, sporting the Elephant fitted New Era cap and the No Mas 1981 Wimbledon T-shirt—then scratch no longer. Pedestrian, a haven for the B-boy haute couture crowd, will have you shaking in your limited edition Jordans before you even arrive. Stocking their shelves with the freshest throwback patterns and indie brands like Mike 23, Eriffs, Mighty Healthy, Lemar and Dauley, and UndrCrwn, your closet will be looking Wild Style in no time. Offering a selection of major and alternative street wear and lifestyle brands, Pedestrian is also filled with hats, books, mags, art supplies, and accessories.

WOMEN'S CLOTHING AND ACCESSORIES

ANTHROPOLOGIE

1801 Walnut St., 215/568-2114, www.anthropologie.com
HOURS: Mon.-Sat. 10 A.M.-8 P.M., Sun. 11 A.M.-6 P.M.

Map 3

This wildly successful national chain began right here in Philly, founded by the same clothiers behind the even better-known Urban Outfitters. The more sophisticated, higher-quality and pricier big sister to Urban, Anthropologie is a fusion of French country and Indian Bazaar–inspired, sophisticated high-end women's wear…or something like that. It's basically filled with pretty, feminine well-made clothes and accessories. Home goods fill the lower level of the three-story historic Rittenhouse Square mansion, a building that epitomizes the lifestyle of many of its well-to-do patrons. Be prepared to shell out big bucks for embellished cotton sundresses in the summer and cozy, intricately detailed woolens in the frostier months.

ECHOCHIC

1700 Sansom St., 215/569-9555, www.echochic.com
HOURS: Mon.-Tues. 11 A.M.-6 P.M., Wed.-Sat. 11 A.M.-7 P.M., Sun. noon-5 P.M.

Map 3

If your personal style is the modern-day equivalent of a classic 1960s French New Wave film, then Echochic is your spot. Picture a ride on the Riviera in a 1965 fire-engine-red Thunderbird convertible on a sun-dappled day, with the accompanying fabulous Missoni bikini, shiny Dior aviators, and vibrant Pucci headscarf. The 1st floor of this upscale Rittenhouse boutique carries plenty of chic items by style heavy-hitters like See by Chloe, Marc Jacobs, and L.A.M.B. The more

adventurous can climb the winding metal staircase (bonus points for doing it in stilettos) for the vintage treasure trove of handbags, shoes, dresses, and bangles from the 1930s–1980s.

GUACAMOLE

422 South St., 215/923-6174
HOURS: Mon.-Thurs. 11 A.M.-10 P.M., Fri.-Sat. 11 A.M.-11 P.M., Sun. noon-9 P.M.

Map 5

Back in the 1990s, this South Street mainstay was a haven for Manic Panic, wallet chains, and angst-ridden teenagers, who could all be found skanking in unison to the rhythm of every Rancid song ever recorded. Today, the evolutionary leap is clear, as the ska-punk past has been substituted by the pop-punk present of Rocket Dog shoes, Dickies tote bags, and a soundtrack of Avril Lavigne playing in the background.

JOAN SHEPP

1616 Walnut St., 215/735-2666, www.joanshepp.com
HOURS: Mon.-Sat. 10 A.M.-6 P.M., Wed. until 8 P.M., Sun. noon-5 P.M.

Map 3

Joan Shepp keeps the ladies of Rittenhouse in the business of high fashion, and the wealthiest, most fashionable ladies of Rittenhouse repay the debt by keeping Joan Shepp in business. This lofty, high-ceilinged store boasts classic wardrobe staples and trendy accents from design houses like Marni, Dries Van Noten, and Yohji Yamamoto. And no silhouette would be complete without a pair of Louboutin or Miu Miu pumps from their drop-dead-gorgeous shoe selection. If you've got cash to burn and appreciate high fashion, go now.

KNIT WIT

1718 Walnut St., 215/564-4760, www.knitwitonline.com
HOURS: Mon.-Sat. 10 A.M.-6 P.M., Wed. until 8 P.M.

Map 3

Chic formal dresses and basic separates line the racks of this upscale retailer. Find the latest pieces from the collections of designers like Roberto Cavalli, Anna Molinari, Piazza Sempione, Rag & Bone, and Collette

Dinnigan, to name just a few. Pick up a supple leather handbag by Il Bisonte or Gryson. Snag a hot new pair of Jimmy Choo pumps for a night on the town, or a more casual pair of hip John Varvatos Converse for stylish everyday wear.

LEEHE FAI

133 S. 18th St., 215/564-6111, www.leehefai.com
HOURS: Mon.-Fri. 10 A.M.-7 P.M., Sat. noon-6 P.M., Sun. 10 A.M.-9 P.M.
Map 3

The hip and often-changing window display will lure you in, and the fabulous and trendy designs from style mavens like Nanette Lepore and Rebecca Taylor will keep you in the dressing rooms. Prices are not cheap for this small boutique's ultra-feminine and flirty frocks, but the staff isn't pushy, and will let you browse at your own pace. Grab a pair of celeb-coveted Rock & Republic designer denims or play dress-up with a fun Betsy Johnson cocktail dress.

PLAGE TAHITI

128 S. 17th St., 215/569-9139
HOURS: Tues.-Fri. 10 A.M.-7 P.M., Sat.-Sun. 10 A.M.-6 P.M.
Map 3

It's no surprise that this selective women's clothing and accessories boutique is a frequent winner of the "Best of Philly" award from *Philadelphia* magazine. Conjured up by the owners of the longstanding Philly fashion hub Knit Wit, Plage Tahiti is known mostly for its colorful bikinis and well-made summer wear. Be on the lookout for staple pieces from designers like Theory, Diane Von Furstenberg, and Ghost. The 2nd floor will appease the more budget-conscious with end-of-season sales and the occasional great bargain throughout the year.

PETULIA'S FOLLY

1710 Sansom St., 215/569-1344, www.petuliasfolly.com
HOURS: Mon.-Sat. 10 A.M.-6 P.M., Wed. until 7 P.M.
Map 3

In architecture, a folly is an ornate and embellished building created to publicly communicate artistic vision and self-expression. In fashion and home accents, Petulia's Folly is the stylish equivalent. With a bevy of high-end but exceptionally unique jewelry, handbags, candles, throw pillows, women's clothing, and shoes, it would be a criminal folly to overlook this one-of-a-kind boutique. If you're on a budget, regular sales mean you can finally pick up the Siegerson Morrison sandals and Katayone Adeli chiffon dress you've been coveting all season.

SMITH BROS.

1728 Chestnut St., 215/988-1838,
HOURS: Mon.-Sat. 11 A.M.-7 P.M., Sun. noon-6 P.M.
Map 3

For some, a simple pair of denim trousers is a plain and utilitarian indulgence. Those people do not shop at Smith Bros. The retailers confound logic with the phrase "high-end casual" to describe their selection of jeans, tops, and accessories. The racks are packed with upscale and hard-to-find denim brands like Citizens of Humanity, Seven, Blue Cult, Chip N Pepper, James, and a savory selection of Juicy Couture. This small local chain has several additional outposts in the suburbs and in New Jersey.

THIRD STREET HABIT

153 N. 3rd St., 215/925-5455,
www.thirdstreethabit.com
HOURS: Mon.-Sat. 11 A.M.-7 P.M., Sun. noon-6 P.M.
Map 1

Most habits are easy to acquire and tough to break; Third Street Habit is no exception to this rule. The Annie Get Your Gun meets Age of Innocence decor is mirrored by the fantastic threads lining the walls. Knowledgeable and friendly staff will work on picking out items that compliment your style with helpful suggestions like: "Like that Ya Ya sweater dress? Then you'll love the Earnest Sewn Cigarette Jean." Sorry wallets, there's a new habit in town, and it isn't cheap.

THREE SIRENS

134 N. 3rd St., 215/925-3548, www.threesirens.com
HOURS: Tues.-Sat. 11 A.M.-7 P.M., Sun. noon-5 P.M.
Map 1

If the mythical three sirens had been outfitted by the Philly boutique bearing the same name, Odysseus would have been a goner. Crooning on sharp rocks all day long necessitates functional fashion, and Three Sirens has got your body covered. Luxuriate in comfy cottons by Vince, designer denims by Paige, and silk sundresses by Vintage Betty. And at these relatively reasonable price points for a quality boutique, you don't have to have epic pockets to dress like a deity.

TOPSTITCH

311 Market St., 2nd fl., 267/322-4057,
www.topstitchboutique.com
HOURS: Mon.-Wed. noon-7 P.M., Thurs.-Sat.
noon-8 P.M., Sun. noon-6 P.M.
Map 1

Walk up the creaky stairs to the 2nd floor of this unassuming Old City store, and prepare to be dazzled by a wide array of hand-picked vintage and original creations. Part art gallery, part sewing studio, and part retail shop, Topstitch is a seamless fusion of all three. When local chic labels Honeymilk, Babooshka, and Kinked Works came together to form Topstitch, local Philadelphians took notice. Search the jewelry cases for nature-inspired feathered earrings or dainty one-of-a-kind brooches. Browse the racks for the perfect retro cocktail dress and a pair of croc pumps to wear when you come back for First Friday. And if you need a quick sewing fix, ask about renting a machine to satisfy your craving. Monthly trunk shows display the work of local artists. While there is more here for women than men, due to popular request Topstich recently added men's clothing and accessories to their great selection.

URBAN OUTFITTERS

1627 Walnut St., 215/567-2780,
www.urbanoutfitters.com
HOURS: Mon.-Sat. 10 A.M.-8 P.M., Sun. noon-6 P.M.
Map 3

Back in 1970, the first of countless Urban Outfitters to follow opened their doors in a small house on the University of Pennsylvania's campus. With the free-love climate of the '60s not far behind, and whiffs of the disco days

of the '70s breezing in, the urban artsy bo-hemian set embraced the avant-garde retailer with open suede-fringed arms. Today, the funky fashion housed in this multimillion-dollar international chain retailer still draws some of its clientele from its original roots, and much of its inspiration from the urban hipster crowd. The beautiful Center City warehouse-like store pays homage to the original dream with retro frocks, vintage-flavored housewares, and ironic T-shirts on four floors. By nature of its large scale, it is no longer quite as cool as it was at the outset, yet the stylish and comfy clothes at this Philadelphia original still attract youngsters in hordes.

VAGABOND

37 N. 3rd St., 215/671-0737,
www.vagabondboutique.com
HOURS: Mon.-Sat. 11 A.M.-7 P.M., Sun. 11 A.M.-5 P.M.
Map 1

With a near-monopoly on the boutique-and-yarn-shop theme with Topstitch, owners Mary Clark and Megan Murphy opened another successful Old City boutique in 2001. Vagabond's large, minimalist space houses the perfect combination of fabulous vintage frocks and ultra-stylish, sleek, and contemporary designs—many from local designers. Check out the back room for yarn, children's clothing, accessories, housewares, and monthly art exhibits. And don't be fooled by the name—while your pants certainly won't be threadbare, your pockets may be after shopping here. Clothes are definitely chic, but certainly not cheap.

SHOES

◀ BENJAMIN LOVELL SHOES

119 S. 18th St., 215/564-4655,
www.benjaminlovellshoes.com
HOURS: Mon.-Thurs. 10 A.M.-7 P.M., Fri.-Sat.
10 A.M.-8 P.M., Sun. noon-5 P.M.
Map 3

"Style never felt so good" is the motto at Benjamin Lovell, a small chain that stocks its shelves with a diverse range of modern footwear, from Mephisto, Ecco, and Dansko to stylish sneaks like Vans and Nike Air Force Ones—the sole unifying theme is their dedication to comfort. Prices can get high, but it's worth every penny for the quality and durability. The Rittenhouse location on 18th Street has a large regular and discount selection, and the South Street branch (Map 5, 318 South St., 215/238-1969, Mon.–Thurs. 10 A.M.–8 P.M., Fri.–Sat. 10 A.M.–9 P.M., Sun. 11 A.M.–6 P.M.) has a great bargain section in the back, where prices are dramatically slashed at the end of the season. There's also a location in Manayunk (Map 9, 4305 Main St., 215/487-3747, Mon.–Thurs. 10 A.M.–7 P.M., Fri.–Sat. 10 A.M.–8 P.M., Sun. 11 A.M.–6 P.M.).

HEAD START SHOES

126 S. 17th St., 215/567-3247, www.headstartshoes.com
HOURS: Mon.-Tues. 10 A.M.-7 P.M., Wed.-Sat.
10 A.M.-7:30 P.M., Sun. noon-6 P.M.
Map 3

The shoes at Head Start are the stuff of folklore and fantasy. If it buckles, snaps, zips, clips, or is covered in studs, you'll find it here. Owner George Patti travels to Italy twice a year to select the unique women's styles, including gravity-defying heels and kinky cowboy boots. Find balance on a pair of Dries Van Noten platform wedges, or walk a straight line with a pair of Via Spiga Mary Janes. All the while you'll be getting a head start on the season's most unique styles.

UBIQ

1509 Walnut St., 215/988-0194, www.ubiqlife.com
HOURS: Mon.-Tues. 11 A.M.-7:30 P.M., Wed.-Sat.
11 A.M.-8 P.M., Sun. noon-6 P.M.
Map 3

A Philadelphia flagship of this selective chain, Ubiq positions itself as sneaker and clothing purveyor, art gallery, and all around urban-youth lifestyle destination. Walk (or skate) up the ramp on the 1st floor and you'll find yourself in sneaker and designer-T heaven. Upstairs, you'll discover a gallery to the left and a sneaker boutique to the right. Popular brands include Jordan's, Air Force Ones, Street Wear, Twelve Bar, The Hundreds, and Royal Fam.

VINTAGE AND THRIFT

BARGAIN THRIFT

5245 Germantown Ave., 215/849-3225
HOURS: Mon.-Tues. and Fri.-Sat. 9:30 A.M.-6 P.M.,
Wed.-Thurs. 9:30 A.M.-8 P.M.
Map 9

With the increasing popularity of high-end vintage and consignment shops, it's hard to find a good old-fashioned dirt-cheap thrift store to root through these days. Well, here it is—a true thrift store in the heart of Germantown. Granted, consignment shop buyers visit regularly and they pick through the best items long before you wake up in the morning, but with new items coming in each day, there is enough good stuff to go around. With an entire branch devoted to furniture a few doors down, you can find some real treasures in both stores, be it clothing, shoes, a couch, or knick-knacks you crave.

BUFFALO EXCHANGE

1713 Chestnut St., 215/557-9850,
www.buffaloexchange.com
HOURS: Mon.-Sat. 10 A.M.-8 P.M., Sun. noon-6 P.M.
Map 3

This nationwide consignment-cum-thrift store aims to reuse and recycle one-of-a-kind fashions. Supply and demand dictates the ever-changing stock, which usually consists of higher-end vintage, designer basics, evening wear, shoes, and accessories. With the store's reasonable prices and items usually in excellent condition, it's likely you won't look like you rolled out of the thrift store. You can also bring in your former-favorite clothing and accessories, which the good people at Buffalo Exchange will buy from you and sell back to the public. The buyers are discriminating, so don't bother trying to sell unless your old duds are in great shape and are still likely to be stylish in someone's mind.

DECADES VINTAGE

615 Bainbridge St., 215/923-3135
HOURS: Mon.-Sat. 1-8 P.M., Sun. 1-6 P.M.
Map 5

Tucked away on a quiet block just south of bustling South Street, this small Bella Vista vintage boutique conjures up ultra-feminine images of glamorous and bohemian high fashion. Amongst the wide array of hand-picked quirky and unusual finds, from higher-end designers as well as lesser-known labels, you can find costume baubles, trendy boots and heels, and one-of-a-kind accessories. Decades is a must for die-hard thrifters who don't want to sift through the trash to find the treasures.

LOST & FOUND
133 N. 3rd St., 215/928-1311
HOURS: Mon.-Thurs. 11:30 A.M.-7 P.M., Fri.-Sat.
11 A.M.-8 P.M., Sun. noon-6 P.M.
Map 1

Thrifters and fashion-forward females rejoice! There is a holy ground where reasonably priced, girly vintage duds and modern ultra-femme dresses, funky shoes, and colorful accessories exist together in peaceful harmony. Fun men's and women's tees (like Shepard Fairey's infamous Andre the Giant Obey print) and hip shoes from makers like Seychelles line the walls in this small, unassuming Old City treasure with a perfect name.

PHILADELPHIA AIDS THRIFT
514 Bainbridge St., 215/922-3186,
www.phillyaidsthrift.blogspot.com
HOURS: Mon.-Thurs. noon-8 P.M., Fri.-Sat. noon-9 P.M.,
Sun. noon-6 P.M.
Map 5

Philadelphia AIDS Thrift (aka PAT) follows the "one man's trash is another's treasure" model. Bring in the wares you no longer need and AIDS Thrift will sell them for you, with a significant portion of the proceeds going to local AIDS/HIV organizations. This eclectic and eccentric spot has everything from used toasters to movie posters, instructional workout videos, children's toys, lamp shades, and winter coats. You might have to dig around a bit to uncover the true gems, but rest assured you'll find them if you have the patience.

SUGARCUBE
124 N. 3rd St., 215/238-0825,
www.sugarcube.us
HOURS: Mon.-Sat. noon-7 P.M., Sun. noon-5 P.M.
Map 1

Sugarcube has a great mix of precious vintage clothing and of-the-moment designs from local and national designers. Stocked with feminine and fashionable dresses and tops and a small but excellent selection of jeans, the prices are often high but worth every penny for unique, quality styles. The shoe selection that has won a "Best of Philly" award and the handbags and accessories, like everything else, are carefully chosen. Best of all, the changing room at Sugarcube is housed in an old bank vault, making you feel very secure and a little spooked while trying on your cool new clothes.

Home Furnishings and Accents

ANASTACIA'S ANTIQUES
617 Bainbridge St., 215/928-9111
HOURS: Thurs.-Sat. noon-6:30 P.M., Sun. noon-5 P.M.
Map 5

A large selection of Victorian collectibles and early-American wares like gas pumps and schoolhouse chalkboards fill this antique-furniture and accessory store. Get lost in the fantastic Bakelite bangles and Lucite-adorned clutches in the vintage jewelry cases. The staff's open and friendly vibe will make you

feel right at home while they help you find the next piece to fit your personal collection—and your personal budget. Prices are reasonable, and if you live nearby, large items can be delivered to your home.

BELLE MAISON
4340 Main St., 215/482-6222, www.belle-maison.com
Map 9

Belle Maison means "beautiful home." Michelle and Bernadette, sisters and co-owners, want to help you make your home beautiful. In their stunning high-end store and showroom in the heart of Manayunk, the grand, ample space is arranged in cozy vignettes to display hand-selected, European-influenced modern and antique pieces. Indoor and outdoor furniture, lighting, accessories, and high-quality linens abound, and interior design and home consultation services are also available. The prices are often steep, but the quality and selection are consistently high.

BRUGES HOME

323A Race St., 215/922-6041, www.brugeshome.com
HOURS: Tues.-Sat. 10 A.M.-7 P.M., Sun. noon-5 P.M.
Map 1

Taking its name from the Dutch port town, Bruges Home is filled with nature-inspired furniture, wall hangings, original art, colorful tableware, and knickknacks from around the world representing various time periods. The store is housed in a bright, restored historic building, making the shopping experience as unique as the offerings. The dazzling scented-candle selection from D.L. & Co, Altru, and Vela Aromatica, to name just a few, is impressive, and if your coffee table is in need of a dose of sophistication, scoop up one of the several Taschen books scattered about.

FOSTER'S URBAN HOMEWARE

399 Market St., 215/925-0950, www.shopfosters.com
Map 1

In Foster's large showroom there is ample space to generously accommodate the humbling variety of cool, cutting-edge items for every room in the home, including kitchen, bedroom, bath, office, living, dining, and playroom. From cutlery to Cuisinarts, decorations to drapes, wine glasses to trash bins, it's all here. While prices aren't rock-bottom, they're not quite as high as at some other high-end home stores.

HELLO WORLD

1201 Pine St., 215/545-7060,
www.shophelloworld.com
HOURS: Tues.-Fri. 11 A.M.-6 P.M., Sat.-Sun. 11 A.M.-5 P.M.
Map 2

While the items found at Hello World's two

locations vary somewhat, both the Rittenhouse (257 S. 20th St., 215/545-5207, Mon.–Fri. 11 P.M.–7 P.M., Sat.–Sun. 11 A.M.–5 P.M.) and Antique Row shops maintain the same standard of quirky and high-end gift and houseware excellence. Retro barkcloth and bakelite bangles dress the windows, while sleek Chadwick door- and placemats keep the floors and tables clean. Save the trip to the flea market and scoop up one of owner and textile designer J. Lamancuso's hand-picked vintage lamps, tables, and chairs. Offering mostly new designs, there is also a small selection of carefully chosen second-hand items. The diverse offerings include pillows, jewelry, handbags, clocks, and cute T-shirts for babies.

MATTHEW IZZO

1109 Walnut St., 215/829-0606, www.matthewizzo.com
HOURS: Furniture store: Mon.-Sat. 11 A.M.-7 P.M. and Sun. by appt.; Clothing store: Mon.-Thurs. 11 A.M.-7 P.M., Fri.-Sat. 11 A.M.-8 P.M., Sun. noon-5 P.M.
Map 2

If its chic, minimalist housewares you crave, then pull up a Jonathan Adler chair and make yourself at home. With a successful high-end clothing boutique under his belt, Izzo has been a trailblazer in the Philly fashion and design scene. This venture in clocks and concrete carries coveted items from Umbra, MoMA Design, and Italian kitchen-accessory favorite Alessi. If the Mandarina Duck purses aren't your bag, check out the full-service hair salon in the back to satisfy your latest personal design fix. Now you can have the complete Matthew Izzo experience all in one stop.

OPEN HOUSE

107 S. 13th St., 215/922-1415,
www.openhouseliving.com
HOURS: Mon.-Sat. 11 A.M.-6 P.M., Wed. until 7 P.M., Sun. noon-5 P.M.
Map 2

How to furnish the contemporary urban living space? Open House has found simple and functional answers that come in the shape of sleek end tables and colorful home accessories. City-dwellers can rejoice at the selection of space-conserving items including stools, side tables, hanging light fixtures, and glass storage jars of all sizes. Soft bedding, decorative rugs, minimalist kitchenwares, and specialty soaps round out the eclectic mix.

🄲 PHAG

1225 Walnut St., 215/545-5645,
www.thephagshop.com
HOURS: Mon.-Sat. 11 A.M.-8 P.M., Sun. noon-6 P.M.
Map 2

Acronyms can be deceiving, and PHAG (Philadelphia Home Art Garden) is no exception. Not your average homosexual-themed novelty gift, home, and garden shop, PHAG offers a wide array of both stylish and quirky furniture, fashions, and garden accessories. Walk beyond the colossal Madonna "Confessions on a Dance Floor Tour" print to the stairs in the back where you'll unearth a hodgepodge of unique gay-themed treasures. Don't miss the dyke dolls (Bobbie comes equipped with her own vibrator), pin-the-tail-on-the-hunk games, or the just-plain-bizarre Judy Garland shrines—all of which position PHAG somewhere truly over the rainbow.

SCARLET FIORELLA

113 S. 13th St., 215/922-1955,
www.scarletfiorella.com
HOURS: Mon.-Fri. 11 A.M.-7 P.M., Sat. 11 A.M.-6 P.M., Sun. noon-5 P.M.
Map 2

Scarlet Fiorella's specialty is their hand-painted art-deco furniture from the 1920s and '40s, but they carry much more. Upon entering, you'll notice plenty of eye-catching housewares and bath and body products. Cute and ironic children's T-shirts, shoes, and accessories also find shelter among the adult offerings, while magnificent vintage chandeliers provide the ideal lighting to showcase the varied hodgepodge.

SCARLETT ALLEY

241 Race St., 215/592-7898,
www.scarlettalley.com
HOURS: Mon.-Fri. 11 A.M.-7 P.M., Sat. 10 A.M.-6 P.M., Sun. noon-5 P.M.
Map 1

Mother-and-daughter owners Mary Kay and Liz Scarlett offer unusual beauty products, home accents, jewelry, and gifts. Check out Voluspa's rich and floral roll-on perfumes and Fresh candles in inviting wake-up fragrances. For the kitsch lover, there are colorful retro-inspired Lexon Mini Dolmen radios or the Toss Designs Pony domino sets. Wander to the back to unearth a sweet collection of lingerie, pajamas, and slippers cozy enough to make you never want to leave the house again. Much of the furniture and shelves in the store are handcrafted by Liz's father and can be special ordered.

WEST ELM

1330 Chestnut St., 215/731-0184,
www.westelm.com
HOURS: Mon.-Sat. 10 A.M.-8 P.M., Sun. 11 A.M.-6 P.M.
Map 2

Minimalist designs and colorful palettes are what you'll find at West Elm, the nationwide home furnishings store with furniture so unique you'll forget it's a chain store. Prices are comparable to the Crate & Barrels of the world, but with an emphasis on more youthful and spare decor. Many of the textiles appeal to a simple, breezy "Far East meets beach house" sensibility, while the lighting and wall fixtures echo a sleeker *Metropolitan Home* aesthetic. The large warehouse-like showroom space displays the wares in color-coded sections.

Gift and Specialty

GOURMET TREATS
GROCERY
105 S. 13th St., 215/922-5252, www.grocery13.com
HOURS: Café: Mon.-Fri. 7:30 A.M.-7 P.M., Sat.
9 A.M.-6 P.M.; Market: Mon.-Sat. 11 A.M.-8:30 P.M.
Map 2

Half café and half specialty upscale food market, there's something for everyone at Grocery, whether you need an on-the-go lunch, snack, or sweet, to purchase a picnic in the park, or find a gift for a foodie friend. Owners Marcie Turney and Valerie Safran, also responsible for the acclaimed Mexican BYOB Lolita across the street, sell several of the restaurant's specialties in the store, including their delicious margarita mix. Flavored oils, spreads, Ciao Bella gelato, and tins of Mighty Leaf tea are offered along with a small but excellent supply of cutting boards and cooking and serving tools.

PREMIUM STEAP
111 S. 18th St., 215/568-2920, www.premiumsteap.com
HOURS: Mon.-Fri. 10 A.M.-5:30 P.M., Sat. 10 A.M.-6 P.M.
Map 3

Relocated from its original suburban Wayne location, Premium Steap now invites city-dwellers to become loose-tea connoisseurs. You'll be intrigued by the long wall of shiny and mysterious canisters whose contents arrive from all over the globe. The knowledgeable and passionate proprietor will encourage you to take one down, remove the lid, and experience the aroma before you select a flavor. Enjoy a premium cup while you're there and take plenty home for later. In addition to the tea itself, the store offers a host of cool teapots, cups, mugs, canisters, strainers, and all things tea.

INTERNATIONAL WARES
BLACK CAT
3428 Sansom St., 215/386-6664,
www.blackcatshop.com
HOURS: Mon. 10 A.M.-9 P.M., Tues.-Sat. 10 A.M.-11 P.M.,
Sun. 11 A.M.-9 P.M.
Map 6

Under the same ownership as the White Dog Café next door, this gift shop is nestled into a row of Victorian brownstones on the fringe of Penn's campus. From handmade candles out of Africa to a stuffed cat made from recycled sweaters and yarns, each item has a story to tell. You'll also find a small, interesting book collection, and toys for both pets and kids. The only common thread among the store's diverse offerings is that all the merchandise was carefully chosen to contribute to the good of the planet. Whether made from recycled materials, supporting the work of local artists and craftspeople, or with a percentage of proceeds supporting other good causes, this is a place where you'll feel good spending your money.

GARLAND OF LETTERS
527 South St., 215/923-5946
HOURS: Daily noon-9:30 P.M.
Map 5

When Mother Earth and Father Sky get busy, they rely on incense from the Garland of Letters to set the mood. Philly's leading purveyor of books on mysticism, philosophy, Eastern religions, nature worship, holistic healing, self-improvement, massage, and more offers a soothing escape from the bustle of South Street. With a good assortment of lotions, oils, music, art, home accessories, crystals, and, of course, incense, the atmosphere is somewhat New Age-y, but in the best possible way. If you need to pick up a book on the meanings of various henna tattoos, recordings of Vedic chanting, or a how-to guide to Tantric sex, this is the place.

TEN THOUSAND VILLAGES
1122 Walnut St., 215/574-2008,
www.tenthousandvillages.com
HOURS: Mon.-Sat. 10 A.M.-7 P.M., Sun. noon-5 P.M.
Map 2

It takes a village, or in this case, ten thousand, to raise a handicrafts store totally dedicated to the support of fair trade and child labor laws in the developing world. There are now approximately 160 retailers of Ten Thousand Villages goods scattered throughout the United States, specializing in unique items ranging from textiles, baskets, and jewelry to musical instruments, ceramics, and handmade soaps—all crafted by artists from every corner of the globe. With a portion of the proceeds benefiting the economic vitality of these artisan communities, you and your newly purchased Bangladeshi recycled tote can shop guilt-free.

MORE SPECIALTY SHOPS

AIA BOOKSTORE AND DESIGN CENTER

1218 Arch St., 215/569-3188, www.aiabookstore.com
HOURS: Mon.-Thurs. 10 A.M.-6 P.M., Fri.-Sat. 10 A.M.-7 P.M., Sun. noon-5 P.M.
Map 2

At this store operated by the American Institute of Architects (AIA), architecture and design buffs will find endless items of interest, though the varied selection spread over two floors offers the layperson plenty to enjoy as well. The selection of specialty books (many ideal for a coffee table) covers a wide range of home and design topics along with collecting, tasting, urban studies, politics, and more. Plenty of quirky gifts are available, including puzzles, ties patterned with maps, watches shaped like postage stamps, screen-printed note cards, and funny baby clothes. This is the store where you can find a gift for that person that already has everything—particularly if that person has a penchant for art or design. A unique collection of greeting cards is available for anti-Hallmark types.

DETAILS

103 S. 18th St., 215/977-9559, www.detailsphiladelphia.com
HOURS: Mon.-Sat. 10 A.M.-5:30 P.M., Wed. until 7 P.M.
Map 3

If you have a thick wallet, an eye for detail, and a desire for fine stationery products, then Details is the store for you. Offering an array of paper products including hand-stitched journals, leatherbound photo albums, eco-friendly stationery, and invitations with serious pizzazz, this store exceeds the expectations of the most discerning papershopper. In-store services include custom design for invitations and announcements and personalized calligraphy, printing, and embossing.

PHILADELPHIA GLASSWORKS

908 N. 3rd St., 215/627-3655, www.phillyglassworks.com
HOURS: Mon.-Sat. noon-8 P.M., Sun. noon-5 P.M.
Map 7

This glass-object gallery and glass-blowing studio is a unique spot where you can watch glassblowers create exquisite masterpieces while you shop. As you wander, look up to see oversized frosted-glass handcuffs and shackles hanging from the ceiling. The many delicate, carefully made items available include jewelry, marbles, paperweights, and vases. And if you're feeling the DIY vibes, sign up for a class in bead-making or lampworking.

R.E. LOAD BAGGAGE, INC.

608 N. 2nd St., 215/922-2018, www.reloadbags.com
HOURS: Tues.-Fri. 11 A.M.-6 P.M., Sat. noon-6 P.M., and Mon. by appt.
Map 7

Former bike messengers Roland and Ellie (the R. and E. in the company name) founded this one-of-a-kind local company in 1998 on their quest to create the perfect messenger bag. Using only the highest-quality materials, R.E. Load Baggage carefully constructs messenger and courier bags, backpacks, and just about any other type of bag that holds stuff. The best part is, each bag is custom-designed and made by hand to reflect the needs and desires of the lucky owner-to-be. Specialized orders can be placed in the store, online, or over the phone, or you can choose from a small ready-made selection. The bags are pricey (upwards of $250), but they are made to last a lifetime, or close anyway. Each has its own special flair chosen by you, so you're not just paying for a bag—you're paying for an extension of your personality to wear over your shoulder. R.E. Load has opened a second store in Seattle and its bags are now sold at select retail stores throughout the country.

SAILOR JERRY

118 S. 13th St., 215/531-6380,
www.sailorjerry.com
HOURS: Mon.-Thurs. 10 A.M.-7 P.M., Fri.-Sat.
10 A.M.-8 P.M., Sun. noon-5 P.M.
Map 2

Norman "Sailor Jerry" Collins is said to be the forefather of the Old School Tattoo. He set up his first tattoo parlor in Honolulu's Chinatown district during the 1930s and his shop became a haven for wayward and often inebriated sailors. The Philly boutique pays homage to the ink legend with locally made T-shirts, shot glasses, lighters, and even custom Chuck Taylor's, all bearing his iconic images. If you start to get seasick from the nautical-themed raised-velvet wallpaper, bamboo trim, and enormous squid chandeliers—outfitted by Philly artist Adam Wallacavage—purchase a bottle of their very own 92-proof rum and it'll be smooth sailing again in no time.

VIA BICYCLE

606 S. 9th St., 215/627-3370, www.bikeville.com
HOURS: Tues. and Thurs.-Sat. 10 A.M.-5 P.M., Wed.
1-9 P.M.
Map 5

The self-proclaimed "most interesting bike shop in the world," Via Bicycle is an excellent resource for buying and selling used bikes and for low-cost repairs. The shop itself is a sight to be seen with its authentic vintage decor filled with well-maintained bikes and accessories. Road bikes, beach cruisers, classics, basics, and rare bikes are available for sale. Or just stop by to fill up your tires outside next to the signature yellow benches where locals do a little fine tuning. The mechanics are knowledgeable and friendly and prices are average.

Malls and Department Stores

In addition to the following malls and shopping centers, which are unique for their size, content, or location, several additional standard suburban malls are located just outside the city. Plymouth Meeting Mall, Willow Grove Mall, and the Cherry Hill Mall (in nearby New Jersey) offer department stores, chain stores, food courts, and movie theaters. For other basics, you can sometimes find great deals on quality goods at the Lord & Taylor department store on City Line Avenue.

FRANKLIN MILLS OUTLET MALL

1455 Franklin Mills Circle, I-95 and Woodhaven Dr.,
215/632-1500, www.simon.com
HOURS: Mon.-Sat. 10 A.M.-9:30 P.M., Sun. 11 A.M.-7 P.M.
Map 10

There aren't too many reasons for visitors to travel to the far corner of Northeast Philadelphia, but Franklin Mills is a good one. The Garden of Eden to the devout discount shopper, the sprawling one-story mall is home to a plethora of outlet stores. Most of the major chains are represented, including the Gap, Banana Republic, J. Crew, and Ann Taylor, along with higher-end manufacturers like Off Fifth (Saks Fifth Avenue), Polo, Ralph Lauren, and Last Call Neiman Marcus—all selling wares at sinfully low prices. There are 200 shops, seven themed restaurants, a 14-screen movie theater, and a bowling alley: Set the entire day aside for your trip; you'll need it.

GALLERY AT MARKET EAST

Market St. between 9th and 12th Sts.,
www.thegalleryatmarketeast.com
Map 2

For those who enjoy both the suburban convenience of mall shopping and the vitality of urban life, Philly offers the Gallery at Market East. Stretching out over three blocks above its eponymous train station, the Gallery holds over 170 stores on four levels, a food court, gym, and even a fish market. Unlike the smaller, upscale Shops at Liberty Place, both the Gallery's shops and clientele better reflect the racial and economic diversity of the city. In addition to the typical mall chains like Foot Locker and Old Navy, the Gallery has a K-Mart and a Burlington Coat Factory, and vendor booths selling spray-painted T-shirts, watches, jewelry, cell phone paraphernalia, and edible treats. While often crowded and loud, the Gallery is a perfectly convenient place to shop. And with the regional rail line underneath the mall, it's easy to make a quick getaway from the urban bustle.

KING OF PRUSSIA MALL

Rte. 202 at Mall Blvd., 610/265-5727,
www.kingofprussiamall.com
HOURS: Mon.-Sat. 10 A.M.-9:30 P.M., Sun. 11 A.M.-7 P.M.
`Map 10`

Some come to the area for the history, others for the nightlife, and others still for the mammoth King of Prussia Mall. The world-famous megalopolis of materialism is home to more than 400 stores and restaurants, eight major department stores, and more than 2.8 million square feet of retail space. The mall website offers tidbits to put this size in perspective—like the fact that the number of sodas sold in the mall each year would be enough to fill five Olympic-sized swimming pools, or that if you walked through every corridor and isle, the distance would be more than walking across Manhattan. In addition to the standard mall stores—think Gap, Bebe, Cinnabon—there are dozens of high-end national and international upscale boutique shops including Versace, Hugo Boss, Donna Karan, Hermes, Thomas Pink, and more. It's almost too much to tackle, which is probably why, in addition to a food court, King of Prussia also offers a separate coffee court for shoppers who need a break and a caffeine buzz. If you're not scared away yet, just be sure to leave your Jimmy Choos at home and wear the walking shoes.

MACY'S

1300 Market St., 215/241-9000, www.macys.com
HOURS: Mon.-Sat. 10 A.M.-8 P.M., Sun. 11 A.M.-7 P.M.
`Map 2`

If you've seen one Macy's, you've seen 'em all, right? Wrong! This Macy's is in a building

that was formerly home to Wanamaker's, considered by many to be North America's first full-fledged department store. Lord & Taylor's followed in this location, then was replaced by Macy's, which opened its doors on this historic landmark site in August 2006. Designed to resemble Paris's Les Halles, the grand building comes complete with marble floors, elegant columns, and gold details around a grand central atrium. It also boasts one of the world's largest playable pipe organs and a 2,500-pound bronze eagle statue from the 1904 St. Louis World's Fair. A light-and-music show of the *Nutcracker* plays hourly in the central atrium during the holiday season; the old Philadelphia tradition has survived the changing of the store's ownership, drawing crowds each year. Be sure to peek inside even if you don't need to buy anything.

THE SHOPS AT THE BELLEVUE

200 S. Broad St., 215/875-8350,
www.bellevuephiladelphia.com
HOURS: Daily 10 A.M.-6 P.M., Wed. until 8 P.M.
`Map 3`

Luxury seeps through the gold-and-marble decor of this two-story shopping center in the heart of Center City's Avenue of the Arts. The high-end options make sense, considering the mall is literally attached to one of the city's finest hotels. If your wallet is fat, this is the place for a good time. Stop at Origins for luxurious creams, lotions, and potions; at Tiffany & Co. for new jewels; Hope Chest for tasteful lingerie; and Nicole Miller for that last-minute cocktail dress. You can also visit the mahogany wonderland of the third-largest Polo Ralph Lauren store in the world, stop at Williams-Sonoma for delectable treats and kitchenwares, or pop into Teuscher to satisfy the most decadent chocolate craving. The lower level offers a food court and the full-service Pierre & Carlo salon and spa.

THE SHOPS AT LIBERTY PLACE

1625 Chestnut St., 215/851-9055,
www.shopsatliberty.com
HOURS: Mon.-Sat. 9:30 A.M.-7 P.M., Sun. noon-6 P.M.
`Map 3`

Somewhere between the over-the-top elegance

of the Shops at the Bellevue and the down-and-sometimes-a-little-dirty Gallery, the Shops at Liberty Place offer yet another indoor urban mall experience. A central atrium is covered by a domed-glass ceiling and several hallways of shops lead toward the street in different directions, occupying two entire floors of a full city block. Above it are endless floors of offices, making the food court a popular stop for the downtown business set at lunchtime. You'll find chain clothing stores including Express, J. Crew, and Victoria's Secret, as well as health and beauty brands Aveda, Crabtree & Evelyn, and The Body Shop, along with shoe stores Nine West, Aldo, and Bellini. You'll also find Borders, Sunglass Hut, Godiva, and an upscale men's hairstylist, Style of Man.

Spa, Bath, and Beauty

BALANCE HEALTH CENTER
112 S. 20th St., 215/751-0344,
www.balancehealthcenter.com
HOURS: Daily 9 A.M.-6 P.M.
Map 3

A true health center, as its name reveals, rather than your typical spa, this isn't a place to go to look better, but a place you go to *feel* better. Rooted in holistic health principles, the spa works with each client to develop personalized feel-better strategies. Offering an array of services to soothe or heal the mind, body, and spirit, Balance offers massage, acupuncture, chiropractic care, hypnotherapy, nutrition counseling, and yoga classes. Traditional Chinese medicine and Ayurveda, a treatment approach rooted in India, are also offered.

BLUEMERCURY APOTHECARY AND SPA
1707 Walnut St., 215/569-3100,
www.bluemercury.com
HOURS: Mon.-Fri. 10 A.M.-7 P.M., Sat. 10 A.M.-6 P.M., Sun. noon-5 P.M.
Map 3

Many of the women you'll see walking around Rittenhouse Square require a certain beauty quotient that can't be unearthed at the local drugstore. Enter Bluemercury. As a purveyor of luxury makeup, lotions, and potions, this upscale apothecary stocks all of the top brands, including Bliss, Bumble & Bumble, NARS, and more. Picture slipping into a luscious Fresh "Sugar" bath, your senses soothed by the scent of the Tocca candles burning all around, followed by a dollop of skin-quenching Laura Mercier Tarte au Citron body lotion. With expert staff and pricey but decadent spa and beauty treatments including facials, wraps, massage, and waxing, Bluemercury goes the extra mile to give the Rittenhouse elite the full pampering experience.

BODY KLINIC
2012 Walnut St., 215/563-8888,
www.thebodyklinic.net
HOURS: Mon.-Sat. 10 A.M.-8 P.M., Sun. 10 A.M.-5 P.M.
Map 3

This small spa provides a wide array of excellent spa services, at lower prices than many of the nearby Rittenhouse-area spas. Offering massage, reflexology, herbal wraps, nail services, waxing, electrolysis, and more, the Body Klinic is probably best-known for their facials, which range from gentle refreshers to the works—complete with microdermabrasion, peels, and so on. Most of the products they use are natural and environmentally friendly, with special offerings that sometimes including fruit and other food products, like cranberry wraps or green-tea and pomegranate scrubs. While there isn't a lot of room for lounging in the small single floor of the converted row house, it is an excellent place to find good, reasonably priced services. Check the website for monthly specials and coupons, including a $5 student discount or $15 off a massage or facial for first-time customers.

SHOPPING

◖ DUROSS & LANGEL

117 S. 13th St., 215/592-7627,
www.durossandlangel.com
HOURS: Mon.-Sat. 11 A.M.-8 P.M., Sun. noon-5 P.M.
Map 2

If smelling deliciously fragrant were your job, you could expect a promotion after a visit to this bath-and-body-product sanctuary. Natural, organic handmade soaps are available in mouth-wateringly sweet scents like coconut clove, banana yogurt, and chocolate-cherry almond, along with more subtle fragrances like black shea and lavender oatmeal. The big hunks of soap on display look good enough to eat. Candles are equally refreshing, in scents of orange blossom, Moroccan cedar, and gardenia, and emollient face and body washes are gentle enough for the most sensitive skin types. Hair products are also top-notch, and the ultra-moisturizing lip balm is simply divine. The local company is committed to using natural products, fair-trade policies for its raw materials, and gift packages of 100 percent recycled paper. Sign up for one of their many workshops to learn how to whip up your own lotions, scrubs, and soaps.

KIEHL'S

1737 Walnut St., 215/636-9936, www.kiehls.com
HOURS: Mon.-Sat. 10 A.M.-7 P.M., Sun. noon-6 P.M.
Map 3

Started as a New York apothecary in 1851, Kiehl's has spread its old-fashioned corrugated tin-ceilings and highly organized shelves to this Walnut Street location. Soothing natural and classically fragrant formulas paired with an unending dedication to customer satisfaction (check out all of the free samples) are what set this hair-and-skin-product haven apart. The unadorned packaging (and maybe also the steep prices) create what could just be a well-marketed illusion that the products provide real medicinal value. Whatever it is, most products do work remarkably well, and smell terrific. Try the signature unisex Original Musk scent, body lotion, or shower gel, infused with essence of Neroli, Bergamot Nectar, Orange Blossom, and Tonka Nut.

RESCUE RITTENHOUSE SPA

255 S. 17th St., 215/772-2766,
www.rescuerittenhousespa.com
HOURS: Mon.-Sat. 9 A.M.-8 P.M.
Map 3

"Beautiful skin is a matter of choice, not chance." These are the words of Danuta Mieloch, owner and founder of Rescue Rittenhouse Spa. When you step off the elevator on the 2nd floor of this Center City office building, you'll enter a tranquil 4,000-square-foot lounge where the simple, soothing decor will put you in the mood for relaxation. Mieloch and her talented staff have won numerous awards for their treatments, most notably their famous transformative facials, including micro-crystal power peels, micro-current, microdermabrasion, and Lumicell Touch. They also offer excellent massage, nail services, waxing, and makeup application. Product lines sold include Biologique Recherche, Valmont, MD Skincare, SkinMedica, Kinerase, Chantecaille, Seda France, Nouveau Derm, Biodroga Systems, Lip Lingerie, and Blinc.

◖ TERME DI AROMA

32 N. 3rd St., 215/829-9769, www.termediaroma.com
HOURS: Tues. noon-8:30 P.M., Wed.-Fri.
11 A.M.-8:30 P.M., Sat. 10 A.M.-7 P.M., Sun. 10 A.M.-4 P.M.
Map 1

This delightful Old City spa specializes in aromatherapy massage, wraps, and facials in an atmosphere that is sweet-smelling bliss. Gentle colors, the sounds of nature, soothing scents, and candlelight surround you from the moment you enter the lobby. Have a cup of tea or juice in the cozy lounge before your treatment. Essential oils are chosen based on your preferences and what you hope to gain from your treatment—be it renewal and relaxation or headache and tension release. The facials are mostly gentle and relaxing, designed so you'll enjoy the process as much as the outcome. Prenatal massage, shiatsu, Reiki, reflexology, and educational seminars on feng shui are also offered, and prices are reasonable, especially considering the prime Old City location.

TOPPERSSPA SALON

117 S. 19th St., 215/496-9966,
http://toppersspa.site.dejazzd.com

HOURS: Mon. 10 A.M.–5:30 P.M., Tues. and Thurs.
10 A.M.–6:30 P.M., Wed. 10 A.M.–7:30 P.M., Fri.–Sat.
9 A.M.–6:30 P.M., Sun. 9 A.M.–4:30 P.M.

Map 3

In the heart of Rittenhouse Square, you'll find a spa and salon offering a diversity of spaces and services within its five floors. The 1st and 2nd floor offers an upscale urban hair and nail salon that belies the more soothing atmosphere waiting on the uppermost levels. There is a cozy Victorian-styled sitting area and changing room on the 3rd floor, along with private massage treatment rooms. The top-floor atrium offers the most unique setting of all in a greenhouse-like atmosphere with a large, windowed ceiling. Umbrellas, chaises, and cabanas offer a lovely place to enjoy a cup of tea or fruit-infused water and completely forget you're in the middle of the city. In addition to the Rittenhouse Square location, this local chain has outlets in Devon and Bucks County, Pennsylvania, and Marlton, New Jersey.

HOTELS

Along with all the standard chain hotels you'd expect in a major city, Philadelphia offers independent and boutique hotels. And even some of the chains have taken up residence in unique, historic buildings—offering more character than their big names might suggest. Intimate bed-and-breakfasts and lively youth hostels round out the diverse mix. Whether you're working with an unlimited expense account or you can barely scrape together change for a cheesesteak, there is a place for you to lay your head here.

The bulk of hotels are located in or just outside of Center City—convenient considering this is where most people spend the majority of their time. You won't be more than a 10-minute drive or a 30-minute walk from the city's major sights, dining, and nightlife anywhere

in Center City. The most expensive places are located here—especially along and near the Avenue of the Arts. If money is no object, stay at one of Philadelphia's drop-dead gorgeous, world-class hotels: The Four Seasons, The Ritz-Carlton, The Park Hyatt at the Bellevue, or the independent and award-winning Rittenhouse Hotel. Even if you can't afford to stay in one of these luxury hotels, you should stop in to check out the elegant lobbies, eat or drink at one of their swank restaurants or bars—or to use some of the nicest bathrooms you've ever seen.

At the opposite end of the spectrum, budget travelers and students have several options, including the Bank Street Hostel in Old City, the restored Chamounix Mansion hostel in Fairmount Park, and the International House in University City. In the mid-range, there are

COURTESY OF MORRIS HOUSE HOTEL

HIGHLIGHTS

LOOK FOR **((** TO FIND RECOMMENDED HOTELS.

((Best Place to Make Friends: Bank Street Hostel offers dorm-style accommodations, a shared kitchen, and common spaces for its mostly international clientele. It's the closest thing Philly has to a European-style hostel for budget travelers (page 171).

((Most Colonial Digs: Two of Benjamin Franklin's contemporaries owned impressive homes in late 18th-century Philadelphia that have since been converted to bed-and-breakfasts named in their honor. Immerse yourself in colonial history at the **Thomas Bond House** in Old City or the **Morris House Hotel** in Society Hill (pages 171, 173).

((Most Remarkable Bed-and-Breakfast: At **Madame Saito Bed & Breakfast,** your talented innkeeper cooks Japanese, Thai, and French cuisine, and teaches sushi-making and ballroom dancing classes in her studio. Come for the affordable digs, but don't leave without trying Madame's sushi (page 173).

((Most Unusual Amenities: Uncle's Upstairs Inn stocks guest bathrooms with condoms and lube for its predominantly gay clientele. An affordable, independent hotel in the heart of the Gayborhood, it is located above a bar (page 174).

((Best Hotel Lobby: Even if you can't afford to blow a week's salary to stay at **The Ritz-Carlton of Philadelphia,** be sure to stop in to see the elegant domed lobby. Enjoy tea, lunch, or drinks in the grand space, or just sneak a peek (page 175).

((Best Place to See Stars: The ultra-elegant, independent **Rittenhouse Hotel** is popu-

PHOTO BY JASON SMITH FOR GPTMC

HOTELS

Westin

lar with celebs who visit Philly or stay long-term while filming movies. It's easy to see why, considering its plush amenities and prime location overlooking Rittenhouse Square (page 176).

((Most Original Hotel Room: Room 414 at the **Westin,** also called the "uwishunu" room, is the result of an impressive collaboration of local artists and designers who set out to create the "Hippest Hotel Room" in Philadelphia. Everything from the funky furniture to the bronze human-hand-like bathroom fixtures was designed to express the unique character of the city (page 176).

((Cheapest Way to Sleep in a Historic Mansion: Just because you're traveling on a budget doesn't mean you can't do it in style. The **Chamounix Mansion** hostel, a converted 18th-century mansion in Fairmount Park, offers private and dorm-style accommodations at the lowest rates in town (page 179).

plenty of chain and independent hotels, bed-and-breakfasts, and rooms in private homes.

It is wise to reserve a room well in advance when visiting at peak times, including summer, festivals, and holidays. The Independence Day celebration is a huge event in Philadelphia, so if you plan to be here for the weeklong festivities, you'd better have a friend in town, a huge wad of money, or a reservation months in advance.

CHOOSING A HOTEL

Old City is the place to be if you're visiting for the historic attractions in and around Independence National Historical Park, but with few exceptions, it is an expensive area for

STAY AWHILE

If you're relocating to Philly temporarily or permanently, you have several good options while you make the transition. For budget travelers, the **International House** in University City is available to students or faculty with valid IDs from any academic institution. Stay for a night, a week, a month, a semester, or the entire school year at a reasonable price. **Windsor Suites** on the Parkway caters to long-term business travelers with fully equipped apartments with large work stations.

And for everyone else, bed-and-breakfasts or rooms rented in a private home are often the best bet. Many owners encourage long-term visitors with reduced rates for stays of a week or more, and even steeper discounts for stays of a month or more. Some to try include **Madame Saito Bed & Breakfast** and **Bella Vista Bed & Breakfast,** which offer standard rooms at great prices, or **La Reserve Center City Bed and Breakfast,** which offers fully equipped studios with kitchenettes near Rittenhouse Square. Two Chestnut Hill bed-and-breakfasts, **Anam Cara** and **Silverstone,** each also rent fully furnished

off-site apartments in the charming residential neighborhood, just a short ride on the regional rail from Center City.

Bed and Breakfast Connections of Philadelphia (800/448-3619, www.bnbphiladelphia .com) lists plenty of additional options in both Philadelphia and nearby. Even if a site doesn't mention it, it's always worth asking the owner and shopping around for long-term rates. Since most are privately owned, there is almost always wiggle room with the price. Many of the small bed-and-breakfasts rent only one or two rooms in their home as an additional source of income, so they might be amenable to having a longer-term resident. There are often reduced rates to stay without breakfast, so inquire about this if you'll be staying awhile and don't need a full meal each day.

And, of course, there is always **Craigslist** (www.craigslist.org), the ultimate site for finding sublets, temporary, permanent, and shared housing, and pretty much any other arrangement you can imagine. If you have the time and determination, you can often find just the right match for your needs and budget.

accommodations. It is jam-packed with families visiting the tourist attractions in summertime, but isn't quite as crowded—or pricey—during other times of the year when many attractions are closed. Anywhere in Center City is convenient for visiting the historic area as well as the rest of the city. It's also just a quick walk to the many museums of the Parkway.

A wealth of bed-and-breakfasts can be found in and around Washington Square West, Society Hill, University City, and Chestnut Hill. Wash West is a great place to stay for gay and straight alike, but is especially popular with gay visitors since it is the center of the city's gay culture. Rooms in the area fill well in advance during the annual Equality Forum in May.

The Parkway is lovely during the day when the museums are open, but can be a bit desolate at night. Home to mostly chain hotels,

it is just steps from Center City. University City and West Philadelphia just across the Schuylkill River are a bit less expensive while still close to Center City. Home to University of Pennsylvania and Drexel University, this area can be a good choice for students with its bustling college scene and affordable bars and restaurants. As a general rule, the closer you stay to the university in West Philly, the safer the neighborhood is and the more there is going on.

If you're staying for a week or more or you're particularly interested in the sights in Northwest Philadelphia or Fairmount Park, you may consider staying in a quieter, more residential part of town. Chestnut Hill offers several options in or near its main business district, and nearby Mt. Airy and Germantown also have a few bed-and-breakfasts but not much in the way of dining, shopping, or nightlife. About a 15-minute drive from Center City, this area is accessible by public transportation, but having a car is convenient as parking is relatively easy and trains stop running before midnight.

All the usual chain hotels can be found near the airport, including the Microtel, Sheraton, the Hilton, and the Philadelphia Airport Marriott, which is directly connected to the airport. There is also a Holiday Inn near the stadium—convenient for those attending events at the sports arenas. Several chain hotels are in the nearby Main Line suburbs just off I-76.

Since chain hotels are so easily found with a few clicks of a mouse, the majority of this chapter is devoted to the lesser-known, unique Philadelphia establishments. Chains are, however, included when there are limited options in a particular area or in some cases because the chains are distinctive or just too beautiful or convenient to leave out. All rates listed in this book are based on double-occupancy in summer (high season). Most hotels offer parking at a daily cost on-site or in a nearby lot, usually for around $20 a day.

The **Greater Philadelphia Tourism and Marketing Corporation** (www.gophila.org) is an excellent resource for additional listings, descriptions, links for reservations, and great discounts, including their **Philly Overnight Hotel Package.** The package includes hotel accommodations, parking, and a free gift and coupon book upon check-in. **Bed and Breakfast Connections of Philadelphia** (800/448-3619, www.bnbphiladelphia.com) has additional offerings.

Old City

Map 1

If you're visiting the historical attractions of Independence National Historical Park, Old City is the ideal place to stay. It doesn't hurt that the area is chock-full of shopping, dining, entertainment, and nightlife options, or that it is one of the prettiest, greenest areas of the city. With the exception of the Bank Street Hostel, and a few of the mid-range chains, this can be an expensive area. Rooms tend to fill quickly, especially in summer, so be sure to reserve well in advance.

UNDER $50
☾ BANK STREET HOSTEL
32 S. Bank St., 215/922-0222,
www.bankstreethostel.com

The vibe here is friendly, laid-back, and communal, so if you're not, this isn't the place for you. But if you don't mind dorm-style beds and a shared bathroom, this is an excellent—and the only—budget option in Old City ($22 for Hostelling International members, $25 non-members). Floor space is available at a reduced rate if beds are full, and no one is turned away—aside from locals, who are not allowed to stay at the hostel. The three floors are divided by sex, except for the 3rd floor, which becomes co-ed when the hostel is full. A communal kitchen, dining area, reading room, pool table, and nightly videos are available. Internet access, lockers, and laundry are available for a fee. There is a curfew of 12:30 A.M. Sunday–Thursday and 1 A.M. Friday and Saturday. This is sometimes extended to 2:30 A.M. in summertime, which allows you just enough time to grab a slice of pizza after the bars close at 2 A.M. No keys are provided, so this is strictly enforced. Check-in 8 A.M.–10:30 A.M. or 4:30 P.M.–12:30 A.M., and bags can be left at the front desk on the morning of check-out if you still have sightseeing left to do.

$100-150
☾ THOMAS BOND HOUSE
29 S. 2nd St., 215/923-8523,
www.winston-salem-inn.com/philadelphia

This charming bed-and-breakfast is in the heart of Independence National Historical Park, adjacent to Welcome Park, where William Penn's home once stood. It has 12 guest rooms, including two large suites with working fireplaces and whirlpool tubs. Built in 1769, the Georgian-style home was named for its first owner, Thomas Bond, acclaimed surgeon and friend of Ben Franklin, who was a regular guest at the home. With period furnishings and personal touches including books, games, complimentary sherry, and fresh-baked cookies, a stay here feels like visiting the home of a colonial-era friend. Rooms start at $115, with the largest suites up to $190. Continental breakfast is served on weekdays and a full breakfast is included on weekends. Complimentary wine and cheese is offered, and all the restaurants of Old City are steps away, including the historic City Tavern across the street.

$150-250

COMFORT INN DOWNTOWN/ HISTORIC AREA

100 N. Columbus Blvd., 215/627-7900 or 800/228-5150, www.comfortinn.com

The Penn's Landing location and reasonable prices ($149–169) are the primary draws for this basic 10-story 185-room chain. While the hotel is on a stretch of highway, the attractions of Old City and Society Hill are all within a short walk and complimentary van service will take you anywhere you want to go in Center City. It has the standard amenities, including WiFi, a bar, a small exercise room, laundry service, an airport shuttle, and a parking lot. A continental breakfast is included. Request a room on an upper floor facing the river for a view of the Benjamin Franklin Bridge.

BEST WESTERN INDEPENDENCE PARK HOTEL

235 Chestnut St., 215/922-4443 or 800/624-2988, www.independenceparkinn.com

You'd never guess that this building—listed on the National Register of Historic Places—is part of the Best Western chain. Combining modern hotel amenities with plenty of character, the 36 comfortable high-ceilinged guest rooms ($222–267) are decked out in Victorian-era furnishings. In a prime spot among Old City's most popular restaurants and bars

and just across the street from Independence National Historical Park, prices at this popular hotel are considerably higher on weekends in summertime. A complimentary continental breakfast with a make-your-own-waffle station is included. Small dogs (weighing less than 10 lbs.) can stay for a $50 non-refundable fee.

HOLIDAY INN HISTORIC DISTRICT

400 Arch St., 215/923-8660 or 800/972-2796, www.holidayinn.com

The slightest hint of the area's colonial history is present in the lobby and room furnishings ($170–190), sprucing up an otherwise-standard eight-story Holiday Inn. The hotel is comfortable and in a central location, but its greatest amenity has to be the rooftop pool that offers much-needed relief from the summer heat. It's a great place to stay with kids, since it's ideally situated for touring Independence Park and taking a break with a dip in the pool.

PENNS VIEW HOTEL

14 N. Front St., 215/922-6600 or 800/331-7634, www.pennsviewhotel.com

This elegant medium-sized boutique hotel in the heart of Old City is family-owned and operated, and it shows in the level of service provided. Built in 1828, the building has been a shipping warehouse, hardware store, and a coffeehouse, and it's on the National Register of Historic Places. The Italian-born Sena family (who also owns a local favorite restaurant, La Famiglia) purchased and renovated the hotel in 1989, and opened Ristorante Panorama and Il Bar on-site. Rooms ($180–229) have a touch of European elegance with large mirrors and armoires, and 12 of them offer whirlpool tubs, marble fireplaces, and views of the Delaware River. Continental breakfast is included.

OVER $250

OMNI HOTEL AT INDEPENDENCE PARK

401 Chestnut St., 215/925-0000, www.omnihotels.com

A steep price (starting around $309) and a prime location make this AAA four-diamond luxury hotel in the heart of the historic district a favorite for well-to-do tourists as well as business travelers. Check the website and travel search engines, as major discounts can sometimes be found. Boasting European-style luxury, the 150 large rooms

offer every amenity along with great views of Independence National Historical Park. The on-site Azalea restaurant serves modern American cuisine for breakfast, lunch, and dinner, and the on-site bar has a sophisticated lounge atmosphere.

Society Hill   Map 1

Society Hill is Old City's neighbor to the south. It offers close proximity to the main historic attractions, but in a quieter, more residential setting. The waterfront Hyatt Regency at Penn's Landing and the Sheraton Society Hill are both fully equipped chain hotels in excellent locations. Several unique bed-and-breakfasts provide nearby alternatives at lower prices.

$50-100
(MADAME SAITO BED & BREAKFAST
124 Lombard St., 215/922-2515

Trilingual Madame Saito does it all out of her two adjoined Society Hill row homes, just a block north of South Street. In addition to running the bed-and-breakfast, she operates a restaurant and catering business specializing in Japanese, French, and Thai cuisine (not fusion, which Madame does not like, just all three cuisines separately). She also teaches ballroom dancing and sushi-making classes in her spare time. For $70–100 a night, you can have a comfortable private room decorated in Japanese and French themes, and discounts are available for stays of a week or more. Some guests stay for months. For an additional fee, you can enjoy a traditional Japanese breakfast cooked by Madame herself.

$100-150
APPEL'S SOCIETY HILL BED & BREAKFAST
414 Spruce St., 215/925-5460

The modern decor of the rooms at this small,

four-room bed-and-breakfast is a contrast to the historic building dating from 1805. Offering an alternative to the bustle of nearby Old City and South Street with rooms and continental breakfast starting at $105 a night, this is a great deal in a pleasant area. It often fills even though the owners do not advertise, so be sure to book in advance, especially in summertime. Each of the basic bedrooms has a private bath, telephone, and air-conditioning, and a minimum two-night stay is required. Saturday and Sunday check-in is discouraged but can be arranged for longer stays.

$150-250
(MORRIS HOUSE HOTEL
225 S. 8th St., 215/922-2446,
www.morrishousehotel.com

The perfect balance of colonial charm and modern amenities, the Morris House Hotel offers period furnishings and WiFi. Built in 1787, this three-story bed-and-breakfast was home to the prominent Morris family for generations. The National Historic Landmark has been beautifully restored; the 15 guest rooms vary in size and price, with doubles starting at $189, suites at $209, and extended luxury suites at $249. Rooms in the new addition next door are attractive and comfortable but quite modern, so if it's colonial ambience you're after, be sure to request a room in the original building. A delicious continental breakfast and afternoon tea is included. When the weather is nice, eat breakfast in the pretty walled garden.

Center City East

Map 2

Broad Street divides Center City into East and West. Center City East lies just west of Old City and Society Hill. It is home to the convention center, Chinatown, and Washington Square West (also called the Gayborhood). There are plenty of good chain hotels on and near Market Street that cater to the convention crowd, including the Wyndham, Hilton Garden Inn, Holiday Inn, and the Marriott. Great bed-and-breakfasts can be found near Antique Row in Washington Square, and there are also a few independent mid-range, mid-size hotels nearby. If it's gay culture you're after, Uncle's Upstairs Inn and the Alexander Inn are two excellent choices.

$50-100
ANTIQUE ROW BED & BREAKFAST
341 S. 12th St., 215/592-7802,
www.antiquerowbnb.com

This popular eight-room bed-and-breakfast is a great deal ($65 s, $110 d) in a great location amidst the shopping and dining of tree-lined Antique Row. Friendly innkeeper Barbara Pope stocks the kitchen with plenty of breakfast fare and she will make it for you or you can opt to do it yourself if you'd rather sleep in. Some rooms share bathrooms and other are fully private. Discounts can be arranged for longer stays.

$100-150
ALEXANDER INN
12th and Spruce Sts., 215/923-3535
or 877/253-9466

This gay-dominated but not exclusive boutique hotel in the heart of Washington Square West is a good deal (starting at $119). Comfortable rooms, a prime location, and friendly staff make the 48-room hotel a popular choice for returning visitors. The modern style is a throwback to cruise ships—a little cheesy without going totally over the top. Some of the rooms are very small, so request a larger one when

available. A 24-hour snack table is available for returning late-night revelers.

◖ UNCLE'S UPSTAIRS INN
1220 Locust St., 215/546-6660

Catering to a predominantly gay clientele, this bed-and-breakfast occupies a 19th-century row home in the heart of the Gayborhood. Most guests begin their nights in the lively downstairs bar, Uncles—a great place to meet fellow travelers. Request a room ($105) on an upper floor if you're not an all-night party animal as rooms directly above the bar tend to be loud until it closes at 2 A.M. A basic continental breakfast is provided.

$150-250
CLINTON STREET BED AND BREAKFAST
1024 Clinton St., 215/802-1334

This charming bed-and-breakfast occupies a historic 1836 brick town house on a tree-lined, primarily residential street. The eight spacious suites ($149 to more than $200 a night) come complete with private baths, kitchens, sitting areas, Internet access, and most have a fireplace. Friendly Innkeeper Kathy Rabun provides the makings for a do-it-yourself breakfast in your suite in case you don't feel like coming to the dining room for the full breakfast. Awarded three diamonds from AAA, it was also voted Philadelphia's best bed-and-breakfast in 2007 by Citysearch.

OVER $250
LOEWS HOTEL
1200 Market St., 215/627-1200,
www.loewshotels.com

The modern, stylish Loews occupies the former PSFS (Philadelphia Savings Fund Society) building, considered by many to be the first modern, international-style skyscraper in the country. Designed by George Howe and William Lescaze, it was constructed in

1932. Despite its modern incarnation today, it retains some original and early details, including Cartier clocks and bank-vault doors. There is also a full-service health spa, high-end seafood restaurant, a business center, spinning room, and lap pool on-site. The hotel is well-equipped for the business traveler with T1 cable lines, modem lines, and electronic safes, but cool enough to be chosen by many leisure travelers for its host of amenities, stylish decor, happening bar scene, and central location. Rooms range from $179–229 depending on size and type.

◖ THE RITZ-CARLTON OF PHILADELPHIA

10 Avenue of the Arts, 215/523-8000, www.ritzcarlton.com

In its prime location on the Avenue of the Arts, the Ritz-Carlton is the epitome of luxury. The five-diamond hotel occupies the historic former Girard/Mellon Bank building. The lobby—with its domed ceiling, marble floors, and grand columns—is absolutely breathtaking. All of the 330 guest rooms offer the ultimate in luxury—as they should, starting at $399 a night. The Ritz is also home to the full-service D'Ambra Day Spa & Salon and the Rotunda lounge in the lobby, offering a full bar, snacks, and an elegant tea service for $40 per person on Sunday afternoons. If you want to either eat or work out in the middle of the night, you can take advantage of the extensive room service menu and fitness center, both available 24 hours a day. The Grill restaurant features upscale American cuisine and the Vault lounge has premium cigars and cocktails. Basically, the Ritz has everything that anyone could possibly desire.

HOTELS

Center City West

Map 3

Most of the accommodations in Center City West are in the Rittenhouse Square area. It is a lovely area to stay in the heart of the downtown shopping, theater, and business district, and an easy walk to the Parkway museums and even Old City. A popular and pricey part of town, it is dominated by high-end chain hotels, but a few mid-range hotels and bed-and-breakfasts can be found as well.

$100-150

LA RESERVE CENTER CITY BED AND BREAKFAST

1804 Pine St., 215/735-1137 or 800/354-840, www.lareservebandb.com

This restored 1850s four-story row house sits on a quiet, residential block in an idyllic location near Rittenhouse Square. There are 12 rooms, including six fully equipped studio and one-bedroom executive suites, which are intended for people staying a week or longer. Rooms start at $120 and suites are $140–180. This is an unbeatable deal for the location, especially for

© DAMIAN KOHUT

La Reserve occupies a historic Center City row house.

HOTELS

long-term stays, with discounts of 10–30 percent depending on the length of stay. There are no TVs in the rooms, creating a more intellectual atmosphere, but a Steinway piano in the parlor and endless activities in nearby Rittenhouse Square keep guests entertained. A full breakfast is served daily in the formal dining room.

THE LATHAM

135 S. 17th St., 215/563-7474, www.lathamhotel.com

This 139-room boutique hotel occupies a busy corner in the heart of the Walnut Street shopping district, and is surrounded by many of the best shops, restaurants, and bars in the city. Also amid the downtown shopping district, it is popular with business travelers as well as vacationers. All the standard hotel amenities are provided in comfortable rooms decked out in pretty, if not entirely authentic, Victorian furnishings. A friendly doorman dressed in traditional British horseback-riding attire creates an air of European sophistication. With doubles starting at $149, this is a good deal for the prime location.

OVER $250

◖ RITTENHOUSE HOTEL

210 W. Rittenhouse Sq., 215/546-9000 or 800/635-1042, www.rittenhousehotel.com

Oprah Winfrey, Bill Clinton, Mark Wahlberg, and Tom Hanks are just a few of the famous guests who have called the Rittenhouse Hotel home during their stays in Philadelphia—and no wonder, considering the ideal location, luxurious accommodations ($300–800), and perfectly attentive yet unobtrusive service. English-born vice president David Benton oversees the independent luxury hotel, bringing a healthy dose of British sophistication to Philadelphia. Consistently ranked in the top 100 boutique hotels in the world, this is *the* place to stay on Rittenhouse Square. Long-term apartment accommodations are available for those with fat wallets. Everything you want can be found on-site—an indoor pool, gym, salon, and two restaurants including Lacroix, one of the most esteemed fine-dining establishments in the city.

RITTENHOUSE 1715

1715 Rittenhouse Square St. (between Locust and Spruce Sts.), 215/546-6500 or 877/791-6500, www.rittenhouse1715.com

You'll be treated to pure elegance and comfort at this 23-room bed-and-breakfast tucked away on a quiet street just off bustling Rittenhouse Square. With rooms starting at $259, junior suites starting at $309, and the crème de la crème—the deluxe, two-level Presidential suite—running as high as $749, this level of luxury obviously does not come cheaply. But if you've got the cash (or credit) and you're looking for a more intimate alternative to the larger luxury hotels, or you want to splurge for a romantic special occasion like an anniversary, Rittenhouse 1715 cannot be beat.

◖ WESTIN

99 S. 17th St., 215/563-1600, www.starwoodhotels.com

With rooms starting at around $339 a night, this deluxe chain in the heart of the downtown business and shopping district is a top choice for business travelers with expense accounts. With clean lines and colors, the rooms and common areas are sleek, stylish, and modern. The 290 guest rooms and 17 suites have all the luxury amenities, but the greatest amenity of all is their signature Heavenly Bed—it is, quite simply, the most comfortable bed in the world. The room decor is soothing but fairly unremarkable, with the exception of room 414, also called the **"uwishunu" room.** A joint effort of the Philadelphia Tourism and Marketing Corporation and numerous local artists and designers, the one-of-a-kind room is both funky and beautiful. Local artists created everything from the light fixtures to the drawer pulls. The crowning jewel is a full wall mural behind the bed courtesy of the Mural Arts Program. Some items in the room are available for purchase, and rotating items mean that the room is an evolving art project. Call ahead for a chance to sleep amid the fantastic art, and don't worry—it still has the Westin trademark Heavenly Bed.

Benjamin Franklin Parkway/Fairmount   Map 4

If you'll be spending a lot of time exploring the city's major museums—including the Philadelphia Museum of Art and the Franklin Institute—this is a great base. An easy walk to Center City West and the Fairmount neighborhood, and close to Fairmount Park, the Parkway itself is home to primarily chain hotels, including the Sheraton, Embassy Suites, Crowne Plaza, and the impressive Four Seasons. The area is very popular with business travelers, but can also make a good base for tourists.

$100-150
BEST WESTERN CENTER CITY
501 N. 22nd St., 215/568-8300, www.bestwestern.com
The lowest-priced hotel in the area (with rooms starting at $124 when booked two weeks in advance) is a standard chain hotel with 183 guest rooms, free parking, a fitness room, gift shop, and an outdoor pool. The decor is a bit outdated, and the outside is an unremarkable block, but it makes a comfortable and affordable base for exploring. There is nothing in the immediate vicinity outside of the on-site sports bar and restaurant, but it's just a short walk from Center City and the restaurants and bars of the mostly-residential Fairmount neighborhood.

$150-250
WINDSOR SUITES
1700 Benjamin Franklin Parkway, 800/617-2893, www.windsorhotel.com
This 24-story hotel sits directly on the Benjamin Franklin Parkway and is easily recognizable by its curved exterior. Offering spacious apartment-style accommodations and large work stations, it is popular with long-term guests in town for business. But considering the reasonable price for the location (studios start at approximately $150 per night), it is a decent option for anyone looking to prepare meals at home and stay near the heart of Center City. A 24-hour fitness facility, free Internet access, a seasonal rooftop pool, and a sundeck are a few of the amenities. Two on-site dining options offer Asian and Mediterranean cuisine.

OVER $250
FOUR SEASONS
1 Logan Sq. (corner of 18th and Race Sts.), 215/963-1500, www.fourseasons.com/philadelphia
Arguably the city's finest hotel, the Four Seasons has earned five diamonds from AAA and was named one of the top 20 U.S. hotels by *Condé Nast Traveler*. Catering to a wealthy and discriminating clientele, the Four Seasons rarely disappoints with its elegant lobby, rooms (starting at $320), and facilities, including a beautiful indoor pool. While this luxury chain has hotels all over the world, each has its own special character. In Philadelphia, the classic design was inspired by the Federal period in early American history. The 365 large, deluxe rooms are equipped with every amenity to ensure your ultimate comfort. Complimentary town car service is available in Center City, and small pets are allowed. The hotel is also home to the elegant Swann Lounge and the Fountain Restaurant, offering some of the most elegant dining and tea service in the city.

HOTELS

HOTELS

South Street/South Philadelphia   Map 5

South Street divides Society Hill from South Philly, and just south of South Street, the Queen Village and Bella Vista neighborhoods are two of the city's most popular areas. Primarily residential, they offer lots of character and plenty of great restaurants. There are no hotels in this part of South Philadelphia, but a few good, reasonably priced bed-and-breakfasts are available, all within a short walk of Center City.

$100-150
BELLA VISTA BED & BREAKFAST
752 S. 10th St., 215/238-1270 or 800/680-1270, www.philadelphiabellavistabnb.com

Just a block from the Italian Market, this converted 1860s townhouse has 10 rooms including seven suites, with rates starting at just $105. Rooms vary in size (from small to spacious) and design (from colonial to contemporary). A continental breakfast with homemade muffins is included in the price. Four apartment units

have kitchens, a sleeping area with a queen bed, a loveseat, and TV, with prices as low as $53 a night for stays of a month or more; breakfast is not included for long-term stays. All rooms have a private bath, satellite TV, and DSL.

SHIPPEN WAY INN
416-418 Bainbridge St., 215/627-7266 or 800/245-4873, www.shippenway.com

Dating from 1750, the building makes up in character what it lacks in fancy amenities. The nine-room bed-and-breakfast occupies a pretty residential street in Queen Village near South Street. The low-ceilinged rooms, at $105–150, are mostly furnished in colonial style and priced depending on their size. Continental breakfast is served in the walled herb and rose garden, weather permitting. A working fireplace warms the living room in winter and in the afternoon tea, wine, and cheese are available daily. There are no televisions in the rooms, but there is one in the common area.

West Philadelphia/University City   Map 6

An affordable alternative to staying in Center City, the area to the west of the Schuylkill River is easily reached via several bridges. Numerous Victorian bed-and-breakfasts with loads of character offer a unique alternative to the two chain hotels, the Hilton Inn at Penn and the Sheraton University City. I've included a few of the best, but there are plenty more worth considering. Check out Inn Between Bed & Breakfast, Spruce Hill Manor, and the University City Victorian for more options.

$50-100
INTERNATIONAL HOUSE
3701 Chestnut St., 215/387-5125, www.ihousephilly.org

There is a lot going on inside this large,

boxy, bland-looking building on the edge of the University of Pennsylvania's campus. The International House offers basic, affordable accommodations for a few days or long-term. Rooms are rented to students, prospective students, faculty, or anyone with an academic affiliation (ID proof is required). Single ($70), double ($90), and efficiency apartments ($115) are rented on a nightly basis when available, but many residents stay for a month ($830) or more. This is where many international students studying at Penn live for a semester or a year. The International House also holds a movie theater showing mostly international films, hosts events and parties, and offers language and other classes to support the local international population.

$100-150
GABLES
4520 Chester Ave., 215/662-1918, www.gablesbb.com

Built in 1889 by prominent Philadelphia architect Willis Hale, this restored Victorian mansion is one of the most popular bed-and-breakfasts in West Philadelphia. Innkeepers Warren Cederholm and Don Caskey create a beautiful, friendly atmosphere in the 10-room mansion decked out in antique furniture. A large wraparound porch is a lovely place to relax and chat with fellow guests. Despite the cozy, historic atmosphere, modern amenities in the rooms include air-conditioning, cable television, phones, VCRs, and WiFi. Most rooms, which range from $105–165, have private baths, but two of them share a bath; see the website for detailed descriptions of each unique space. A computer station, refrigerator, and microwave are available for guest use in the common area, and the homemade breakfast is excellent.

$150-250
CORNERSTONE BED & BREAKFAST
3300 Baring St., 215/387-6065,
www.cornerstonebandb.com

This restored 1865 Victorian mansion has only six beautifully appointed rooms ($145–190), including two suites. Located near the campuses of the University of Pennsylvania and Drexel, it offers a nice alternative to visiting parents or students in town to check out the schools. The wraparound porch surrounded by a lovely garden is the setting, weather permitting, for a wine-and-cheese hour on Saturday 5–6 P.M. Rooms have a mix of antique and contemporary furniture, and include modern amenities like large flat-screen televisions. A full breakfast is served in the dining room, but if you're in a rush in the morning they will pack it to go at your advance request.

THE HILTON INN AT PENN
3600 Sansom St., 215/222-0200,
www.theinnatpenn.com

In the heart of the University of Pennsylvania's campus, this is the primary hotel for visiting parents, faculty, and guests of the university. The AAA four-diamond hotel is managed by Hilton but retains its own character. The 238 comfortable rooms and suites, starting at $229, are comfortable and as high-tech as you'd expect from an Ivy League–affiliated establishment. The Italian restaurant, Penne, is on-site, and plenty of additional dining, shopping, and entertainment options are just outside the door around the campus. Rooms fill early during the beginning and end of the semester and especially during graduation in May.

Fairmount Park   Map 8

UNDER $50
◖ CHAMOUNIX MANSION
3250 Chamounix Dr., 215/878-3676 or 800/379-0017,
www.philahostel.org

A one-of-a-kind mansion turned youth hostel, Chamounix (pronounced CHAM-ah-nee) occupies a bucolic setting in the heart of Fairmount Park. Originally built as a country home for Philadelphia merchant George Plumstead in 1802, the restored mansion offers clean, air-conditioned dorm accommodations, with several private rooms available, at an unbeatable price of $20 for Hostelling International members with valid ID, $23 for non-members, and $8 for children under 16 traveling with their family. A public SEPTA bus runs into the city from a stop just a short walk from the hostel, but a car or bike is useful for greater flexibility and safety at night. Free bikes are available for guests to explore Fairmount Park. There is a midnight curfew and alcohol and smoking are not permitted on-site. Included in the common areas is an Internet kiosk, a TV/VCR lounge with a video library, and a recreation room with table tennis, a piano, and foosball. Linens, pillow, and blanket are provided and stays are generally limited to three nights. A washer and dryer, towels, and lockers are available for a fee. Check-in is 8–11 A.M. or 4:30 P.M.–midnight. There is a daily lockout 11 A.M.–4:30 P.M. when the office is closed. Reservations must be secured with Visa, MasterCard, or money order.

Northwest Philadelphia
Map 9

Northwest Philadelphia accommodations options are primarily in Chestnut Hill, with a few bed-and-breakfasts in Germantown and Mt. Airy. Chestnut Hill has one full-service hotel and several bed-and-breakfasts, all located on or near the Germantown Avenue business district.

CHESTNUT HILL
$100-150
ANAM CARA
52 Wooddale Ave., 215/242-4327,
www.anamcarabandb.com

Meaning "soul friend" in Celtic, Anam Cara lives up to its name with a friendly and welcoming atmosphere. Just a short walk from Germantown Avenue in the heart of Chestnut Hill, the cozy bed-and-breakfast is run by Irish-born Teresa Vesey and her husband, Jack Gann, a licensed masseur who offers on-site massage. There are three attractive rooms, starting at $110 a night, in the main house and two spacious self-catering "extended stay" apartments on a pretty block nearby. Reduced rates are offered for weekly and monthly stays and there is a two-night minimum on weekends.

CHESTNUT HILL HOTEL
8229 Germantown Ave., 215/242-5905,
www.chestnuthillhotel.com

Built in 1864, the current building replaced an inn in the same location that dated from 1772. The only full-service hotel in Chestnut Hill, this pleasant hotel offers all the modern amenities on Germantown Avenue, an excellent base for exploring the area. The area is bustling during the day with shoppers, and there are several great dinner options nearby, but it gets relatively quiet at night. The AAA three-diamond establishment has hosted its fair share of celebrities including Kate Hudson, Billie Jean King, and Cuba Gooding Jr. Standard doubles start at $109 and suites start at $140. Three on-site restaurants happen to be some of the neighborhood's very best, but there are a myriad of other choices nearby as well.

SILVERSTONE BED AND BREAKFAST
8840 Stenton Ave., 215/242-3333 or 800/347-6858,
www.silverstonestay.com

Three beautifully decorated guest rooms ($85–125) are available in this 19th-century stone mansion. The Victorian-style rooms are complete with quilts, floral patterns, and lace—but the effect is cozy and warm, not stuffy or over the top. Innkeeper and registered nutritionist Yolanta Roman uses herbs and vegetables she grows in her sprawling backyard to prepare a full breakfast for guests each morning. A shared kitchen and laundry room are also available. Roman also rents out private two- and three-bedroom apartments nearby (no breakfast included). Each fully equipped unit ($130–150) includes use of an outdoor pool and fitness center and rates are reduced for long-term stays.

GERMANTOWN
$100-150
TWELVE CHIMNEYS
BED AND BREAKFAST
136 W. Tulpehocken Ave., 215/438-7307

Three rooms are available for rent in this 1859 mansion on a quiet historic street. An in-ground pool in the shaded back garden is a highlight, as is the spooky basement complete with secret tunnels believed to have been part of the Underground Railroad. Friendly hosts and a tasty breakfast make this a pleasant and intimate place to stay, and with doubles at $110 and suites at $165, the price is right.

Greater Philadelphia

Map 10

There are plenty of places to stay outside of the main neighborhoods, and most of them are chains. There's a cluster of hotels conveniently located near the airport as well as some near the many colleges in the Greater Philadelphia area. With the exception of the Conwell Inn on Temple University's campus, a car is necessary to get around. Included here are a few alternatives to the big chains.

$100-150

CONWELL INN

1331 W. Berks St., 215/235-6200,
www.conwellinn.com

The only hotel in North Philadelphia is part of Temple University's campus. Just a quick subway ride from Center City, it's a great option for visitors to the university, but there isn't any other reason to stay in this part of town, since it's further from most of the attractions. While the campus is generally considered safe, many parts of North Philadelphia are considered sketchy at night and there isn't much in the way of dining and cultural attractions. That said, the 22-room hotel ($135–159) is perfectly nice, and it's smack in the middle of campus on Broad Street.

GENERAL LAFAYETTE INN

646 Germantown Pike, Lafayette, 610/941-0600,
www.generallafayetteinn.com

Just beyond Chestnut Hill in Montgomery County, the historic General Lafayette Inn is home to a cozy five-bedroom guest house, restaurant, bar, and brewery. Rooms ($109–159) are comfortable and include antiques, televisions, and a self-service continental breakfast. It was built and has been operated nearly continuously since 1732, and was named for General Lafayette, who led troops in the nearby battle of Barren Hill during the Revolutionary War. Its storied history is fodder for quite a few ghost stories.

RADNOR HOTEL

591 E. Lancaster Ave., St. Davids, 610/688-5800 or
800/537-3000, www.radnorhotel.com

This independent full-service hotel located in the upper-crust Main Line suburb of St. Davids is just 20 minutes from downtown Philadelphia. Its 171 rooms and suites ($149–269) are comfortable and well appointed, but the main reason to stay here is if you're visiting the nearby colleges, including Haverford, Bryn Mawr, and Villanova. The suburban location will require you to drive anywhere you want to go, but it is a convenient base for visiting Valley Forge National Historical Park or the King of Prussia Mall.

HOTELS

EXCURSIONS FROM PHILADELPHIA

You'll never run out of things to do in Philadelphia, but if you get the chance to take a day or weekend trip beyond the city, there is plenty more to see and do within just a short distance. The Brandywine Valley, Bucks County, and Pennsylvania Dutch (Amish) Country are the most popular nearby destinations, and they're only 45–90 minutes away by car. In all three destinations, charming towns, villages, and farms are sprinkled amidst the bucolic Pennsylvania landscape; some straddle the river into New Jersey and Delaware, in Bucks County and the Brandywine Valley respectively. Bucks County and the Brandywine Valley are home to estates, museums, gardens, wineries, galleries, and antiques. A bit farther west, the lush, rolling farmlands of Pennsylvania Dutch County beckon visitors to experience the lifestyle of our unique non-electricity-using, horse-and-buggy-riding Amish neighbors. And in each area you'll find cozy bed-and-breakfasts, a diversity of dining options, opportunities for recreation, and shopping galore—from outlets to antiques to fine art to handmade crafts.

As you explore, you'll learn about the long, rich history, of each area—many aspects of which are linked with Philadelphia's history. There are several key Revolutionary War sites in the Brandywine Valley and Bucks County regions, and Pennsylvania Dutch Country developed when persecuted Amish communities came to Pennsylvania from Germany because of William Penn's pledge of religious freedom.

And while the three excursions detailed in this chapter are some of the best and closest,

HIGHLIGHTS

LOOK FOR  TO FIND RECOMMENDED SIGHTS, ACTIVITIES, DINING, AND LODGING.

◖ Best Place to See the Brandywine Valley in Still Form: The **Brandywine River Museum** displays American art in a former 19th-century grist mill on the Brandywine River. Among the excellent collection are many paintings of the local landscape by renowned Andrew Wyeth, who is credited with bringing much fame to the area with his renderings (page 186).

◖ Best Historic Gardens: One of the best estate gardens and horticultural showcases in the world, **Longwood Gardens** offers more than 1,000 acres of landscaped gardens, a large greenhouse, and a small museum and display in the former family home of the founders of the estate. It is yet another local du Pont family legacy (page 187).

◖ Best Decorative Arts Collection: One of several lavish du Pont family estates in the Brandywine Valley, **Winterthur Museum, Garden, and Library** boasts America's most esteemed collection of decorative arts. In addition, 1,000 lush acres are filled with rolling hills, streams, and gardens to explore (page 191).

◖ Most Charming Town: The artist enclave of **New Hope** straddles the Delaware River and attracts hordes of Philadelphians and New Yorkers alike. They come for the shops, restaurants, art galleries, antiques, and bed-and-breakfasts that offer bustling culture in a small-town setting (page 194).

◖ Best Castle Museum: The **Fonthill Museum** in Bucks County was built in a mix of architectural styles. Inside the mazelike interior, the collections of its former owner, famed local Henry C. Mercer, are on display (page 195).

◖ Best Way to Cool Off on a Hot Day: Several Bucks County companies offer **water sports on the Delaware River.** Two to try for tubing, rafting, canoeing, and kayaking are Delaware River Tubing Co. on the New Jersey side of the river, and Bucks County River Country on the Pennsylvania side (page 197).

◖ Best Market: Lancaster's **Central Market** is reminiscent of Philadelphia's Reading Terminal Market, but with lower prices and even more homemade Amish goods and crafts for sale among its diverse offerings. Originally an outdoor market in the 1730s, it is the oldest continually-operating market in the country (page 200).

◖ Most Historic Theater: Take a tour – or even better, see a show – at Lancaster's historic **Fulton Theatre,** built in 1852. The intimate venue has seen many a famous actor grace its stage, including most of the Barrymore family, Sarah Bernhardt, W. C. Fields, and Mark Twain (page 200).

EXCURSIONS

© KARRIE GAVIN

Longwood Gardens

EXCURSIONS

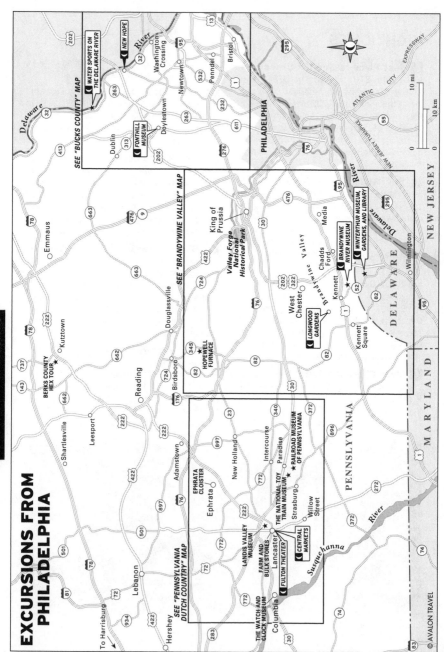

EXCURSIONS FROM PHILADELPHIA

SEE "BUCKS COUNTY" MAP

◄ WATER SPORTS ON THE DELAWARE RIVER

◄ NEW HOPE

Washington Crossing

◄ FONTHILL MUSEUM

Dublin

Doylestown

Newtown

Penndel

Bristol

PHILADELPHIA

NEW JERSEY

ATLANTIC CITY EXPRESSWAY

NEW JERSEY TURNPIKE

10 mi

10 km

SEE "BRANDYWINE VALLEY" MAP

Emmaus

King of Prussia

Valley Forge National Historical Park

Media

◄ WINTERTHUR MUSEUM, GARDENS, AND LIBRARY

◄ BRANDYWINE RIVER MUSEUM

Brandywine Valley

Chadds Ford

Kennett

Wilmington

DELAWARE

Kutztown

Douglassville

West Chester

◄ LONGWOOD GARDENS

Kennett Square

BERKS COUNTY HEX TOUR

Reading

Birdsboro

HOPEWELL FURNACE

Leesport

Shartlesville

MARYLAND

SEE "PENNSYLVANIA DUTCH COUNTRY" MAP

Adamstown

New Holland

Intercourse

Paradise

★ RAILROAD MUSEUM OF PENNSYLVANIA

EPHRATA CLOISTER

Ephrata

Strasburg

Willow Street

★ THE NATIONAL TOY TRAIN MUSEUM

PENNSYLVANIA

To Harrisburg

Lebanon

LANDIS VALLEY MUSEUM

FARM AND BULK STORES

◄ CENTRAL MARKETS

◄ FULTON THEATER

Lancaster

Susquehanna River

Hershey

THE WATCH AND CLOCK MUSEUM

Columbia

© AVALON TRAVEL

there is plenty more to do. Anyone visiting in the summer should follow the stream of locals who head "down the shore"—local vernacular for the New Jersey beach towns. And for all lovers of winter sports, no winter trip to the area is complete without a trip "up the mountains" to the Poconos in northeastern Pennsylvania. Whether you're just visiting Philadelphia or you live here and you're looking for a break, take advantage of the wealth of vastly different cultural opportunities all within a short distance.

PLANNING YOUR TIME

Each of these destinations can be experienced in a day trip if that is all the time you have, but an overnight—or even better, a weekend—will make for a more relaxing and in-depth experience. The Brandywine Valley is closest to Philadelphia (around 45 minutes), followed by Bucks County (about an hour) and Pennsylvania Dutch Country (an hour and a half). Since it is the farthest away and also the most spread out, Pennsylvania Dutch Country is the destination in which you'll most want to spend a night. While the Brandywine Valley and Bucks County are each very doable in a day trip, the great wealth of historic inns in both areas make them lovely places to spend

a night as well. The Brandywine Valley and Pennsylvania Dutch Country are in roughly the same direction west of Philadelphia, so they may be planned in coordination if you want to visit both. If you can only choose one, Pennsylvania Dutch Country is the most unique, since there is no other place where Amish culture is so alive and well.

The best way to travel to any of these areas is by car, although parts of each are accessible by public transportation if you have patience and no other option. Biking is another excellent option in all three areas when the weather is nice, especially in Bucks County, which is well known for scenic trails and paths.

All of the side trips are year-round destinations, with a climate similar to Philadelphia and plenty to do no matter when you go. The summer tends to be more crowded in all three. There are a multitude of holiday decorations and events during the winter season, but you will not be able to experience outdoor attractions, like tubing on the Delaware in Bucks County—a popular summer activity. Similar to Philadelphia, the most pleasant time to visit is in either the spring or fall. This is when the gardens are in bloom or the gorgeous Pennsylvania foliage is colorful, and temperatures are generally mild and pleasant.

EXCURSIONS

Brandywine Valley

The Brandywine Valley, spanning southeastern Pennsylvania and northern Delaware, is only around 30 miles southwest of Philadelphia. Central towns include Chadds Ford, Kennett Square, West Chester, and Wilmington, any of which makes a fine base for exploring. Many of the Brandywine Valley's major attractions include the lavish, historic estates and gardens of generations of du Ponts, one of the wealthiest and most prominent American families in history. The local landscape has been immortalized by world-renowned painter Andrew Wyeth, and a visit to the Brandywine River Museum is

a chance to see many of these works in the place that inspired them. Home to charming towns, Revolutionary War sites, museums, and wineries, the Brandywine Valley is a romantic destination.

SIGHTS
Chadds Ford and Kennett Square
Route 1 runs through Chadds Ford and Kennett Square, and the area's primary sights are just a short drive from one another along or near the main road. At the heart of Chadds Ford, at the intersection of Routes 1 and 100, you'll find the **Chadds Ford Barn Shoppes,**

© KARRIE GAVIN

fall foliage in the Brandywine Valley

about a dozen shops including boutiques, an art gallery, an inn, and several restaurants. Kennett Square also offers plenty of shopping, dining, and entertainment in a small-town setting. Be sure to sample some mushrooms while you're in the "mushroom capital" (aka Kennett Square).

BRANDYWINE BATTLEFIELD HISTORIC SITE

The largest Revolutionary War battle in the area was fought on this site just off Route 1 on September 11, 1777. The British won, the American army lost thousands of soldiers, and the remaining American troops retreated to Valley Forge while the British went on to occupy Philadelphia. Despite the devastating outcome, history buffs enjoy exploring the grounds and visiting the two restored homes that served as headquarters for George Washington and General Lafayette as they camped here. The **Visitor Center** (878 Baltimore Pike, 610/459-3342, www.ushistory .org/Brandywine, Tues.–Sat. 9 A.M.–4:30 P.M.,

Sun. noon–4:30 P.M. Mar.–Nov.; Thurs.–Sat. 9 A.M.–4:30 P.M., Sun. noon–4:30 P.M. Dec.–Feb.) has a small museum containing artifacts, exhibits, and a gift shop. The grounds are always free and open to the public, but there is a fee for admission into the museum and a guided tour of the grounds and historic homes ($5 adult, $3.50 senior, $2.50 child 13–18, free 12 and under). Tours are offered daily throughout the year, with the exception of March when they are offered on weekends only; last tour is at 3 P.M.

C BRANDYWINE RIVER MUSEUM

This museum (100 Creek Rd., 610/388-2700, www.brandywinemuseum.org, daily 9:30 A.M.–4:30 P.M., $8 adult, $5 senior, student, and child 6–12, free child under 6) contains three floors of art. The river can be seen through floor-to-ceiling windows, making it the perfect setting for the impressive showcase of mostly local art. Among more than 3,000 works on display are a wealth of impressive still lifes and illustrations, many from the Wyeth family,

especially Andrew, probably the most famous Wyeth, for his moving, realistic portrayals of the Brandywine landscape. As you stroll the galleries, you'll be fascinated by the similarities and differences in the works of three generations of Wyeth painters, including Andrew's father, N. C., and his son Jamie. Works of other early American artists are also on display.

LONGWOOD GARDENS

The gardens at Longwood (1001 Longwood Rd., Kennett Square, 610/388-1000, www

.longwoodgardens.org, $16 adult, $14 senior, $6 student and child, free 4 and under) are credited to Pierre S. du Pont, great-grandson of Eleuthère Irénée du Pont, a French immigrant who founded the DuPont chemical company when he arrived in the area in 1800. Pierre expanded the corporate empire of his family's business and devoted some of his great wealth to the development of Longwood Gardens in 1906. A wealth of trees had already been planted by the Quaker Peirce family, the earliest owners of the land since the

WINE TRAILS OF THE BRANDYWINE VALLEY AND BUCKS COUNTY

Both the Brandywine Valley and Bucks County have gained increasing respect as East Coast producers of quality wine. Visiting any of the six wineries that make up the Brandywine Valley Wine Trail or the eight that make up the Bucks County Wine Trail is a lovely way to spend a day. Each winery is different in size, style, and varieties of wine produced, and each has its own unique story. All are relatively small, making for an intimate visit, and most are family-owned and -operated. In either area, you'll pass rolling farmlands, quaint towns, antiques shops, restaurants, and historic inns and bed-and-breakfasts as you drive between the wineries. See each winery's website to learn more about their history, wine, and special events throughout the year. Most offer tastings and tours for free or a small fee. The **Bucks County Wine Trail** website (www.buckscountywinetrail.com) offers a map and links to all of its wineries, and the **Brandywine Valley Wine Trail** website (www.bvwinetrail.com) has a map as well as information on special events, discounts, and packages.

BRANDYWINE VALLEY WINERIES

Chaddsford Winery: 632 Baltimore Pike, Chadds Ford, 610/388-6221, www.chaddsford.com, daily noon-6 P.M.

Folly Hill Vineyards: 700 Folly Hill Rd., Kennett Square, 610/388-5895, www.follyhillvineyards.com, daily 11 A.M.-6 P.M.

Kreutz Creek Vineyards: 553 S. Guernsey Rd., West Grove, 610/869-4412, www.kreutzcreekvineyards.com, Sat.-Sun. 11 A.M.-6 P.M.

Paradocx Vineyard: The Shoppes at Longwood Village, Rte. 1, Kennett Square, 610/444-9003, www.paradocx.com, Sun.-Thurs. 11 A.M.-7 P.M., Fri.-Sat. 11 A.M.-8 P.M.

Twin Brook Winery: 5697 Strasburg Rd., Gap,

717/442-4915, www.twinbrookwinery.com, Mon.-Sat. 10 A.M.-6 P.M., Sun. noon-5 P.M.

Va La Vineyards Family Farmed Wines: 8820 Gap Newport Pike (Rte. 41), Avondale, 610/268-2702, www.valavineyards.com, Thurs.-Fri. noon-5:30 P.M., Sat.-Sun. noon-6 P.M.

BUCKS COUNTY WINERIES

Buckingham Valley Vineyards: 1521 Rte. 413, Buckingham, 215/794-7188, www.pawine.com, Tues.-Sat. 11 A.M.-6 P.M., Sun. noon-4 P.M.

Crossing Vineyards & Winery: 1853 Wrightstown Rd., Washington Crossing, 215/493-6500, www.crossingvineyards.com, daily noon-6 P.M.

New Hope Winery: 6123 Lower York Rd., Rte. 202, New Hope, 215/794-2331, www.newhopewinery.com, daily 10 A.M.-5 P.M.

Peace Valley Winery: 300 Old Limekiln Rd., Chalfont, 215/249-9058, www.peacevalleywinery.com, Wed.-Fri. and Sun. noon-6 P.M., Sat. 10 A.M.-6 P.M., daily in Dec.

Rose Bank Winery: 258 Durham Rd., Newtown, 215/860-5899, www.rosebankwinery.com, Thurs.-Sun. 11 A.M.-5 P.M.

Rushland Ridge Vineyards: 2665 Rushland Rd., Rushland, 215/598-0251, www.rushlandridge.com, Thurs.-Fri. 3-6 P.M., Sat. noon-6 P.M., Sun. noon-4 P.M.

Sand Castle Winery: 755 River Rd. (Rte. 32), Erwinna, 800/722-9463, www.sandcastlewinery.com, Mon.-Sat. 10 A.M.-6 P.M., Sun. 11 A.M.-6 P.M.

Wycombe Vineyards: 1391 Forest Grove Rd., Furlong, 215/598-9463, www.wycombevineyards.com, Fri.-Sun. noon-6 P.M., closed Jan.-Feb.

© KARRIE GAVIN

Brandywine Battlefield Historic Site

early 1700s. Pierre purchased it in 1906 to save it from destruction. While the gardens have continually evolved, Pierre is credited with much of what exists today. In addition to more than 1,000 acres of lush, beautifully landscaped gardens, there is a sprawling multiroom greenhouse and a museum where you can learn about the early history of the gardens and the family that lived on the site in the **Peirce-du Pont House.** Dating from 1730, the house is the oldest building on the grounds, and was the home of the Peirce family until 1905. It was later the weekend residence of Pierre du Pont from 1906 until his death in 1954. A short video plays inside, and there are several rooms of exhibits about the history of the estate. The hours of the gardens, like the blooms and the exhibits, change seasonally. It is normally open daily 9 A.M.–5 or 6 P.M., with extended hours from late May to early September (Mon.–Wed. and Sun. 9 A.M.–6 P.M., Thurs., Fri., and Sat. 9 A.M.–10 P.M.) and during the winter holidays (daily 9 A.M.–9 P.M. late Nov.–early Jan.).

MORE CHADDS FORD SIGHTS

The **Chadds Ford Historical Society** (1736 North Creek Rd., 610/388-7376, www.chaddsfordhistory.org, Mon.–Fri. 9 A.M.–2 P.M. year-round, Sat.–Sun. noon–5 P.M. in summer, free) has a small shop and exhibit room, and operates two nearby historic homes. The **John Chads' House,** built in 1725, and the **Barns-Brinton House,** built in 1714, are open for tours (Sat.–Sun. 1–5 P.M. May–Sept., $5 adult, $3 child), offering a glimpse into the lives of early settlers to the area.

Just down the road is the **Christian C. Sanderson Museum** (1755 Creek Rd., 610/388-6545, www.sandersonmuseum.org, Sat.–Sun. 1–4:30 P.M. Mar.–Nov., free). Sanderson, born in 1882 in Montgomery County, was an avid collector of early Americana. His former home contains his 4,000-plus-item collection, including an autograph of Helen Keller and the only pastel drawing by Andrew Wyeth.

In nearby Glen Mills, the 1704 **Newlin Grist Mill** (Cheyney Rd. and Baltimore Pike, Glen

Mills, 610/459-2359, www.newlingristmill .org, office open daily 9 A.M.–4 P.M., park open daily 8 A.M.–dusk) is the only operating 18th-century grist mill in the Commonwealth of Pennsylvania. The 150-acre park is devoted to the history of the people who lived here and the techniques used to power the mill. The park is free, but there is a $5 admission charged for a tour of the historic buildings on-site. Fishing and picnic grounds are also available.

West Chester

This small, quaint town has a concentrated area of shops and restaurants, along with a few interesting sights. The **Chester County Historical Society** (225 N. High St., 610/692-4800, www .cchs-pa.org, Tues.–Sat. 10 A.M.–5 P.M., Sun. noon–5 P.M., $8 adult, $6 senior, $5 student and child 6–17, free under 5) has a small museum, library, and shop that make a good starting point to the area. The museum contains over 60,000 items celebrating the area's history, including furniture, clothing, and other artifacts. Galleries offer permanent and rotating collections. For more local history, visit the **William Brinton 1704 House and Historic Site** (21 Oakland Rd., 610/399-0913, www.brinton-family.org, Mon.–Fri. 10 A.M.–2 P.M., Sat.–Sun. noon–5 P.M. May–Oct.), a restored Quaker home furnished in medieval English style.

The **American Helicopter Museum and Education Center** (1220 American Blvd., 610/436-9600, www.helicoptermuseum.org, Wed.–Sat. 10 A.M.–5 P.M., Sun. noon–5 P.M., $6 adult, $5 senior, $4 child and student) is the premier museum devoted exclusively to helicopters in the country. Pennsylvania is considered the birthplace of the helicopter, and this museum displays more than 35 civilian and military helicopters, autogiros, and convertaplanes to celebrate this slice of local history. The artifacts and exhibits span from the earliest machines to the latest military technology.

Baldwin's Book Barn (865 Lenape Rd., 610/696-0816, www.bookbarn.com, Mon.–Fri. 9 A.M.–9 P.M., Sat.–Sun. 10 A.M.–6 P.M.) is more than just a bookstore. Not just for book lovers, the barn is worth seeing as much for the building and grounds as for the books and antiques inside. The original dairy barn, built in 1822, has been headquarters for the Baldwin family's used book and collectible business since 1946. The dairy barn has since been converted to a residence and the large stone barn is now the bookshop. Today, its five floors are filled with more than 300,000 used and rare books, manuscripts, maps, paintings, prints, antiques, and collectibles. Exposed wood ceiling beams, cozy reading nooks, and a wood-burning stove create a lovely atmosphere for perusing the books and antiques.

Wilmington and Vicinity

The city of Wilmington, Delaware, and the surrounding area has quite a few museums, including the Delaware History Museum, Delaware Center for Contemporary Arts, Natural History Museum, Sports Museum and Hall of Fame, and even the Toy and Miniature Museum. If you have time to do it all, visit the visitors center in downtown Wilmington for more details about the many great options. If you only have a day or a weekend, the biggest must-see attractions are several estates, homes, and gardens left by the du Ponts, the area's most famous—and wealthy—residents through history.

HAGLEY MUSEUM AND LIBRARY

One of the major du Pont family historic sites in the area, the Hagley Museum and Library (200 Hagley Rd., 302/658-2400, www.hagley .org, $11 adult, $9 student and senior, $4 child 6–14) was founded by E. I. du Pont in 1802. The 235-acre estate along the Brandywine River was home to a gunpowder mill and the community of workers that operated it. The family home of the du Ponts is perched high on a hill overlooking the village and mill. A bus runs continually through the picturesque estate, allowing you to stop and explore the home and mills, with tour guides posted throughout to explain the sites. There is also a three-story museum attached to the visitors center where you can watch a short movie about the du Pont family company's many inventions, from gunpowder to pantyhose to

© KARRIE GAVIN

Brandywine Creek on the site of Hagley Museum and mills

countertops. The sprawling grounds are open daily 9:30 A.M.–4:30 P.M. A bus makes a continuous loop through the park throughout the day, with the last bus departing for a tour of the du Pont residence at 3:30 P.M. The only exception is on winter weekdays (Jan.–mid-Mar.), when the park is only open for one guided tour at 1:30 P.M.

NEMOURS MANSION

If you want to delve even deeper into the lavish lives of one of the earliest, wealthiest families in America, take a tour of Nemours Mansion (1600 Rockland Rd., 800/651-6912, www .nemours.org, call for hours, $12, ages 12 and over only), which was built in the early 20th century for industrialist, inventor, and philanthropist Alfred I. du Pont. The nearly 50,000-square-foot French château–style mansion shares its 300 acres with the operational Alfred I. du Pont Hospital for Children. Guests are allowed to enter by guided tour only (offered May–Dec.) and reservations are required. You'll spend a minimum of two hours exploring the

formal gardens and lavish mansion filled with antiques and works of art. You'll even get to see the family's antique cars in the garage.

◖ WINTERTHUR MUSEUM, GARDEN, AND LIBRARY

The du Pont family has left its mark all over the area, and the world, with its many inventions and accomplishments. A tour of any of their remarkable, lavish estates and gardens is an experience to remember. Winterthur (5105 Kennett Pike, 800/448-3883, www .winterthur.org, Tues.–Sun. 10 A.M.–5 P.M., $20 adult, $18 student and senior, $10 child 2–11, free under 2) was designed by Henry Francis du Pont (1880–1969), an avid antiques collector and horticulturist, and his father, Henry Algernon du Pont, in the spirit of 18th- and 19th-century European country houses. Part of the estate has been converted into a museum with artifacts and exhibits about mostly local history. A walk or trolley ride through the grounds and gardens when they are in bloom is spectacular.

RESTAURANTS
Chadds Ford

Just down the road from the Brandywine River Museum and other sights of Chadds Ford, you'll find upscale cuisine in a stylish yet relaxed setting at (**Brandywine Prime** (Rtes. 1 and 100, 610/388-808, www .brandywineprime.com, Mon. 5–10 P.M., Tues.–Thurs. 11:30 A.M.–10 P.M., Fri.–Sat. 11:30 A.M.–11 P.M., Sun. 10 A.M.–2 P.M. and 4–9 P.M., bar open daily from 11:30 A.M.). Serving lunch, brunch, and dinner, the restaurant's specialty is seafood and perfect cuts of meat, but don't miss the fresh oyster bar, or the elaborate Sunday brunch buffet on weekends ($18.95 adult, $10.95 child).

If you're looking for a more casual breakfast, lunch, or brunch spot, head to the classic greasy-spoon diner **Hank's Place** (Rtes. 1 and 100, 610/388-7061, www.hanks-place.net, Mon. 6 A.M.–4 P.M., Tues.–Sat. 6 A.M.–7 P.M., Sun. 7 A.M.–3 P.M.) across the street. The near-constant line out the door speaks volumes about its popularity; some Philadelphians make the trip on a weekend for the packed omelettes, blueberry pancakes, and the Pennsylvania favorite, scrapple. While breakfast is the star, you can also get plenty of cheap, tasty soups, salads, and sandwiches.

For an elegant and traditional afternoon tea service, visit **The SpecialTeas Tea Room and Gift Shop** (100 Ridge Rd., Chadds Ford, 610/358-2320, www.specialteastearoom.com, Mon. noon–3 P.M., Tues.–Sat. 11 A.M.–4 P.M.). The shop is part of the **Old Ridge Village Shoppes** which include jewelry, crafts, quilts, and several restaurants.

West Chester

In West Chester, **Gilmore's** (133 E. Gay St., 610/431-2800, www.gilmoresrestaurant.com, Tues.–Sat.) is a popular upscale French BYOB in the heart of town. There are just two seatings at 6 P.M. and 8:30 P.M.; be sure to make reservations, as it is one of the area's most acclaimed restaurants.

Or you can head off the main drag just a short drive on a quiet road to **Four Dogs Tavern** (1300

W. Strasburg Rd., Rte. 162, 610/692-4367, Mon.–Wed. 11:30 A.M.–10 P.M., Thurs.–Sat. 11:30 A.M.–11 P.M., Sun. 11 A.M.–10 P.M.) for a more casual atmosphere for reasonably priced salads, burgers, and dinner entrées in an upbeat atmosphere. The bar stays open until midnight on weekdays and 1 A.M. on weekends, and there is usually live entertainment on Thursday and Sunday nights. Nab a seat on the outdoor patio when the weather is warm.

Another star in West Chester dining is **Simon Pearce** (1333 Lenape Rd., Rte. 52 N., 610/793-0948, Mon.–Sat. 11:30 A.M.–9 P.M., Sun. 11 A.M.–8:30 P.M.). A destination restaurant, it offers modern, upscale cuisine in a beautiful setting on the Brandywine River. Sunday brunch features live classical music, and while you're there, you can visit the handmade glass and pottery workshop and home retail store.

Wilmington

Moro (1307 N. Scott St., 302/777-1800, Tues.–Sat. 5–11 P.M.) is a popular Wilmington restaurant that serves upscale New American cuisine for dinner. The creative chef changes the menu daily to utilize the freshest ingredients, and the wine list contains 900 selections.

HOTELS

There are countless charming inns and bed-and-breakfasts in the area, and one of the very best is the (**Inn at Montchanin** (Rte. 100 and Kirk Rd., Montchanin, DE, www .montchanin.com). Ideally situated for visiting Winterthur, Nemours, and Hagley museums and estates, the award-winning inn was once part of the Winterthur estate. Today, it offers every modern convenience in its elegant yet cozy rooms and suites. The village-like setting offers loads of character, and the on-site fine-dining restaurant, **Krazy Kat's**, offers quality, creative cuisine for breakfast, lunch, and dinner. The 28 rooms start at $179 a night, and special packages are sometimes offered online. The inn was named "the world's best hotel for under $250" by *Travel + Leisure* magazine.

For a more rural experience, stay at the **(Sweetwater Farm Bed & Breakfast** (50 Sweetwater Rd., Glen Mills, 610/459-4711, www.sweetwaterfarmbb.com). It's not easy to find even though it's just a short drive from the sights of Chadds Ford—and that's exactly the point. A few remote country roads lead to the sprawling 50-acre estate, and you can't see another property from the grounds. There are seven rooms in the main stone house and seven additional private cottages. Rooms offer every amenity, including refrigerators and fireplaces, and some have oversized whirlpool tubs. The main house has a pool table and comfortable sitting areas, along with a dining room where a gourmet breakfast is served each morning. Owned by the nephew of Grace Kelly, the property oozes charm and grace, just as she did. Pictures of the Kelly family, as well as the cast and crew of M. Night Shyamalan's *The Village* (who stayed here while filming) can be seen in the main house. Rates start at $135 weekdays and $160 weekends.

The Brandywine River Hotel (Rtes. 1 and 100, 610/388-1200, www.brandywineriver-hotel.com) offers a convenient resting place from which to explore the many nearby sights. Rooms are quite nice, if a bit more like a typical hotel, and rates start at just $129 per night.

GETTING THERE AND AROUND

The Brandywine Valley is about 30 miles, or a 45-minute drive, southwest of Philadelphia. It is easily accessible via major routes I-95, I-476, U.S. Routes 30 and 322, and the Pennsylvania and New Jersey Turnpikes. The major roads running through the area are Routes 202, 1, 100, and 52. A car is the best way to get around, since attractions are spread out, driving on the country roads is pleasant, and parking is abundant. If that isn't an option, **SEPTA** (215/580-7800, www.septa.org) provides limited bus and regional rail service from Philadelphia to West Chester and some other nearby areas. **SCOOT** (Southern Chester County Organization on Transportation, 877/612-1358, www.tmacc.org) offers service between West Chester, Chadds Ford, Kennett Square, and other locales. **DART** (800/652-DART, www.dartfirst-state.com) offers local service in and around Wilmington.

INFORMATION

Delaware County's **Brandywine Conference and Visitors Bureau** (Chadds Ford, 800/343-3983, www.brandywinecvb.org) has a useful website with loads of information. The **Chester County Conference and Visitors Bureau** (Kennett Square, 800/228-9933, www.brandywinevalley.com) also has a great website, and you can visit their conveniently located facility adjacent to Longwood Gardens on Route 1 for more information and maps (daily 10 A.M.–6 P.M. Apr.–Oct., daily 10 A.M.–5 P.M. Nov.–Mar.). Both of these sites offer information, maps, and links to the area's sights, accommodations, dining, recreation, shopping, and more. For additional bed-and-breakfasts, the **Brandywine Valley Bed and Breakfast** site (www.bvbb.com) offers information and online booking.

EXCURSIONS

Bucks County

Only about 35 miles north and an hour's drive from Philadelphia, Bucks County offers a unique blend of rural countryside filled with farms, creeks, and covered bridges, along with a bustling arts and cultural scene. Local towns of interest include Doylestown, Lahaska, and New Hope in Pennsylvania, and Lambertville in New Jersey, all located within a short drive from one another along Route 202.

SIGHTS
◖ New Hope

The town of New Hope is the most popular destination in Bucks County and a lovely place to stroll. It is situated along the Delaware River just across a small auto/pedestrian bridge from Lambertville, New Jersey, another charming town. New Hope has a rich history and strong artistic roots and is home to many unique shops, restaurants, and art galleries. The action centers around Bridge Street, which connects New Hope with Lambertville, as well as Union Street in Lambertville and Main Street in each town. There is also a thriving gay culture, including a few gay bars and gay-owned inns and restaurants.

In addition to exploring on foot, another great way to see the area is to take a 50-minute ride on the **New Hope and Ivyland Railroad** (32 W. Bridge St., New Hope, 215/862-2332, www.newhoperailroad.com) between New Hope and Lahaska, pulled by a steam locomotive.

A branch of the James Michener Museum in Doylestown is in New Hope, **The Michener in New Hope at Union Square** (Union Square on Bridge St., 215/862-7633, www.michenermuseum.org, Wed.–Sun. 11 A.M.–5 P.M. Jan.–Mar., Tues.–Sun. 11 A.M.–5 P.M. Apr.–Dec., until 6 P.M. Sat. in summer, $5 adult, $4 senior, $2 child 6–18, free under 2). With the same

A boat tour of the Delaware River departs from the charming town of New Hope.

PHOTO BY G. WIDMAN FOR GPTMC

EXCURSIONS

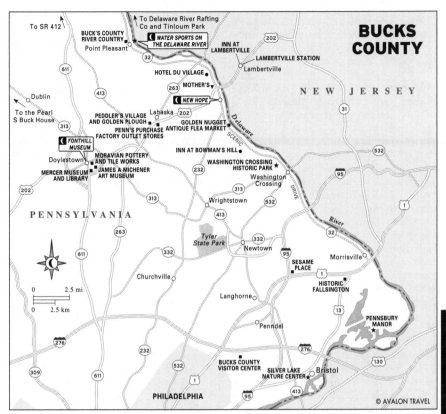

goal of highlighting local art, this branch is home to two permanent exhibits: *The Artists Among Us* and *Creative Bucks County,* along with rotating exhibits featuring historic and contemporary artists.

Doylestown Museums

Another charming town and cultural center, Doylestown is home to several impressive museums. Three of them, all National Historic Landmarks, are within a short distance of one another in what has become known as Mercer Mile. They all celebrate the life, work, and collections of Henry Chapman Mercer (1856–1930), a local archaeologist, writer, anthropologist, ceramist, scholar, antiquarian, and collector who spent his life in

the area. Mercer built three memorable structures: Fonthill, the Moravian Pottery and Tile Works, and the Mercer Museum.

(FONTHILL MUSEUM

Mercer's castle-like home, Fonthill Museum (525 E. Court St., 215/348-9461, www.fonthillmuseum.org, Mon.–Sat. 10 A.M.–5 P.M., Sun. noon–5 P.M., guided tour only, last tour 4 P.M., $9 adult, $8 senior, $4 child, $12 includes admission to Mercer Museum) was built 1908–1912. Modeled after a 13th-century Rhenish castle, it is a mix of medieval, Gothic, and Byzantine styles designed by Mercer himself. Constructed of poured reinforced concrete, the ornate, mazelike interior contains 32 stairways and 44 rooms, each in a different shape. Mercer's collection of books, prints, and Victorian engravings are on display, and the ceilings and walls are embedded with handcrafted tiles made in Mercer's kilns.

MORAVIAN POTTERY AND TILE WORKS

A more in-depth look at Mercer's famous tiles produced during the American arts and crafts movement can be seen at the Moravian Pottery and Tile Works (130 Swamp Rd., 215/345-6722, daily 10 A.M.–4:45 P.M., $3.50 adult, $3 senior, $2 child) on the grounds of Fonthill. The working history museum continues to produce tiles and mosaics in a similar manner to Mercer's original works. Tours of the 1912 factory are offered every half hour and consist of a 17-minute video and a self-guided walk where you can see original installations and various displays about tile production.

MERCER MUSEUM AND LIBRARY

In 1916, Mercer built another six-story concrete castle, which is now the Mercer Museum (84 South Pine St., 215/345-0210, www.mercermuseum.org, Mon.–Sat. 10 A.M.–5 P.M., Tues. until 9 P.M., Sun. noon–5 P.M., $8 adult, $7 senior, $4 child). The impressive structure is filled with themed rooms containing Mercer's collection of tools, folk art, and articles from early America. Mercer collected more than 40,000 items in all, fearing that the advance of industrialization would wipe out original tools. He made it his mission to preserve evidence of America's early productivity when everything was made by hand.

JAMES A. MICHENER ART MUSEUM

This museum (138 S. Pine St., 215/340-9800, www.michenermuseum.org, Tues.–Fri. 10 A.M.–4:30 P.M., Sat. 10 A.M.–5 P.M., Sun. noon–5 P.M., $6.50 adult, $6 senior, $4 student and child 6–18, free under 6) is named for another famous Doylestown local, a Pulitzer Prize–winning author, philanthropist, and teacher. The museum displays a collection of 20th-century American art and sculpture, including a world-class collection of Pennsylvania Impressionism. Occupying the former Bucks

County Prison, the nonprofit cultural institution is dedicated to preserving, interpreting, and exhibiting the art and heritage of Bucks County.

More Bucks County Sights

HISTORIC FALLSINGTON

Historic Fallsington (4 Yardley Ave., Fallsington, 215/295-6567, www.historicfallsington.org, Tues.–Sat. 10:30 A.M.–3:30 P.M. mid-May–mid-Oct., Mon.–Fri. 10:30 A.M.–3:30 P.M. Nov.–Apr., $5) is a 300-year-old preserved Quaker village on the National Register of Historic Places that evolved around a central Quaker meeting house built in 1690. There are nearly 90 structures, mostly simple in design, and you can enter several on a guided tour. The rest are privately owned, but you can wander around the village and see them from the outside.

PENNSBURY MANOR

Pennsbury Manor (400 Pennsbury Memorial Rd., Morrisville, 215/946-0400, www.pennsburymanor.org, Tues.–Sun., hours change seasonally, $5 adult, $4.50 senior, $3 child 6–17) is William Penn's re-created 17th-century country manor and farm. Penn preferred the tranquility of country living to crowded urban dwellings, and at the peaceful 43-acre Pennsbury Manor, it is easy to see why. Visitors can tour the manor house, brew house, workman's cottage, smokehouse, blacksmith shop, and barn, and see farm animals including oxen, horses, and sheep. On Sundays from April through October there are costumed interpreters at the site that make it easy to imagine the working colonial farm.

SESAME PLACE

Sesame Place (100 Sesame Rd., Langhorne, 215/752-7070, www.sesameplace.com) is the only theme park in the world based on the popular television series *Sesame Street*. Catering to children ages 2–13, it offers amusements, a three-story netted jungle gym, live stage shows, and a water park of more than 14 acres. Costumed Sesame Street characters wander around to interact with kids. Open daily 10 A.M. in May–October; it closes anywhere from 5 to 9 P.M. depending on day and time of year. An all-day pass costs $44.50 for adult and child, $39.50 for senior and AAA member, and free for children under 2. A reduced "twilight admission" costs $26.50 and allows three or four hours of park time (enter after 4 P.M. when the park closes at 8 P.M. or after 2 P.M. when it closes at 5 or 6 P.M.). Call ahead for specific closing hours.

WASHINGTON CROSSING HISTORIC PARK
Washington Crossing Historic Park (1112 River Rd., 215/493-4076, www.ushistory.org/washingtoncrossing, Tues.–Sat. 9 A.M.–5 P.M., Sun. noon–5 P.M., $5 adult, $4 senior, $2 child) commemorates the spot where General George Washington and his troops crossed the Delaware River on Christmas night in 1776, considered a pivotal moment in the Revolutionary War. The troops marched on to win a victory at Trenton, which paved the way for the subsequent final victories that would lead to defeat of the British army and the forming of an independent nation. The park is preserved as a historic site and nature area. A 17-minute orientation film, *Of Dire Necessity,* plays throughout the day, and guided tours of various park areas and structures are offered. A reenactment is performed each Christmas Day.

RESTAURANTS
◖ **Marsha Brown** (15 S. Main St., New Hope, 215/862-7044, www.marshabrownrestaurant.com, Mon.–Thurs. 5–10 P.M., Fri. 5–11 P.M., Sat. 2–11 P.M., Sun. 2–9 P.M.) occupies a large, stone former church. More than 125 years old, it features many stunning details and furnishings. Despite the stylish, bustling atmosphere, it is easy to imagine the former incarnation, especially on the 2nd floor, with its two-story arched ceilings, original woodwork, large stained-glass windows, and a step-up dining area where services were once led. Louisiana-bred owner Marsha Brown created a sophisticated Southern fine-dining experience. Along

with an ample raw bar, her New Orleans–inspired menu features upscale versions of classics like jambalaya and inventive new creations using only the best cuts of meat, fresh seafood, and vegetables. A happening downstairs bar serves a variety of cocktails.

Mother's (34 N. Main St., New Hope, 215/862-5857, www.mothersnewhope.com, Mon.–Thurs. 11 A.M.–9 P.M., Fri. 11 A.M.–10 P.M., Sat. 10 A.M.–10 P.M., Sun. 10 A.M.–9 P.M.) has been a popular local spot for more than 30 years, despite several changes in ownership. The casual, affordable restaurant and bar has a friendly atmosphere and quality food, from hearty sandwiches and salads for lunch to fresh meat, fish, and pasta dinner entrées. Their excellent desserts and reasonably priced wine list are highlights, as is the bar, which offers live music on Friday nights.

Lambertville Station (11 Bridge St., Lambertville, 800/524-1091, www.lambertvillestation.com, Mon.–Thurs. 11:30 A.M.–3 P.M. and 4–9:30 P.M., Fri.–Sat. 11:30 A.M.–3 P.M. and 4–11 P.M., Sun. 10 A.M.–3 P.M. and 4–9:30 P.M.) occupies a restored former train station, with tracks lining one side of the restaurant. Just across the bridge from New Hope, it is a local favorite for breakfast, lunch, and dinner, serving excellent new American cuisine. Lunch is casual with à la carte dining that's great for people-watching. Dinner inside offers a more upscale environment. The popular **Inn at Lambertville Station** is attached, with rooms decked out in antiques in themes of different cities from around the world—some offering lovely views of the river.

RECREATION
◖ **Water Sports on the Delaware River**
Several different companies offer tubing, rafting, canoeing, and kayaking along the Delaware River throughout the summer—a lovely way to spend a hot day. Sometimes called the "Eden of the East," the Delaware River moves at an average speed of 1.5 miles per hour, is about five feet deep, and often near

80 degrees all summer. There aren't many rapids in the area, so be prepared for more of a lazy, gentle float than an adrenaline-pumping journey.

Delaware River Tubing Co. (2998 Daniel Bray Hwy., Frenchtown, NJ, 866/938-8823, www.delawarerivertubing.com) offers great prices on tubing and rafting, with rates starting at $9.95 for a tube or $14.95 for a raft, with an additional $5 for a meal package. At a stand part-way through the trip, your meal ticket will get you a burger or dog, chips or candy bar, and a drink. In addition to offering tubes and rafts at slightly higher rates than Delaware River Tubing Co., **Bucks County River Country** (2 Walters La., Point Pleasant, PA, 215/297-5000, www.rivercountry.net) on the Pennsylvania side of the river offers kayak and canoe rentals. Both follow similar routes and offer comparable experiences, and if you go with Bucks County, you can still buy food from the other company's food stand.

SHOPPING

One of the biggest draws to Bucks County for Philadelphians and New Yorkers is the unique shopping. New Hope and Lambertville have shops galore lining Main Street in New Hope and Lambertville, Union Street in Lambertville, and Bridge Street, which traverses both towns across a small driving and walking bridge. Shops include antiques, art galleries, and collectibles, along with contemporary clothing, furniture, and home accessories. Just outside of New Hope in Lahaska, **Peddler's Village** (U.S. 202 and Rte. 263, 215/794-4000, www.peddlersvillage.com) is also a local favorite, with around 75 unique shops connected by brick walkways spread over a quaint 42-acre village. Here, you can also stay overnight in the **Golden Plough Inn,** choose from six on-site dining options, and keep kids entertained in the Grand Carousel and a children's play area, **Giggleberry Fair.** Just across the street from Peddler's Village, the **Penn's Purchase Factory Outlet Stores** (5881 York Rd. at U.S. 202, 215/794-0300) offers more than 40 name-brand shops with discount prices.

Nearby, **Rice's Market** (6326 Greenhill Rd., Solebury, 215/297-5993, www.ricesmarket.com, Tues. 7 A.M.–1:30 P.M. year-round, Sat. 7 A.M.–1:30 P.M. Mar.–Dec.) is an open-air market selling antiques, collectibles, new and used clothing, and gourmet treats. The **Golden Nugget Antique Flea Market** (1850 River Rd., 609/397-0811, www.gnmarket.com, Wed. and weekends 6 A.M.–4 P.M.) is another unique market. On Sundays, the busiest day, sometimes as many as 400 vendors set up shop selling a wide variety of antiques, crafts, and more.

HOTELS

There are so many great bed-and-breakfasts in Bucks County that choosing one can be difficult. One of the most luxurious bed-and-breakfasts in the world is located here in New Hope, just 2.5 miles from the center of town. The **◖ Inn at Bowman's Hill** (518 Lurgan Rd., New Hope, 215/862-8090, www.theinnatbowmanshill.com) has just four romantic rooms and two dramatic, elegant extended suites on a private five-acre estate. The inn was voted one of the "top 10 most romantic inns" by *American Historic Inns* in 2006, among countless other accolades. When the weather is warm, a pool offers a lovely place to swim, and when it's colder, the in-room fireplaces and in-room and outdoor whirlpool tubs offer luxurious warmth. A gourmet breakfast is included in the rate, and in-room massage is available for a fee. With rooms and suites from around $295–525 per night, a stay here does not come cheap, but for a romantic getaway or special occasion, there is no place better.

The Lambertville House (2 Bridge St., Lambertville, 609/397-0200, www.lambertvillehouse.com) in the heart of Lambertville, just steps from the bridge into New Hope, has 26 rooms offering every modern amenity. Most rooms have in-room fireplaces, some have oversized whirlpool tubs, and all have ultra-comfy beds. Listed on the National Register of Historic Places, it was built in 1812, and has provided rest to Presidents Andrew Johnson and Ulysses S. Grant, among other notable guests, on their travels between New York and Philadelphia.

The Inn at Lambertville Station overlooks the Delaware River.

Have a drink on the pretty front porch of the cozy bar **Left Bank Libations,** perfect for people-watching. Rates start at $200.

Hotel du Village (2535 River Rd., New Hope, 215/862-9911, www.hotelduvillage.com) is a unique, affordable alternative about a mile outside of New Hope. There are 20 rooms on the grounds of what was formerly a prep school for young girls and boys. There is a cozy, upscale French restaurant on-site, and rates range $130–155 with breakfast included.

In Doylestown, try the **Doylestown Inn** (18 W. State St., 215/345-6610, www.doylestowninn.com). Built in 1902, it has been updated with a modern look and amenities. A brand-new bar and grill opened in 2007, and rates range $145–220 depending on the time of year, with prices considerably cheaper January–March.

There are also plenty of campgrounds nearby that range from rustic sites to modern compounds with pools and mini-golf courses. **Tinicum Park** (901 E. Bridgetown Pike, Erwinna, 215/348-6114) is a popular one, for camping as well as hiking and other outdoor activities.

GETTING THERE AND AROUND

Only about 30 miles north of Philadelphia, and an hour or less by car, Bucks County is easily accessible by I-95, Routes 1 and 13, and the Pennsylvania Turnpike. **Amtrak's** regional rail lines travel through Bucks County with stops in Trenton, NJ, and other nearby locations (800/872-7245, www.amtrak.org). **SEPTA** (215/580-7800, www.septa.org) has regional rail lines throughout Bucks County with stops in Doylestown and in Trenton, NJ. Once in Bucks County, it is possible to get between major points on public transportation, but most people prefer to drive or ride bikes in the nice weather, which is essential for getting to some of the more off-the-beaten-path sights. If you plan on staying in New Hope or Lambertville, everything is within an easy walk, but you'll need a car to explore outside of these towns.

INFORMATION

The **Bucks County Conference and Visitors Bureau** (3207 Street Rd., Bensalem, www .buckscountycvb.org, 9 A.M.–5 P.M. Sept.–May, 8:30 A.M.–5:30 P.M. June–Aug.) offers lots of information and maps of the area, along with a theater featuring a 16-minute orientation film, a gift shop, and a rotating art exhibit featuring the work of local artists. The website offers a wealth of information about the area's attractions, lodging, dining, and more, and offers a function to create your own itinerary.

Pennsylvania Dutch Country

The people and culture are the primary tourist draw in Pennsylvania Dutch Country, the largest Amish and Mennonite settlement in the world, and plenty of attractions have been created to allow visitors a glimpse into their way of life. It can sometimes be difficult to sift through the tourist traps and find more legitimate cultural experiences, so it always helps to ask a local, like a friendly innkeeper, to point you in the right direction. Taking a horse-and-buggy ride with an Amish or Mennonite guide is a good way to have your questions answered and take in the landscape. And while the Amish are the primary draw, the area also offers more contemporary attractions like theaters, fine dining, and antiques. The city of Lancaster makes a good base for exploring, or if you prefer a more small-town experience, check out Lititz, Ephrata, Bird-in-Hand, Adamstown, Paradise, Strasburg, or Intercourse.

SIGHTS
City of Lancaster

Quaint and quiet in comparison to Philadelphia, Lancaster is bustling and lively compared to the rest of rural Lancaster County. It also hosts museums and attractions that pay homage to the Amish experience and offers the largest choice of accommodations and dining.

◖ CENTRAL MARKET

The Central Market (23 N. Market St., 717/291-4723, Tues. and Fri. 6 A.M.–4 P.M., Sat. 6 A.M.–2 P.M.) is an excellent place to stop for a bite and shop for locally made goods and food. The current redbrick building was built in 1889, and the market features over 60 stalls including a wide variety of fresh produce and meat from local farms, along with fresh-cut flowers, seafood, handcrafted quilts, handmade fudge, baked goods, and international cuisine. An example of the great prices: a bag of fruit for about $1, an apple fritter for $0.60, or an empanada for $1.50.

◖ FULTON THEATRE

While you're in town, see a show at the historic Fulton Theatre (12 N. Prince St., 717/397-7425, www.thefulton.org) if you get the chance, or at least stop in for a tour. The Victorian gem is the oldest continuously operating theater in the country and one of just eight National Historic Landmark theaters. Quality musicals, comedies, and dramas are shown in the elegant venue. Hour-long tours are available at 11:00 A.M. weekdays and on weekends by appointment.

LANCASTER HERITAGE CENTER MUSEUM

The Lancaster Heritage Center Museum (5 W. King St., 717/299-6440, www.lancaster-heritage.com, Mon.–Sat. 9 A.M.–5 P.M., free) is just across the walkways from the market. The compact three-story museum is committed to preserving local history with a permanent collection, annual exhibitions, and rotating exhibits. The 1st floor explains aspects of the Pennsylvania Dutch history and culture in a way that makes it simple to understand, with a few interactive displays for kids. Don't miss the Masonic Hall ceiling mural on the 2nd floor in a room containing an array

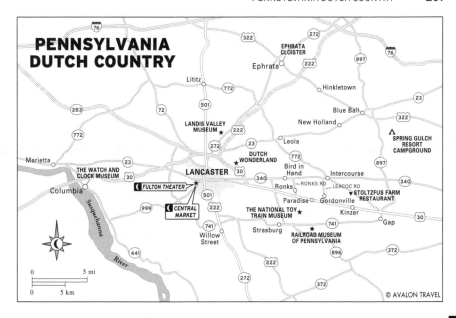

of decorative arts and antiques; it was painted in 1933 by G. L. Zambon of Philadelphia and has been restored. The Heritage Center also operates the nearby **Lancaster Quilt & Textile Museum** (37 Market St., 717/299-6440, Mon.–Sat. 9 A.M.–5 P.M., and first Fridays 5–9 P.M., $6 adult, $4 student, free 17 and under). A collection of Lancaster County Amish quilts from the 18th century to the present makes up the majority of the permanent exhibition.

More Nearby Sights
DUTCH WONDERLAND

If you have young kids and you're visiting in summer, visit the "kingdom of kids," Dutch Wonderland (2249 Lincoln Hwy. E., 717/291-1888, www.dutchwonderland.com, $28.95, free under 2). There is nothing very Dutch about the place, but the small amusement park has about 40 rides great for children 12 and under. It's a pleasant, easy-to-navigate park, with mini-golf and play areas. In the summer it is open daily 10 A.M.–8:30 P.M. early June–late August. Hours vary

and are reduced in fall, winter, and spring; check the website.

EPHRATA CLOISTER

The Ephrata Cloister (632 W. Main St., Ephrata, 717/733-6600, www.ephratacloister.org, Mon.–Sat. 9 A.M.–5 P.M., Sun. noon–5 P.M., closed Mon. in Jan.–Feb., $7 adult, $6.50 senior, $5 child 6–17, free under 6) was founded in 1732 as the home of a German religious community, one of the first of its kind. Today it is a National Historic Landmark managed by the Pennsylvania Historical and Museum Commission to highlight the unique history of the people that lived and worshipped here. At its peak, in the 1740s and '50s, about 300 people lived and worked here. The group believed in spiritual rewards and shunned earthly pleasures, including sexual intercourse. The community is known for accomplishments in creating self-composed a cappella music; developing a form of Germanic calligraphy, Frakturschriften; and building a publishing center that included a paper mill, printing office, and book bindery.

PENNSYLVANIA DUTCH WAY OF LIFE

The Pennsylvania Dutch (also called Pennsylvania Germans or Pennsylvania Deutsch) are the descendants of early German immigrants to Pennsylvania. They arrived, mostly before 1800, to escape religious persecution in Europe in William Penn's unique colony founded on the principle of religious freedom. Today, the Pennsylvania Dutch speak a variation of their original German language, as well as English. They are made up of Amish, Mennonite Lutheran, German Reformed, Moravian, and other groups that share some beliefs while differing in others. While there are communities living in many parts of the United States and Canada today, by far the largest settlement is here in Pennsylvania, concentrated in and around Lancaster County.

It is unusual in the United States for the people and culture to be the primary tourist draw of a place, as it is in the area often referred to as Amish Country. But it is no surprise that visitors want to witness a lifestyle so different than their own. Observing the culture, free from modern technology like telephones, computers, and cars, offers a window into a time long past. And while many local Pennsylvania Dutch welcome and have come to rely on the tourist industry for their livelihood, it is important to remember that they are real people going about their daily lives and to be respectful of their privacy. All visitors should know that among their many unique beliefs that shun vanity, the Amish people do not believe in having their photograph taken.

The many different sects of Pennsylvania Dutch vary from strict followers of the Old Order to more modern groups who have allowed certain aspects of modernity into their lives. Some do not use battery-powered electronics, while others now use phones or cars. Each sect has their own rules ranging from guidelines for dress and hair length to buggy styles and farming techniques. Most Pennsylvania Dutch wear traditional clothing that is simple, unadorned, and made by hand. Jewelry is not worn – not even wedding bands; unmarried men are usually clean-shaven while married men have beards. The Amish are generally averse to anything that could chip away at the family or close-knit community structure, which is of the highest importance. This includes most modern technology, and education beyond the eighth grade, which they feel can lead to unnecessary egoism and separation. Mennonites hold many of the same beliefs but tend to be somewhat less conservative in dress codes and in the use of technology.

It would take an entire book to delve into the fascinating heritage of the Pennsylvania Dutch, but there is no better way to get a glimpse into their unique way of life than a visit to the area. You'll learn much through your own observation, and through the many museums and sites dedicated to preserving local culture. Many Pennsylvania Dutch tour guides are willing to answer your questions. Many are also constantly having to reassess their beliefs and choose what to incorporate from the modern world into their lives, without sacrificing their core values. It is best not to generalize, as every family and sect is different. Times have changed, and continue to change, for the Pennsylvania Dutch, if at a much slower pace than for many of us.

LITITZ FOOD TOURS

In the small town of Lititz, you can visit two different historic food institutions. The **Wilbur Chocolate Company's Candy Americana Museum & Store** (48 N. Broad St., 717/626-3249, www.wilberbuds.com, Mon.–Sat. 10 A.M.–5 P.M., free) has a display of antique candy molds and paraphernalia; on a tour you can watch the chocolate-making process and try delicious samples. The **Julius Sturgis Pretzel House** (219 E. Main St., 717/626-4354, www.juliussturgis.com, Mon.–Sat. 9:30 A.M.–4:30 P.M. mid-Mar.–mid-Jan., Mon.–Fri. 10:30 A.M.–3:30 P.M. mid-Jan.–mid-Mar., $3 adult, $2 child) was established in 1861 as America's first commercial pretzel bakery. While most of the production has moved into a larger facility, you can still tour its original location for a guided tour. You'll get to twist your own pretzel and learn about the history and symbolism involved in pretzels. A store offers all kinds of pretzels, including chocolate-covered, and other treats.

STRASBURG RAILROAD
Founded in 1832, the Strasburg Railroad (Rte. 741 E., Strasburg, 717/687-7522, www .strasburgrailroad.com, seasonal hours, call ahead, $11 adult, $6 child) is America's oldest short-line railroad. The Victorian-style wooden passenger train is pulled by a coal-burning steam locomotive. On a 45-minute ride to the town of Paradise and back, you'll pass the area's quintessential scenic rolling farmlands. For an additional fee, you can have lunch in the dining car, or the swanky first-class car. There are several displays and shops at the station. Across the street, you can see more trains, locomotives, and engines at the **Railroad Museum of Pennsylvania** (300 Gap Rd., Strasburg, 717/687-8628, www

.rrmuseumpa.org, Tues.–Sat. 9 A.M.–5 P.M., $8 adult, $7 senior and youth, free under 6).

WHEATLAND
Wheatland (1120 Marietta Ave., Lancaster, 717/392-8721, www.wheatland.org, Mon.–Sat. 10 A.M.–4:30 P.M., Sun. noon–4:30 P.M. Apr.–Oct.; Mon., Fri., and Sat. 10 A.M.–4:30 P.M., Sun. noon–4:30 P.M. Nov.–Dec., $7 adult, $6 senior, $5 student, $2 child 6–11, free under 2) is one of the few historic sites that has nothing to do with Amish culture. The home of President James Buchanan for 20 years, it served as Democratic headquarters during the 1856 presidential campaign. Buchanan gave his first campaign address on the front lawn. On a tour, you'll see the restored home and grounds, and learn much about the era in American history when he lived and served as president.

WORKING AMISH VILLAGES
The **Amish Farm and House** (2395 Lincoln Hwy. E., Lancaster, 717/394-6185, www.amish-farmandhouse.com, daily, 8:30 A.M.–4 P.M.

EXCURSIONS

© KARRIE GAVIN

the historic steam locomotive at the Strasburg Railroad

© KARRIE GAVIN

lush farmlands in Amish country

Nov.–Mar., 8:30 A.M.–5 P.M. Apr.–May and Sept.–Oct., 8:30 A.M.–6 P.M. June–Aug., $7.50 adult over 12, $6.75 senior, $5 child 5–11) is a replicated traditional Amish village. Self and guided tours are offered of the stone farmhouse and working barn, built in 1805, and the blacksmith shop. On a tour, you'll learn about the customs, history, and religion of the Old Order Amish, and seasonal buggy rides are available.

The **Landis Valley Museum** (2451 Kissel Hill Rd., 717/569-0401, www.landisvalleymuseum.org, Mon.–Sat. 9 A.M.–5 P.M., Sun. noon–5 P.M., $9 adult, $7 senior, $6 child 6–17, free under 6) is also a re-created village of Pennsylvania Dutch life, with more than 40 historic structures on 100 acres. The buildings have docents stationed to explain and demonstrate a village at work, including a blacksmith's shop, gun shop, tavern, and homes showing pottery, weaving, cooking, and quilting demonstrations in realistic settings. There are also tours, wagon rides, and a short film that runs in the visitors center explaining the site.

RESTAURANTS

There are plenty of traditional Pennsylvania Dutch restaurants where you'll eat family-style all-you-can-eat meals that are hearty and plentiful, with lots of the stick-to-your-ribs variety of mostly meat and potatoes. Two to try are **Stoltzfus Farm Restaurant** (3716A East Newport Rd., 717/768-8156, Intercourse, www.stoltzfusmeats.com, Mon.–Sat. 11:30 A.M.–8 P.M. Apr.–Oct., Fri.–Sat. 11:30 A.M.–8 P.M. Nov., closed Dec.–Mar.) or **Plain and Fancy Farm Restaurant** (3121 Old Philadelphia Pike/Rte. 340, Bird-in-Hand, 717/768-4400, www.plainandfancyfarm.com, daily 11:30 A.M.–7 P.M.), which offers an all-you-can-eat feast or an à la carte menu, as well as lodging and tours.

Strawberry Hill (128 W. Strawberry St., Lancaster, 717/393-5544, www.strawberryhillrestaurant.com, daily 5–10 P.M.) is a long-time popular Lancaster spot. The old Victorian house on a hill just outside of the action of the city has been a hotel, tavern, speakeasy, brothel, corner bar, steak house, and, since 1986, the

Strawberry Hill restaurant. Delicious, creative dishes are served in a cozy, friendly setting, and the extensive wine list earned it the title of "Pennsylvania's top wine destination restaurant" by *Wine Spectator.*

If it's fine dining you're after, try (**Donecker's Restaurant** (333 N. State St., Ephrata, 717/738-9501, www.doneckers .com, Mon.–Thurs. 11 A.M.–9 P.M., Fri.–Sat. 11 A.M.–10 P.M., Sun. noon–4 P.M., closed some Sun. and Wed. in winter, call ahead, reservations recommended). Delicious contemporary cuisine is served in a traditional, elegant setting, with fine arts and antiques decorating the place and live piano music on weekend evenings.

SHOPPING

There are plenty of places to shop for authentic local goods and foods. The **Kitchen Kettle Village** (Rte. 340, Intercourse, 717/768-2708, www.kitchenkettle.com, Mon.–Sat. 9 A.M.–5 P.M.) offers a unique shopping experience, with 42 shops featuring a wealth of locally made products. In 1954, the Burnley family started a canning business out of their garage that has expanded into the quaint shopping center it is today. Don't miss the Jam 'n Relish Kitchen, where Amish and Mennonite cooks make an array of delicious spreads and treats. Quilts, ironwork, folk art, pottery, and designer leather can also be purchased along with an array of food items. There is a variety of on-site lodging starting at around $89 per night, and several sit-down dining options. For more local goods, the **Olde Mill House Shoppes** (105 Strasburg Pike, Lancaster, 717/299-0678, www .oldemillhouse.com) offers handcrafted home accessories and arts and crafts from local and national artists. The town of **Adamstown** (www.antiquescapital.com) offers a wealth of antiques shops in a concentrated area, mostly along Route 272.

If you prefer name-brand clothing, jewelry, and shoes at rock-bottom prices, you're also in luck. The area has great outlet shopping at **Tanger Outlet Center** (311 Stanley K. Tanger Blvd., Lancaster, 717/392-7260, www.tangeroutlet.com) and **Rockvale Square Outlets** (35 S. Willowdale Dr., Lancaster, 717/293-9595, www.rockvaleoutletslancaster.com).

HOTELS

There are a host of unique accommodations in the area, including numerous excellent bed-and-breakfasts. (**King's Cottage Bed and Breakfast** (1049 E. King St., Lancaster, 717/397-1017, www.kingscottagebb.com), a distinguished Select Registry Inn, is one of the best. Just a short drive from the heart of the city, the Spanish-style 1913 mansion is a National Historic Landmark offering every modern amenity. Each room is unique, and many have fireplaces and large whirlpool tubs. The friendly innkeepers, Janis and Ann, are happy to help you plan your visit, and they know all there is to know about the area. Prices range about $150–325 depending on room and time of year, and a delicious homemade gourmet breakfast is included.

For a unique, modern hotel in the heart of the city, try the **Lancaster Arts Hotel** (300 Harrisburg Ave., Lancaster, 717/299-3000, www.lancasterartshotel.com). Housed in a former tobacco warehouse, this boutique hotel has tons of character with original brick and stone walls, exposed wooden beams, and locally made furniture and artwork. There is also a 1st-floor art gallery and a restaurant and bar. Rates for the 47 rooms and 16 suites start around $159.

The **General Sutter Inn** (14 E. Main St., Lititz, 717/626-2115, www.generalsutterinn .com) is a popular spot in the heart of Lititz. Built in 1764, it has been a local institution at the intersection of the two main drags for 250 years. A restaurant and tavern on the 1st floor draws a steady stream of locals, while visitors love the rooms decked in elegant Victorian antiques. Despite its age and creaky floorboards and windows, the hotel is in great shape and the beds are remarkably comfortable. Rates start at around $100 per night, and with several connecting rooms it is a great place for families.

For those who prefer roughing it, there is a great RV and tent campground, **Spring Gulch Resort Campground** (475 Lynch Rd., New Holland, 717/354-3100, www.springgulch.com).

GETTING THERE AND AROUND

The heart of Dutch Country is about 65 miles, or 1.5 hours by car, from Philadelphia. It can be reached via I-76 West (Schuylkill Expressway) to U.S. 202 South to U.S. 30 West, or by taking I-76 to the Pennsylvania Turnpike. Since much of the area is wide-open roads and farmland, it is best to have a car for a leisurely tour. However, there is a train that runs from Philadelphia into the city of Lancaster (Amtrak, 800/872-7245, www.amtrak.com), and local bus service within Lancaster and nearby towns, including Ephrata and Lititz (Red Rose Transit Authority, 717/397-4246, www.redrosetransit.com).

INFORMATION AND TOURS

The **Pennsylvania Dutch Visitors Center** (501 Greenfield Rd., 800/723-8824, www.padutchcountry.com, Mon.–Sat. 8:30 A.M.–5 P.M., Sun. 9 A.M.–5 P.M., with extended hours in summer and fall) is an excellent source of information about the area. The website lists attractions, accommodations, dining, shopping, and more, along with suggested itineraries and a function that lets you create your own itinerary to save and print. There are also discounts offered on the website.

There are walking, buggy, and bus tours to give you an up-close look at Amish life. A **Historic Lancaster Walking Tour** (100 S. Queen St., 717/392-1776) departs on select days April–October. The **Amish Experience** (3121 Old Philadelphia Pike/Rte. 340, Bird-in-Hand, 717/768-3600, ext. 210, www .amishexperience.com) offers two-hour guided bus tours of the area, which can be combined with other attractions at a discount. They also have an "experiential" theater that features scenes from Amish history re-created with multiple projection screens, special effects, and a three-dimensional set (40 minutes). The **Mennonite Information Center** (2209 Millstream Rd., Lancaster, 800/858-8320, www.mennoniteinfoctr.com, two-hour tour for up to 7 people $36) offers personalized guides that ride with you in your car while telling you everything you wanted to know about the local culture. There are many different people offering buggy rides of the countryside by an Amish or Mennonite guide. Try **Abe's Buggy Rides** (2596 Old Philadelphia Pike/Rte. 340, Bird-in-Hand, 717/392-1764, www.abesbuggyrides.com). For an exhilarating tour experience, you can take in the beauty of Pennsylvania Dutch Country from up above in a hot-air balloon. The **United States Hot Air Balloon Company** (800/763-5987, www.ushotairballoon.com) offers a variety of flights from Bird-in-Hand; call to schedule.

BACKGROUND

The Setting

GEOGRAPHY

The original city of Philadelphia outlined by founder William Penn consisted only of the area that is today known as Center City. The rectangular grid occupied approximately two square miles bordered by the Delaware and Schuylkill Rivers to the east and west, Vine Street to the north, and South Street to the south. It wasn't until 1854 that the city consolidated and all the boroughs, townships, and districts of the County of Philadelphia were incorporated into the city. Today, the city and county are one and the same, covering approximately 135 square miles. In addition to that neat grid of city blocks, the city now also includes hills, valleys, winding roads, rivers, creeks, and woodlands.

Water occupies just over 5 percent of the total area of Philadelphia, and parks and woodlands cover around 10 percent of the land area. The lowest point of the city is 10 feet above sea level at the meeting of the Delaware and Schuylkill Rivers in Southwest Philadelphia. The highest point is in Chestnut Hill, at 444 feet above sea level. In addition to the two major rivers, the Delaware and the Schuylkill, smaller bodies of water include the Wissahickon, Cobbs, and Pennypack Creeks. Covering more than 9,200 acres, Fairmount Park is considered the largest urban municipal park in the world. The

PHOTO BY K. CIAPPA FOR GPTMC

PENN'S FIVE ORIGINAL SQUARES

In one of the earliest examples of thoughtful city planning, William Penn and his surveyor, Thomas Holme, laid out a detailed plan for Philadelphia. It was drawn more than 300 years ago but much of it remains in place today. This is because it not only factored in the conditions of the time, but also considered the effects of the growth and expansion that would ultimately occur. The area we now know as Center City was originally the entire city of Philadelphia. Its symmetrical grid of streets between the two rivers also contained five strategically placed squares, or parks. There was one at the center and one in each of the four quadrants. Penn recognized the importance of having preserved green spaces to break up the expanses of buildings long before that concept came into vogue. While their names and appearances have changed over time, his five original squares continue to anchor the city and play an important role in Philadelphia today.

Center Square is now the home of City Hall. While it's the only square that is no longer green, it is the most important one of all as home to the main offices of city government, including the mayor's office. It is located at the geographic center of the city at the intersection of its two main thoroughfares, Market Street and Broad Street. While City Hall wasn't built here until about a century later, it fulfilled Penn's intentions. The city offices were originally in Old City at the State House (now Independence Hall), but Penn thought they should move here when the city grew westward and this became the new center, as he predicted it would.

The other four well-landscaped squares are primarily spots for rest and relaxation in several bustling areas of the city, and each has plenty of green space, park benches, sculptures, and monuments. Originally named for their locations, Southwest, Southeast, Northwest, and Northeast Squares are today called, respectively, **Rittenhouse Square, Washington Square, Logan Square,** and **Franklin Square.** Franklin Square underwent a massive makeover in 2006, and is now a popular Old City attraction complete with an old-fashioned carousel and a Revolutionary-themed mini-golf course.

largest continuous sections of the park are East and West Fairmount Parks, on either side of the Schuylkill River, the Wissahickon Valley Park in the northwest section of the city, and Pennypack Park in the northeast, but the park system includes a total of 63 regional and neighborhood parks, including the five central city parks—Center, Franklin, Logan, Rittenhouse, and Washington—that were laid out in Penn's original plan. Pretty much every patch of green in the city is part of Fairmount Park.

The second-largest city on the East Coast and the sixth-largest in the nation, Philadelphia is conveniently located in the middle of the Northeast Corridor. By car, Philadelphia is approximately two hours from New York City and two and a half hours from Washington, D.C. It is an hour's drive from Lancaster County, also known as Amish Country, and an hour from Atlantic City, New Jersey, with the rest of the New Jersey shore points just beyond. The area known as the Greater Philadelphia region consists of five counties in southeastern Pennsylvania (Bucks, Chester, Delaware, Montgomery, and Philadelphia). The four counties in southern New Jersey (Burlington, Camden, Gloucester, and Salem) and New Castle County in Delaware are also sometimes included when referring to the Greater Philadelphia region.

CLIMATE

Philadelphia's four distinct seasons offer very different experiences and activities. Summers are often very hot and humid, while winters can be extremely cold. Fall and spring are generally mild and pleasant. While each season offers its own advantages, you will need to plan your day and dress accordingly if you visit in one of the more extreme seasons. Average temperatures in

PHILLY FIRSTS

In addition to being considered the birthplace of the United States of America, Philadelphia claims countless landmark "firsts" in America's history. It also boasts many of the biggest and best in numerous categories. Listed below are just a few of its many distinguished accomplishments.

FIRSTS

- 1681   First parks made for the pleasure of people, three of Penn's original squares
- 1690   First paper mill in North America, built near Germantown by William Bradford
- 1685   First almanac, *America's Messenger* by William Bradford
- 1698   First public school in the American colonies
- 1728   First botanical gardens, by John Bartram on the Schuylkill River
- 1731   First lending library, the Library Company of Philadelphia
- 1736   First voluntary fire squad in the United States, the Union Fire Company
- 1743   First institution devoted to science and philosophy in North America, the American Philosophical Institution
- 1751   First Hospital, Pennsylvania Hospital
- 1752   First fire insurance company, Philadelphia Contributionship
- 1776   First reading of the Declaration of Independence
- 1777   First United States flag on record, and first Fourth of July celebration
- 1780   First Bank, Pennsylvania Bank
- 1790   First stock exchange, Philadelphia Exchange

- 1790-1800   First capital of the United States, Philadelphia
- 1799-1802   First row houses, Carstairs Row
- 1802   First public water supply project, Philadelphia Water Works
- 1805   First art museum and school, Pennsylvania Academy of the Fine Arts
- 1812   First natural history institution, The Academy of Natural Sciences
- 1854   First Consolidation Act by a city and its townships
- 1874   First zoo
- 1876   First department store, Wanamaker's
- 1920   First Thanksgiving Day Parade
- 1934   First professional football game (Philadelphia Eagles beat Cincinnati Reds, 64-0)
- 1946   First computer (ENIAC), constructed at University of Pennsylvania

OTHER DISTINCTIONS

- Oldest street in continuous use: Elfreth's Alley, since 1702
- Most murals in any city in the world, with more than 2,800
- Oldest theater in continuous use in the English-speaking world: Walnut Street Theatre, since 1809
- Oldest and largest outdoor market: the Italian Market
- Largest landscaped city park: Fairmount Park, with 9,200 acres
- Oldest African American newspaper: *The Philadelphia Tribune,* since 1885
- Largest masonry building in the world: City Hall
- Longest-running parade: the Mummers New Year's Day Parade, since 1901

July range 67–86°F (20–30°C), but severe heat waves can bring temperatures up to 95°F (35°C) with the heat index as high as 110°F (43°C). While this usually only lasts for a few days each summer, it is very unpleasant to do anything outdoors during a heat wave. In January, the average temperature is 23–38°F (3–5°C), with occasionally frigid temperatures, severe snowfall, and icing that can make driving dangerous. This is the exception rather than the rule, however, and on most winter days, bundling up in warm clothes will make it possible to get between destinations without too much trouble.

The classic Northeast Fall is quite beautiful in Philadelphia, complete with leaves changing colors and falling from the trees as the heat of summer gives way to cooler weather. Spring is mostly filled with many perfectly comfortable, pleasant days. Rainfall is moderate with 42 inches annually. Seasonal snowfall varies from a light dusting to the occasional blizzard with an average of 21 inches a year. Precipitation is generally spread throughout the year, so a light rain jacket will come in handy. A local current weather report and forecast is available 24 hours a day by calling 215/936-1212.

History

Philadelphia has one of the oldest and richest histories of any U.S. city, along with a great wealth of monuments and attractions that keep that history alive. Considered the birthplace of the nation, Philadelphia is most famous for its central role in the Revolutionary War. The seeds of Revolution, major battles, and the drafting of the Declaration of Independence and Constitution all took place right here, and Philadelphia was the nation's capital for the first ten years.

But while the late 18th century was undeniably one of the most fascinating periods in Philadelphia's history, that is only part of the story. Beginning before William Penn arrived and continuing with the rebirth taking place today, the city's tumultuous and storied past spans more than 300 years. This chapter merely scratches the surface. Visiting the city's many historic sights will reveal still more, but history buffs should also be sure to check out the *Suggested Reading* list in this book's *Resources* (most notably *Philadelphia: A 300-Year History*).

WILLIAM PENN'S VISION

Before William Penn arrived, the area that would become Philadelphia was inhabited by Native Americans, and later by other European settlers. The Lenni-Lenapes, also known as "the Delaware Indians," were the earliest known residents. Many were pushed west by the advance of Swedish, Dutch, and English settlers in the early 1600s, but others remained. In the 1630s and 1640s, the Swedes and Dutch spent approximately 17 years arguing over claims to land along the Delaware River, but the dispute over ownership was never resolved, and it ultimately fell under British rule.

William Penn negotiated to take ownership of the land west of the Delaware from King Charles II of England, as partial payment for a debt owed to Penn's deceased father, who was a wealthy, high-ranking naval officer, admiral, and courtier. The 45,000 square miles that would become Pennsylvania were primarily woodlands, stretching from the Allegheny Mountains to the Delaware River. The king was happy to pay off his debt with land that was not of major importance to him, but perhaps even happier to see the rebellious young Quaker and many of his followers leave England.

Quakers were not generally well regarded by proper English society, as their rejection of a hierarchal system clashed with the lavish wealth and strict monarchy of English society and government. Penn was imprisoned several times in England for expressing his religious beliefs and insisting on religious freedom as a moral right.

© KARRIE GAVIN

These signs posted throughout the city reveal much about the history of many historic sites.

In 1661, he was expelled from Oxford for failing to properly honor the Church of England, and shortly thereafter, he became a Quaker, much to the displeasure of his wealthy, traditional family. He was purportedly beaten by his father, whom he fiercely battled when it came to religion.

Penn wanted to found a society where not only Quakers, but people of all religions, could practice without persecution. This was an unprecedented idea for the colonies of the time, and a stark contrast to the Puritanical zeal of the settlers in Boston and New England, who longed for stricter religious control over settlers in their communities. Penn began to carry out his "holy experiment" in his new city of Philadelphia. His ship, the *Welcome,* was one of 23 shiploads of immigrants to arrive in the first year of Philadelphia's founding.

Penn hired his cousin William Markam to help him plan "a large Towne or City in the most Convenient place upon the [Delaware] River for health & Navigation." He hoped for a "greene Country Towne, which will never

be burnt, and always be wholesome." Penn envisioned a city that bore a closer resemblance to some of the rural towns of England, which he preferred to the overcrowded cities he knew such as London, which were more susceptible to disease and fire damage because of people living in such close proximity. Exhibiting one of the first examples of thoughtful city planning in the New World, Penn and his helpers laid out a grid with large lots, wide streets, and space for gardens and orchards, including the five central city parks that remain an important part of life in Philadelphia today. His design served as an example for numerous cities to follow.

In the spring of 1682, Penn wrote the Frame of Government for Pennsylvania. He consulted with Algernon Sidney and John Locke; the former complained he was keeping too much power for himself and the latter that he was giving too much to the people. Penn's Frame survived and was later studied by Benjamin Franklin, Thomas Paine, and others. Parts of it were used as a model for many

WHAT'S IN A NAME?

There is an interesting story behind the names of both Pennsylvania ("Penn's woods") and Philadelphia ("city of brotherly love"). Can you guess which one was named by William Penn? If you guessed Pennsylvania, you're wrong. William Penn was given the colony of Pennsylvania by King Charles II of England, to repay a debt the king owed to Penn's deceased father, wealthy, high-ranking naval officer Admiral Penn. The 45,000-square-mile tract of land consisted primarily of woodlands stretching from the Allegheny Mountains to the Delaware River. William Penn wanted to name the colony "Sylvania" after the woods, but the king insisted on adding Penn to the name, in honor of Admiral Penn. William Penn wasn't crazy about the name. As part of the Society of Friends, or Quakers, who denounce excess and self-promotion, Penn considered it egotistical to name land after oneself. He knew that people would assume the colony was named after him, and many do to this day.

The young William Penn, however, did choose the name for the city that would shape his colony, a name rooted in his own ideals and plan for the city. He set out to found a society where not only Quakers, but people of all religions, could practice without persecution. An unprecedented idea at the time, he called it his "holy experiment," and named his city Philadelphia. Based on the Greek *philos* for "love" and *adelphos* for "brother," Philadelphia means the city of "brotherly love."

state governments to follow, and many of its principles influenced the content of the United States Constitution. Useful features of this early document include the call for religious liberty, an assembly elected by the people to make the laws, trial by jury, and a penal system designed to reform, not just to punish.

COLONIAL ERA

When Penn arrived, many of the early residents in Philadelphia lived in caves dug out of the Delaware River banks. Penn made an unprecedented move in buying, rather than taking, land already claimed, setting a new standard for colonial settlers' treatment of indigenous peoples. Popular legend has it that Penn made a treaty of friendship with the Lenape chief Tammany under an elm tree at Shackamaxon, present-day Kensington. The famous painting *Penn's Treaty with the Indians* by Benjamin West immortalized the scene. The giant statue of William Penn that stands on top of City Hall was positioned to point to the location of the signing of the treaty. Whether or not the exact event took place in that spot is debatable, but what it represents—Penn's peaceful relationship with the natives—is well supported.

Documents show that he wrote to the Indians, asking for peaceful relations and acknowledging the mistakes of previous European settlers. Penn even learned their language so he wouldn't need a translator to communicate with them.

Penn advertised for the purchase of large tracts of land at reasonable prices all over Europe, and people came to the city in droves seeking economic opportunity and religious freedom. In 1683, there were just a few hundred inhabitants and by 1701, there were around 2,500. The freedom of religion brought not only English, Welsh, German, and Dutch Quakers to the colony, but also Huguenots (French Protestants), Mennonites, Amish, Lutherans from Catholic German states, Irish Catholics, and Jews, among others. A group of German Quakers established the first German settlement in America in present-day Germantown.

The vast majority of those first land purchasers settled along the Delaware River, concentrated in what is today known as Old City and Society Hill. Despite Penn's hope for westward expansion and plans for large lots surrounded by gardens, nearly all the lots were subdivided multiple times and resold. Smaller alleys were built in between the main streets to accommodate additional homes and people. While his goals were admirable, he had to compete with the reality of a city's natural growth, and immigrants from other large cities who were inclined to replicate what they were accustomed to. Until 1704, few people lived west of Fourth Street, and it would be many more years before they spread west towards the Schuylkill River.

While Penn was largely responsible for the way Philadelphia would eventually develop due to careful, conscious planning, he barely spent any time there. While a visionary, he was not the best businessman and spent much of his life trying to get his finances in order in England. Penn's final significant act before returning to England for good on October 25, 1701, was issuing the Charter of Privileges, also known as the Charter of 1701. This established Philadelphia as a city and gave the mayor, aldermen, and councilmen the authority to issue laws and ordinances and to regulate markets and fairs. It also officially granted the religious freedom that was already practiced. Penn attempted to sell Pennsylvania back to the English Crown, but in 1712 he had a stroke and could no longer speak. The deal was never made and the colony remained his property, under the control of his mostly ineffective, uninvolved offspring, in the years until the Revolutionary War.

SEEDS OF REVOLUTION

The city prospered in the first half of the 18th century. Streets were paved and gas lights installed, making the streets brighter and safer at night. Schools and theaters were formed and by the 1750s, Christ Church and the Pennsylvania State House, now known as Independence Hall, were built. Philadelphia had developed into a true city, but as it became increasingly established, accomplished, and self-sufficient, a need for change also became evident.

In the 1760s, resentment towards British rule was mounting among many residents. England incurred a large debt during the Seven Years War, and attempted to impose unprecedented taxes on the colonies to help pay those debts, without the consent of the colonials. The British felt that since the outcome of the war was beneficial to the colonies, they should bear some of the tax burden, but, under the Magna Carta, colonies were entitled to a vote in the policies that affected them. By 1764, the British Parliament was realizing the increasing importance of the colonies and attempted to gain more control. Meanwhile, colonists were increasingly frustrated that they had no voice in the governmental decisions of a distant ruler and were starting to wonder if their relationship with the crown did them more harm than good. Tensions escalated with the Stamp and Townshend Acts of 1765 and 1767 respectively, in which the British imposed a direct tax on stamps and an import tax on products including lead, paper, paint, glass, and tea. In both cases, colonists revolted and successfully boycotted the importation of British goods until the acts were repealed. The phrase "no taxation without representation" became popular during this time.

After the boycotts, the only remaining food tax imposed by England was on tea—but not for long. In 1773, the famous Boston Tea Party took place in Boston Harbor. The massive protest was a response to the Tea Act, which allowed England to sell tea in the colonies with no import taxes. Revolutionaries broke into a British ship the night before it was scheduled to arrive in Boston and dumped an estimated 90,000 pounds of tea overboard. The radical act of defiance further inspired revolt among colonists along the eastern seaboard.

The British government was outraged and responded by passing five acts that became known as the Intolerable Acts. While their action was an attempt to regain power and order and scare the colonists into submission, it backfired, and incited the other colonies to unite in support of Massachusetts and resolve to not be taken advantage of by England. Benjamin Franklin, who considered himself a loyal British subject until then, was staunchly against what he called the "capricious English policy."

BEN FRANKLIN: PHILLY'S FAVORITE SON

When Benjamin Franklin arrived in Philadelphia in October 1723, he was just a 17-year-old runaway from Boston. No one could have possibly guessed at the significant contributions he would make to the development of the city, the nation, and the world. A man of many talents, he was an author, political theorist, politician, printer, scientist, inventor, civic activist, and diplomat. As a scientist he is best-known for his discoveries and theories regarding electricity, by way of experimenting with lightning and a kite. As a political writer and activist he was one of the major players to fight for and articulate the hopes and meaning of an independent American nation. As a diplomat during the American Revolution, he was largely responsible for securing support from France that ultimately led to victory. Among Franklin's many accomplishments in Philadelphia, he established postal routes between Philadelphia, New York, Boston, and other locations; founded the Union Fire Company to help protect the city from destruction by fire; set up a volunteer group for defense; built two batteries in case the city should be attacked; raised money to build the first hospital in the colonies; and founded the first lending library and the oldest philosophical society. His accomplishments are too great to list them all, but Franklin was involved in practically every significant accomplishment, decision, and invention that took place in Philadelphia during the most critical time in the city's — and ultimately the nation's — history.

The tide was quickly turning and there was a call for a general congress of the colonies to meet and discuss the issues. The First Continental Congress was held in September 1774 in Carpenters' Hall in Philadelphia, chosen because it was centrally located to all the colonies. The 55 delegates represented all the colonies except Georgia, and as a result of the meeting, the Articles of Association, a formal agreement to boycott British goods, was drafted on October 20, 1774. It was wildly successful; imports from Britain dropped 97 percent the following year, showing that the colonies could be powerful when they banned together. The Congress agreed that if the Intolerable Acts were not repealed, the colonies would cease to provide exports to Britain after a certain date. They also planned for a Second Continental Congress in Philadelphia for May 10, 1775.

REVOLUTIONARY WAR

Most members of the First Continental Congress hoped a commercial boycott would persuade the British government to grant their demands and the colonies would remain part of the British Empire, but this was not to be. Instead, they were quickly thrust into what would become the Revolutionary War. The King of England declared Massachusetts in a state of rebellion due to their boycott of the Intolerable Acts, and trade was severely restricted throughout New England. Acts of protest, picketing, and even the burning of several British ships took place in the colonies. On April 19, 1775, British troops advanced at Concord and Lexington in Massachusetts and fired at colonists what became known as "the shot heard around the world." Word quickly spread, marking the unofficial beginning of the Revolutionary War.

When the Second Continental Congress met in 1775 at the Pennsylvania State House, now Independence Hall, they declared war and formed a Continental Army with George Washington as commander. They met here from May 10, 1775, to March 1, 1781, and this is where the Declaration of Independence and Articles of Confederation were adopted. During the war, this Congress essentially acted as the government of the country-to-be, making all the leadership decisions for the now-united colonies.

In March of 1776, the British began a blockade of the Delaware Bay and were moving south through New Jersey. By December, half of Philadelphia's population had fled and the Continental Congress went to Baltimore for fear the city was about to be invaded. American troops pushed back the British at the Battles of Princeton and Trenton and most refugees and Congress returned to the city. By late spring of 1776, the Americans forced the British to evacuate Boston, and by July all of the British Royal officials had fled and the patriots were ready to declare victory—but the British weren't ready to give up.

DECLARATION OF INDEPENDENCE

Meanwhile in 1776, while the war was still being fought, a committee including John Adams, Benjamin Franklin, and Thomas Jefferson was assigned to draft a Declaration of Independence. It declared that the 13 colonies in North America were "free and independent states" and that "all political connection between them and the State of Great Britain, is and ought to be totally dissolved." The final document was the result of much debate and multiple drafts; Adams wrote the bulk of it, but Franklin made several key edits. The delegates voted and the document passed in Congress on July 4, 1776. As legend has it, the Liberty Bell sounded to summon citizens to hear the first public reading of this revolutionary document on July 8, 1776.

In September 1777, American troops could no longer hold off the British, who invaded Philadelphia from the south. Washington tried to stop them at the Battle of Brandywine but was driven back. Residents fled into other parts of Pennsylvania and to New Jersey, and Congress fled to Lancaster and later to York. British troops claimed the city, abandoned by all residents who had the means to flee, for 10 months. But eventually, as battles ensued in other areas, the British troops pulled out of Philadelphia on June 18, 1778, to try to defend New York City. With the help of the French army, who had recently joined the American cause, American troops began reoccupying Philadelphia. The city government returned a week later, and the tides around the colonies had shifted. The Continental Congress returned in early July, and the city was no longer under serious threat. The war was essentially won, though it wasn't official until 1783, when the Treaty of Paris recognized U.S. sovereignty.

THE CONSTITUTION

Under the Articles of Confederation, the Congress only had power over colonial governments, not the citizens themselves. After the war ended, this system grew problematic, especially since any change to the Articles of Confederation required a unanimous vote by all of the colonies. This was nearly impossible since they each acted independently and there was much refusal to participate for the common good. The country could not pay the debts it accrued over the war, while each colony was busy issuing independent and conflicting laws and rules. In 1787, delegates of the 13 colonies held the Constitutional Convention in Philadelphia and immediately voted to drop the Articles of Confederation. They spent many months debating the form that their new government should take, until they finally found a brilliant compromise, and adopted the U.S. Constitution.

This seminal document unified and guided the laws and principles of the new country's government, as it does to this day. Philadelphia was the U.S. capital from 1790 to 1800 and George Washington served as the nation's first president. The northern colonies petitioned Congress to keep the capital in Philadelphia or New York, but—after a debate that Thomas Jefferson called the "most bitter and angry contest ever known in Congress, before or since the Union of the States"—the northerners were forgiven some heavy debts in return for agreeing to move the capital city to a site along the banks of the Potomac River, in what is now Washington, D.C. The Pennsylvania state government left in 1799 and the U.S. government the following year.

POST-REVOLUTIONARY ERA

The city's economy and population experienced rapid growth as the country stabilized and had time to focus on things other than war. However, two massive yellow fever outbreaks in the 1790s caused thousands to flee, virtually shutting down trade and commerce for short periods of time. The yellow fever epidemic of 1793 killed nearly one in ten residents, while most of the upper class fled to the suburbs. Benjamin Rush, the most famous American physician of his time, gained renown during the epidemics when he refused to flee the city and insisted on treating as many patients as possible. The work of Rush, along with that of Phillip Syng Psysick (the "father of American surgery") and the success of Pennsylvania Hospital all contributed to making Philadelphia the leading center for the study and practice of medicine in the United States. By 1800, Philadelphia had largely recovered from the epidemic, and became one of the United States' busiest ports and the country's largest city with almost 68,000 people in the city and nearby suburbs.

However, as the largest city in the country, it was among the most heavily affected by international events. As the British and French warred against each other, the United States tried to stay neutral, but could not. Maritime trade was interrupted by the Embargo Act of 1807, when the United States tried to stop trading with both Britain and France, and by the War of 1812, when the United States went to war against the British in an effort to reassert its independence. Philadelphia's shipping industry never recovered, and New York soon became the United States' busiest port and largest city.

While the embargo was initially bad for the city, it ultimately helped shape Philadelphia into the United States' first major industrial city. Many goods were not available due to trade embargos, so factories were established to make those goods at home. Manufacturing plants were built and the city became an important center for paper, leather, shoes, and boots. Coal and iron mines and the construction of new roads, canals, and railroads helped the city grow into an industrial power. Major projects included the Water Works, a gasworks, and the U.S. Naval Yard. Philadelphia also became the financial and cultural center of the country. Chartered and private banks including the First and Second Banks of the United States and the first U.S. Mint opened. The Pennsylvania Academy of the Fine Arts, the Academy of Natural Sciences, the Athenaeum, and the Franklin Institute were created and public education became available after the Pennsylvania General Assembly passed the Free School Law of 1834.

CRIME AND CONSOLIDATION

The population grew rapidly as immigrants, mostly from Germany and Ireland, continued to arrive. The wealthy finally moved west of 7th Street, and the poor moved into their former homes near the Delaware River, many of which were now converted into tenements and boarding houses. With crowded row houses filling tiny streets and alleys, this area grew filthy and smelly—like areas of London that Penn hoped his city would never resemble.

During the 1840s and 1850s, hundreds of people died each year from malaria, smallpox, tuberculosis, and cholera. The poor were affected the worst because when disease broke out in the city, the rich found respite in second homes in areas like Germantown. Violence, lawlessness, and gangs became serious problems during these years. Many of the volunteer fire companies were infiltrated by gangs, and brutal fights broke out between rival gangs at fire sites, all wanting to be paid for putting out the fire.

As the city grew into an industrial metropolis, ethnic tensions also grew. In addition to the Swedish, German, and British immigrants who had first established homes in the city, Philadelphia was home to strong Irish Catholic and African American communities in the early part of the 19th century. These communities established mutual aid societies, churches, and other institutions, while facing a great deal of opposition from the Nativists of the time.

Rampant racism and violence against immigrants, especially Irish Catholics, was common in the 1840s and 1850s. The Nativist Riots between Protestant Nativists and Irish Catholic immigrants began in 1844 over a question of religious practice in public schools and resulted in injury, death, and much property damage. Violence against African Americans was common, and African American homes and churches were sometimes burned.

The city didn't have the structure or government in place to handle all its problems, and additional tax revenue was required to put programs and institutions—including a police force—in place. The Act of Consolidation was passed on February 2, 1854, which united all of Philadelphia County's districts, townships, and municipalities into one big city. Through this act, 5 of the 30 largest cities in the country at the time were formed into a single municipality. This dramatically increased the size and tax base of the city, and the population grew from about 125,000 to more than 500,000. The total area of the city grew from 2 square miles to 129 square miles. In addition to the crowded area along the Delaware, there were more than 1,500 farms, woods, and wetlands in Philadelphia's new boundaries. The city included the townships and villages (which we now know as neighborhoods) of Germantown, Manayunk, Roxborough, Frankford, Northern Liberties, and Kingsessing. Enough money would be generated to pay the new and much-needed police force, as well as many other public services including water, streets, and transportation.

CIVIL WAR

When the Civil War began in 1861, Philadelphia was initially divided over allegiances. The number of blacks living in the city was just 4 percent, or 22,000—small by modern standards but far greater than in any other northern city at the time. Philadelphia served as an important stop on the Underground Railroad, housing the largest free black population in the north. Large networks of African Americans and whites, especially among the fiercely abolitionist Quakers, assisted many slaves on the way to freedom. However, many Philadelphians were against the anti-slavery movement and abolitionists were sometimes the target of violence; some Quaker meeting houses were burned to the ground.

Ultimately, Philadelphia joined the Union and the city went on to play an important role in the war by supplying soldiers, ammunition, war ships, and army uniforms. More than 157,000 soldiers and sailors were treated within the city—many at Satterlee Hospital, the largest Army Hospital in the world at the time, which stood in West Philadelphia near the site of today's Clark Park. The Mower General Hospital in Chestnut Hill also treated hundreds of thousands of injured soldiers. Philadelphia began to prepare for invasion in 1863, but the southern army was held off at Gettysburg and ultimately the war was won. Philadelphia was less impacted by the Civil War than many other places, because it avoided the major physical destruction that many cities in the south suffered, as well as the major political and social upheavals that took place in other northern cities.

A GROWING CITY

After the Civil War, immigrants continued to arrive in the city and by 1870, 27 percent of the population was foreign born. By the 1880s, immigration from Russia, Eastern Europe, and Italy rivaled immigration from Western Europe. In 1881 there were around 5,000 Jews in the city and by 1905, the number grew to 100,000. The Italian population increased from around 300 in 1870 to 18,000 in 1900, and the majority settled in South Philadelphia, which remains an Italian stronghold. In 1876 there were around 25,000 blacks in the city and by 1890, this number was near 40,000. During the 1880s, the people moving into the city were mostly poor, working-class immigrants, and the wealthy were beginning to leave. The suburbs along the Main Line of the Pennsylvania Railroad just west of the city became a popular destination, and the area remains one of the wealthiest and most elite in the region today.

Over the course of the late 19th century, industry grew in the modern metropolis despite a great deal of political corruption and setbacks. Philadelphia became a city of homeowners, distinct from cities like New York and Chicago, where large groups of people rented tenements. The city developed to include row after row of single-family homes, which provided affordable housing for the middle class. The police department improved and volunteer fire companies were finally replaced by a paid fire department. Education reforms were implemented that served to protect the education system from corrupt politics. Opportunity for higher education improved when the University of Pennsylvania moved to West Philadelphia and Temple University, Drexel University, and the Free Library were all founded.

One of the biggest events in the history of the country took place in Philadelphia in 1876. The Centennial Exposition was a World's Fair held in Fairmount Park to celebrate the United States' Centennial. Nine million people came to the city over a six-month period to take part in the carnival atmosphere and to see the landmark science exhibits, including Alexander Graham Bell's telephone and the Corliss Steam Engine. Millions of dollars went into planning the incredible event, but unfortunately many of the buildings constructed for it were left abandoned with no real purpose once the fair ended.

Other major developments of the growing city included the construction of City Hall at the center of the city at Broad and Market Streets. The architectural marvel took 23 years to complete, and for 100 years, was the tallest building in Philadelphia. An unofficial agreement kept it the tallest building until the 945-foot One Liberty Place snatched that crown in 1987, soon to be followed by seven other skyscrapers.

Another key element to the city's growth was the Pennsylvania Railroad, which expanded westward to connect Philadelphia with the entire East Coast and the Midwest. This was also the era when major department stores including Wanamaker's and Strawbridge & Clothier came to the city. As automobile use increased, new roads and bridges were built, including the Northeast (Roosevelt) Boulevard in 1914, the Benjamin Franklin Parkway in 1918, and the Delaware River (Benjamin Franklin) Bridge—which connects the city with Camden, New Jersey—in 1926. New skyscrapers were built and wired for electricity, and the first subway was constructed in 1907. The Philadelphia Museum of Art opened in 1928. The city was growing in every way imaginable.

THE GREAT DEPRESSION AND WORLD WAR II

While several economic depressions and recessions of the 19th and early 20th century certainly hurt the city, their effect was somewhat hampered in Philadelphia compared with other cities because of its variety of industry. But in 1929, when the Great Depression hit, Philadelphia—like the rest of the country—could not withstand the blow. The effects were devastating to the functioning of commerce and to the well-being of residents. In the three years that followed the stock market crash, 50 banks closed and thousands of residents couldn't pay mortgages, making foreclosures commonplace. More than half of the savings and loan associations went out of business. In 1933, the unemployment rate was at its highest; blacks were affected worse than whites, and immigrants worst of all.

The mayor at the time, J. Hampton Moore, was considered unsympathetic to the plight of the people, blaming them for laziness. He fired 3,500 city workers, instituted pay cuts, forced unpaid vacation, and reduced the number of contracts. Many groups of workers united and not long after, Philadelphia became a strong union city, which it remains to this day.

There was a great deal of corruption and fraud in the city government throughout this period. Many had no faith in what they saw as the GOP machine. Mob activity was high, especially during Prohibition, and the city slowly started to shift towards the Democratic Party in hopes of change. The government was exposed on multiple counts of corruption and stealing and in the 1951 election, Joseph S.

Clark became the first Democratic mayor in 80 years. Philadelphia has remained staunchly Democratic ever since, with not a single Republican mayor or congressman elected in Philadelphia in more than 50 years.

The beginning of World War II helped bring Philadelphia out of the Depression as new jobs, many in the defense industry, offered new opportunity. More than 30,000 workers found jobs at the Naval Ship Yard. When the United States became involved in the war in 1941, many Philadelphia men went to serve, while women, African Americans, and workers from outside the city, who had been excluded by unions, filled in for the missing labor force. At the end of the war in 1945, there were around 184,000 Philadelphians in the U.S. armed forces.

A SHRINKING CITY

The city's population peaked at over two million residents in 1950; ever since, the numbers have declined while suburban counties have grown. After World War II, Philadelphia experienced a serious housing shortage, with many of its homes more than 100 years old and in poor condition. The phenomenon known as "white flight" began, and has continued ever since, in Philadelphia as in many other U.S. cities. Many economically disadvantaged African Americans, Puerto Ricans, and other groups moved into the city while middle and upper-middle class families, mostly white, moved out. Between 1950 and 2000, the city lost 26.7 percent of its population, in keeping with national trends—Chicago lost 20 percent and Baltimore lost 31.4 percent during this time, according to U.S. census data. Philadelphia was shrinking at a startling rate, and many manufacturing and other businesses were leaving the city or shutting down entirely, so there were no jobs for the people coming in.

The 1960s was a turbulent decade in Philadelphia, as it was across the nation. Crime had become a serious problem, with drug-related gang warfare plaguing the city. A 1970 City Planning Commission survey noted crime as the city's number one problem. Police Commissioner Frank Rizzo was a controversial figure who was both loved and hated, depending on whom you asked. He had a reputation as an aggressive police officer, quick to use force, especially against African Americans, but also as a strong proponent of law and order. He was elected mayor in 1971, after serving four years as police commissioner, and was given credit for keeping violence in check, if only by comparison to other cities at the time. He was reelected in 1975, and police and fire departments and some cultural institutions were well taken care of. Meanwhile, other areas, including the Free Library, the Department of Welfare and Recreation, the City Planning Commission, and the Streets Department experienced major cuts. Rizzo was a public figure who divided the city perhaps more than any other in its history.

Crime continued through the 1980s, with mafia warfare taking place, mostly in South Philadelphia. Drugs, gangs, and crack houses existed in many of the city's poorest neighborhoods, and the murder rate skyrocketed. In 1984, Wilson Goode became Philadelphia's first African American mayor. Throughout the decade, development continued in some areas of the city, including Old City, South Street, and Center City, which saw several massive skyscrapers built. But due to a combination of massively reduced federal spending on cities, a shrinking tax base, and generous labor contracts, among other things, the city finances worsened throughout the 1970s and 1980s. When Goode left office at the end of the 1980s, the city was nearly bankrupt.

The very least shining moment of the entire Goode administration had to be the highly publicized MOVE incident. The police had several prior run-ins with the radical group MOVE, and a major clash in 1978 resulted in the tragic death of a police officer and nine MOVE members going to prison. The second major incident occurred in 1985 during a stand-off at the group's headquarters in Southwest Philadelphia. The police had no idea how to handle the situation, and eventually dropped a satchel bomb from a helicopter onto the house, setting off a fire that killed 11

MOVE members, including five children, and destroyed 62 neighboring houses. The handling of this unbelievable event was a shameful disgrace to the police, the administration, and the entire city.

A CITY REBORN

When Ed Rendell, now governor of Pennsylvania, was elected mayor in 1992, he had a hard road ahead to fix the financial and social mess the city was in at the time. The vast problems included numerous unpaid bills, the lowest bond rating of the top 50 largest U.S. cities, and a budget deficit of $250 million. With charm and determination, Rendell somehow attracted investment in the city, stabilized finances, and even produced small budget surpluses.

Revitalization took place in many parts of the city through the 1990s, and in 1993, the new convention center was built. Seventeen new hotels opened between 1998 and 2000 as a result. The city began to work harder to promote its historic sites, festivals, and entertainment, and it worked. Increasing numbers of visitors came to the city and local pride was revitalized in some respects.

Former city council president John F. Street was elected mayor in 1999 and many aspects of the city's revitalization have continued into the 21st century, although some locals don't give Street much credit for the momentum created by the Rendell administration. There were accusations of typical Philadelphia-style of scandals in Street's administration, including awards, insider deals, and poor money management. There has also once again been a rise of violent crime after a decline for a short time in the 1990s. It should be noted, however, that both the decline and increase have matched changes in cities throughout the country.

Many neighborhoods continued to revitalize during Street's two terms in office and the city saw considerable progress in many areas, while it suffered in other areas. The population of Center City grew from 78,000 to 88,000 during the years 2000–2005, partly due to a condominium boom created by tax breaks. The number of households grew by 24 percent and the overall population decline of the city, while not stopping, is finally slowing, with under a 5 percent drop so far this decade.

PHILADELPHIA TODAY

To look around Center City Philadelphia today is to have no doubt that the city is growing and improving in many ways. The revitalization that began during the Rendell era continues today. The skyline continues to expand, with the brand new Comcast Center now the tallest building between Chicago and New York. The city has seen a rebirth in arts and culture, with brand-new additions to the Avenue of the Arts including the modern Kimmel Center and the Suzanne Roberts Theatre. As a result of the updating, expanding, and marketing of many attractions, tourism has become a major industry and Philadelphia has garnered much national attention in the past decade. It was the only U.S. city chosen to host the multinational rock concert Live 8 in 2005, and MTV's *The Real World* finally came in 2004. Perhaps we were their 15th choice of location and yes, we almost lost the deal due to MTV's challenges in working with local labor unions, and it was the worst cast in the show's history, but regardless, the attention from media and young people was a positive for the city.

Construction projects are taking place around the city, and the slowing of the population decline is evidence that fewer people are leaving the city, while new people, many of them young, are moving in. Many neighborhoods, including Fairmount, University City, Northern Liberties, Graduate Hospital, Manayunk, and Fishtown continue to experience a rebirth, while empty lots have been transformed into homes and condominiums, and new businesses have come to economically underdeveloped areas. As is typical with gentrification, there is concern over long-term residents being priced out of their homes, and a multitude of other concerns that fall in line with the division of the city along class lines. Yet most Philadelphians have felt a change was long overdue and there is generally great enthusiasm around the development.

The vast majority of residents are enthusiastic about the current mayor, Michael Nutter, whose term began in 2008. Endorsed by the local media and elected in a landslide, the West Philadelphia native has positioned himself as a true reformer. As a city councilman, Nutter was a key leader in instituting the smoking ban and fighting proposed cuts to hours of city libraries and other important community resources, in the face of much opposition. Only time will tell, but the general consensus is that Nutter is prepared to address the needs of the entire city—not just Center City or the outlying neighborhoods, and not just of the rich or poor—as some of his predecessors have been accused. He is taking a stronger, and long overdue, stance on vital city issues, including crime—which is probably the city's largest challenge. If what Nutter says is true, and many, including myself, have great optimism that it is, he has the ability and determination to begin to address many of the city's major problems, and to see Philadelphia continue to reach towards its full potential.

Recent estimates predict that the city's population will stop shrinking and begin to grow again in a few years. The reasons some cite include: an increase in new transplants from foreign destinations and from pricier nearby Northeast cities, the 10-year tax abatement on some types of new housing, a historically undervalued housing market, improvements to the waterfront, and continuing redevelopment throughout the city. Here's hoping that the predictions are right, and the momentum and growth of the past two decades continues.

Government and Economy

GOVERNMENT

Philadelphia is by far the most Democratic county in Pennsylvania. In May of 2007, there were 993,334 registered voters. Democrats made up about 76 percent, and Republicans just 15 percent. In 2004, John Kerry received 80 percent of the local votes to George W. Bush's 19 percent. Since 1932, Philadelphia has voted Democrat in every presidential election, and it has often been the only county in the entire state to do so. Philadelphia's own resident Arlen Specter received less than one-third of the Philadelphia vote in the 2004 race for State Senate, which he won easily on the state level.

From the Civil War until 1951, Philadelphia was staunchly Republican. For many years, Philadelphia was dominated by a corrupt political machine. The Republican Party rode the successes of Lincoln and the Civil War to hold onto the mayor's office through the 1950s despite wave after wave of reform movements by city activists. The machine controlled the city through voter fraud and intimidation, and through extensive patronage. Reform efforts slowly changed city government, with the most significant change in 1950 when a new city charter strengthened the position of mayor and weakened the Philadelphia City Council. Other northern industrial cities elected Democratic mayors in the 1930s and 1940s, but Philadelphia didn't join the trend until 1951. While the city switched allegiances to the Democratic Party in the 1950s, the reputation of Philadelphia as a city that is "corrupt but contented" survives to this day in the minds of many.

Philadelphia once had six congressional districts, but as a result of the city's declining population it now has only four—all of which are Democratic. A Republican has not represented a significant portion of Philadelphia in any office since 1983.

ECONOMY

Philadelphia was a leading agricultural center early in its history, surrounded by rich Pennsylvania farmlands. Due to its location at the meeting of the Delaware and Schuylkill Rivers, shipyards were very successful. Farm goods were traded for sugar and rum in the West Indies, and these products were in turn exchanged for goods from England and elsewhere. Abundant natural resources, including coal and iron, helped Philadelphia become an early industrial leader, and by the 1770s Philadelphia was one of the most important business centers in the British Empire, with printing, publishing, papermaking, and textiles leading the way. Despite the government leaving Philadelphia in 1800, the city remained the cultural and financial center of the country for some time. It also became one of the first and strongest industrial powerhouses.

The face of industry has changed drastically since its early days, in Philadelphia and in other parts of the world. From 1990 to 2006, the average annual growth rate in employment was 0.8 percent. But the private services-providing sectors, which are now the leading industries (including trade, transportation & utilities, information, financial activities, professional and business services, education, health, leisure, and hospitality), grew by 1.4 percent, while the goods-producing sectors (including natural resources and mining, construction, and manufacturing) fell by 1.8 percent. This shows a move away from the traditional manufacturing economy. Today, Philadelphia has some of the very best education and health systems in the world, with a wealth of top-rated schools and hospitals. The tourism industry continues to grow, and new businesses form each year to meet the needs of the increasing numbers of visitors.

People and Culture

DEMOGRAPHICS

Philadelphia is the sixth-largest city in the country, with approximately 1.45 million people as of the 2006 census estimate. It was recently demoted from its long-standing position as fifth-largest when Phoenix surpassed it in population. Center City has the third-largest downtown residential population in the entire country. The Greater Philadelphia region is also the fourth-largest metropolitan region in the United States, following New York, Los Angeles, and Chicago. The region was home to 6.1 million as of 2005, and there are a total of 45.7 million people living within just 200 miles of Philadelphia—second only to New York City's total of 48.8 million within 200 miles. Approximately one-fourth of the total U.S. population lives within a six-hour drive of Philadelphia.

As of the latest census estimate, the population is 47.4 percent white, 45.4 percent African American, 10.2 percent Hispanic and Latino, and 5.2 percent Asian. It is interesting to note that while Philadelphia has almost equal numbers of whites and African Americans, the statistic is drastically different for the state of Pennsylvania, where African Americans represent only 10.6 percent and whites 86 percent.

It is also worth noting that two of the most subjugated ethnic groups in the city during the mid-19th century, African Americans and Irish Americans, today make up the largest groups in the city. While Philadelphia has long been considered a largely "black and white" city compared with other major cities, the number of Hispanics and Asian Americans has increased over the past two decades. Philadelphia also has the second-largest Irish, Italian, and Jamaican populations in the entire United States.

The number of foreign-born residents increased by 34,000 between 1990 and 2000. Puerto Ricans constitute over 76 percent of the Latino population, although the Mexican population is growing. Asian communities have been long-established in Chinatown; parts of Northeast Philadelphia have large Korean American communities and Vietnamese Americans have a strong presence in South Philadelphia, especially near the Italian Market

PHILLY-SPEAK

Philly-speak is one of a kind. You'll surely notice the unique accent and terminology – unless, of course, you were born here. Many locals aren't aware that we say things differently from the rest of the country until we leave town and someone tells us. There are plenty of additional variations between different neighborhoods, classes, and ethnic groups, with the most typical Philly expressions prevalent in the longest-established blue-collar communities. However, many of the terms cut across boundaries and are just distinctively Philly. Here are some of the most common:

- **The Blue Route:** I-476, the highway that cuts through Philadelphia's suburbs, including Delaware and Montgomery Counties

- **down the shore:** New Jersey beach towns, including Ocean City and Wildwood, where Philadelphians go in the summer. Usage: "I'm going down the shore this weekend," not to be confused with going "up the Poconos," where Philadelphians vacation in winter.

- **The Drive:** Kelly Drive or East River Drive

- **The Expressway:** the Schuylkill Expressway (pronounced "skookil"), the section of I-76 that runs through Philadelphia

- **hoagie:** a sandwich (or samwich in Philly) on a long roll filled with meat, cheese, and top-pings, referred to as a "sub" in many other parts of the country

- **Iggles:** Philadelphia Eagles professional football team

- **jawn:** any person, place, or thing. Usage: "Pass me that jawn" (anything from a beer to the remote control); "You goin' to that jawn?" (often a party or club, but works for any event); or "That jawn is fly" (the jawn being an attractive person).

- **jimmies:** small chocolate or rainbow-colored candy that you sprinkle onto ice cream, known in most places as sprinkles

- **lager:** Yuengling lager; when you order a "lager" in Philly, it implies the locally brewed Yuengling brand.

- **wit/witout:** When ordering a cheesesteak, "wit" (with) means with onions and "witout" (without) means no onions, so "Whiz wit" is a cheesesteak with Cheese Whiz and onions.

- **wooder:** local pronunciation of water, as in "I'll have a cherry wooder ice," when ordering the sweet, flavored, slushy ice treat popular in Philly

- **youse** or **yiz:** plural for you, when addressing more than one person, as in "What're youse/yiz doin' tonight?"

and Washington Avenue. Countless highly concentrated immigrant enclaves can be found throughout the city, including many Africans and West Indians in Cedar Park in West Philly, Poles in Port Richmond, and many Russians, Greeks, and Ukrainians in the Near Northeast and parts of Fairmount. Nine percent of the city's population is foreign born.

The median household income in the city is just under $31,000, with males at a median income of around $34,000 versus $28,500 for females. Of all housing units, 590,071 (89.1 percent) were occupied and 71,887 (10.9 percent) were vacant. Out of occupied housing units, 349,633 (59.3 percent) are owned and 240,438 (40.7 percent) are rented.

RELIGION

Since its founding, the only colony that practiced religious tolerance has attracted a wide diversity of religious sects. Founder William Penn was a Quaker and many other Quakers followed him to the new city to escape English persecution. Their influence can be seen in the many Quaker Friends' schools and meeting houses that still exist.

PHILLY 'TUDE

A nasty rumor has somehow spread that Philadelphians are unfriendly, boorish, and sometimes even downright mean. Well, I'd like to set the record straight. Many locals are a little rough around the edges, but that is part of the local charm; this is a traditional blue-collar town after all. But unless you insult our sports teams, loudly root for another team in front of us, or play for one of our sports teams and blow the season, you shouldn't be the target of any more rude behavior than you would in any other East Coast city. (Hmmm, perhaps that isn't saying too much?)

Granted, we can be loud at times, and maybe a little impatient – especially if you're holding up traffic while staring at a map – but beneath the tough exterior, Philadelphians are, by and large, warm, helpful, and down-to-earth people. We like to think we're just more honest here than others. We don't bother much with fake pleasantries, so you'll always know where you stand. If people are being nice to you, they probably really like you, and if not, they're just not in the mood to bother with you, so move on to ask someone else for directions.

And just to be safe, anything negative you have to say about Philly should be said in private. While locals insult the city (and the sports teams) quite freely, visitors rarely earn the right. Oh, and one last thing – you might want to learn how to order a cheesesteak at the fast-lane cheesesteak joints so you don't hold up the line. (See *Cheesesteaks 101* in the the *Restaurants* chapter for help.)

Today, Christianity is the dominant religion in the city, with Protestants and Roman Catholics making up the two largest sects in similar numbers. There is a significant Eastern Orthodox population, and since the early 1800s, there has been a large Jewish population that has continued to grow as Eastern European Jews have immigrated to Philadelphia. Many of the Jewish communities left the city for the suburbs during the period 1950–2000, and some synagogues were converted to mosques and Baptist churches.

Smaller religious groups include Islam and Hinduism, with an increase in immigration from the Middle East, Pakistan, Bangladesh, and India. There is also a small Muslim community, about 85 percent of which is African American.

The Arts

Philadelphia is one of the artistic and cultural capitals of the country, and has been since its earliest days. In the 19th century, while New Yorkers flocked to dime museums and tawdry circus acts, Philadelphians attended art galleries and public libraries. Once referred to as "The Athens of America," Philly was North America's first nexus of culture. The bustling cosmopolitan center in a rapidly growing young country was home to dozens of cultural innovations including America's first library, art school, museum, university, hospital, and much more. The evolving artistic and cultural scene continues to thrive in the 21st century, with the sparkling Avenue of the Arts and a vibrant independent arts scene.

ARCHITECTURE

Philadelphia is a living gallery for more than 300 years of architectural history—and not all of it is made from the ubiquitous red brick. More than 100 buildings are designated National Historic Landmarks, with outstanding examples of practically every notable style represented. Renowned architects who have left their marks on the city include William Strickland, Frank Furness, Daniel Burnham, George Howe, Louis I. Kahn, Robert Venturi, I. M. Pei, Frank Lloyd Wright, and Cesar Pelli.

Those who are interested in learning more about the city's architecture should take one of the Open House tours offered by the Friends of Independence or the Architectural Landmarks tours offered by the Philadelphia Society for the Preservation of Landmarks. And anyone who appreciates architecture should visit the Athenaeum, the world's premier landmark devoted to American architecture 1800–1945. For still more information and background, Philadelphia Architects and Buildings maintains an excellent online database (www.philadelphiabuildings.org/pab/) with a wealth of information about the city's architectural gems and the innovative architects who were responsible for them.

17th Century

Many of the city's very first settlers lived in caves built into the riverbanks, followed by log cabins, which were introduced by early Swedes. People soon began building with wood and brick, with the first brick house completed in 1684. Old Swedes' (Gloria Dei) Church, completed in 1700, is the oldest surviving building in Philadelphia today. The church reflects the Quaker aesthetic for simplicity and symmetry, as do many of the city's first buildings that still survive. The largest of the Quaker-style buildings is the Arch Street Friends Meeting House in Old City.

18th Century

The 18th century brought an array of new, more elaborate styles in architecture, including Georgian and federal. Many of the structures in Old City and Society Hill today represent some variation of these styles. Named after several generations of kings of England named George, the Georgian style was characterized by proportion and balance. Classic examples are made of red brick with white trim, including Independence Hall and Christ Church.

The Carpenters Company was formed in 1724 to instruct builders on these new styles of architecture.

After the Revolution, there was a deliberate move away from English style in many regards, including architecture. An influx of new styles came to Philadelphia, including Classical revival, seen in the First Bank of the United States, and Romanesque revival, as can be seen in Mother Bethel A.M.E. Church.

The federal style was named for the federal period in American history, when it gained popularity. During the late 18th century, the founders of the United States, after rejecting the authority of the English crown, were inspired by the ancient democracies of Greece and Rome. Marked by an intricate interior and a simple, conservative exterior, one of the city's best examples of federal architecture is the Central Pavilion of Pennsylvania Hospital, completed in 1805. The American eagle was a popular emblem, and many buildings you'll see with this mark were built during this period. The style became a symbol of the nation's wealthy and elite.

19th Century

The beginning of the 19th century brought the Greek revival style to Philadelphia, along with leading architects William Strickland and Robert Mills. Strickland was responsible for the Second Bank of the Unites States, modeled on the Parthenon, and the impressive Merchant's Exchange, which offered a modern twist on classic Greek styles.

The early 1800s also saw the start of a new housing innovation: the inexpensive and efficient row house. The first row houses in the United States were part of Carstairs Row (now Jewelers' Row), named for builder and architect Thomas Carstairs. They provided quality housing not yet available in cities like New York and Boston. The style became known as "Philadelphia rows." As the city industrialized in the 1830s and 1840s, the Delaware riverfront was lined with tenements, warehouses, and factories, some of which survive today as converted "luxury lofts."

John Haviland also worked during this period; his 1829 Eastern State Penitentiary was the first structure that so deliberately melded structure and function, and he also designed the Atwater Kent Museum, Walnut Street Theatre, St. George's Episcopal Church, and the University of the Art's Hamilton Hall.

As the 19th century progressed, commercial buildings increased in size and splendor, and architects like William L. Johnson and G. P. Cummings made their marks. Heavily ornamented Victorian and Gothic revival architecture came into vogue, bringing ornate homes, especially to West Philadelphia and Center City. Two large-scale examples include the Pennsylvania Railroad's Broad Street Station and the Pennsylvania Academy of the Fine Arts' main building, both designed by architect Frank Furness.

City Hall deserves a paragraph of its own in Philadelphia's—and the world's—architectural history. Designed by John MacArthur Jr., the mammoth structure is one of the finest examples of French Second Empire architecture in the world. It is the country's largest governmental building and the world's tallest masonry building. Sculptor Alexander Milne Calder created more than 250 statues to adorn the edifice, including the 37-foot-tall statue of William Penn. Construction of City Hall took 30 years (1871–1901), due in part to municipal corruption and cost overruns. Originally intended to be the world's tallest building at 548 feet, it had already been superseded by the Eiffel Tower and Washington Monument by the time it was completed. Just north of it stands the Norman-Romanesque-style Masonic Temple and the Gothic revival-style Arch Street United Methodist Church, also built during this period.

20th Century

The largest suspension bridge in the world at the time, the Benjamin Franklin Bridge was built in Philadelphia in 1926. A few years later, the building that now houses the Philadelphia Museum of Art was built by Julian Abele, who drew inspiration for the design while traveling in Greece. The Beaux Arts–style Free Library of Philadelphia was constructed on the Parkway in 1927, followed by 30th Street Station and the Franklin Institute in the 1930s.

A notable Philadelphia skyscraper is the PSFS Building. Built in 1932 by William Lescaze and his partner George Howe, it is considered America's first International-style skyscraper. West of City Hall, the office megacomplex Penn Center rises on the site of former train tracks (and Furness's Broad Street Station) while I. M. Pei's 1963 Society Hill Towers stand as modernist beacons in colonial Society Hill. Liberty Place was the first skyscraper built taller than City Hall, in the late 1980s.

21st Century

Philadelphia remains at the cutting-edge of architecture. The magnificent, modern Kimmel Center on the Avenue of the Arts opened in 2001, and west of the Schuylkill, the 28-story glass Cira Center by Cesar Pelli was completed in 2005. The Comcast Center is the tallest building between New York and Chicago at 975 feet. As of its 2008 completion, it is also the tallest LEED platinum-certified building in the United States, in keeping with the trend towards more environmentally friendly building practices.

FINE ARTS

Philadelphia's fine arts tradition can be traced back to its earliest days. Before the American Revolution, the wealthy merchant class began to patronize the arts, especially the portrait painters. No proper high-society home was complete without a portrait of its owners hanging on the walls. Due to high demand, fine artists gravitated to the burgeoning city, including William Williams, his son William Joseph Williams, Benjamin West, Gilbert Stuart, and Charles Wilson Peale. Peale painted portraits of many notable historic figures including George Washington, John Hancock, Thomas Jefferson, and Alexander Hamilton; many are on display today in a gallery housed in the Second Bank of the Unites States.

In 1805, the Pennsylvania Academy of the Fine Arts was founded by Charles Wilson Peale, sculptor William Rush, and others in the city's arts and business communities. One of the nation's leading art schools, it is known for its vast holdings of 19th- and 20th-century paintings and for playing a central role in the education of generations of American artists.

The Philadelphia Museum of Art, one of the world's greatest art museums, was founded as the "Pennsylvania Museum and School of Industrial Art" as part of the 1876 Centennial Exposition. The landmark building dates from 1919, and its collection now includes almost a quarter of a million pieces. The Art Museum (as it's locally known) is also the starting point for two local institutions of higher education. Philadelphia University, formerly the Philadelphia Textile School, started by offering textile manufacturers a polished education, while the University of the Arts traces the origins of its fine arts program to the Art Museum's original school.

Public art is a major part of the Philadelphia landscape. The Fairmount Park Art Association ensures that the main municipal park is a showcase for sculpture and architecture, and the much-copied One Percent for Art program requires any construction project with city funding to include public art. Meanwhile, the Mural Arts Program has created nearly 2,800 murals across the city—more than in any other city in the world.

LITERATURE

Philadelphia has had an important presence in the literary world dating all the way back to Benjamin Franklin. The statesman, printer, inventor, scientist, political theorist, and author published his *Poor Richard's Almanack* annually 1732–1758. It contained the standard information normally found in an almanac, as well as Franklin's own doses of wit and wisdom, much of which has resulted in sayings that still exist in American vernacular.

The 19th century transformed Philadelphia into a center of publishing, with major publishers like J. B. Lippincott playing a major role in

local industry for decades. Philadelphia writers at the time included Charles Brockden Brown, a pioneer in the development of the American novel. Meanwhile, interlopers such as Edgar Allan Poe and Louisa May Alcott made the city a brief stop during their illustrious careers. Noted African American scholar, activist, and historian W. E. B. Du Bois wrote his social history *The Philadelphia Negro* in 1899, and Walt Whitman, the father of American poetry, spent much time in the city, just a quick trip from his native Camden, New Jersey, across the Delaware River.

The Curtis Publishing Company was one of the largest publishers in the country during the early 20th century. It ran its magazine empire from its historic Curtis Center building in Society Hill, publishing the *Ladies' Home Journal* and *The Saturday Evening Post,* the country's oldest magazine. Though the major publishing houses today are largely centered in nearby New York City, some domestic and international publishers still have outposts in Philly.

PERFORMING ARTS

Philadelphia's most famous performing arts space is undoubtedly the Walnut Street Theatre, America's oldest surviving and the world's most-subscribed-to theater. The building, at the corner of 9th and Walnut Streets, opened as a circus in 1809 and went through several incarnations before becoming the nonprofit regional theater it is today. Though few theaters from the 19th century remain today, the Forrest, Plays & Players, and Merriam theaters date from the beginning of the 20th century, when powerful national theater syndicates like the Shubert controlled the country's live entertainment.

In the music world, the Philadelphia Orchestra, founded in 1900, has established its reputation as one of the United States' "Big Five" orchestras. Several opera companies competed for attention, and in 1975, the last two merged into the current Opera Company of Philadelphia.

After Broadway tryouts left Philadelphia

in the 1960s, innovative young theater companies, including the Wilma Theater and the Philadelphia Theatre Company, began filling in the gaps. In the 1990s, Mayor Ed Rendell spearheaded the Avenue of the Arts initiative, which focused on turning the stretch of Broad Street spanning out from City Hall into a true center for performing arts. At the time, the Academy of Music was essentially a loner, but since then theater groups have flocked to the new and renovated theater spaces, including the Arts Bank in 1994, Clef Club in 1995, Wilma in 1996, the Prince Music Theater in 1999, and Suzanne Roberts' Philadelphia Theatre Company in 2007. Meanwhile, Freedom Theater improved its space on North Broad. And, of course, the Kimmel Center opened in 2001, giving a grand home to the Philadelphia Orchestra and several other resident companies.

ESSENTIALS

Getting There

BY AIR

The **Philadelphia International Airport** (800/745-4283, www.phl.org) is approximately seven miles from Center City and offers frequent service for more than 25 major airlines and several discount airlines. It is a major hub city for US Airways (www.usairways.com), and discount carrier Southwest Airlines (www.southwest.com) offers daily nonstop flights from Philadelphia to numerous cities including Chicago, Las Vegas, Orlando, Phoenix, Providence, and Tampa. Millions of dollars in renovation projects in the past decade have resulted in a much more pleasant airport experience. The Marketplace now consists of more than 150 national and local shops offering food, beverages, and merchandise, so there is plenty to do while you wait for your flight—which you often will, as delays occur frequently.

Getting to and from the airport on public transportation is easy on SEPTA's R1 regional rail line, which directly links the airport to Center City and 30th Street Station for $7 one way. It runs every 30 minutes daily 5:25 A.M.–11:25 P.M., and connects with other rail lines that can get you practically anywhere within the city and nearby suburbs. Taxis charge a flat rate of $26.25 for travel to and from Center City from the airport

PHOTO BY ANTHONY SINAGOGA FOR PCVB

PHILADELPHIA TO NEW YORK ON THE CHEAP

Many locals and visitors regularly make the trip to our neighboring city, the Big Apple. The most luxurious way to get there in a hurry is to take the Amtrak train, but tickets start at $43 each way, so the only people who regularly use Amtrak are business types and the independently wealthy. The good news is, your options are varied and you can get to New York for as little as $20 round-trip.

The cheapest way to New York, and hence the method preferred by many locals, is to take what is known as **"the Chinatown bus"** for $12 one-way and $20 round-trip. Originally used primarily by Chinese food purveyors buying products in New York to sell in Philly, today it is used by commuters, students, and just about everyone on a budget. It's actually run by a variety of different companies (www.chinatown-bus.org, www.2000coach.com, and www.ivymedia.com are just a few) that offer service from Chinatown in Philly (many buses depart from N. 11th St., between Arch and Race Sts.) to Chinatown in New York. The trip takes 2–2.5 hours depending on traffic, and service to Washington D.C. is also offered ($15 one-way/$28 round-trip).

Depending on where you're traveling from in Philly and where you need to get to in New York, you may find the pick-up and drop-off locations more appealing with the **P2P Circulator** (917/217-8485, www.p2pcirculator.com).

Their buses depart from outside Amtrak's 30th Street Station (30th and Market Sts.) and drop passengers at New York's Penn Station. Not a lot of people know about this yet, so for now, it's less crowded and the buses are generally nicer for a few dollars more ($15 one-way, $25 round-trip). A frequent-commuter discount is available at a great price ($110 for 12 one-way trips).

In an effort to compete, **Greyhound** (10th and Filbert Sts., 215/931-4075 or 800/231-2222, www.greyhound.com) often offers rates on par with these buses, and drops off at Port Authority, so it is worth checking their rates if these departure and arrival locations are preferable.

If you like to travel by rail, but can't afford Amtrak, another option is to take a combination of **SEPTA** and **NJ Transit.** SEPTA's R7 line to Trenton departs from the major downtown stops, including 30th Street, Suburban Station, and Market East. In Trenton, you'll wait about 20 minutes and transfer onto NJ Transit's line to Penn Station in New York, for a total travel time of about 2.5 hours. For travel from 30th Street Station, the trip costs around $20 one-way depending on time of day. It costs a bit more than the bus, but the advantage, aside from being on rails (which means no traffic and no bumps), is more flexibility in departure stations and arriving in Penn Station.

and are waiting just outside the baggage claim area.

Alternative airports include Newark International (Newark, NJ, 85 miles), Baltimore-Washington International (Baltimore, MD, 109 miles), JFK International (Jamaica, NY, 105 miles), and La Guardia (Flushing, NY, 105 miles). You'll often find the best fares directly to Philadelphia, especially once you factor in time and money spent traveling from the other airports, but it is worth investigating airfares from these nearby cities, especially if you're planning a multi-city visit in the area.

BY TRAIN

Since the early days of rail transport in the United States, Philadelphia has been a hub for the Pennsylvania Railroad and the Reading Railroad. Today, Philadelphia is a hub of the semi-nationalized **Amtrak** (30th and Market Sts., 800/872-7245, www.amtrak.com). The station is a primary stop on the Washington–Boston Northeast Corridor route and the Keystone Corridor, which connects to Harrisburg and Pittsburgh. It also offers either direct or connecting service to Atlantic City, Chicago, and many other cities in the United States and Canada. All trains traveling outside the city depart and arrive at Amtrak's 30th Street Station. The train is the most pleasant, but also the most expensive, method of public transportation to nearby cities like New York and D.C., although you can check the website for fare specials, and ask about discounts for seniors or people with disabilities.

The Southeastern Pennsylvania Transportation Authority, or **SEPTA** (215/580-7800, www .septa.org), has regional lines serving the suburbs of Philadelphia. It also connects to New Jersey Transit in Trenton via the R6 line, which continues to Newark, New Jersey, and New York City. Regional Rail also extends south of the city to Wilmington, Delaware.

BY BUS

The **Greyhound Bus Terminal** (10th and Filbert Sts., 215/931-4075 or 800/231-2222, www.greyhound.com) offers direct and connecting service all over the country. **NJ Transit** (800/772-2222, www.njtransit.com) buses travel between Philadelphia and South Jersey, including the Jersey shore as far as Cape May at the southernmost tip. **SEPTA,** in addition to providing extensive local service, also offers service to some parts of southeastern Pennsylvania.

BY CAR

Philadelphia is easily accessible by car, connected to several major highways including the PA Turnpike (I-276), I-76, I-476, I-95,

inside Amtrak's 30th Street Station

PHOTO BY G. WIDMAN FOR GPTMC

U.S. 1, and the New Jersey Turnpike. I-676 is the section of I-76 that runs through Center City and continues across the Ben Franklin Bridge into New Jersey. The Walt Whitman Bridge and the Tacony-Palmyra Bridge also connect Philadelphia to New Jersey. The usual car rental agencies can be found at the airport or in Center City, including Avis, Hertz, and Enterprise.

Getting Around

You have plenty of options for getting around in Philadelphia, between public transportation, taxis, and the easy-to-navigate, grid-like streets that are great for walking and biking. There is rarely a reason to drive your car in Center City when you factor in the difficulty of parking in the busiest parts of town. It's usually best to ditch the keys unless you're traveling outside of Center City, where limited public transit and ample parking make driving convenient.

PUBLIC TRANSPORTATION

The extensive public transportation network includes buses, subways, trolleys, and regional rail lines, all operated by SEPTA. While locals are quick to complain about increasing fares and delays, and the public transit system certainly has its flaws compared with other major cities, it will generally get you to most places you need to go in the city without any major trauma. However, it can

RIDE THE 23 BUS

Not a tour bus by any stretch of the imagination, this is an outing for someone who really wants to see a glimpse of an interesting cross-section of the city, not just the tourist spots. This former trolley route is SEPTA's most traveled surface route, averaging more than 20,000 riders daily in 2006. It runs all the way from the sprawling, upscale suburb-like enclave of Chestnut Hill in the far northwest section of the city into the far reaches of South Philadelphia – the historically Italian, working-class part of town. Along the way, it passes through many other diverse parts of the city including Germantown and Mt. Airy, filled with historic homes and some of the most racially diverse neighborhoods in the country; and North Philadelphia, which has some of the city's most impoverished pockets. It cuts through Center City East and past the Reading Terminal Market before continuing into deep South Philly. As you move through the different areas, you'll notice the make-up of the commuters changing along with the landscape. A straight-through ride of the entire route takes about an hour, and is a good way for newcomers to get a quick intro to much of the city. If you have a day to play, hop on and off and explore whenever you see something interesting. Keep in mind, however, this a regular commuter line, so if

© DAMIAN KOHUT

you want to snag a seat and avoid crowds, you should avoid traveling during the morning or evening rush hours. And since the bus is not intended for hopping on and off, you'll have to pay the fare each time, or purchase a One-Day Convenience Pass, which will get you eight trips in one day for $6.

be confusing, as some trips in Philly may require a combination of bus, subway, and/or regional rail lines. The farther away from Center City you travel, the fewer direct routes you'll find, but within the central areas it is generally quick and easy to get around. In general, all you need is a little patience and willingness to figure out the system, or ask someone for help. The SEPTA website lets you enter departure and arrival information with the "Plan My Trip" feature and will give you the best way to get from A to B—a good idea if you have Internet access and time to plan. Some SEPTA "Night Owl" routes run

all night, but with a limited schedule after 8 P.M. Many lines, including the regional rail, stop running at midnight.

Buses, trolleys, subways, and subway surface cars cover the city, especially in Center City. Regional rail lines run within the city to the far northeast and northwest sections including Germantown, Manayunk, and Chestnut Hill, and to many suburbs. The eight rail lines (R1-Airport through R8-Chestnut Hill West/Fox Chase) can all be accessed through Center City stations at Market East, Suburban, and 30th Street Stations. These routes connect with many of the subway and bus lines, but fares must be paid separately and cost is dependent on distance or number of "zones" traveled. Fares increase during peak hours, weekdays 6–9:30 A.M. on trains heading towards Center City and 4–6:30 P.M. on all trains leaving from Center City.

Fares

Buses, trolleys, and subways cost $2 per ride and an additional $0.75 for a transfer, which is good for an additional ride on a different line continuing in the same direction. Up to two transfers can be purchased for any one trip, and are not required when transferring from one subway line to another, but are required between buses or when switching between modes of transport (like from bus to subway). If you'll be using a lot of public transportation, consider the One Day Convenience Pass, which will get you eight trips on any buses or subways in one day for $6. Buying tokens also saves money ($1.45 each, 2 for $2.90, 5 for $7, and 10 for $14.50). They can be purchased in any major subway station, including Suburban, 30th Street, and Market East, and at over 400 retail locations in the city, including some newspaper stands. A weekly TransPass gets you unlimited rides on all modes of public transit in a calendar week for $20.75; a pass for unlimited rides in a calendar month is $78. Trips on some regional rail lines require a surcharge if used with a pass. Discounts are available for seniors, riders with disabilities, children, K–12 students, some college students, families, and groups.

Disabled Access

Every SEPTA bus line is equipped with some vehicles with a wheelchair lift or ramp that can be lowered by the driver. The majority of vehicles include automated route and stop announcements that can be heard inside and outside of the bus. Route information is also displayed electronically on the front and side of buses.

Regional rail cars are accessible to those with mobility devices and many stations are ADA accessible, with additional facilities currently under construction to become accessible. Many of the major regional rail stations, including Temple University, Market East, Suburban, 30th Street, and University City, are ADA accessible. Primary subway and trolley stations including Frankford Transportation Center, 69th Street Station, Fern Rock, and Olney are accessible and provide easy connections to many bus routes. A toll-free 24-hour elevator-status number (877/737-8248) is updated when changes in elevator service occur and an Alternate Accessible Service list on the SEPTA website provides alternative options.

Customized Community Transportation (CCT Connect) provides ADA paratransit services to individuals with disabilities who are unable to use regular services, along with a Shared-Ride paratransit program for senior citizens (215/580-7145).

IMPORTANT NUMBERS

- **Philadelphia Airport:** 800/745-4283, www.phl.org

- **Amtrak** (train): 30th and Market Sts., 800/872-7245, www.amtrak.com

- **SEPTA** (bus, subway, and regional rail): 215/580-7800, www.septa.org; disabled access: 877/737-8248 (elevator status in stations), 215/580-7145 (paratransit service).

- **Greyhound** (bus): 10th and Filbert Sts., 215/931-4075 or 800/231-2222, www.greyhound.com

- **Taxis:** Olde City Taxi: 215/708-8888; Philadelphia Airport Shuttle: 215/969-1818; Quaker City Cab: 215/728-8000; United Cab Association: 215/238 9500; Yellow Cab Co.: 215/922-8400; Philadelphia Taxi Co.: 215/232-2000

CAR SHARE

If you're relocating to the area and you don't own a car, never fear; Philadelphia has another option. Since most city-dwellers only drive occasionally – to get to the supermarket, suburban malls, or for day and weekend trips – there is no need for many to own a car. There's a way to save tons of money on insurance and maintenance, and still have a car at your fingertips whenever you need one. **Philly Car Share** (215/730-0988, www.phillycarshare .org) is recognized as one of the best car-share programs in the world for its ease, affordability, and low rates.

Environmentally friendly, car-sharing programs are sweeping the world, and Philly's program is at the forefront. Rates start at just $2.90/hour or $29/day, including insurance, maintenance, parking, and gas. To be eligible, you must be at least 21, have had a valid driving license for at least two years, maintain a clean driving record, and if you don't have a PA license, you must get one within 60 days of joining. Once you have an account, you can call or go online to find out where the nearest available vehicle is parked. Then, with advanced technology, a device inside the car is synched with your key card, so you can get in without having to go pick up a key anywhere. The number of users, vehicles, and designated Car Share parking spaces is constantly increasing, so no matter where you live, you're never far from a car or parking spot.

A similar service is offered by **Flexcar/Zipcar** (www.flexcar.com), two major car-sharing companies that merged in late 2007.

GETTING TO NEARBY NEW JERSEY

For travel to nearby New Jersey, including Collingswood and Haddonfield, **PATCO** (856/772-6900, www.ridepatco.org) offers a regular service from several Center City stations. **Camden Riverlink** (215/925-5465, www.riverlinkferry.org) offers a scenic option for getting across the river to Camden. It departs every hour on the hour from Philadelphia and on the half hour from Camden, with plenty of additional departures during events at the Susquehana Bank Center. It runs May–September and costs $6 for adults and $5 for children and seniors.

BICYCLING AND WALKING

Bicycling magazine rated Philadelphia as one of the best large cycling cities (population more than one million) in the country and *About Inc.* rated it as one of the top walking cities in the country. Center City is compact and the grid-like streets are easy to navigate. Active types will enjoy spending the day walking or biking around the city, especially when the weather is mild. In addition to allowing you to enjoy the scenic trails in Fairmount Park, bicycling is a quick way to get around without having to worrying about parking or traffic. As in any major city with car traffic, bicyclists should exercise caution when riding on busy city streets and a helmet should always be worn. While somewhat limited, there is an increasing network of wide bike-friendly streets with designated bike lanes. A map of routes can be found at the visitors center or online at the Streets Department website (www.phila.gov/streets/), and these routes should be used whenever possible.

The **Bicycle Club of Philadelphia** (www .phillybikeclub.org) is a great resource for bike enthusiasts. The club sponsors recreational cycling activities open to everyone for a small fee. It also promotes bicyclists' rights and safe biking practices. See the *Arts and Leisure* chapter for specific trails and repair and rental locations.

DRIVING AND PARKING

While driving and parking in Center City can be somewhat difficult, you'll usually find a parking meter even in the busiest parts of town if you're willing to search for up to 20 minutes and walk a few blocks. The Philadelphia

Parking Authority's website (www.philapark .org) provides a directory of parking lots and garages. There are garages all over Center City, especially near the convention center and Avenue of the Arts, but they can be expensive.

Most central areas have metered street parking. The time limit varies depending on the area but is usually only good for 1– 4 hours. Meters accept Smart Cards and coins. The size of a credit card, Smart Cards fit in your wallet so you don't have to carry change. Once you insert the card into the meter, it deducts $0.25 increments until you remove it or the maximum time limit is reached. They are available in $20 and $50 denominations, and can be purchased at any Shop Rite and 7-Eleven, or online from the Parking Authority (www.philapark.org). Be aware that some areas that have no meters still have time limits. Pay close attention to signs, especially in Center City, or you may get a ticket.

TAXIS

It's usually easy to hail a taxi anywhere in Center City, but the best places to find one is in front of a hotel or on any busy corner. Rides are metered, with the exception of the flat fee of $26.25 for trips between Center City and the airport. If you're in an area without a lot of activity, it's best to call a cab and go outside when it arrives. It generally shouldn't take more than 15 minutes, except during rain showers or at 2 A.M. when the bars close and everyone is clamoring for one. Fares are regulated, and taxis should always have a meter running so you can see how much you're paying. Fares are based on distance traveled with small increases for wait time during traffic. Your driver should be able to give you an estimate of how much it will cost to get to a specific destination. See the *Important Numbers* sidebar for taxi company numbers.

Conduct and Customs

ALCOHOL

The drinking age is 21 in Pennsylvania, and is strictly enforced in most bars in the city. If you look young, you will get carded everywhere, with the exception of a few complete dives (which will remain unnamed for their sake). Purchasing alcohol in Pennsylvania is not always simple. Beer distributors and state-run Wine & Spirits shops are located throughout the city and keep limited hours. See the sidebar *Bring Your Own Bottle* in the *Restaurants* chapter for more information.

SMOKING

Non-smokers no longer have to leave the bar reeking of smoke. In 2007, a smoking ban went into effect in all restaurants and bars in Philadelphia. There is the occasional dive bar, remote neighborhood bar, or private club where smoking is still allowed, but they are the exception. It is still acceptable for smokers to light up at most al fresco bars, restaurants, and coffee shops, as well as in subway stations

and in parks. Smoking is not as taboo here as in many West Coast cities, but the recent ban has certainly changed the bar culture—for the better, according to most.

BUSINESS HOURS

Most offices, including banks, are open 9 A.M.–5 or 5:30 P.M. on weekdays. Shop hours vary greatly, but with the exception of smaller boutiques or antiques stores, which often have limited hours, most stores are open at least 10 or 11 A.M.–6 or 7 P.M. Monday–Saturday, and are closed or have very limited hours on Sunday. Many downtown shops stay open as late as 9 P.M. on Wednesday evening to accommodate after-work shoppers. Most restaurants serve food until 9 or 10 P.M. on weeknights and until 10 or 11 P.M. on weekends, with some restaurants in the most active parts of town (like Rittenhouse Square, Old City, South Street, Northern Liberties, and Manayunk) offering late-night menus. Many bars serve food until midnight or 1 A.M. and some Chinatown restaurants stay open until 3 A.M. Other than that, late-night dining is generally limited to diners and cheesesteak and pizza joints—some of which are open 24 hours. With the exception of a few private clubs and after-hours clubs, bars in Philadelphia close at 2 A.M. sharp.

TAXES AND TIPPING

There is a hotel tax of 14 percent, with 6 percent going to state tax and 8 percent to city tax. There is a 7 percent tax on dining out and most general sales and a 10 percent tax on liquor, but there is no tax on items considered essential, including clothing.

Philadelphians were rated the nation's best tippers in the 2007 *Zagat Restaurant Guide*, with restaurant tips averaging 19.4 percent. A 15 percent tip is usually the minimum, even when people are not particularly impressed with service. When all is good, most locals drop 20 percent. The 15–20 percent tipping rule usually applies to taxi cabs, although with more flexibility; a $1–2 tip will cover most rides within the city. For a ride to the airport, especially when luggage handling is involved, the standard is closer to $5. Bell hops and valet parkers generally get $1–2 per bag or per vehicle, and slightly more at the city's ritziest establishments.

Tips for Travelers

BUSINESS TRAVELERS

For the increasing numbers of travelers who come to the city for business—especially since the new convention center was built—most hotels have on-site facilities like fax machines and in-room Internet access. There are various 24-hour **FedEx Kinko's,** including those at 1201 Market Street (215/923-2520) and 2001 Market Street (215/561-5170). For shipping, call the local **UPS service** (215/567-6006, www.ups.com).

INTERNATIONAL TRAVELERS

Philadelphia has become an increasingly popular destination for international travelers. It is in the Eastern time zone, the same as New York and three hours ahead of the West Coast. English is the language spoken and U.S. dollars are the currency. There is an American Express office at 16th Street and John F. Kennedy Boulevard (215/587-2300), where you can cash travelers checks or change money. The **International House** (2701 Chestnut St., 215/287-5125, www.ihouse-philly.org) on the University of Pennsylvania campus also serves as a great resource for international visitors. It offers information, social and cultural programming, language

lessons, and affordable short- and long-term accommodations for students or anyone affiliated with a university.

SENIOR TRAVELERS

Philadelphia is a hospitable destination for older travelers, although some may choose to avoid the hottest summer months and the coldest winter months. Senior citizens with proof of age (65 and older) ride buses and subways for free all the time and regional rail for free during off-peak hours (before 6 A.M., from 9 A.M.–3 P.M., and after 6 P.M.). Discounts are available at many attractions and AARP discounts are available at many hotels. The **Independence Visitor Center** (6th and Market Sts., 215/965-7676, www.independencevisitorcenter.com) offers additional resources and information for seniors.

STUDENTS

The Greater Philadelphia region has the second-largest number of colleges in the nation and the second-largest concentration of college students living on the East Coast. There are around 120,000 students attending college in the city and nearly 300,000 in the entire metropolitan area. Including colleges, universities,

GAY PHILLY

With a vibrant gay community, new gay-owned restaurants opening all the time, and several new bars and clubs set to debut in the next year, Philadelphia presents a wealth of choices. Though not as large or visible as in New York or San Francisco, there has long been a thriving gay community in Philadelphia. As far back as the 1930s and '40s, underground gay house parties and social networks existed not only in Center City but also in West Philadelphia, Germantown, and other areas. There was also a group of mob-owned gay bars centered around 13th and Locust Streets – the area that remains the nexus of gay culture in Philly today. This east-of-Broad, south-of-Market neighborhood, Washington Square West, is commonly called the Gayborhood.

A pivotal change occurred in Philadelphia in 1965 when a group of protesters began an annual July 4th march in front of Independence Hall. Four years before the Stonewall riots in New York ignited the worldwide modern gay rights movement, this period began the era of openness in the city. Gays and lesbians began to come out in increasing numbers and to claim their rightful place in the community.

Today, Philly's gay community is a highly visible and important part of the city, with several dozen clubs, bars, lounges, bookstores, boutiques, restaurants, and shops catering to the community. Local politicians court the LGBT crowd for support and dollars, and the media gives wide coverage to various pride festivals and events, including Equality Forum and Blue Ball in late April and early May, the Pride Parade in June, and OutFest in October.

Outside of Center City, the gay community is a little more circumspect, and unfortunately flashiness and PDA can draw unfriendly attention in some places. Gay travelers to the city would do well to visit the Gay and Lesbian section of the Tourism Board website (www.gophila.com\gay) for information, to book particularly gay-friendly hotel accommodations, or learn about special hotel and event packages. There are several hotels and bed-and-breakfasts in the Gayborhood, with plenty others nearby. The William Way LGBT Community Center (1315 Spruce St., www.waygay.org) is the city's largest gay and lesbian center; or visit www.phillygaycalendar.com for the most comprehensive guide to events, venues, organizations, and clubs. The *Philadelphia Gay News* is a publication that offers a calendar of events and articles and is available in print or online (www.epgn.com).

and trade and specialty schools, there are more than 80 schools in the region. The biggest colleges and universities include: University of Pennsylvania, Temple University, Drexel University, The Art Institute of Philadelphia, Villanova University, Arcadia University, Bryn Mawr College, Haverford College, La Salle University, and St. Joseph's University.

Students should check for student discounts at many sights and movie theaters throughout the city. If you're considering studying in the area, be sure to check out **One Big Campus** (www.onebigcampus.com) for valuable information and resources. **Campus Philly** (www.campusphilly.org) offers a wealth of information and resources to students.

TRAVELERS WITH DISABILITIES

Those using a wheelchair or who have difficulty walking should exercise caution on Philadelphia's sometimes older, cracked, or bumpy sidewalks and walkways. Most of the major streets in Center City have curb cuts and handicapped parking, although parking spaces can be limited near major attractions, so allow extra time to find one. Most attractions, theaters, and all the stadiums and newer, larger hotels in Philadelphia have elevators or ramps, but due to their old age, some of the historic buildings are ill-equipped. When in doubt, call ahead before arriving to be sure a location is accessible.

The **Mayor's Commission on People with Disabilities** (215/686-2798, www.phila.gov/mcpd) offers resources and a wealth of information including help finding accessible parking, ATMs, health centers, and cultural events. **ARTREACH, Inc.** (215/568-2115, www.art-reach.org) connects people with disabilities to services and arts in the area and offers an online and print access guide with information on more than 75 of the region's theaters, performing arts centers, and museums. Listings include wheelchair accessibility of entrances and restrooms, phone numbers, and information on large-print or Braille materials or assistive listening devices. The guide is also available on audiocassette for the blind.

SEPTA provides detailed information on their website (www.septa.org); also see *Disabled Access* in the *Getting Around* section of this chapter. The **Independence Visitor Center** (6th and Market Sts., 215/925-6101, www.independencevisitorcenter.com) is helpful in providing additional information and resources.

TRAVELING WITH CHILDREN

Philadelphia is an extremely popular destination for families with children. The many kid-friendly, interactive attractions make it a favorite for school trips or for parents to teach their kids about history. With the exception of the very high-end restaurants, kids can be found dining out with parents in most of the city's restaurants. When traveling with children in the hot summer months, consider booking a hotel with a pool or take a visit to one of the city's public pools.

TRAVELING WITH PETS

Philadelphia is a pet-friendly town, especially in Center City and in the northwest section of the city. With plenty of green spaces, and several specifically designated dog parks, there are plenty of places to walk your dog. Several hotels also allow pets, but you should always check in advance, as there may be a surcharge or limited rooms available. Most restaurants and bars with outdoor seating allow well-behaved pets to sit with you while you eat and drink. Friendly servers will often offer your dog water. Visit www.dogfriendly.com for listings of dog parks and dog-friendly accommodations and businesses, or check out the *Dog Lover's Companion to Philadelphia*, published by Avalon Travel.

WOMEN TRAVELING ALONE

As with most places, women traveling alone should exercise extra caution, especially at night. Most, but not all, parts of Center City are generally well lit and filled with people except very late at night. When venturing out after dark, it's always best to travel in groups or take a cab. Muggings and purse snatchings do occur, so be alert and hold your purse tightly, or better yet, don't carry one at all at night if you can avoid it. As a general rule, whenever you don't feel safe for any reason, step inside the nearest open business and wait there while you call a cab. See the general safety information for more information.

Health and Safety

HOSPITALS AND PHARMACIES

Philadelphia is home to several of the world's best hospitals and medical research facilities. For medical emergencies or short- or long-term care, you will find as good treatment in Philadelphia as anywhere. There are too many to name them all here, but just a few of the most renowned hospitals include Pennsylvania Hospital, University of Pennsylvania Hospital, Thomas Jefferson University Hospital, Hahnemann University Hospital, Wills Eye Hospital, and Temple University Hospital. Most hospitals are located in Center City and University City. Independent and chain pharmacies can be found everywhere in the city and you're never very far from a Rite Aid, CVS, or Walgreens. Among others, there is a 24-hour **CVS** in Center City West (1826 Chestnut St., 215/972-0909).

CRIME

If there is one statistic that Philadelphia is least proud of and most in need of changing, it is the murder rate—the highest among the nation's 10 largest cities. The murder rate peaked in 1990 at 503, at a rate of 31.5 murders per 100,000 residents. There was an average of about 400 murders a year for most of the 1990s; the number dropped to 288 in 2002, but is on the rise again. Violent and property crime has grown at a rate that exceeds the national average. Criminologists blame the high rate on many social and economic problems including unemployment, gang activity, increased illegal gun trafficking, reductions in youth programs, poverty, and single-parent households. While it is impossible to pinpoint the cause or predict the future, it is a dire situation in some parts of the city, and we can only hope that this trend will change soon. Many residents are hopeful that new stricter policies and crime-fighting tactics planned for the mayoral administration of Michael Nutter will bring positive change.

It would be remiss to say that tourists are completely safe from the violence that plagues some parts of Philadelphia, but it also must be noted that the vast majority of these crimes, especially murders, are taking place in areas most visitors and many locals never visit. While infrequent murders have taken place in practically every area of the city, most are in economically downtrodden pockets of North, Southwest, and West Philadelphia. Many of the crimes involve drugs and many innocent people that live in drug-infested areas have fallen victim.

The most likely crimes that people outside of these areas encounter are muggings, purse snatchings, and car theft, which happen mostly at night in desolate areas. You should always exercise caution and be alert to your surroundings, especially when leaving bars, clubs, and parking garages. When in doubt, always take a cab to your destination. If you don't feel safe, get to a well-lit, populated area or step inside the nearest business and wait for a cab. Trust your instincts and travel in groups whenever possible at night.

Information and Services

COMMUNICATIONS AND MEDIA

Phones

When the number of phone numbers in the city got too large for the 215 area code to accommodate, the 267 area code became a second Philadelphia area code. The number of public pay phones has decreased dramatically as it has in most places with the advent of cell phones. The few that still do exist cost $0.50 for local calls, and most accept coins and calling cards. Dial "1" before calling toll-free numbers (those starting with 800, 888, 877, etc.). Prepaid phone cards are available at many convenience stores and cell phone stores.

Internet Services

Many parts of Philadelphia are now served by **Wireless Philadelphia** (www.wireless-philadelphia.org), a citywide initiative to provide wireless Internet access to everyone. The goal is to make Internet available throughout the entire city, and the coverage area is continually expanding. The program offers free wireless in several hot spots and community centers, and free or low-cost plans for individuals. Free hot spots, some of which are already operational and others in the works, include: Love Park, the Benjamin Franklin Parkway, the "Historic Square Mile," Penn's Landing, Cobbs Creek Environmental Center, Hunting Park, Wissahickon Environmental Center, Pennypack Environmental Center, Bartram's Garden, FDR Park, and Penn Treaty Park. There has been much talk of Philadelphia becoming the first city to have free wireless service everywhere, but as of yet, it hasn't happened. It isn't difficult to find free wireless access at many coffee shops and libraries throughout the city.

If you don't have your own computer, public libraries are a good option for residents, but aren't much help to non-residents since you need a library card to access the system and only residents can obtain one. Many hotels and youth hostels have a computer available for free or cost for short-term use. The **ING Direct Café** (17th and Walnut Sts., 215/731-1410, Mon.–Fri. 7 A.M.–7 P.M., Sat. 10 A.M.–7 P.M., Sun. 10 A.M.–5 P.M.) has computers available for Internet surfing.

Mail Services

Post offices are located all over the city and the main branch (2970 Market St., 215/895-8989) next to 30th Street Station has a limited-service window that stays open nightly until 10 P.M.

Newspapers and Periodicals

Philadelphia has two main daily newspapers, the *Philadelphia Inquirer* (www.philly.com) and the *Daily News* (www.philly.com/dailynews). The *Inquirer* is considered the more serious paper, offering balanced coverage of local, national, and international news. While its popularity and ratings wax and wane, it is often considered in the top tier of daily papers in the country. Check out the Friday "Weekend" supplement for listings of entertainment and events. The *Daily News,* not generally regarded as serious journalism, is concentrated mostly on local news, with extensive sports coverage; some locals are avid fans of the easy, fun read. The *Metro* (www.metro.com), a free daily available at many SEPTA stations, is filled with short snippets of news and entertainment that range from important to entertaining to completely inane.

Many locals, especially the younger set, get their information and news from the free alt weeklies *PW* (www.philadelphiaweekly.com) and City Paper (www.citypaper.net). Most stories are locally based, and both offer good listings of events, concerts, restaurants, bars, and more. You'll find them in newspaper boxes all over Center City. While many locals have their favorite, the verdict isn't out, and both are very popular. *Philadelphia* magazine (www.phillymag.com) is the award-winning monthly lifestyle magazine for the city and suburbs, sold at bookstores and newsstands. It is an entertaining read, offering a mix of interesting features, sensational local-interest stories, and useful service journalism. Many read it for its local style, dining, and arts and entertainment coverage. The *Philadelphia Gay Times* is geared towards issues, news, and events affecting the gay community and the *Philadelphia Tribune* is an African American weekly newspaper, the oldest of its kind in the country.

The *Philadelphia Independent Media Center* (www.phillyimc.org) is a grassroots news organization serving Philadelphia and the surrounding areas. It also serves as the local organizing unit of the global Indymedia network and was among the first of over 200 Indymedia centers in cities across the United States and worldwide. The organization's goal is to create alternatives to corporate media, with a website, online radio station (Radio Volta), community center, performance space, and an upcoming newspaper.

Radio

The independent and world music station WXPN (88.5 FM) is a very popular local station operated out of World Café Live in University City. Here are some of the other local stations:

- news: WKYW (1060 AM)
- rock: WMMR (93.3 FM)
- classic rock: WYSP (94.1 FM) and WMGK (102.9 FM)
- oldies: WOGL (98.1 FM)
- top 40: WIOQ (102.1 FM)
- country: WXTU (92.5 FM)
- hip-hop and R&B: WUSL (98.9 FM)
- R&B and classic soul: WDAS (1480 AM)
- classic and jazz: WRTI (90.1 FM)
- smooth jazz: WJJZ (106.1 FM)
- National Public Radio: WHYY (91.0 FM)

MAPS AND INFORMATION

The best place to find maps and a wealth of information about what to do and where to go in Philadelphia is at the **Independence Visitor Center** (6th and Market Sts., 215/965-7676 or 800/537-7676, www.independencevisitorcenter.com). It is conveniently located in Old City near the major historic attractions. The large facility has knowledgeable staff and volunteers, as well as exhibitions, a film theater, café, gift shop, and bookstore.

RESOURCES

Suggested Reading

Avery, Ron. *A Concise History of Philadelphia.* Philadelphia: Otis Books, 1999. If you don't have a month to devote to the next book listed, this is a good primer on Philadelphia history, a quick and easy read at just under 100 pages. Written by a native Philadelphian and former newspaper journalist, it's well researched and informative, spanning Philadelphia history from pre–William Penn through the late 20th century. An additional chapter highlights the African American experience in the city.

Barra Foundation. *Philadelphia: A 300-Year History.* New York: W. W. Norton & Company, 1982. This is the most comprehensive account of the history of Philadelphia ever written, produced over 15 years from conception to publication. The mammoth 800-plus-page volume is a collaboration of more than 20 scholars and historians. Each chapter is written by a different expert, and offers a compelling and colorful narrative of a slice of Philadelphia's history, beginning with The Founding, 1681–1701, and culminating with The Bicentennial City, 1968–1982. It is required reading for anyone really interested in local history.

Bissinger, Buzz. *A Prayer for the City.* New York: Vintage, 1998. This compelling account of a critical period in Philadelphia history was written by Pulitzer Prize–winning author and former *Philadelphia Inquirer* journalist Buzz Bissinger. It intimately follows Ed Rendell, arguably Philadelphia's most esteemed and fascinating mayor ever—personally and politically—through his first four-year term in office. The author was granted behind-the-scenes access to city government around the clock, and he provides a candid account of the mayor, city politics, and the lives of several other diverse Philadelphians in the 1990s. A compelling read for anyone interested in the complex problems facing American cities in general, and certainly for anyone interested in Philadelphia, the book is disturbing, hopeful, and real. It is however, a decade out of date, so it serves as a slice of Philadelphia history rather than a current report. Fortunately, many positive improvements have taken place since it was published.

Booker, Janice L. *Philly Firsts: The Famous, Infamous and Quirky of the City of Brotherly Love.* Philadelphia: Camino Books, Inc. 1999. This fun, entertaining little book reveals much about Philadelphia's history through its many "firsts." The city was the first in the country in so many landmark accomplishments, from major achievements like hosting the first hospital and the first university, to the more inane, like its claim as the birthplace of bubble gum and licorice.

Du Bois, W. E. B. *The Philadelphia Negro.* Philadelphia: University of Pennsylvania Press, 1996. Originally published in 1899, this sociological study was the first of its kind to look closely at black urban Americans. It examines the lives and communities of blacks in Philadelphia at the end of the 19th century. The book was sponsored by the University of Pennsylvania, and some suspected its underlying purpose was to show how the black community was responsible for many social problems of the time, but this was not the result. A novel concept at the time, the study did not presume that blacks lived in poor conditions due to an innate shortcoming of the race. The writer was a civil rights activist and scholar and the first black man to receive a PhD from Harvard University. A cofounder of the NAACP, Du Bois also wrote *Black Folk, Then and Now* (1899) and *The Negro* (1915).

Isaacson, Walter. *Benjamin Franklin: An American Life*. New York: Simon & Schuster, 2003. In nearly 600 pages, you will learn more than you ever thought you wanted to know about Benjamin Franklin, but you'll be glad you did. The detailed, entertaining account of Philadelphia's favorite son portrays the complex figure's shortcomings, as well as his numerous accomplishments over his fascinating lifetime. Franklin spent much of his life in Philadelphia and played a key role in many monumental events in the city's history, so you will learn much about the city through the life of its most prominent historical figure.

Internet Resources

INFORMATION AND EVENTS

Campus Philly
www.campusphilly.org

With more than a quarter million students attending more than 80 local colleges and universities, there are plenty of resources to support the student population and enhance the college experience. The best place to start is with Campus Philly, a non-profit organization that sponsors student-oriented events and programs. Their website contains feature articles, events, special student discounts, and networking opportunities. You can also check out **One Big Campus** (www.onebigcampus. com, 877/887-4452), which offers information about visiting local schools and the surrounding city, as well as special hotel and transportation discounts for prospective students and their families.

City of Philadelphia
www.phila.gov

The official website of the City of Philadelphia is a useful resource for new residents to the city. This is the place to go to find out where to sign up for gas and electricity or how to find hospitals and other emergency services. A news section offers updates on events in the city and local government, and the site also offers links to many other useful sites, including public transportation, education, and employment resources.

Greater Philadelphia Tourism and Marketing Corporation
www.gophila.com

Philadelphia's tourism and marketing board is the ultimate online resource for visitors to the city and the surrounding region. The website offers nearly comprehensive listings and informative descriptions of everything the city has to offer, from historic sights to restaurants, nightlife, and shopping. It also offers suggested itineraries and tours for visitors with varied interests, including couples, families with children, gay, and African American visitors, among others. You can also book online to get great discounts for hotels, events, and travel packages.

Philly Fun Guide
www.phillyfunguide.com

This is the place for comprehensive entertainment and other event listings in the area. Offering a wide range of leisure activities, including music, dance, sports, fairs, festivals, outdoor activities, tours, parades, dining, and more, it is coordinated by the Greater Philadelphia Cultural Alliance, whose mission is to increase participation and support for arts and culture organizations in the area. Sign up to receive FunSavers, discounted ticket offers on many of the best visual and performing arts shows and exhibits in the area, delivered to your email inbox every Thursday.

NEWS

City Paper and PW
www.citypaper.net and
www.philadelphiaweekly.com

Read articles from these free alternative weeklies, browse event listings, check restaurant reviews, and more.

Metro
www.philly.metro.us

If you can't get to a SEPTA station to pick up a *Metro,* you'll find similar content online.

Philadelphia Magazine
www.phillymag.com

Get the latest news, read articles from this month's issue, and more on *Philadelphia*'s website.

Philadelphia Independent
Media Center
www.phillyimc.org

This is the website for the local independent media source.

Philadelphia Inquirer and Daily News
www.philly.com

Philadelphia's two main daily newspapers are owned by Knight Ridder and can both be read online.

Philadelphia Gay Times
www.epgn.com

This is the online branch of the print paper for the gay community. It has personals, classifieds, and events listings. Plenty of additional events can be found at www.phillygaycalendar.com.

Philadelphia Tribune
www.phillytrib.com

This site provides news geared towards the African American community.

HISTORY AND ARCHITECTURE

Philly History
www.phillyhistory.org

This award-winning site contains an extensive archive of photographs spanning Philadelphia's history. One of the country's largest municipal archives, it has an estimated two million photographs dating from the late 1800s. A number of different search options make it possible to find photographs from a specific time period, locale, or topic.

Philadelphia Society for the
Preservation of Landmarks
www.phand.org

The group began in 1931, when the historic Powel House was set to be demolished and Frances Anne Wister and other supporters set out to save the house. They were successful, and later acquired Grumblethorpe, the Physick House, and Waynesborough. Today, the organization manages the four historic museum homes and is involved in other programs that support historic preservation.

Philadelphia Architects
and Buildings Project (PAB)
www.philadelphiabuildings.org

It's certainly the ultimate resource for architectural scholars, but the easy-to-use, accessible website is also an excellent resource for anyone interested in architecture. The website brings together the collections, data, and images of The Athenaeum of Philadelphia, the University of Pennsylvania Architectural Archives, the Philadelphia Historical Commission, the Pennsylvania Historical and Museum Commission, and many other important architectural organizations. The site contains more than 35,000 images of structures and more than 2,500 biographies of architects, with an ever-growing database. If there is a local building you want to know more about, this is where to look.

U.S. History
www.ushistory.org

The site is hosted by the Independence Hall Association (IHA), an organization founded in 1942 in conjunction with the creation of Independence National Historical Park. Their mission is to educate the public about the Revolutionary and colonial era in Philadelphia and this website does just that with detailed, interesting information about the sites and history of Independence Park.

PARKS AND RECREATION

Fairmount Park
www.fairmountpark.org

Outdoor lovers will want to check out this website offering a vast amount of information on the history, arts, culture, environment, and recreational activities available in Fairmount Park. Detailed maps include listings of all facilities.

Friends of the Wissahickon
www.fow.com

This nonprofit is dedicated to Wissahickon Park, the part of Fairmount Park in the northwest section of the city. The site offers information on trails, maps, activities, and events.

BEST PHILLY BLOGS

Foobooz
www.foobooz.com

With a name derived from "food" and "booze," you can guess what this blog is all about. Foobooz keeps up-to-date on the latest restaurant and bar openings, events, and all things food and booze in Philly. It also features great deals around the city. Every Wednesday Foobooz editor Arthur Etchells contributes a food column, "The Bite," to *Metro Philadelphia*.

Philebrity
www.philebrity.com

A local blog covering arts, style, gossip, and media in the city, Philebrity is irreverent, entertaining, and even useful at times. They rely on reader tips for their gossip, so it can't be taken too seriously, but it is often a fun read, and the young-oriented arts and event listings are solid.

Philly Blog
www.phillyblog.com

No matter what your local interests, questions, or concern, there is someone on phillyblog willing to discuss them with you. Since 2002, this has been a popular local forum. Offer your own two cents, or just read what others have to say about the city. Whether choosing which neighborhood to live in, where to find the best cheesesteak, or looking for information on local zoning codes, there is a thread on this site for you.

Uwishunu
www.uwishunu.com

"Uwishunu" is not a foreign word, but a subtly hip rendering of the words "you wish you knew," all smooshed together. The younger, hipper offshoot of the Greater Philadelphia Tourism and Marketing Corporation (www.gophila.com), Uwishunu offers an insider's look at Philadelphia. Written in blog form by GPTMC staff and other local contributors, it highlights the latest and greatest places to eat, drink, shop, and more. Their mission is to "enable visitors to hang like locals and locals to hang like insiders."

Young Philly Politics
www.youngphillypolitics.com

This progressive political blog offers a forum for young, socially aware individuals to discuss, or just read about, issues and politicians in the city, region, and state. The active bloggers on the site are passionate about (mostly local) politics, and often have interesting things to say. Anyone can contribute by signing up for a username.

Index

Restaurants Index

Nightlife Index

Shops Index

Hotels Index

Acknowledgments

Writing this book has been incredibly fun, interesting, and completely exhausting at times. I simply could not have done it, and certainly not have enjoyed it so much, without a lot of help. I'd like to thank everyone who contributed in ways large and small, and everyone who helped me maintain a sense of humor and my sanity along the way.

It has been a pleasure to work with each and every one of the talented people at Avalon Travel and I am honored to be part of such an amazing team. Special thanks to two of the best, most supportive, patient editors I have ever worked with: Acquisitions Editor Grace Fujimoto and my editor Naomi Adler Dancis. Your insightful feedback and constant encouragement made this book what it is and helped me grow as a writer. Grace—thank you for choosing me to write this book in the first place and helping shape my jumble of early ideas into a solid outline. Naomi—thank you for knowing when to let me make my own decisions and when to step in and rescue me from myself; I couldn't have asked for a better person to guide me on this journey.

To the countless people who provided information, photographs, and hosted me, thank you for your time and generosity. To everyone at the Greater Philadelphia Tourism and Marketing Commission, thanks for your assistance, photographs, and for doing a terrific job of promoting Philly.

Thanks to all my friends for your support and enthusiasm and for taking me away from my work when I needed it most. To Michi, Val, and Laurie, I don't know where I'd be without your friendship. Laur, thanks also for your editing help and the countless conversations about William Penn and Fairmount Park. To Gary Davidoff, Kenzo Nakawatase, Ned Rauch-Mannino, Leslie Young, Amos Huron, Julie Zied, Rob Huff, and Ethan Birchard, thanks for your time and talent; your insights about sports, music, fashion, gay culture, and other specialties make this book stronger.

To my large, wonderful family—thanks for making Philadelphia home in the truest sense of the word. Mom and Dad—thanks for instilling me with the confidence to pursue my dreams. Dad—thanks for reading rough stages of this book and contributing your sports knowledge. Mom—I am glad your sense of adventure has rubbed off on me. To my sisters, Molly and Julie—thank you for your terrific writing, photos, and friendship. To my brother Ben—you're one of my favorite people in the world. To both Grandmoms, Uncle Joe and Terry, Scott, and Baby, I love and miss you.

To Damian, my husband and best friend, you contributed in so many ways. There were few decisions I didn't bounce off of you, and your ideas and opinions are on many of these pages. Thanks for listening, offering advice, doing far more than your share around the house, and putting up with me when I was stressed. Your faith in me, encouragement, and awesome love are driving forces in everything I do.

Last, thanks to all the people, past and present, who make Philadelphia such a fascinating place to live in and to write about.

MOON PHILADELPHIA

Avalon Travel
A member of the Perseus Books Group
1700 Fourth Street
Berkeley, CA 94710, USA
www.moon.com

Editor: Naomi Adler Dancis
Series Manager: Erin Raber
Copy Editor: Amy Scott
Graphics Coordinator: Stefano Boni
Production Coordinator: Sean Bellows
Cover Designer: Stefano Boni
Map Editors: Albert Angulo, Brice Ticen
Cartographer: Chris Markiewicz
Indexer: Greg Jewett

ISBN-10: 1-59880-138-4
ISBN-13: 978-1-59880-138-5
ISSN: 1942-406X

Printing History
1st Edition – September 2008
5 4 3 2

Printed in U.S.A. by RR Donnelley

KEEPING CURRENT

If you have a favorite gem you'd like to see included in the next edition, or see anything that needs updating, clarification, or correction, please drop us a line. Send your comments via email to feedback@moon.com, or use the address above.

MAP SYMBOLS

Symbol	Name	Symbol	Name	Symbol	Name	Symbol	Name
Expressway		Highlight		Airfield		Golf Course
Primary Road		City/Town		Airport		Parking Area
Secondary Road		State Capital		Mountain		Archaeological Site
Unpaved Road		National Capital		Unique Natural Feature		Church
Trail		Point of Interest		Waterfall		Gas Station
Ferry		Accommodation		Park		Glacier
Railroad		Restaurant/Bar		Trailhead		Mangrove
Pedestrian Walkway		Other Location		Skiing Area		Reef
Stairs		Campground				Swamp

CONVERSION TABLES

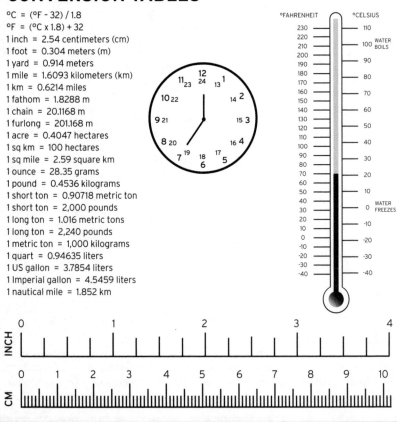

$^\circ C = (^\circ F - 32) / 1.8$

$^\circ F = (^\circ C \times 1.8) + 32$

1 inch = 2.54 centimeters (cm)
1 foot = 0.304 meters (m)
1 yard = 0.914 meters
1 mile = 1.6093 kilometers (km)
1 km = 0.6214 miles
1 fathom = 1.8288 m
1 chain = 20.1168 m
1 furlong = 201.168 m
1 acre = 0.4047 hectares
1 sq km = 100 hectares
1 sq mile = 2.59 square km
1 ounce = 28.35 grams
1 pound = 0.4536 kilograms
1 short ton = 0.90718 metric ton
1 short ton = 2,000 pounds
1 long ton = 1.016 metric tons
1 long ton = 2,240 pounds
1 metric ton = 1,000 kilograms
1 quart = 0.94635 liters
1 US gallon = 3.7854 liters
1 Imperial gallon = 4.5459 liters
1 nautical mile = 1.852 km

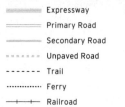

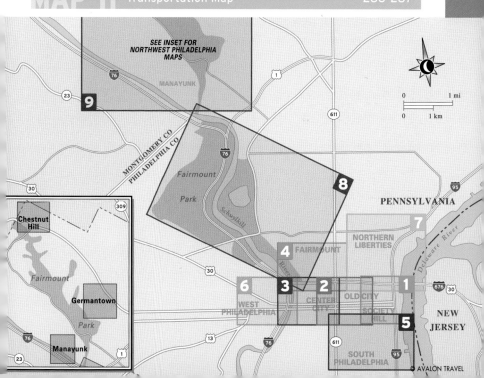

CHINATOWN

SEE MAP 7

Chinatown

Franklin
Square
1 ⊙

⊙ SIGHTS

1	FRANKLIN SQUARE	78	TODD HOUSE
3	NATIONAL CONSTITUTION CENTER	79	FIRST BANK OF THE UNITED STATES
4	FREE QUAKER MEETING HOUSE	80	INDEPENDENCE LIVING HISTORY CENTER
5	U.S. MINT	82	PHILADELPHIA MERCHANT'S EXCHANGE
6	CHRIST CHURCH BURIAL GROUND	85	WELCOME PARK
17	BETSY ROSS HOUSE	88	PENN'S LANDING
18	ARCH STREET FRIENDS MEETING HOUSE	94	ATHENAEUM
23	ELFRETH'S ALLEY	96	OLD ST. JOSEPH'S CHURCH
26	INDEPENDENCE VISITOR CENTER	97	PHILADELPHIA CONTRIBUTIONSHIP
27	PRESIDENT'S HOUSE	98	OLD ST. MARY'S CHURCH
29	FRANKLIN COURT	100	BISHOP WHITE HOUSE
39	CHRIST CHURCH	101	POWEL HOUSE
45	DECLARATION HOUSE (GRAFF HOUSE)	103	PENNSYLVANIA HOSPITAL
51	LIBERTY BELL	104	MOTHER BETHEL A.M.E. CHURCH
52	INDEPENDENCE HALL	106	OLD PINE STREET PRESBYTERIAN CHURCH
53	SECOND BANK OF THE UNITED STATES	107	
74	CURTIS CENTER AND DREAM GARDEN MOSAIC	108	THADDEUS KOSCIUSZKO NATIONAL MEMORIAL
75	PHILOSOPHICAL HALL AND LIBRARY HALL	109	ST. PETER'S EPISCOPAL CHURCH
76	NEW HALL MILITARY MUSEUM	111	HEADHOUSE SQUARE
77	CARPENTERS' HALL		

⊙ RESTAURANTS

31	FORK	62	PHILADELPHIA FISH & CO.
33	PATOU	64	AMADA
34	GIANFRANCO PIZZA RUSTICA	68	CAFÉ SPICE
38	OLD CITY COFFEE	71	LA FAMIGLIA
44	FRANKLIN FOUNTAIN	73	OCEANAIRE
48	MORIMOTO	81	FARMICIA AND METRO CAFÉ
50	JONES	83	CITY TAVERN
55	THE BOURSE FOOD COURT	86	POSITANO COAST BY ALDO LAMBERTI
58	BUDDAKAN	110	XOCHITL
60	HARU	113	MOSHULU

⊙ NIGHTLIFE

30	GIGI	67	32°
37	SUGAR MOM'S	69	EULOGY BELGIAN TAVERN
49	LAS VEGAS LOUNGE	70	THE PLOUGH AND THE STARS
65	KHYBER PASS		
66	BLEU MARTINI		

⊙ ARTS AND LEISURE

2	AFRICAN AMERICAN MUSEUM IN PHILADELPHIA	56	RITZ AT THE BOURSE
9	TEMPLE GALLERY	59	NATIONAL LIBERTY MUSEUM
10	PAINTED BRIDE ART CENTER	72	BLUE CROSS RIVER RINK AT PENN'S LANDING
15	SNYDERMAN GALLERY AND THE WORKS GALLERY	87	RITZ EAST
19	F.U.E.L. COLLECTION	89	JAM ON THE RIVER
20	ARDEN THEATRE COMPANY	90	INDEPENDENCE SEAPORT MUSEUM
21	FIREMAN'S HALL MUSEUM	91	PHILADELPHIA CITY SAIL
22	CLAY STUDIO	93	WASHINGTON SQUARE PARK
24	MUM PUPPETTHEATRE	95	ROSE GARDEN AND MAGNOLIA GARDEN
46	ATWATER KENT MUSEUM	99	POLISH AMERICAN CULTURAL CENTER AND MUSEUM
47	PHILADELPHIA BIKE TOURS	102	RITZ 5
54	NATIONAL MUSEUM OF AMERICAN JEWISH HISTORY		

National
Constitution
Center
⊙ 3

2 ⊙

Free Quaker
Meeting House ⊙ 4

U.S.
Courthouse

Independence
Visitor
Center ⊙ 26

5th

Declaration
House ⊙ 45

President's
House ⊙ 27

Liberty Bell
⊙ 51

RAINSTEAD

CHESTNUT

49 50

Independence Hall
52

SANSOM

Philosophical Hall
and Library Hall ⊙ 75

Curtis Center and
Dream Garden Mosaic
⊙ 74

Independence
Square

WALNUT

73

92

Washington
Square
Park

93

94 ⊙
Athenaeum

MARSHALL

9th
LOCUST

SPRUCE

Pennsylvania
Hospital
103

PINE

WASHINGTON
SQUARE WEST

ADDISON ST

LOMBARD

Mother
Bethel A.M.E.
Church
104 ⊙

Starr
Garden
Park

SEE MAP 2

SEE MAP 5

BRADFORD ST

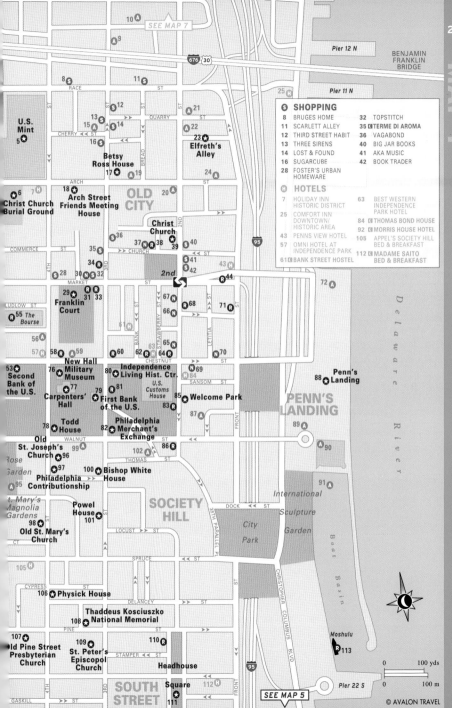

SEE MAP 7

BENJAMIN
FRANKLIN
BRIDGE

Pier 12 N

Pier 11 N

U.S.
Mint

RACE ST

QUARRY

CHERRY ST

Betsy
Ross House

Elfreth's
Alley

BREAD

2ND

SHOPPING

8	BRUGES HOME	32	TOPSTITCH
11	SCARLETT ALLEY	35	TERME DI AROMA
12	THIRD STREET HABIT	36	VAGABOND
13	THREE SIRENS	40	BIG JAR BOOKS
14	LOST & FOUND	41	AKA MUSIC
16	SUGARCUBE	42	BOOK TRADER
28	FOSTER'S URBAN HOMEWARE		

HOTELS

7	HOLIDAY INN HISTORIC DISTRICT	63	BEST WESTERN INDEPENDENCE PARK HOTEL
25	COMFORT INN DOWNTOWN/ HISTORIC AREA	84	THOMAS BOND HOUSE
43	PENNS VIEW HOTEL	92	MORRIS HOUSE HOTEL
57	OMNI HOTEL AT INDEPENDENCE PARK	105	APPEL'S SOCIETY HILL BED & BREAKFAST
61	BANK STREET HOSTEL	112	MADAME SAITO BED & BREAKFAST

Christ Church
Burial Ground

Arch Street
Friends Meeting
House

OLD
CITY

Christ
Church

ARCH

COMMERCE ST

CHURCH

MARKET ST

Franklin
Court

2nd ST

LUDLOW ST

The
Bourse

New Hall
Military
Museum

Independence
Living Hist. Ctr.

U.S.
Customs
House

Welcome Park

Second
Bank of
the U.S.

Carpenters'
Hall

First Bank
of the U.S.

Philadelphia
Merchant's
Exchange

Todd
House

CHESTNUT ST

SANSOM ST

PENN'S
LANDING

Penn's
Landing

Delaware River

Old
St. Joseph's
Church

WALNUT

Philadelphia
Contributionship

Bishop White
House

THOMAS ST

SOCIETY
HILL

St. Mary's
Magnolia
Gardens

Powel
House

Old St. Mary's
Church

LOCUST ST

Rose
Garden

International
Sculpture
Garden

City
Park

SPRUCE ST

Boat Basin

Physick House

CYPRESS ST

DELANCEY ST

Thaddeus Kosciuszko
National Memorial

PINE ST

Old Pine Street
Presbyterian
Church

St. Peter's
Episcopol
Church

STAMPER ST

Headhouse

Moshulu

CHRISTOPHER COLUMBUS BLVD

SOUTH
STREET

Square

GASKILL ST

SEE MAP 5

Pier 22 S

0   100 yds

0   100 m

© AVALON TRAVEL

SEE MAP 4

SEE MAP 7

Race-Vine

Hahnemann University Hospital

611

RACE ST

SPRING ST

CHINATOWN

10 R

SEE MAP 3

CHERRY ST

1 A

Arch Street United Methodist Church

2

ARCH

R 7

8 N

Chinese Friendship Gate

11

9 A

JFK Plaza

Thomas Paine Plaza

Masonic Temple

3

4 A 5 S

Reading Terminal Market

6

FILBERT ST

3

JOHN F KENNEDY BLVD

Penn Square

City

City Hall

15th

3

Juniper

13th

11th

21 N

CENTER CITY EAST

LUDLOW ST

16

17 N

S 19

Macy's

S 22

23

St. Stephen's Episcopal Church

18 A

24 A

CHESTNUT ST

25

26

27

S 28
S 29
S 31
R 33
N 35

R 20

Thomas Jefferson University Hospital

S

30 R
32

34 S

SANSOM ST

38 R

39 R

S 36

N 37

42 S

48 S

WALNUT ST

Walnut-Locust

41 N

40 N

44 A

N 43

45 N

46 S A 47

Thomas Jefferson University

12th

LOCUST ST

15th/16th

50 A

611

52

Library Company of Philadelphia

N 53

55

56

N 58

N 61

57

SPRUCE ST

51 A

54 R

59 R

N 60

CYPRESS ST

Kimmel Center

62 A

66 N

12TH

CLINTON ST

69 N

N 65

67 S

68 S

PINE ST

ANTIQUE ROW

SEE MAP 3

WAVERLY ST

WASHINGTON SQUARE WEST

63 A

LOMBARD ST

Seger Park

Lombard-South

NAUDAIN ST

RODMAN ST

RODMAN ST

64 R

SOUTH ST

© AVALON TRAVEL

Chinatown
13 R

14 R

2 R

CHERRY ST

Franklin Square

FRANKLIN ST
8TH ST

National Constitution Center

U.S. Mint

676 30

SEE MAP 1

QUARRY ST
BREAD ST
3RD ST
4TH ST

Independence Mall

FILBERT ST

U.S. Courthouse

15 S
Gallery at Market East
8th

Independence Visitor Center

MARKET ST

5th

Liberty Bell

Independence Hall

JEWELER'S ROW

Independence Square

A 49

Washington Square

9th

Pennsylvania Hospital

MARSHALL CT

ADDISON ST
ADDISON ST

Starr Garden Park
BRADFORD ST
RODMAN ST

SEE MAP 5

GASKILL ST

SOUTH STREET

SEE MAP 1

0   100 yds
0   100 m

✪ SIGHTS

2 ARCH STREET UNITED METHODIST CHURCH	16 **CITY HALL**
3 **MASONIC TEMPLE**	23 ST. STEPHEN'S EPISCOPAL CHURCH
6 **READING TERMINAL MARKET**	52 LIBRARY COMPANY OF PHILADELPHIA
11 CHINESE FRIENDSHIP GATE	

◗ RESTAURANTS

7 VIETNAM	32 LOLITA
10 SINGAPORE CHINESE VEGETARIAN	33 CAPOGIRO
12 SZECHUAN TASTY HOUSE	38 **XIX/NINETEEN**
13 LAKESIDE CHINESE DELI	39 NAKED CHOCOLATE CAFÉ
14 RAY'S CAFÉ AND TEA HOUSE	54 VALANNI
20 1225 RAW SUSHI AND SAKE LOUNGE	59 MERCATO
	64 MS TOOTSIE'S SOUL FOOD CAFÉ

◖ NIGHTLIFE

8 TROCADERO THEATRE	53 BUMP
35 VINTAGE	55 UNCLES
37 **FERGIE'S**	57 TAVERN ON CAMAC
40 **SISTERS**	58 12TH AIR COMMAND
41 **WOODY'S**	61 **TRIA**
43 PURE	65 DIRTY FRANK'S
45 THE BIKE STOP	

◬ ARTS AND LEISURE

1 PENNSYLVANIA ACADEMY OF THE FINE ARTS	47 FORREST THEATRE
4 FABRIC WORKSHOP AND MUSEUM	49 WALNUT STREET THEATRE
9 SPACE 1026	50 **ACADEMY OF MUSIC**
18 PRINCE MUSIC THEATER	51 WILMA THEATER
24 LUCKY STRIKE LANES	62 **KIMMEL CENTER**
44 12TH STREET GYM	63 PHILADELPHIA THEATRE COMPANY/SUZANNE ROBERTS THEATER

◉ SHOPPING

5 **AIA BOOKSTORE AND DESIGN CENTER**	29 OPEN HOUSE
15 GALLERY AT MARKET EAST	30 ROBIN'S BOOKSTORE
19 MACY'S	31 SCARLET FIORELLA
22 SOUND OF MARKET STREET (JAZSOUND)	34 SAILOR JERRY
25 WEST ELM	36 **DUROSS & LANGEL**
26 **MITCHELL & NESS**	42 **PHAG**
27 I. GOLDBERG	46 TEN THOUSAND VILLAGES
28 GROCERY	48 MATTHEW IZZO
	67 HELLO WORLD
	68 GIOVANNI'S ROOM

◎ HOTELS

17 **THE RITZ-CARLTON OF PHILADELPHIA**	60 ALEXANDER INN
21 LOEWS HOTEL	66 ANTIQUE ROW BED & BREAKFAST
56 **UNCLE'S UPSTAIRS INN**	69 CLINTON STREET BED & BREAKFAST

SEE MAP 6

0 ___ 100 yds
0 ___ 100 m

Amtrak
Station

22nd

R RESTAURANTS

3	MAMA'S VEGETARIAN
4	FUJI MOUNTAIN
6	VIC
9	CAPOGIRO
13	LA COLOMBE
18	DIBRUNO BROS.
25	TONY JR.'S
28	LEBUS
33	REMEDY TEA BAR
36	SANSOM ST. OYSTER HOUSE
47	BRASSERIE PERRIER
50	LE BEC-FIN
51	SUSANNA FOO
55	LOS CATRINES RESTAURANT & TEQUILA'S BAR
56	MONK'S
59	ROUGE
60	THE BLACK SHEEP
68	SNACKBAR
69	TWENTY MANNING
66	SEAFOOD UNLIMITED
67	AUDREY CLAIRE
72	DARLING'S CAFÉ
74	ANTS PANTS
76	PUMPKIN
78	JAMAICAN JERK HUT

N NIGHTLIFE

2	FIRST UNITARIAN CHURCH
8	TINTO
10	THE BARDS
14	LOIE
26	TRIA
35	NODDING HEAD BREWERY
39	WALNUT ROOM
42	DENIM
53	GOOD DOG
54	McGLINCHEY'S
75	TEN STONE
77	BOB & BARBARA'S

A ARTS AND LEISURE

1	MUTTER MUSEUM
5	ADRIENNE THEATRE
17	DHYANA YOGA STUDIO
59	CURTIS INSTITUTE OF MUSIC
60	CONCERTS IN THE PARK
61	RITTENHOUSE SQUARE
63	SCHUYLKILL BANKS RIVER TOURS
64	RITTENHOUSE ROW FESTIVAL
65	RITTENHOUSE FITNESS CLUB
70	CIVIL WAR AND UNDERGROUND RAILROAD MUSEUM
73	ODUNDE AFRICAN AMERICAN STREET FESTIVAL

S SHOPPING

7	BALANCE HEALTH CENTER
11	BODY KLINIC
12	BORN YESTERDAY
15	TOPPERSSPA SALON
16	BOYD'S
19	BUFFALO EXCHANGE
20	SMITH BROS.
22	THE SHOPS AT LIBERTY PLACE
23	DETAILS
24	PREMIUM STEAP
27	BENJAMIN LOVELL SHOES
29	LEEHE FAI
30	JOSEPH FOX BOOKSHOP
31	ANTHROPOLOGIE
32	ECHOCHIC
34	PLAGE TAHITI
37	PETULIA'S FOLLY
38	KIEHL'S
40	KNIT WIT
41	BLUEMERCURY APOTHECARY AND SPA
43	CHILDREN'S BOUTIQUE
44	HEAD START SHOES
46	URBAN OUTFITTERS
48	JOAN SHEPP
49	UBIQ
52	THE SHOPS AT THE BELLEVUE
57	RESCUE RITTENHOUSE SPA

H HOTELS

21	WESTIN
45	THE LATHAM
58	RITTENHOUSE 1715
62	RITTENHOUSE HOTEL
71	LA RESERVE CENTER CITY BED AND BREAKFAST

RITTENHOUSE

River

Schuylkill

Water

Park

LOCUST ST

CYPRESS ST

CYPRESS

MANNING ST

DELANCEY

DELANCEY ST

PANAMA ST

WAVERLY ST

LOMBARD

NAUDAIN ST

TANEY

26TH

25TH

24TH

23RD

22ND

73

SEE MAP 8

SEE MAP 8

Girard College

GIRARD AVE

FRANCISVILLE

POPLAR

N 1

PARRISH ST

FAIRMOUNT

2 A

BROWN ST

28TH

27TH

26TH

25TH

24TH

23RD

CAPITOL

ST

Eastern State
Penitentiary

4 ◄ ▶ 5

ASPEN

3 R

MEREDITH

PENNSYLVANIA DR

KELLY

6 R

FAIRMOUNT

R 7

N 8

Fairmount

MOUNT

VERNON

9 ★

Fairmount Water Works
Interpretive Center

Park

GREEN

Philadelphia
Museum
10 ★ of Art

BRANDYWINE

SPRING

FRANKLINTOWN

76

Eakins
Oval

11 ◄ ▲ 12

R 13

HAMILTON

SPRING GARDEN ST

BENJAMIN

PARK TOWNE PL

14

FRANKLIN

Schuylkill River

WINTER

ST

Franklin Institute
Science Museum

17 A

SUMMER ST

SPRING ST

0   100 yds

16 R

RACE

0   100 m

23RD

22ND

21ST

CHERRY

SEE MAP 6

© AVALON TRAVEL

SEE MAP 3

ARCH

SEE MAP 7

Girard

GIRARD AVE

HARPER ST

611

POPLAR ST

SPRING GARDEN

BROWN

Fairmount

FAIRMOUNT AVE

NORTH ST

WALLACE ST

POPLAR

MOUNT VERNON ST

Spring Garden

Community College of Philadelphia

CALLOHILL

ree Library of Philadelphia

676 30

Logan Fountain Square

Race-Vine

18 A 19 20

LOGAN SQUARE

611

Cathedral of Saints Peter and Paul 22

JFK Plaza   Thomas Paine   SEE MAP 2

◎ SIGHTS

4 ◖ EASTERN STATE PENITENTIARY

9 FAIRMOUNT WATER WORKS INTERPRETIVE CENTER

10 ◖ PHILADELPHIA MUSEUM OF ART

11 EAKINS OVAL

15 FREE LIBRARY OF PHILADELPHIA

22 CATHEDRAL OF SAINTS PETER AND PAUL

◎ RESTAURANTS

3 ◖ BRIDGID'S

6 LONDON GRILL

7 JACK'S FIREHOUSE

8 MUGSHOTS COFFEEHOUSE AND CAFÉ

16 DARLING'S CAFÉ

20 FOUNTAIN AT THE FOUR SEASONS

◎ NIGHTLIFE

1 NORTH STAR BAR

◎ ARTS AND LEISURE

2 WAKE UP YOGA

5 TERROR BEHIND THE WALLS AT EASTERN STATE PENITENTIARY

12 I-GLIDE TOURS AND RENTALS

14 RODIN MUSEUM

17 ◖ FRANKLIN INSTITUTE SCIENCE MUSEUM

18 ACADEMY OF NATURAL SCIENCES

◎ HOTELS

13 BEST WESTERN CENTER CITY

19 FOUR SEASONS

21 WINDSOR SUITES

MAP 5

SOUTH STREET/SOUTH PHILADELPHIA

☯ SIGHTS
1 ISAIAH ZAGAR'S MAGIC GARDEN
40 GLORIA DEI (OLD SWEDES' EPISCOPAL CHURCH)

ⓡ RESTAURANTS
2 CHAPTER HOUSE CAFÉ
4 ⓒ HORIZONS
9 BEAU MONDE
15 COQUETTE
17 MARRAKESH
19 JIM'S STEAKS
25 ANSILL
27 SAM'S MORNING GLORY DINER
28 RALPH'S
30 FAMOUS 4TH ST. DELICATESSEN
31 DMITRI'S
32 ISGRO PATICCERIA
33 ⓒ SABRINA'S CAFÉ
34 ANTHONY'S ITALIAN COFFEE HOUSE
35 MOLCAJETE MIXTO
36 JOHN'S WATER ICE
37 SHANK'S AND EVELYN'S
41 NAM PHUONG
42 PLAZA GARIBALDI

ⓝ NIGHTLIFE
8 L'ETAGE
11 TATTOOED MOM
20 FLUID
22 FILLMORE AT THE TLA
39 ROYAL TAVERN

ⓐ ARTS AND LEISURE
29 FLEISHER ART MEMORIAL
38 ITALIAN MARKET FESTIVAL
43 MUMMERS MUSEUM
44 UNITED ARTISTS RIVERVIEW STADIUM 17

ⓢ SHOPPING
3 VIA BICYCLE
5 ANASTACIA'S ANTIQUES
6 DECADES VINTAGE
7 SOUTH STREET
10 GARLAND OF LETTERS
12 REPO RECORDS
13 ⓒ PHILADELPHIA RECORD EXCHANGE
14 PHILADELPHIA AIDS THRIFT
16 GUACAMOLE
21 BRICKBAT BOOKS
23 ⓒ BENJAMIN LOVELL SHOES
24 PEDESTRIAN

ⓗ HOTELS
18 SHIPPEN WAY INN
26 BELLA VISTA BED & BREAKFAST

SEE MAP 2

WALNUT

Thomas Jefferson University

9th ST

LOCUST ST

WASHINGTON SQUARE WEST

Washington Square

SPRUCE

Pennsylvania Hospital

CYPRESS ST

CLINTON ST

PINE

WAVERLY ST

LOMBARD

Starr Garden Park

Seger Park

RODMAN

SOUTH ST

KATER

Isaiah Zagar's Magic Garden

BAINBRIDGE

FITZWATER

CATHARINE

CHRISTIAN

CARPENTER

MONTROSE

WASHINGTON

LEAGUE

ELLSWORTH

ANNIN

FEDERAL

WHARTON

ROOSEWOOD

611

12th & Reed Street Park

WHARTON

PASSYUNK

SEE MAP 1

SOCIETY HILL

International
Sculpture
Garden

City
Park

Boat Basin

Delaware River

FRONT ST
DOCK ST
LOCUST ST

MARSHALL CT

DELANCEY ST
DELANCEY ST

ST

5TH
4TH
3RD

Headhouse
Square

GASKILL
SOUTH STREET

10
11 12 13 16 17 18 19 20 21 22 23 24 25

FABRIC ROW

MONROE

FITZWATER

30 31

ITALIAN MARKET

QUEEN

CHRISTIAN

2ND
FRONT

CHRISTOPHER COLUMBUS BLVD

Pier 30 S

Pier 34 S

Pier 36 S

Pier 38 S

Pier 40 S

40
Gloria Dei
(Old Swedes'
Episcopal Church)

Pier 46 S

Pier 48 S

Jefferson
Square
Park

MOYAMENSING

43

Pier 53 S

MANTON ST

TITAN ST

SEARS ST

Pier 55 S

Pier 56 S

0   100 yds

0   100 m

Pier 57 S

✪ SIGHTS

3 30TH STREET STATION
20 UNIVERSITY OF PENNSYLVANIA
29 WOODLANDS CEMETERY AND MANSION

ⓡ RESTAURANTS

2 RAE
10 LA TERRASSE
11 WHITE DOG CAFÉ
23 MARIGOLD KITCHEN
24 THE GREEN LINE CAFÉ
25 VIENTIANE CAFÉ
26 DAHLAK

Ⓝ NIGHTLIFE

6 CAVANAUGH'S
12 NEW DECK TAVERN
15 WORLD CAFÉ LIVE
19 ROTUNDA

Ⓢ SHOPPING

9 BLACK CAT

Ⓐ ARTS AND LEISURE

4 INTERNATIONAL HOUSE
8 INSTITUTE OF CONTEMPORARY ART
13 UNIVERSITY OF PENNSYLVANIA ARENA
14 TROPHY BIKES
16 THE BRIDGE: CINEMA DE LUX
17 STRIKES BOWLING LOUNGE
18 NEIGHBORHOOD BIKE WORKS
21 UNIVERSITY MUSEUM OF ARCHAEOLOGY AND ANTHROPOLOGY
22 PENN RELAYS
28 CLARK PARK

Ⓗ HOTELS

1 CORNERSTONE BED & BREAKFAST
5 INTERNATIONAL HOUSE
7 THE HILTON INN AT PENN
27 GABLES

Lee Park

46th
MARKET

40th

LUDLOW

CHESTNUT

SANSOM

WALNUT

LOCUST

LOCUST WALK

SPRUCE

WEST PHILADELPHIA

PINE

OSAGE

LARCHWOOD

HAZEL

CEDAR

BALTIMORE

Clark Park

Woodlands Cemetery and Mansion
29 ✪

0   200 yds

0   200 m

© AVALON TRAVEL

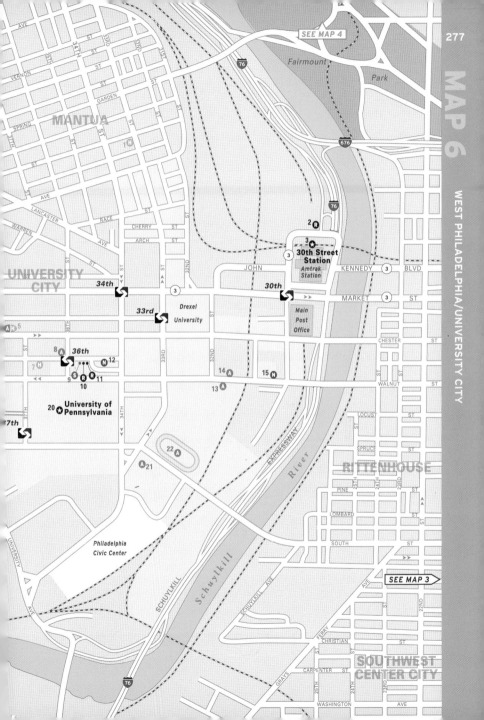

SEE MAP 4

Fairmount
Park

MANTUA

UNIVERSITY
CITY

34th

33rd

36th

University of
Pennsylvania

17th

Drexel
University

30th Street
Station

Amtrak
Station

JOHN

30th

Main
Post
Office

KENNEDY

MARKET

BLVD

ST

CHESTER

WALNUT

ST

ST

LOCUST

SPRUCE

RITTENHOUSE

PINE

LOMBARD

SOUTH

SEE MAP 3

Philadelphia
Civic Center

River

EXPRESSWAY

Schuylkill

SCHUYLKILL AVE

SCHUYLKILL

FERRY

CHRISTIAN

CARPENTER

WASHINGTON

SOUTHWEST
CENTER CITY

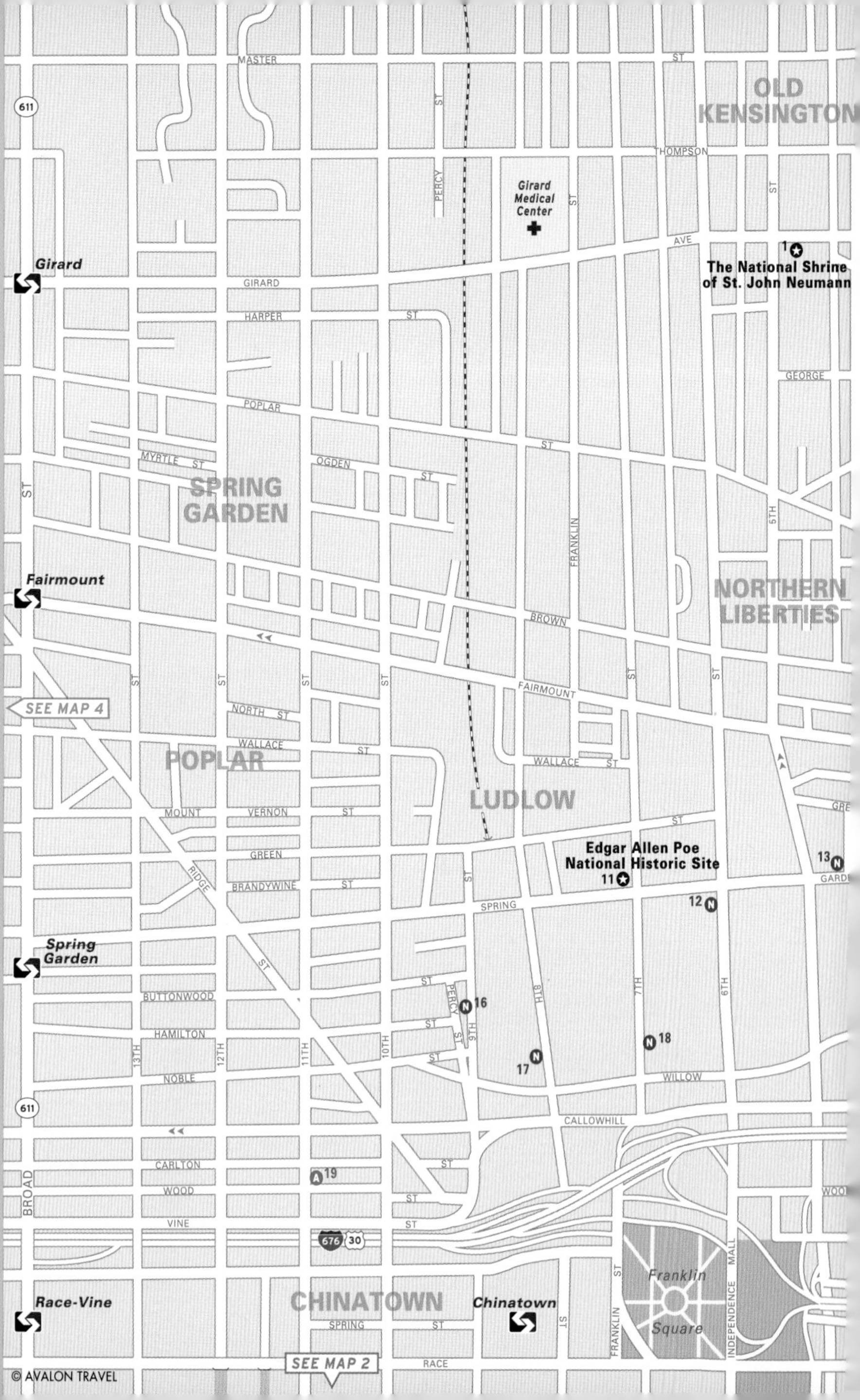

MAP 7

OLD KENSINGTON

THOMPSON

Girard Medical Center

1 The National Shrine of St. John Neumann

Girard

GIRARD

HARPER

GEORGE

POPLAR

MYRTLE ST

OGDEN

SPRING GARDEN

Fairmount

FRANKLIN

NORTHERN LIBERTIES

BROWN

FAIRMOUNT

SEE MAP 4

NORTH ST

WALLACE

WALLACE

POPLAR

LUDLOW

MOUNT

VERNON

GREEN

Edgar Allen Poe National Historic Site
11

13

BRANDYWINE

12

SPRING

Spring Garden

BUTTONWOOD

16

HAMILTON

17

18

NOBLE

WILLOW

611

CALLOWHILL

CARLTON

19

WOOD

VINE

676 30

Franklin Square

Race-Vine

CHINATOWN

Chinatown

SPRING

SEE MAP 2

RACE

© AVALON TRAVEL

FISHTOWN

Girard

Penn
Treaty
Park

Piers 37 N to 57 N

Delaware River

Pier 35 1/2 N

Spring
Garden

Pier 12N

BENJAMIN FRANKLIN
BRIDGE

676 30

SEE MAP 1

Pier 11N

0   100 yds

0   100 m

★ SIGHTS

1 THE NATIONAL
SHRINE OF ST. JOHN
NEUMANN

11 EDGAR ALLEN POE
NATIONAL
HISTORIC SITE

® RESTAURANTS

3 BAR FERDINAND

6 HONEY'S SIT N' EAT

8 NORTH 3RD

10 ⊂STANDARD TAP

ℕ NIGHTLIFE

4 JOHNNY BRENDA'S

7 ⊂ORTLIEB'S JAZZHAUS

12 TRANSIT

13⊂SILK CITY

14 700 CLUB

16 STARLIGHT BALLROOM

17 SHAMPOO

18 ELECTRIC FACTORY

Ⓐ ARTS AND LEISURE

2 ART STAR

9 ⊂NORTH BOWL

19 VOX POPULI AND
KHMER GALLERY

ⓢ SHOPPING

5 PHILADELPHIA
GLASSWORKS

15⊂R. E. LOAD
BAGGAGE, INC.

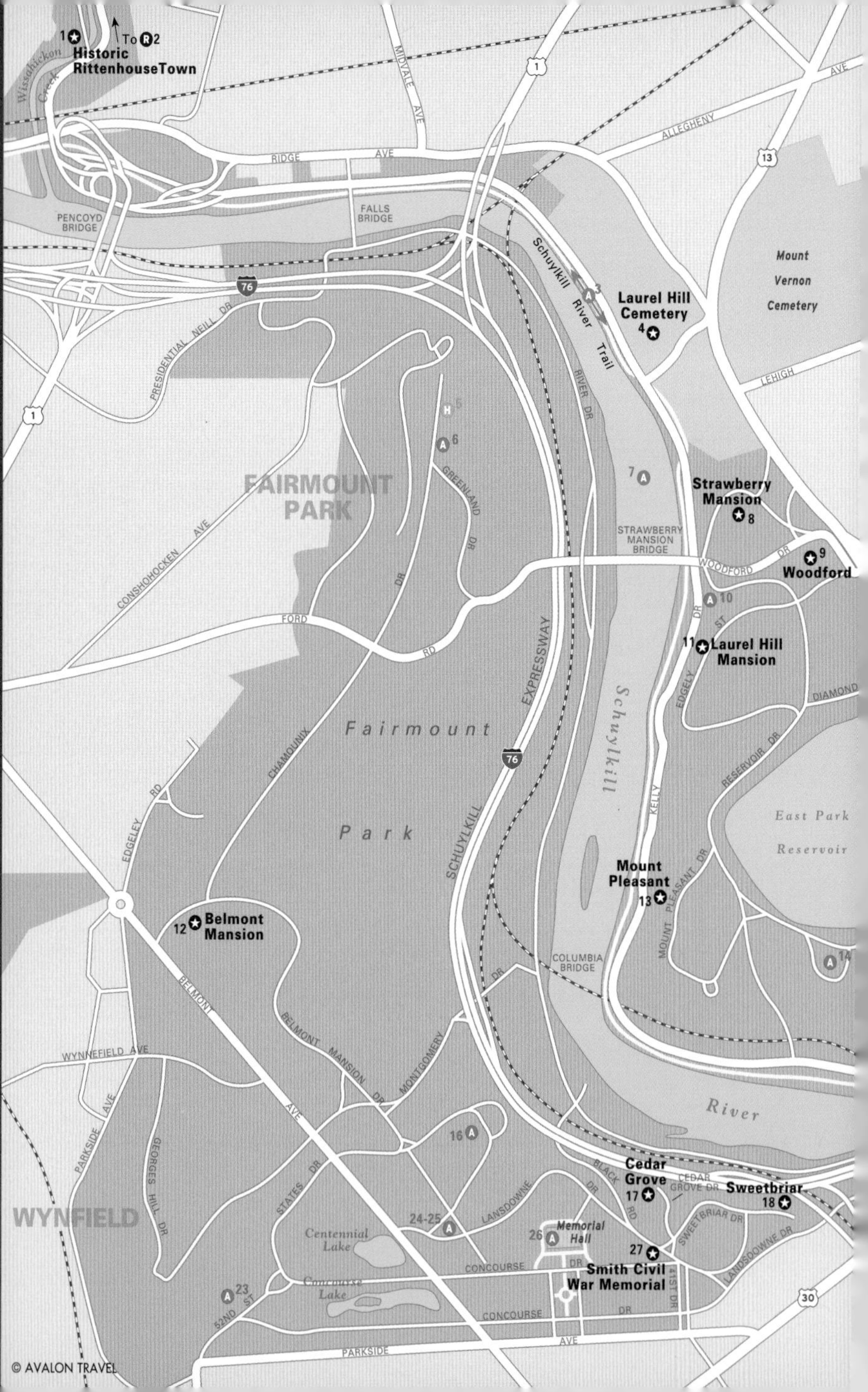

MAP 8

1 Historic RittenhouseTown
To 2

Wissahickon Creek

RIDGE AVE

PENCOYD BRIDGE

FALLS BRIDGE

76

Schuylkill River

River Trail

3

Laurel Hill Cemetery
4

Mount Vernon Cemetery

PRESIDENTIAL NEILL DR

LEHIGH

ALLEGHENY

13

1

CONSHOHOCKEN AVE

FAIRMOUNT PARK

H 5

6

GREENLAND DR

7

STRAWBERRY MANSION BRIDGE

Strawberry Mansion
8

WOODFORD

9 Woodford

10

11 Laurel Hill Mansion

FORD RD

CHAMOUNIX DR

EGGLEY RD

Fairmount

Park

Schuylkill

EDGELEY DR

KELLY DR

DIAMOND

RESERVOIR DR

East Park Reservoir

12 Belmont Mansion

EXPRESSWAY

76

Mount Pleasant
13

MOUNT PLEASANT DR

14

BELMONT AVE

WYNNEFIELD AVE

PARKSIDE AVE

GEORGES HILL DR

BELMONT MANSION DR

MONTGOMERY DR

COLUMBIA BRIDGE

DR

River

WYNFIELD

STATES DR

LANSDOWNE DR

16

24-25

26 Memorial Hall

23

52ND ST

Centennial Lake

Concourse Lake

CONCOURSE DR

BLACK RD

Cedar Grove
17

CEDAR GROVE DR

27 Smith Civil War Memorial

SWEETBRIAR DR

18 Sweetbriar

LANSDOWNE DR

30

CONCOURSE DR

PARKSIDE AVE

© AVALON TRAVEL

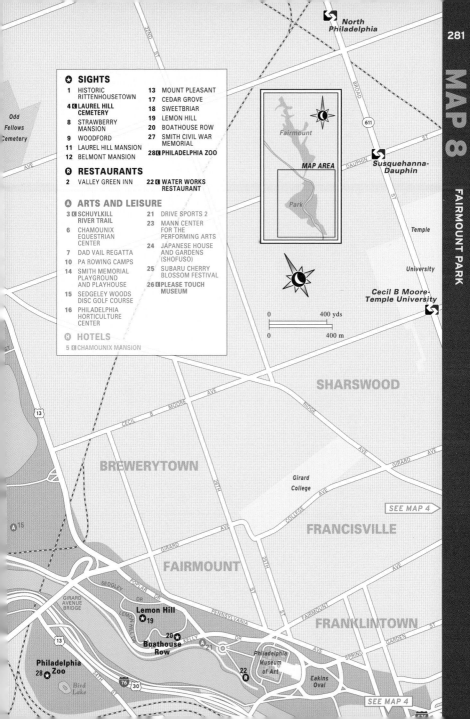

SIGHTS

1	HISTORIC RITTENHOUSETOWN	13	MOUNT PLEASANT
4	LAUREL HILL CEMETERY	17	CEDAR GROVE
		18	SWEETBRIAR
8	STRAWBERRY MANSION	19	LEMON HILL
9	WOODFORD	20	BOATHOUSE ROW
11	LAUREL HILL MANSION	27	SMITH CIVIL WAR MEMORIAL
12	BELMONT MANSION	28	PHILADELPHIA ZOO

RESTAURANTS

2	VALLEY GREEN INN	22	WATER WORKS RESTAURANT

ARTS AND LEISURE

3	SCHUYLKILL RIVER TRAIL	21	DRIVE SPORTS 2
6	CHAMOUNIX EQUESTRIAN CENTER	23	MANN CENTER FOR THE PERFORMING ARTS
7	DAD VAIL REGATTA	24	JAPANESE HOUSE AND GARDENS (SHOFUSO)
10	PA ROWING CAMPS		
14	SMITH MEMORIAL PLAYGROUND AND PLAYHOUSE	25	SUBARU CHERRY BLOSSOM FESTIVAL
15	SEDGELEY WOODS DISC GOLF COURSE	26	PLEASE TOUCH MUSEUM
16	PHILADELPHIA HORTICULTURE CENTER		

HOTELS

5	CHAMOUNIX MANSION

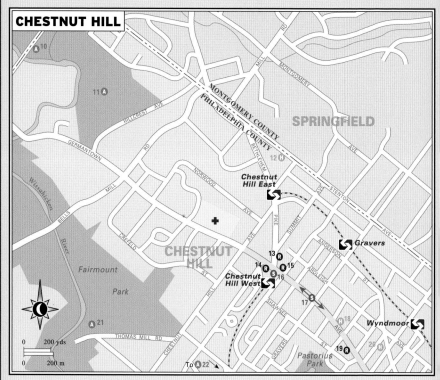

CHESTNUT HILL

MANAYUNK

© AVALON TRAVEL

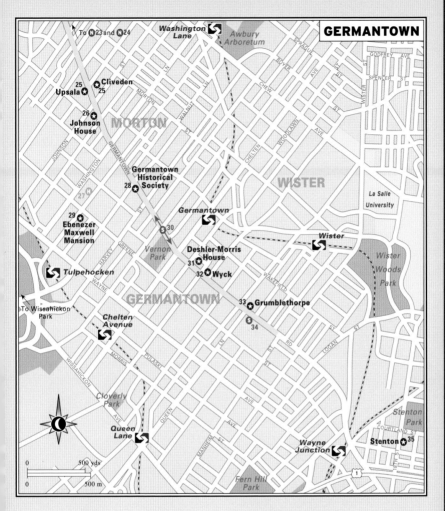

GERMANTOWN

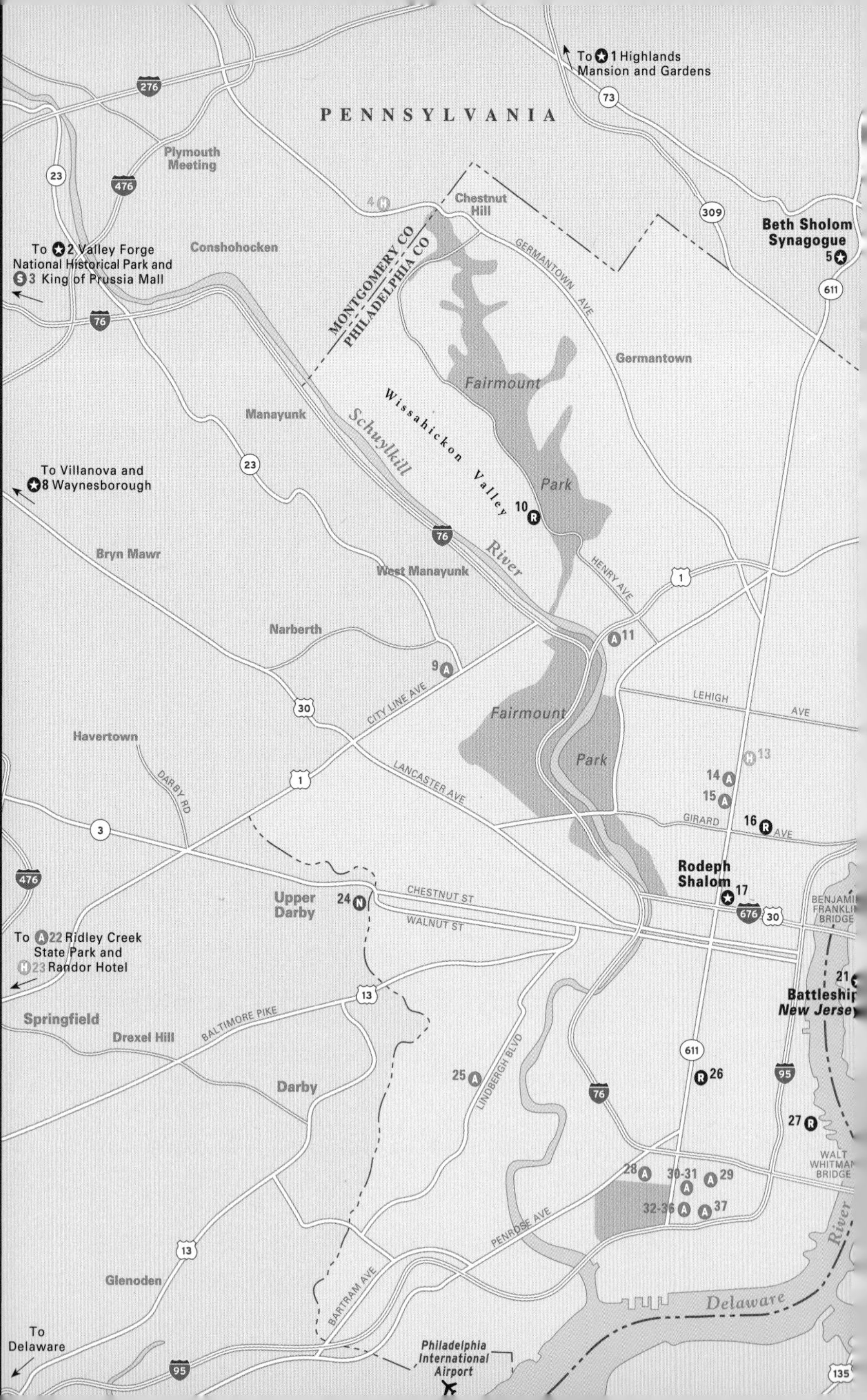

MAP 10

GREATER PHILADELPHIA

To ★1 Highlands
Mansion and Gardens

73

PENNSYLVANIA

276

23

476

Plymouth
Meeting

Chestnut
Hill

4 H

309

**Beth Sholom
Synagogue**
5 ★

Conshohocken

GERMANTOWN AVE

611

To ★2 Valley Forge
National Historical Park and
$3 King of Prussia Mall

76

Germantown

Manayunk

Fairmount

Wissahickon Valley

23

Schuylkill River

To Villanova and
8 Waynesborough

Park

Bryn Mawr

10 R

West Manayunk

HENRY AVE

76

1

Narberth

A 11

30

9 A

CITY LINE AVE

LEHIGH   AVE

Fairmount

H 13

Havertown

DARBY RD

1

LANCASTER AVE

Park

14 A
15 A

3

GIRARD   AVE

16 R

476

**Rodeph
Shalom**
17

Upper
Darby

24 H

CHESTNUT ST

676   30

BENJAMIN
FRANKLIN
BRIDGE

To A22 Ridley Creek
State Park and
H23 Randor Hotel

WALNUT ST

13

Springfield

Drexel Hill

BALTIMORE PIKE

21

**Battleship
New Jersey**

Darby

25 A

LINDBERGH BLVD

611

95

26 R

76

27 R

WALT
WHITMAN
BRIDGE

28 A   30-31   29
         A   A

32-36   37
A   A

13

Glenoden

To
Delaware

95

Philadelphia
International
Airport

Delaware River

135

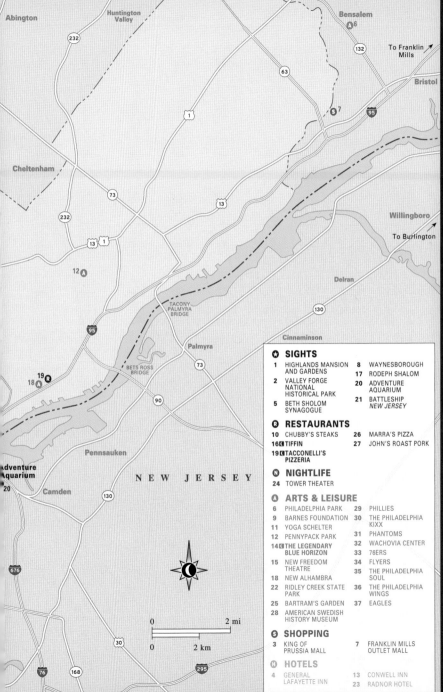

Abington

Huntington Valley

Bensalem

To Franklin Mills

Bristol

Cheltenham

Willingboro

To Burlington

Delran

TACONY PALMYRA BRIDGE

Cinnaminson

Palmyra

BETS ROSS BRIDGE

Pennsauken

NEW JERSEY

Adventure Aquarium

Camden

	SIGHTS		
1	HIGHLANDS MANSION AND GARDENS	8	WAYNESBOROUGH
2	VALLEY FORGE NATIONAL HISTORICAL PARK	17	RODEPH SHALOM
		20	ADVENTURE AQUARIUM
5	BETH SHOLOM SYNAGOGUE	21	BATTLESHIP *NEW JERSEY*

	RESTAURANTS		
10	CHUBBY'S STEAKS	26	MARRA'S PIZZA
16	TIFFIN	27	JOHN'S ROAST PORK
19	TACCONELLI'S PIZZERIA		

	NIGHTLIFE		
24	TOWER THEATER		

	ARTS & LEISURE		
6	PHILADELPHIA PARK	29	PHILLIES
9	BARNES FOUNDATION	30	THE PHILADELPHIA KIXX
11	YOGA SCHELTER		
12	PENNYPACK PARK	31	PHANTOMS
14	THE LEGENDARY BLUE HORIZON	32	WACHOVIA CENTER
		33	76ERS
15	NEW FREEDOM THEATRE	34	FLYERS
18	NEW ALHAMBRA	35	THE PHILADELPHIA SOUL
22	RIDLEY CREEK STATE PARK	36	THE PHILADELPHIA WINGS
25	BARTRAM'S GARDEN	37	EAGLES
28	AMERICAN SWEDISH HISTORY MUSEUM		

	SHOPPING		
3	KING OF PRUSSIA MALL	7	FRANKLIN MILLS OUTLET MALL

	HOTELS		
4	GENERAL LAFAYETTE INN	13	CONWELL INN
		23	RADNOR HOTEL

0   2 mi

0   2 km

© AVALON TRAVEL

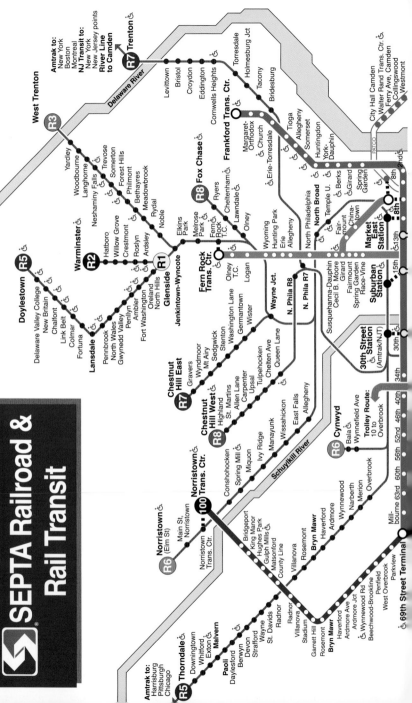

SEPTA Railroad & Rail Transit

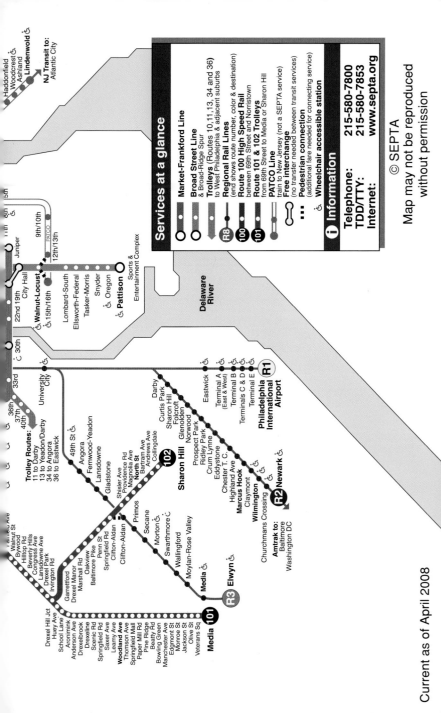

Services at a glance

Market-Frankford Line

Broad Street Line
& Broad-Ridge Spur

Trolleys (Routes 10,11,13, 34 and 36)
to West Philadelphia & adjacent suburbs

Regional Rail Lines
(end shows route number, color & destination)

Route 100 High Speed Rail
between 69th Street and Norristown

Route 101 & 102 Trolleys
from 69th Street to Media or Sharon Hill

PATCO Line
train to New Jersey (not a SEPTA service)

Free interchange
(no transfer needed between transit services)

Pedestrian connection
(additional fare needed for connecting service)

& **Wheelchair accessible station**

ⓘ Information

Telephone:	215-580-7800
TDD/TTY:	215-580-7853
Internet:	www.septa.org

© SEPTA
Map may not be reproduced
without permission

Current as of April 2008

www.moon.com

DESTINATIONS | ACTIVITIES | BLOGS | MAPS | BOOKS

MOON.COM is ready to help plan your next trip! Filled with fresh trip ideas and strategies, author interviews, informative travel blogs, a detailed map library, and descriptions of all the Moon guidebooks, Moon.com is all you need to get out and explore the world—or even places in your own backyard. While at Moon.com, sign up for our monthly e-newsletter for updates on new releases, travel tips, and expert advice from our on-the-go Moon authors. As always, when you travel with Moon, expect an experience that is uncommon and truly unique.

MOON IS ON FACEBOOK—BECOME A FAN!
JOIN THE MOON PHOTO GROUP ON FLICKR